To George & Mary,
Valued friends
& great citizens.
Affectionately

Vaughan

Canadians want "their" MPs, not parties, to represent them in the House of Commons. We should insist that this realizable democratic aspiration be adopted now! The door would then be opened to significant social and economic accomplishments that are impossible with a government that, to be realistic, belongs to a party.

POWER *SHIFT*

Party Rule ➤ Real Rep. Democracy

From Party Elites
to Informed Citizens

Vaughan Lyon

Professor Emeritus,
Trent University, Political Science

Foreword by **Alan Cairns**

Past President of the Canadian
Political Science Association

iUniverse, Inc.
Bloomington

Power Shift
From Party Elites to Informed Citizens

iUniverse books may be ordered through booksellers or by contacting:

iUniverse
1663 Liberty Drive
Bloomington, IN 47403
www.iuniverse.com
1-800-Authors (1-800-288-4677)

Because of the dynamic nature of the Internet, any web addresses or links contained in this book may have changed since publication and may no longer be valid. The views expressed in this work are solely those of the author and do not necessarily reflect the views of the publisher, and the publisher hereby disclaims any responsibility for them.

ISBN: 978-1-4620-3763-6 (sc)
ISBN: 978-1-4620-3765-0 (hc)
ISBN: 978-1-4620-3764-3 (e)

Printed in the United States of America

iUniverse rev. date: 12/23/2011

For dear Nonie

"Let me count the ways"

Elizabeth Barrett Browning

CONTENTS

FOREWORD

Professor Alan Cairns

That the political systems of the democratic world and the institutions that channel political life in Canada, and elsewhere, are in trouble will surprise no one. Vaughan Lyon's contribution to the agonised introspections triggered by the crisis is distinguished by the comprehensiveness of his critique and its accompanying thesis that piecemeal tinkering or adhockery cannot provide the transformative change that is required.

Very little emerges unscathed from his probing and well-documented critique. The public service bureaucracy, the Senate, the House of Commons, the role of the prime minister, the first-past-the-post electoral system, a disempowered citizenry and diminished voter turnout, party finance, and the institutions of direct democracy—all are held up to the light and found wanting. His prime focus is the party system, isolated by party discipline in the legislature from the citizenry it is supposed to serve. The thesis that parties are instruments of democratic citizenship is a great delusion. In fact, they are a barrier to a 21st-century democracy.

In his devastating critique of where we are now and how we got there, he is insistent that patching up an obsolete system will not eliminate the democratic deficit; nor will it give citizens the greatly enhanced role that he argues is necessary. The consequence of our decline, which he hopes to reverse, is governments with ever-declining legitimacy, governments incapable of responding to the crises on our agenda because they cannot mobilize an apathetic citizenry disenchanted with its leaders.

Vaughan Lyon's goal is an empowered citizenry, the necessary support for the strengthened government needed to grapple with 21st-century challenges. The alienation of citizens from government is to be reversed, with government "firmly rooted in the citizenry."

Vaughan Lyon is an institutionalist. He understands that why we behave as we do is because the institutions that channel our political actions induce us to do so. He does not blame individuals for behaviour that contributes to the survival of a faltering regime. The solution, accordingly, is to change the institutions and thus to change the behaviour of those who operate them. Current reform proposals are dissected and shown to be inadequate to salvage an obsolete system from further decline.

The centrepiece of his reform proposals is an elected constituency parliament in each constituency across the country, which will hold members of Parliament accountable and weaken party discipline in the House of Commons. This is no small change, and the author knows that the inertia of established institutions and the timidity of those who control them are barriers that only a mobilized reform movement can overcome. This proposal, which is both innovative and radical, invites the reader's close and sympathetic attention.

A major book should shake us out of our complacency or shatter us out of our despairing indifference that we are trapped in a failing system in which all the exits to an improved future are locked. Vaughan Lyon is part of the company of academics, journalists, and concerned citizens who seek to modify our public arrangements when they appear to be in disarray—when they are seen as responses to yesterday, not to today and tomorrow.

Lyon's concern is not the construction of rarefied theory to advance the discipline of political science but the search for practical democratic improvements in the political system of the country in which he lives—Canada. He advocates a "quiet Canadian democratic revolution." He invites the reader to accompany him on that path to the future.

Alan Cairns
Past-President, Canadian Political Science Association

PREFACE

The world suffers under a dictatorship of no alternatives.
Although ideas all by themselves are powerless to overthrow
this dictatorship, we cannot overthrow it without ideas.

Roberto Mangabeira Unger

I suffered under the "dictatorship of no alternatives" for part of my life. Politics based on parties battling for power, rather than on citizens working together to further common interests, always seemed undemocratic, but the way "democratic politics" had to be. But then, gradually, extensive experience as a party activist, a career as a political scientist, and membership in a society whose members were alienated from their elected representatives and the governments they formed, convinced me that there must be a more democratic way to organize our politics. It was not hard to find.

For most of the century, whenever given the opportunity, Canadians have expressed a strong desire to have the person they elected to represent them in the House of Commons do so, i.e., for constituency representation, rather than "representation" by an MP committed to following the leadership of his or her party. By the time I started to give voice to that desire and work on a practical model to make it feasible, 83 percent of Canadians told pollsters they thought constituency rather than party representation would improve the quality of our political life.[1] Strongly agreeing, I set out to

---

1   These propositions were put by pollsters to Canadians: "We would have better laws if members of parliament were able to vote for what people in their riding thought was best rather than having to vote the same way as their party." A full 83 percent of respondents agreed. Paul Howe and David Northrup, "Strengthening Canadian Democracy: The Views of Canadians," IRPP [Institute for Research on Public Policy] *Policy Matters* 1, 5 (July 2000): 23. More recently, 89 percent of candidates for office "strongly agreed" or "agreed" with the proposition that MPs should be allowed to vote freely in

show that, despite its dismissal by most politicians and parties engaged in politics-as-usual, constituency representation could be organized simply. Most importantly, it could change the relationship of citizen to politics from alienation and rejection to constructive engagement. That is the genesis of *Power Shift*.

In the chapters that follow I shall show that the vast majority of Canadians who prefer constituency representation are fully justified in thinking that this form of representation would serve them better than party representation; that they need not remain trapped in the present political system. We are not the same people, and our world is dramatically different from that of the 19th century when our political system, based on citizens delegating their civic responsibilities to a party leader they chose occasionally, became established. That system is too deeply flawed to be successfully adapted to modern demands, and a practical, responsible model that embraces our desire for constituency representation is readily available. Adoption of constituency representation—properly organized—would lead at once to a long-overdue transfer of power from party elites to informed, responsible citizens.

*****

The root cause of the alienation, and the resulting lack of public support that hobbles government, is our dependence on political parties to represent and govern us. The style of politics they impose—exaggeratedly competitive, adversarial, and divisive—is ill suited to modern governance. It should be replaced with one that fosters a collaborative relationship between citizens, their elected representatives and government based on them, and the civil service.

Compared to authoritarian regimes, our system is representative, but the system falls very far short of the claims made for its representativeness. As will be shown, there is a major gap between the values and priorities of citizens and their governing politicians. We need to put much more substance behind the "representative democracy" rhetoric used to describe our system. The key element in representation is that the representative acts with the

the Commons. Jerome H. Black and Bruce M. Hicks, "Strengthening Canadian Democracy: The views of parliamentary candidates," IRPP *Policy Matters* 7, 2 (March 2006): 36. www.irpp.org.

agreement or *consent* of the represented.[2] Further, the agreement should be informed and freely given to be worthy of respect by the representative. Constituency representation would replace delegation with agreement or consent in the citizen-representative relationship.

The current political system is best described as a *partyocracy*, drawing attention to the dominant role parties play in it.[3] These organizations are devoted, above all else, to winning power in competitive elections for their leaders and the interests with which they identify. They are self-appointed spokespersons for "the people," but functioning in a competitive setting, they can offer us only a very limited form of representation. Most party MPs willingly help their constituents with any problems they might have with government bureaucracies. On the important policies before parliament, however, they are required to follow the "line" laid down by their leader and, in a reversal of the role they claim to perform, represent that position to their constituents.

That is not the kind of representation Canadians want. A genuine representative democracy would enable Canadians to play a much more significant and responsible role in determining the actions of government, through MPs actually representing them. Citizens want their MP to represent them as a lawyer acts for clients. The clients and the lawyer deliberate, pooling information and ideas. The lawyer then carries the position agreed on forward on behalf of the client. In the case of an MP, he or she would carry the views of constituents to the House of Commons.

With partyocracy generating widespread dissatisfaction across all

---

2   Formally, *representation* has been defined as "a relation between two persons, the representative and the represented or constituent, with the representative holding the authority to perform various actions that incorporate the agreement of the represented." David Sills, ed., *International Encyclopaedia of the Social Sciences,* vol. 13 (New York: Macmillan and the Free Press, 1968), 461. A system of *representative government* has been defined as "one in which representatives of the people share, to a significant degree, in the making of political decisions." A. Birch, *Representative and Responsible Government* (Toronto: University of Toronto Press, 1964), 14.

3   "Partyocracy" is a concept taken from Giovanni Sartori, who writes, "Political parties have indeed become such an essential element in the political process that in many instances we might legitimately call democracy not simply a party system but a 'partyocracy' (partitocrazia)." Giovanni Sartori, *Democratic Theory* (New York: Frederick A. Praeger, 1965), 120

elements of the population, including many politicians, how does it survive? Briefly, well-entrenched institutions are notoriously difficult to change or remove.[4] That difficulty is compounded when the major power holders in society on whom we depend to make changes have a significant stake in preserving the status quo. I propose avoiding some of the difficulties involved in directly changing institutions by adding a vitally important new institution that would allow citizens to speak for themselves. Its impact would then cause "adjustments" by those institutions that exist now and, particularly, by parties.

Most of us believe that MPs should really represent their constituents' views in the House of Commons.[5] However, we also accept the mistaken notion that political parties are inevitable if we are to have a democracy.[6] These views clash, one neutralizing the other, making it possible for party leaders to ignore our desire for genuine representation, unmediated-by-parties. They have no interest in designing institutions that would incorporate constituency representation and they dominate the policy dialogue in the country. The result is a lack of any real-life or convincing virtual models to show that there are alternatives to politics dominated by disciplined, hierarchically organized parties, each of which has its own agenda.

---

4   Political scientist Michael Atkinson reflects the prevailing view: "Most political institutions are the product of responses to previous crises. Unless another crisis occurs, institutional change is likely to be slow and indecisive. "What Kind of Democracy Do Canadians Want?" *Canadian Journal of Political Science* 27, 4 (December 1994): 743.

5   "Three quarters (75 percent) of all Canadians are convinced that the 'Canadian parliamentary system is in need of major reform.' Only 16 percent do not share this opinion." Pollster Michael Adams reporting on 1986 poll results in "Canadian Attitudes Towards Legislative Institutions," in *Canadian Legislatures, The 1986 Comparative Study*, Robert J. Fleming, ed. (Queen's Park, Toronto: Office of the Assembly, 1986), 27. Commenting on a 2004 poll in which Canadians endorsed "Effecting significant changes to Canadian political institutions to make them much more open and democratic …" Bob Rae, then Chairman of the Canadian Unity Council, its sponsor, observed, "these results show that if and when political institutions do move toward change, Canadians will certainly be ready." *Opinion Canada* 4, 35 (December 2004). http://www.opinion-canada.ca/en/articles/print_122.html

6   Asked by pollsters to agree or disagree with the statement, "Without political parties there cannot be true democracy," 68.5 percent strongly or somewhat agreed while 23 percent somewhat or strongly disagreed." Source: "Survey conducted for the Institute for Research on Public Policy," April 2000. (Location: CORA Queen's University.) www.queensu.ca.cora/

Given this lack, it is easy to understand the public's inability to imagine an alternative to party representation. It is, however, less easy to understand the dogmatic assertion that "parties are inevitable in democracy," found in most writing by political scientists in Canada and elsewhere.[7] The observation of Vernon Bogdanor, a reform-minded British political scientist, is typical. He leads off his book on political change with the comment: "Any contemporary discussion of the party system must begin from the realization that parties are essential to democracy . . . in every democracy in the world, political parties compete for the right to form a government. So any attack upon the party system which called for the abolition of parties would be entirely futile."[8]

I do not call for the abolition of parties—freedom of association is a cornerstone of our liberties. But I do advocate making it possible for MPs to represent their constituents, taking that function away from "party" MPs. With this new mode of representation parties would be pushed to the margins of our politics, hastening their current decline in Canada as in all the other industrialized democracies.[9]

The unhealthy current situation is that parties decline but no substitute for them is proposed. Rather, most reformers urge the parties to perform their functions differently and "better." Parties do what wins elections, not what outsiders advise.

Bogdanor starts from the premise that "democracy" exists and parties are necessary to maintain it. The understanding underlying this study and widely shared by other citizens is, however, that while progress toward democracy has been made, partyocracy is merely a way station. The track to a fuller democracy will progressively allow citizens to assume more responsibility for their own governance. Seen from that perspective, power-

---

7   Michael Parenti writes, "The most subtle form of 'political education' is the treating of events and conditions which are in fact amenable to change as though they were natural events." *Power and the Powerless* (New York: St. Martin's Press, 1978), 125. A great deal of this kind of political "education" continues to take place.

8   Vernon Bogdanor, *The People and the Party* (Cambridge: Cambridge University Press, 1981), 2.

9   See Russell Dalton and Martin P. Wattenberg, **Parties without Partisans: Political Change in Advanced Industrial Democracies.** (Oxford: Oxford University Press, 2000).

monopolizing parties are a barrier to rather than an essential attribute of democracy.

Challenging the dogmatic belief in the inevitability of political parties is vitally important. Partyocracy is unable to produce the quality of informed citizenship or strength in government that is essential to meet the unprecedented difficulties and opportunities that we are facing in Canada and abroad. It must be replaced.

*****

Democracy and *democratic citizenship*, key concepts in this study, are defined in many different ways to suit the purposes of those using them. There will be more discussion of the use and abuse of political terminology later, but at the outset, let it be clear that *democracy* and *citizenship* will be used in this study as they are commonly understood.[10] In a few eloquent lines, which I will refer to again, Joseph Tussman, an American political theorist, captured the essential characteristics of both terms:

> The essential feature of a democratic polity is its concern for the participation of the member in the process by which the community is governed. It goes beyond the insistence that politics or government be included among the careers open to talent. It gives to each citizen a public office, a place in the sovereign tribunal and, unless it is a sham, it places its destiny in the hands of that tribunal. Here is the ultimate decision-maker, the court of last appeal, the guardian of the guardians, government "by the people."[11]

The discontinuity between the democratic values expressed by Tussman and the values embodied in party representation and governance is striking. It is not our choice to trust a handful of party politicians, preoccupied with their struggle for power, to make crucially important public policy. We were born into an ongoing system and have been given no opportunity to

---

10   "Democracy" is a rich mine of conceptual complexity for political scientists, but for the citizen its meaning is plain. People easily distinguish the democratic ideal—"government by the people"—from the existing political system.

11   Joseph Tussman, *Obligation and the Body Politic* (New York: Oxford University Press, 1960), 105–6.

consider an alternative that might better suit our needs and values in the 21st century.

*****

This book presents the case for a truly representative democracy. I make an urgent plea that we reject the conditioning to passivity to which we have been exposed and insist on having the mode of representation that we believe is both desirable and needed. We have the right to choose our representative system as well as our particular representative. Political stability demands the infrequent exercise of this right, but there are moments when a revitalization of our political life demands it. With citizen support for existing political institutions declining at the same time that governments need more support, this is clearly such a moment.

*****

Meeting the parties-are-inevitable-if-we-are-to-have-democracy dogma head-on, the first of the following chapters outlines an alternative model of representation based on a new foundational institution—an elected constituency parliament in each riding. Its members would deliberate with their MP to develop a local position on issues that the member could then represent in the House of Commons as the authentic view of the majority of his or her constituents. Citizens would not only choose their leaders, they would also shape the agenda of government. Policy democracy based on constituency parliaments added to the electoral democracy we have now would move democratic government to a higher level in Canada.

Little serious attention is now paid to the citizenry's desire for constituency representation, yet it seems obvious that adopting this citizen-supported mode of representation is key to increasing political participation and support for government. Instead of considering that option, however, we struggle along with a system based on parties—by virtually every account almost the least respected of our social institutions. They provide only a shaky foundation for a political system facing unprecedented challenges.[12]

---

12   On the basis of surveys of public opinion, the authors of *Political Choice in Canada* conclude, "In general, the parties and politicians who run the political system are regarded with distaste by most of the public." H. D. Clarke, L. LeDuc, J. Jenson, and J.

The presentation of the model of constituency representation in chapter 1 is not merely an academic exercise. Many Canadians are more than ready to move beyond the general discussion of our political ills to specific proposals for fundamental change. The policy democracy/constituency parliament model is offered as a rallying point for them.

Since the proposed model will involve the transfer of power from elites to citizens, some of those who are politically advantaged by and comfortable with the present system will vigorously oppose it. They will be following the example of previous generations of the politically advantaged who opposed allowing "the masses"—men, then women—to choose their political leaders in competitive elections. When their opposition was overcome, and the franchise expanded, the development was quickly recognized as progress.

Shortly after its adoption and a breaking-in period, people will also wonder why policy democracy based on constituency parliaments was not instituted earlier. With the benefit of hindsight, its "appropriateness," too, will seem obvious.

In the second chapter, we will examine the existing representative system, its origins, features, and weaknesses. Assessing partyocracy as a representative system only partially captures its essence, however. To round out the description of it, we need to examine the structure of leadership found in partyocracy. Our government is prime ministerial. That phenomenon is put under a spotlight in chapter 3.

The weak representative system and the style of leadership it supports result in few of us seeing government as ours—a we/they relationship exists between citizens and the political leadership of the country. Consequently, citizens offer government only qualified support, while they place heavy demands on it. The imbalance in demands and supports results in the trend toward bankruptcy, considered in chapter 4.

The inability of partyocracy to support good government is illustrated in chapters 5 and 6. As party government in the liberal democracies has grown dramatically more intrusive, expensive, and necessary, its weaknesses have become more apparent and less tolerable. Some of those weaknesses can be

H. Pammett, eds., *Political Choice in Canada* (Toronto: McGraw-Hill Ryerson, 1979), 30-31.

attributed to the co-optation and demoralization by the party in office of the supposedly neutral and professional bureaucracy.

These weaknesses are reflected in the government's performance of all the tasks expected of it. However, the inability of government to guarantee the integrity of the country stands out. The ongoing struggle to maintain the federation is considered in chapter 7. The analysis of partyocracy's weaknesses as government, with the alternative model in mind, will show that adopting that model promises a quantum leap in the quality of democratic citizenship, governance, and national unity.

In the following three chapters, 8–10, I consider the significance of the many current proposals to strengthen partyocracy. Over many years, the limited amount of the time and energy people have available for political reform has been invested in trying to overcome the weaknesses of partyocracy with incremental reforms ("patches"). Currently, an unprecedented number of such reforms are being considered seriously—a reflection of the concern that so many, at all levels, feel about the deficiencies of the existing system. The scope of these reforms is, however, limited by the dogma that democracy requires parties.

The time and energy spent on the reform of partyocracy is poorly invested. Despite modest incremental reforms, debilitating political alienation has increased. The failed "reform" experience is summarized in chapter 11. More hopefully, in the same chapter, it is shown that almost all the prerequisites for an alternative, more promising approach to change are present at this moment in our history. The only prerequisite missing is an irresistible demand for it from citizens. A combination of a new awareness that a viable model of constituency representation exists and modern communications that will permit the organization of engaged citizens will produce that demand. It will be welcomed by many politicians who have experienced the failings of the system first-hand and who are citizens before they are partisans.

*****

The analytic approach adopted in this study is *institutional*. Grammatical purists will object to personalizing institutions. Parties, parliaments, etc., will be said to act, while of course, it is really individuals who are doing so within the framework of one of those institutions. When, however, the institutions are such a powerful force in determining individual actions, it seems appropriate, on most occasions, to emphasize their significance by attributing behaviour directly to them rather than to political actors who come and go.

Demonizing politicians—holding them personally responsible for our political ills—does not further an understanding of political phenomena nearly as much as focusing on institutions does. What so often leads public figures to disappoint us is not their lack of altruism, ability, or will. Rather, it is primarily the system of rewards and punishments built into the system. Public figures engage in demagoguery, distribute patronage to allies, defer obsequiously to powerful lobbies, and so on because, given the way the system is organized, that behaviour is rewarded.

The institutional reforms proposed in this book would bring with them a different set of incentives. These would encourage politicians to adopt behaviour that would draw public support. Rather than feeling widespread alienation from all things political, many citizens would then experience interest and engagement.

*****

A personal final note: This book is dedicated to answering the what-is-to-be-done question and to dealing with our uncertainty about how best to reform the political system. I embrace the task with both passion and reticence. *Passion* because, as a parent, citizen, former party activist, and political scientist, I can think of nothing that is of greater importance. Our existing liberal democratic political system has contributed immeasurably to the quality of life of generations. Think of the human misery avoided and the opportunities provided for most Canadians to live dignified, satisfying lives, because a few in earlier generations pressed for change from autocratic rule. A truly representative system, engaging citizens in their governance, would set similar progress in motion if it were adopted now.

Reticence, because I feel presumptuous claiming to articulate the aspirations of Canadians and intimidated because it is so important that outlining the logical democratic alternative to the present system on their behalf be done convincingly. I will be considering the transformation of a political system that places control of the government in the hands of a tiny minority to one that is vastly more open to the contributions of millions of Canadians, one that allows us to share responsibility for setting public policy with those we elect as our representatives in the House of Commons.

In short, we will be considering a peaceful and orderly second democratic revolution! The first gave citizens the right to choose their rulers; the second will also allow Canadians to deliberate with those leaders and share in determining what policies they adopt. This dramatic extension of democracy is long overdue in all the now-stalemated liberal democracies. We, however, will content ourselves with considering reform in our country—Canada.

The Alternative to Party Representation and Government

Policy Democracy Based on Constituency Parliaments

Imagining alternatives can be tough.

Rick Salutin

The prime difficulty ... is that of discovering the means
by which a scattered, mobile, and manifest society may so
recognize itself as to define and express its interests.

John Dewey

What we call necessary institutions are often no more than
institutions to which we have grown accustomed ... in matters of
social constitution, the field of possibilities is much more extensive
than men living in the various societies are ready to imagine.

Alexis de Tocqueville

Introduction: An Overview of Constituency Parliaments

In the 19th and early 20th centuries, we finally won the universal right
to elect our representatives to the House of Commons and, in doing so,
to indirectly choose who and what party would govern. Now it is urgent

that we take the next step to a fuller democracy, one where citizens will participate directly with their elected leaders in determining the policies the government will adopt. This participation requires an institution that will fill the space— now unsatisfactorily occupied by parties—between citizens and those we elect. Ideally, this institution should create a close working relationship between us, our elected representatives, the governments they form, and the civil service. We *can* create such an institution. It would be quite simple in structure and modest in cost. The difficulty in establishing it lies in mobilizing the strong (but still only latent) support for constituency representation. We have been socialized into leaving politics to the politicians, but we must now assume responsibility ourselves for fundamental changes in the system. Our politicians will not make them without a strong push from us.

Canadians are now alienated from politics and politicians, feeling powerless in a system purporting to be a democracy.[1] The importance of that alienation is not to be ignored, downplayed, or finessed. It lowers our support for government. That, in turn, has a negative impact on the administration's desire and ability to serve our interests.

The most impressive contemporary evidence supporting the desire of Canadians for a new politics was provided by the Citizens' Forum on Canadian Unity (the Spicer Commission) appointed by Conservative PM Brian Mulroney. After listening to thousands of Canadians from coast to coast, it summarized our views this way: "Since election campaigns do not constitute a vote by the people on ... policies, and since elected representatives seem to have little or no influence or freedom to represent constituents' views, there is a perceived need for mechanisms which will (a) require members of parliament to consult their constituents on major issues; and, (b) either give them more freedom, or require them to vote according

---

1   The conclusion reached by Ekos Research on the basis of an intensive analysis of public opinion is similar to that of other surveys: "There is a widespread belief that governments are self-serving, inefficient and ineffectual. The strength of these responses would suggest an underlying rage but for the fact that these negative sentiments have been evident for too long a period to characterize them as rage. Perhaps deep resentment and frustration would be better descriptors of the current public mood." Ekos Research Associates Inc., *Rethinking Government '94: An Overview and Synthesis* (Ottawa: Ekos Research Associated Inc., 1995), 3.

to their constituents' wishes. A group in Ontario reflected the consensus of most Forum discussions in reporting: "The government must be changed. We must have a system whereby our elected representatives truly represent and reflect the wishes of their constituents."[2]

It cannot be argued that only reform-minded people were heard by the Commission and that the "silent majority" is satisfied with the existing representative system. As already noted, polling and party promises have, for at least the past century, also reflected the desire of Canadians to have their representatives carry forward their views to the House of Commons, i.e., to have constituency rather than party representation. Even elected MPs and party candidates for office agree, by overwhelming majorities, that they should be allowed to represent the views of their constituents in the Commons.

Our preference for that mode of representation has been ignored or merely exploited by our political leaders, however. No serious thought has been given to how constituency representation might be organized, because it is not in the interests of the parties monopolizing political life to consider alternatives to their dominance. That institution has been allowed to dictate to us!

How legitimate or worthy of our support can government be when it is based on a (party) system of representation that lacks the support of the overwhelming majority of its citizens? Who does the political system belong to—the people whom it claims to serve, or the tiny group of political practitioners working in the system?

To initiate our consideration of moving Canada to a higher level of democracy, I will present a viable, responsible model embracing the constituency representation we want and need. The model would enable citizens to direct, as well as elect, their governments, taking that power away from parties and, in particular, their leaders. Adoption of the model would institute *policy democracy*. This advanced form of democracy would be based on the constituency parliaments described below.

I might be expected to conclude the book, after considering all the reasons why the existing system of representation must be democratized,

---

2   Canada, Citizens' Forum on Canada's Future, *Report to the People and Government of Canada* (Ottawa: Minister of Supply and Services Canada, 1991), 101–2.

with this description of constituency parliaments. That order is reversed for an important reason. The parties have, as mentioned, convinced many that they are inevitable. If this belief is not effectively challenged by showing how representation could be organized without parties, it would be difficult for many people to accept my critique of their performance. What would be the point of doing so if we believe that we must have them and, especially, if we feel the features of the party objected to are largely beyond reform?

On the other hand, if we consider the functioning of the existing system with a practical alternative to it in mind, we can assess its current performance against that alternative. At the end of this comparative assessment, we should be able to conclude whether the old or the new would best serve our interests. If the *new* represents enormous political progress, as I hope to show, then the issue remaining is how do we bring about change to constituency representation? I address that in the final chapter.

The model set out below will, of course, be denounced as impractical, as pie in the sky, by those who have a vested interest in the existing system. Others, lacking that interest, may still find the model outside the range of changes they are used to discussing. I hope, however, that all Canadians who feel alienated by the current system and who would like to participate in building a more democratic political system supporting a more efficient and responsive government—for themselves and for future generations—will approach the model with an open mind. If we were free of the past and constructing a democratic system from scratch for today, wouldn't it look very much like the one described below?

Requisites of a Realistic Proposal for Empowering Citizens

Constituency representation must meet three conditions to be successful. First, there must be an elected body of citizens in a constituency who can legitimately claim to represent their neighbours. This body would establish (aggregate) the majority viewpoint of those neighbours on policy issues of particular interest to them. Their MP would then carry these views forward to the House of Commons, converting what is now an increasingly discredited party battleground into a forum of MPs representing citizens.

Second, the constituency viewpoint reached in deliberations of the body representing the citizens in a constituency must be informed, so that it is worthy of respect and representation by the MP. Third, the citizens elected by their neighbours to represent them in the local parliament would be expected to accept responsibility for the consequences flowing from their contribution to public policy—responsibility would accompany empowerment.

These three conditions cannot be met by party MPs holding occasional town-hall meetings, circulating questionnaires, or even sponsoring constituency-wide referenda. A substantive majority viewpoint can only be determined in the deliberations of elected representatives of constituents who have full access to relevant information and the time to deliberate on it. There must be a new institution to facilitate the deliberations.

Constituency Parliaments: An Overview

Let it be clear that I am not proposing immediate full participatory democracy. To move from a system where one person, i.e., the prime minister, dominates government to one where everybody participates extensively on an ongoing basis in setting public policy is unrealistic. The idea is a "straw-man" advanced only to discredit the idea of significantly increased participation. But it is both realistic and necessary to significantly extend participation to include a "base" of elected citizens to deliberate on issues and determine the majority's view on them. Formal citizen participation has not been expanded since the universal franchise was established in the 1920s and never beyond voting.[3] There is a mismatch between that record, the rapid expansion of government in the last century, and a concentration of power in the office of the prime minister. We "grow" centralized government but not citizen participation.

I am advocating establishing a network of elected constituency parliaments (CPs), one in each of Canada's 308 constituencies.[4] It would be the key representative and deliberative institution that would make

---

3   The voting age was reduced from 21 to 18 in 1970.
4   This study considers policy democracy/constituency parliaments in the context of national politics. The arguments apply to the provincial scene, as well, but with less force. As will be discussed (chapter 7), alienation from the national administration is more intense and damaging than the hostility to, and mistrust of, provincial politicians.

constituency representation possible. The members of each CP, working closely with the constituency's member of the House of Commons, would develop a majority position on the issues on which they want to be heard. The MP would then represent those views in the Commons and, on most occasions (see below), support them with his or her vote if that opportunity presents itself.

Local deliberation on national and international issues, plus the ability of any citizen to seek election to the local parliament, or influence its members, would fundamentally alter our system of representation. A citizen-excluding system would become citizen-inclusive. Policy direction would predominantly flow up from us to our leadership, rather than down, as is currently the case. The change is indicated in these diagrams.

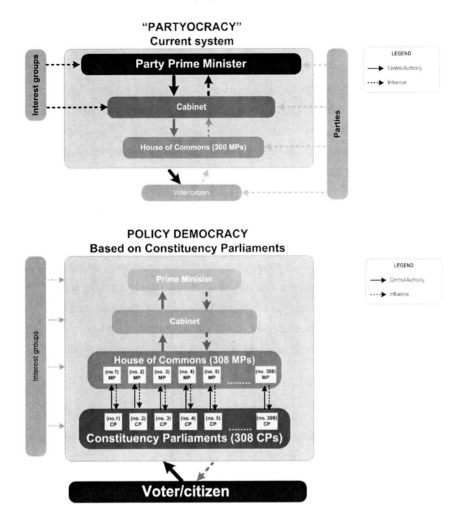

A major barrier to the adoption of constituency representation will be the lack of trust that many of us now have in the political judgment of our fellow citizens. Some now think of our quite conservative, dominant middle class in 19th-century terms—as a potentially dangerous mob that, given more power and responsibility, would threaten our liberties or take from the rich to give to the poor. We should credit most of our neighbours with being responsible and trust that the views of their elected local representatives, formulated in the deliberations of the constituency parliaments, would be well informed. As an integral part of the national policy-making and governing team, the CP members would have a strong incentive, indeed obligation, to master the issues being discussed locally. John Stuart Mill made the case for responsibility stimulating social learning when the right to vote was being extended in his time:

> He [the citizen] is called upon, while so engaged, to weigh interests not his own; to be guided, in case of conflicting claims, by another rule than his own private partialities; to apply at every turn principles and maxims which have for their reason of existence the common good; and he usually finds associated with him in the same work minds more familiarized than his own with these ideas and operations, whose study it will be to supply reasons to his understanding and stimulate his feeling for the general interest.[5]

Constituency Parliaments: Features

Elections. Members of constituency parliaments would be elected in each riding on the basis of one constituency parliament member for every thousand voters. The local assemblies would, therefore, on average, have approximately one hundred members. They would be elected from wards— the neighbourhoods making up the constituency.[6] The timing of the election of members—whether they would be held separately from or concurrent with general elections—and other details, while important, could be decided when CPs are established.

Participation and socialization. In the 2011 general election, there were roughly 24 million registered voters. On the basis of one representative per

---

5   John Stuart Mill, *Autobiography,* ed. Jack Stillinger (Boston: Houghton Mifflin, 1969), 103–4.

6   Four of five Canadians now live in urban Canada, and that percentage is grow-ing. Canada, Statistics Canada (Ottawa: Statistics Canada, 2009). Special arrangements would have to be made in the model to accommodate citizens who live far from urban centres. With the help of modern communications, this would be possible.

thousand registered voters, establishing constituency parliaments would create formal positions for 24,000 constituency parliamentarians meeting in their constituencies.[7] Over time, the normal turnover of members would result in a substantial body of citizens with constituency parliament experience. The very real possibility would exist that, at some point in his or her life, an interested citizen could play a formal political role in local parliament. The constituency parliaments could promote still wider involvement by appointing committees of non-members to assist in their review of policy issues. Experts on many of the subjects dealt with in parliament live in most constituencies and could have a voice on public policy through their local CP. A study group on foreign policy at the local community centre would, for example, have a significant place where it could express its members' views. They would probably find parliament too geographically remote, inaccessible, and intimidating to carry their views to its members.

With constituency parliaments in place, issues that now seem beyond the control of the ordinary citizen would be brought home with deliberation in the CPs. People would be encouraged to consider the relevance of national and international matters to their lives and to develop informed opinions about them. Further, the political content of the local news media and the new media, i.e., the Internet, would spark higher levels of activity from community-based interest groups as they reported on the constituency parliament sessions.

Citizens who now consider issues in isolation from others would be brought together to exchange views in the CPs. In an era when newspaper readership and party membership is declining, and cocooning is becoming increasingly common, institutions that bring people into face-to-face contact are needed more than ever to build social solidarity and expand the perspectives of individuals.

In addition to increasing local political involvement, constituency parliaments would add balance to the representation of political interests because its members would be elected from wards within the constituency. Since they often live in the same neighbourhood, citizens of low socio-economic status and ethnic minorities, now grossly under-represented at

---

7   The figure is based on the number of persons registered to vote in the 2011 federal election. Source: Elections Canada. www.electionscanada.ca

all levels of government, could be elected to CPs and gain a voice on public policy.

Women, another under-represented group, would be given significant additional opportunities for political participation. Government would be "brought home" for politically engaged women. They would not have to go to Ottawa to participate significantly in making national policy. Women have proven themselves skilful at organizing locally, and they might easily be the dominant gender in most constituency parliaments, balancing off male domination of the House of Commons.

Establishing constituency parliaments would do far more to empower women than enfranchising them did in the 1920s. The unsatisfactory attempt to deal with the issue of increasing female representation in the House of Commons politics by establishing quotas for their representation could be abandoned.

Retired and young persons, an enormous untapped reservoir of experience and energy, might also find membership in a constituency parliament practical and attractive. Aboriginal persons, perhaps the most difficult group of Canadians to engage in the formal political system, would also have more access to government through constituency parliaments.[8]

Many constituency parliament members could come from the ranks of those who are already politically engaged but in ways they find unsatisfactory and limiting. Those citizens deserve a more personally satisfying role in the policy-making process than their membership in parties and in interest groups offer.

If one considers the very small number of people now holding elective office, and the even smaller number dominating the policy-making process, the enlargement of the policy-making community that would accompany the establishment of constituency parliaments is impressive. Future generations would be born into a society where taking an interest in politics, modelled by their parents and neighbours, would be more common and intense. The trend of turning away from politics, particularly noticeable among young Canadians, would be reversed.

---

8   The record of aboriginal non-participation in the electoral process is set out in a series of articles in *Electoral Insight*, 5, 3 (Ottawa: Elections Canada, November 2003)..

Modus Operandi

Initially, the constituency parliament (CP) might meet full-time for a period of approximately one month per year. For this regular annual session, the CP would set its own agenda. It could both respond to issues before the Commons that it selected for local consideration and initiate action on others that its members thought should be put before the House of Commons.

A one-month-long session might appear too brief for serious local deliberation. Until recently, however, when most provincial legislators promoted themselves from part- to full-time status, the elected representatives in even our largest province met for only two to three months a year to transact business. The CP as a representing body would not be charged with adopting legislation or becoming engaged in many of the activities of senior parliamentarians. Additional constituency parliament meetings could be scheduled by the local parliament itself, by its MP, or by the government, as required.

Consultation. If a wide consultation of informed public opinion on any issue was deemed desirable by the national government, the network of elected constituency parliaments would be there, with a real mandate to represent Canadians. They could provide an informed, responsible view on developments that come up suddenly, such as proposals that Canada participate in peacekeeping missions or that it adopt certain measures to deal with an economic emergency.

A public consultation, based on constituency parliaments, could be seen as a form of referendum. Unlike a conventional referendum, however, it could be quickly arranged; offer more informed, responsible, and nuanced advice; and be less subject to manipulation. The existence of constituency parliaments would minimize the need for expensive polling and other forms of consultation. The financial savings from this alone might meet most or all of the cost of CPs (see below).

The existing gap between us, our elected representatives, and government would be bridged by CPs. "Heavy traffic"— information, proposals, ideas— would travel back and forth over that bridge from all parts of the country and from all segments of the population. Local parliamentarians could establish direct contacts on common concerns with members of similar bodies across provincial, regional, linguistic, and other divides. A system emphasizing those concerns, rather than those of competing parties, would promote social cohesiveness and national unity.

Role of elected representatives. Demands are frequently made by diverse groups and individuals and by backbench MPs themselves that they be given a more significant role in developing public policy. They would find that role in organizing and playing a major part in the deliberations of the local constituency parliament. In addition to performing the usual constituency duties, the MP would help CP members to become informed. They would share ideas and in-depth information on current issues with their constituency parliament's members. The MPs would be accountable to these citizens, who would be in a good position to assess their performance in the constituency, and also in Ottawa acting as their spokesperson in the House of Commons. The latter role would assume new importance, since the MP carrying the mandate of his or her constituents would no longer be subject to control by party whips. Political executives could no longer take his or her support for granted.

An MP could chair CP sessions, unless members of the local assembly decided it would be better for the MP to be free to participate more fully in discussions. One of the local parliament's members could then be elected its speaker.

Integration with senior government. Politics are now centered on the ongoing party competition for our support that climaxes on election day. But in policy democracy, the primary focus of Canadians would be on the ongoing development of public policy at the local and national levels. Policy message(s) would be conveyed to Ottawa between elections from constituency parliaments through their MPs. The ballot would be used almost exclusively to choose between candidates for office. Particular policies would "really" be mandated by citizens as they were considered in constituency parliaments, or in the Commons alone when they did not "make it" to the agenda of constituency parliaments. It is proposed that the CPs would select only a few significant policy issues to consider.

Candidate(s) in general elections in policy democracy would be nominated by the constituency parliaments, run as independents or as party candidates in the unlikely event that parties survived after the new system of representation was adopted. General elections would lose much of their significance in policy democracy. If an MP were working closely and effectively with the local constituency parliament, what reason would voters have to remove him or her from office? If individual cabinet ministers, or the executive as a whole, were efficiently implementing the program developed collaboratively with CP members and the Commons, why would either be replaced?

If it were necessary to "refresh" the executive with new or superior talent, its members individually or collectively could be replaced at any time by MPs to whom they would be responsible, in more than just theory. There would be no need to wait for, or use, an election to change political leadership and, at the same time, possibly impose an inexperienced governing team on the country with all the uncertainty that causes.

With the new constituency parliament model, many citizens would miss the melodramatic aspects of competitive party politics with its heightened theatrics during election campaigns. The struggle of party leaders for power is exciting and interesting. It does reward the advertising industry with higher profits. But I think most citizens would gladly trade all the sound and fury involved in elections, and competitive party politics generally, for a representative system that gave them a significant role in directing the actions of what would be *their* government.

The cabinet's role would also be different in a system where the House of Commons, truly representing the citizenry, was a major power centre. The workload of cabinet members would still be extremely heavy. It would be unreasonable to expect them to add to their other responsibilities by acting as chairpersons of, or even just participants in, their constituency parliaments.

If we decided to continue the present practice of having some constituency MPs serve as cabinet ministers, there are at least three ways to avoid burdening them with CP responsibilities.[9]

9   Additional reasons for changing the role played by members of the cabinet will be considered in a later chapter.

- Each candidate for the office of MP could run with an alternate, a practice now followed in several countries.[10] In the event that an MP's term was interrupted by death, resignation, or appointment to the cabinet, the alternate would assume his or her responsibilities. In the latter case, the minister would continue to sit in the House and participate in the debates as a member of the executive but would not have a vote.

- An even better Canadian solution, one which would enhance the status of constituency parliaments, would be for the local assembly to elect one of its members to replace an MP serving in the cabinet.

- We could follow the American model some distance and have cabinet members chosen from the community by MPs consulting with their CPs. The PM might be chosen first and be given a voice in the composition of the executive team he was to lead.

Meetings of the constituency parliaments would need to be coordinated with sessions of the House of Commons. To accomplish this, it would be desirable, although not immediately essential, to alter some House of Commons procedures. Most of those that would be affected are already recognized by parliamentarians as in need of change.

The cabinet could, for example, be required to introduce its legislative and spending proposals in the early weeks of a parliamentary session. The only exception would be emergency bills, the nature of which would be carefully spelled out. Then legislation would be submitted to thorough committee scrutiny in the House of Commons. After the scrutiny, parliament would adjourn, and with all the information collected by the Commons committees available to them, the CP members, along with their MP, would meet to consider the legislation of interest to them and the matters for which they feel action should be proposed. Following these deliberations, the MP would return to the Commons, participate in further discussions with colleagues, and cast final deciding votes. With this procedure in place, the

---

10   These include Brazil, Denmark, and France. See *Inter-Parliamentary Union, Parliaments of the World* (London: Macmillan, 1976), 195.

constituency parliament would be an integral part of the legislative process and could have a major impact on policy.

Power and the constituency parliament. The election of constituency parliaments would give their members a unique degree of legitimacy among bodies seeking to influence public policy. But the void that now exists between us and our elected representatives would not be filled satisfactorily if CPs only have *influence*. We need more than this if we are to shift the balance of political power from party to citizen.

The obvious way of ensuring that a power shift takes place would be to make it mandatory for MPs to vote as directed by their CPs—but this would not be desirable or feasible. The local groups would focus their attention on only a few issues and leave others to their MP's judgment. Further, MPs returning to Ottawa from meetings with their CPs should listen and respond to the views of colleagues from other parts of the country. Those views, and others, should all be factored into their final voting decision. The House of Commons cannot be a real forum for the discussion and negotiation of public questions if the members arrive at sessions with fixed positions on issues that were established elsewhere.

While not legally bound, an MP would be morally obligated to convey the views of constituents on the issues that the CP had taken a position on—and on others for which he or she could reasonably anticipate what the CP's response would be. In most cases, the MP would also support that position with his or her vote. However, if the MP, after making the position of his or her constituency clear, then decided to express a different position in voting, he or she might later be able to convince constituency parliament members that the deviation from their viewpoint was justified. If the representative failed in this, the MP would not necessarily lose the general confidence of the CP. People who respect one another can often agree to disagree and continue a good relationship.

On the other hand, the MP might articulate views that differed significantly from those of the CP members on many issues or on one or more of great importance to local parliamentarians. In this circumstance, the constituency parliament members could demand the MP's resignation as the constituency's representative. If it were not tendered, they could decide to urge voters to defeat the MP at the next election. Or perhaps the constituency parliament should be able to initiate a recall election of the MP in those circumstances.

It is possible that an MP criticized by his or her CP might win a recall-forced or general election. The member could then argue that his or her representation of the constituency was superior to that of the CP. The election would then be tantamount to a vote of lack of confidence in the CP or the majority of its members. Voters would have reason to consider carefully who they elected in the next CP election. Obviously, every CP will not always perfectly represent the considered views of the citizens it is supposed to represent. The views of all CPs, as aggregated in the Commons, will, however, provide an excellent overall representation of informed opinion in the country.

A study of the role of MPs in the Commons identifies two challenges that must be met by advocates, like myself, of a "semi-delegate" role for them: "They face the challenge of providing a convincing account of how individual representatives can serve as credible proxies for highly pluralistic publics, in which there may be no clear consensus on individual issues, and they also need to explain how a system of riding delegates can be responsive to the needs of groups that are not territorially based, including national, religious, ethnic, linguistic and social minorities."[11]

In the policy democracy/constituency parliament model, the majority view of that pluralist public would be identified through "deliberative discussion" and voting. The needs of groups that are not territorially based would be provided for by not tying MPs strictly to a delegate role, i.e., by supplementing local deliberations with the freedom to consider and act in the Commons on the needs of non-territorially based interests. The absence of parties, if that proves the case, would not stop the current practice of MPs organizing lobbies to press particular causes.

In my discussions with MPs about constituency parliaments, some expressed the view that the role proposed for them would be demeaning—making them mere "letter-carriers" from the CP to the House of Commons.

---

11   Jack Stilborn (prepared by), "The Roles of the Members of Parliament in Canada: Are They Changing?" (Ottawa: The Library of Parliament, May 2002), 11. http://www.parl.gc.ca/information/library/PRBpubs/prb0204-e-htm

Some of the same people who loyally reflect the views of their party leaders in the Commons believe it would be demeaning to act as spokespersons for an informed body of their constituents! Do lawyers find it humiliating to represent their clients?

Unlike that of some MPs, the general reaction of citizens to whom I have talked about policy democracy based on constituency parliaments has been enthusiastic. The prospect of the MP carrying forward the views of informed representatives of the constituency to the House of Commons, and then working with colleagues and the executive to govern the country, was seen as natural—the way it should be. This view confirmed polling on the subject of political representation. At the same time, however, those citizens were sceptical about the possibility of achieving constituency representation in the face of opposition from entrenched interests, an issue that will be discussed in later chapters.

Support for Constituency Deliberation

The authority of CPs must be bolstered beyond the election of its members by providing them with two important resources, time and information. To ensure that their views cannot be dismissed as uninformed, members of constituency parliaments must be able to analyse public policy issues in depth.

Information. Constituency parliament members would be informed from several sources, with House of Commons committees being the most important. Members would need to have access to the same information available to MPs if they are to be confident and assertive in their relations with them. MPs must not be able to play the if-you-knew-what-I-know-you-would-agree-with-me game with the local representatives.

The information sharing would be an important step in countering the "culture of secrecy" described by the now-disbanded Economic Council of Canada, which still exists, despite freedom-of-information laws: "At present, public involvement in policy-making suffers under a large handicap. By and large, the general public does not know, even after the fact, the arguments and evaluations on which public decisions are based."[12]

The party in office often believes it improves its competitive position to keep significant information from parliament, the media, and us, and it often relies on exclusions in the Access to Information Act to do so![13] It would, however, be disadvantageous for the country's executive to refuse to release information if MPs and CP members were empowered, and their support was necessary if the executives' policy recommendations were to be adopted.

As background for their deliberations, the constituency parliament members could have complete transcripts and/or tapes and videos of all the evidence provided to parliamentary committees. They could, in addition, hear direct representations from nationally and locally based interest groups, experts, and concerned citizens. Each constituency parliament would be an empowered study group. After deliberation based on all this input, the constituency parliament's members could be as fully informed as its MP.

Even with the best and fullest information sources, there will, of course, be important but very complex issues on which, like the cabinet itself, constituency parliament members will defer to the judgment of experts.[14]

Time. The constituency parliament model could not succeed if its members were expected to serve on a volunteer basis any more than the senior parliament could. If members of the CP were not remunerated many people

---

12   Economic Council of Canada, "Design for Decision-Making, Eighth Annual Review" (Ottawa: Information Canada, 1971), 85.

13   The evasions of the Access to Information Act are discussed in chapter 8.

14   Commenting on the argument that citizens should be excluded from the policy-making process because many of the issues faced by government will be beyond them, political scientist Sir Ivor Jennings writes, "What is needed … is not so much knowledge as plain common sense, the ability to seize the point of an argument when it is presented in an elementary fashion. [PM Chrétien was known to demand one-page presentations on even complex issues.] If the State had to decide nice points in the theory of knowledge or consider the composition of matter, it could do no more than leave the question to its philosophers and scientists. Fortunately, the general questions of public policy are not of this order, and for those aspects of it, such as the precise relationship between a currency and its gold backing, which are, the ordinary individual usually has enough sense to rely on the experts." *Party Politics: The Growth of Parties* (Cambridge: Cambridge University Press, 1961), 6.

would be unable to stand for election weakening the claim of the CP to be the authentic voice of the constituency. Further, its members need time to study and discuss issues in depth if their views are to be taken seriously by the MP who is to carry them forward to the House of Commons.

I fear that, with current feelings about government being so negative, some will be inclined to dismiss out-of-hand the idea of an extension of government to include significant citizen participation by paid representatives between elections. As readers follow the critique of the existing system in the following chapters, however, and see how the addition of constituency parliaments would deal with the system's weaknesses, they may change their minds. But to meet cost concerns head on let me note now how I think the adoption of the constituency parliament model might be adequately financed.

The financing issue, like other important details relating to the organization of constituency parliaments, would, of course, be subject to change by citizens once the principle of constituency parliaments was accepted and work begun on its implementation. My calculations, based on figures published by Elections Canada, are intended only to show what could be the cost to individual Canadians.

It would, I think, be appropriate to tie the remuneration of constituency parliament members to that of their Ottawa colleagues. The basic salary of an MP is $157,731 (2011) for what is a full time, 12-month position for most. Meeting for one month a year, the members of constituency parliaments might be paid one twelfth of the MPs salary — $13,144 in salary plus $2500 for information and other general CP expenses for total of $15,644.

Each of the 308 constituency parliaments would represent an average of 77,707 registered voters. (23,933,743 total reg. voters ÷308 constituencies).

The individual constituency parliament's 77,707 registered voters would, on the basis of one CP member for each thousand citizens, have to support an overall CP cost of $1,220,232. (78 CP members × $15,644. salary plus expenses=1,220,232.) The constituency would have, on average, 77,707 registered voters sharing this cost/tax. Assuming a common tax rate, the cost to each of these registered voters, you and me, would be $15.70 per year. ($1,220,232 ÷ 77,707 =15.70) That cost figure, and much more, could easily be offset by improvements in government as a result of increased citizen involvement.

Some members of the constituency parliaments would find their $13,144 salary attractive while, for others, it would represent a financial sacrifice, as is the case with members of the House of Commons.

Looked at from a strictly cost point of view, the Constituency Parliaments could be seen as a bargain. But, for most of us, a significant advance of popular democracy, with all the values it incorporates, cannot be measured in monetary terms.

Currently, we invest significant public funds in maintaining our dysfunctional system of representation but virtually nothing in citizens to ensure that arrangements are in place so that they/we can be truly represented. Change in political institutions is dramatically lagging behind social and economic developments – as we shall discuss.

Constituency Parliaments and Other Political Actors

The establishment of constituency parliaments would precipitate adjustments in the structure and functioning of existing formal and informal representative agencies. I will consider these in subsequent chapters. To round out the description of the CP model in this chapter, however, some preliminary comment on these probable changes might be helpful.

Parties. In my discussions of the policy democracy/constituency parliament proposal with other citizens, they frequently suggest that parties would extend their pattern of top-down control to local assemblies, undermining their credibility as spokespersons for their constituents. They assume that with constituency parliaments established, parties would survive in their present form, with their leaders enjoying their current ability to manage MPs.

In a policy democracy based on constituency parliaments, however, the really important relationship for MPs would be with their constituency parliament, not with a party. Voters cannot compete for a party MP's loyalty now because they are not organized. But with the establishment of a constituency parliament, it would be virtually mandatory for the MP to represent the views of constituents.

In the very unlikely event that parties survived, the MP would be directly faced with a serious decision, i.e., whether to respect the views of his or her neighbours and colleagues in the constituency parliament or to follow the direction of an autocratic party leader. At the very least, the cross-pressures on all MPs up to and including party leaders from fellow citizens and party would force a relaxation of party discipline, enabling members to respond to local opinion.

Again, assuming the survival of parties, politicians now join them because of what the party can do for them, i.e., provide an election organization, offer positions in the Commons hierarchy, and other perks. None of these would be relevant to a candidate for a seat in a constituency parliament. He or she could personally contact all his or her voters easily without financial or other help from a party.

We accept parties as a necessary evil in federal and provincial elections because we are conditioned to believe that we must have them to have democracy.[15] Individuals seeking public office accept them and their discipline because (a) they are the "only show in town," and (b) because they need party support to organize and finance a campaign. However, parties are seen as an electoral handicap where the system can work without them, i.e., in most local government, in Nunavut, and in almost all large "democratic" organizations. Commenting on Nunavut and the Northwest Territories, political scientist Nelson Wiseman notes, "they have constructively demonstrated contrary to conventional wisdom that representation, electoral democracy, and the Westminster model can move forward without parties."[16]

---

15   Asked to evaluate the party system, the majority of Canadians found them dysfunctional in 10 of 11 categories. The evaluation was (mildly) positive in response to the statement "Political parties and democracy always go together—no parties, no democracy." Fifty percent of respondents agreed, 26 disagreed, and 24 percent "don't know." Harold D. Clarke and Allan Kornberg, "Evaluations and Evolution: Public Attitudes toward Canada's Federal Political Parties, 1965-1991," *Canadian Journal of Political Science* 26, 2 (June 1993): 291..

16   Nelson Wiseman, review of *Political Parties, Representation, and Electoral Democracy in Canada,* ed. William Cross, *Canadian Journal of Political Science* 35, 4 (De-

Parties are more likely to disappear in a policy democracy than they are to be a continuing force that would take control of constituency parliaments. MPs would break free of party control, and constituency parliament members would never be subject to it.

Parliament. The impact of constituency parliaments on parliament would be significant. Responsible cabinet government would be brought into line with the idealized vision we now hold of it. It is recognized as largely myth that the cabinet is responsible to the House of Commons and the Commons to the people. The familiar reality is that the prime minister, relying on the support in the House of a disciplined party team, manages his or her MPs. We are left significantly unrepresented. Leaders of opposition parties control their MPs, too, but less firmly.

With the input of empowered citizens, represented in Ottawa by their MP, the present top-down distribution of power would be largely reversed. In the absence of parties to provide leadership to the government, the members of the Commons, consulting with their CPs, would elect a prime minister and cabinet from their ranks; from outside the ranks of elected members, as in the United States; or a combination of both.[17]

A variety of executive arrangements is found in the liberal democracies, and we would adopt one that fit with the policy democracy/constituency parliament model.[18] Demands and support would flow from us, through constituency parliaments, to MPs in the Commons, and from them to the executive headed by the PM. MPs, with a secure base in their constituencies,

cember 2002): 902.. These examples may be dismissed as insignificant because of the small number of citizens in each jurisdiction. Still, it is interesting that when these new governments were formed they were non-party. If Canada were starting over, would parties be assigned the responsibility for representing citizens and their governance?

17   In charging the Commons with the responsibility for appointing a PM, we would be returning to the pre-1919 pattern. The Liberals in that year instituted the practice of assigning the choice of leader, and sometimes the PM, to a convention. With the policy democracy model in place, constituency representatives—members of CPs—would play a role in appointing the PM in consultations with their MPs.

18   The desirability of choosing the executive from outside parliament will be discussed more fully in later chapters. For an example of how very different the organization of executive authority can be in liberal democracies, consider the collegial executive of Switzerland. www.swissinfor.ch/eng/politics/political_system

would be in a position to insist that the cabinet be really responsible to them. The arbitrary powers of the prime minister would be checked. Under our current system, we have no formal means through which we can hold MPs or governments accountable, other than an election—a crude and disruptive tool. With constituency parliaments in place, we would have the means to hold both continuously accountable.

A government based on constituency representation would, of course, still require strong executive leadership. The character of that leadership would be fundamentally different in policy democracy, however. The executive would be implementing an agenda developed in collaboration with our representatives rather than imposing its own. And it would be directing a bureaucracy that would truly be a public service, rather than one that was required to further the interests of the party in office as a by-product of its work.[19]

Interest groups. Along with parties, interest groups unsatisfactorily fill the representational vacuum that now exists between us and our governors. In policy democracy, interest groups of whatever kind will no longer be able to claim that they speak for us, because we will have the means to speak for ourselves.

Many special interests will find they must lobby through constituency parliaments—a new and important power centre—to influence policy. Depending on access to a small group of policy makers will no longer be effective. Public-interest groups will find that the upward flow of power from citizens to the executive means that they have significant access to national policy makers through constituency parliaments.

Refocusing interest-group activity and bringing some of the now-behind-the-scenes pressure out into the open would have a powerful educative effect on more than just constituency parliament members. Lobbyists, and those they represent, would have to learn more about and would have to respond to public concerns in order to be effective.

Media. The media's reports on politics focus heavily on party leaders and, particularly, on the prime minister, because that is where power lies. With the

---

19   This point is discussed fully in chapter 6.

redistribution of that power occasioned by the introduction of constituency parliaments, the number of power holders and sites would be substantially increased. Discussions in the Commons and its committees would gain new significance when MPs are no longer team players following the directions of their party's leadership. Constituency parliaments would also constitute an important new locus of power and a forum for the local discussion of national and international issues. Local media, often parochial in their orientation, would be drawn into devoting time and space to a wider range of issues as they reported on their community's CP sessions.

Constituency parliaments and policy democracy would affect the media in two less obvious ways. First, to the extent that the CPs raised the general level of political sophistication, the media would face a more critical audience and need to adjust their coverage to it. Second, the power wielded by a small number of corporate media owners has been a long-standing subject of concern and the topic of two post World War II commissions of enquiry. People with extensive media experience were members of both. In the face of hostile media owners in a strong position to protect their interests, elected governments quickly shelved their commissions' significant recommendations. Electoral democracy does not generate the level of trust and support the party in office needs if it is to make highly sensitive decisions touching on freedom of the press—or of media owners, depending on one's political perspective. Unorganized, we citizens were in no position to provide countervailing support to government had it wished to act on the recommendations of the commissions—although these were important to the health of our democracy.

In a policy democracy, citizens could decide on the most appropriate model of ownership and control of the mass media. At the same time, ownership would be less important, since a large number of citizens would be participating directly in government. They would not be as dependent as they are now on the media for information and opinion.

Conclusion

Most of us agree that the present political system is obsolete. We tell those who ask that we want our MP to represent us, free of party control. Policy democracy based on constituency parliaments would, responsibly, provide that mode of representation. It would give government roots in the citizenry, from which it could draw support, as it pursued the public interest as we defined it.

The model proposed in this chapter recognizes that adequate institutional means must be provided to support wider political participation. Constituency parliaments would provide those means. Elected CP members would be given the required status, time, and information—all at little cost— so that they could execute their role effectively.

The policy democracy/constituency parliament proposal is *conservative* in that it simply realizes in practical terms the mode of representation that the vast majority of us already believe is appropriate in a democracy. But it is *radical* in that the local parliaments would fundamentally alter the existing distribution of political power. Party representation supporting party government would give way to constituency representation supporting citizen-based government. Power would be devolved from a small party elite to a popular base of constituency parliament members. Without resorting to much hyperbole, we could say that power was shifted to the people. Popular input to policy, added to the existing system of electing representatives, would move the system to a new level of democracy. Social and economic achievements would then be possible that we can only dream of now, while we are preoccupied with keeping the existing archaic political system functioning.

Postscript: Edmund Burke, Champion of Constituency Parliaments?

No discussion of representation is complete without reference to the ideas of Edmund Burke, the eloquent 18th-century spokesperson of British conservatism. Burke is commonly cited as support for opposition to the idea that the member of the Commons should reflect the views of constituents. He expressed his opposition over two centuries ago in a world as different from our own as "chalk from cheese." But that does not stop people relying still on his criticisms of delegate representation.

In his time, Burke argued that it would be wrong for constituents to make their MP a delegate, because they would then (a) deprive themselves of the benefit of his judgment and (b) cause decisions made in parliament to be based on the opinions of people hundreds of miles away, who were ignorant of the issues and did not bear responsibility for the well-being of the nation. He extolled the merits of a trustee role, i.e., one where the MP acted on the basis of his best judgment of the interests of the country. When he was writing, however, disciplined parties curbing the independent views of MPs; a well-educated, assertive population with easy access to a vast amount of current information; and large, intrusive government were all far off.[20]

With constituency parliaments in place, while the MP would adopt a semi-delegate role, his or her constituents would gain the benefit of the MP's independent advice, expressed in a local forum. The country would similarly gain from its expression, enriched by that local discussion, in the House of Commons. The pressure from party leaders to parrot a party line or be a party delegate would be effectively countered by the insistence of CP members that their MP contribute their and his or her critical thinking to the policy-making process at the local and national levels. Further, with the establishment of CPs, the views the MP would be expected to represent would be informed. As office-holders in government, CP members would be expected to accept their share of responsibility for the consequences flowing from Ottawa's policies.

First the trustee and now the current party delegate roles have been made dysfunctional by political developments. Today, Burke would likely recognize the need for (necessarily) large governments to have a strong base of citizen support to function effectively. Indeed, if he were alive today to respond to changes in the political world, Burke might well be a strong supporter of an institutional arrangement, such as policy democracy based on constituency parliaments, that would bring leaders and led into a close, mutually respectful working relationship.

---

20   Edmund Burke, "Speech to the Electors of Bristol," in *The Philosophy of Edmund Burke,* eds. L. I. Bredvold and Ralph G. Ross (Ann Arbor: University of Michigan Press, 1960), 147–48.

Citizens Systematically Under-Represented, Misrepresented, and "Dumbed Down"

Today, a person is deemed to be politically "represented" no matter what, i.e., regardless of his own will and actions or that of his representative. A person is considered represented if he votes, but also if he does not vote. He is considered represented if the candidate he has voted for is elected, but also if another candidate is elected. He is represented, whether the candidate he voted for or did not vote for, does or does not do what he wished him to do. And he is considered politically represented, whether "his" representative will find majority support among all elected representatives or not.

Hans-Hermann Hoppe

Any system that allows the people to speak without permission is profoundly distressing to professional politicians. There is nothing they hate more than to hear the people answering a question they were never asked. Hence the great scarcity of political systems that allow the people to speak for themselves.

Jean-Francois Revel

Introduction

We desperately need the policy democracy/constituency model of representation. Living in what is described as a "representative democracy," citizens tell pollsters they feel powerless, unrepresented. That is an exaggeration, but it reflects the frustration experienced by citizens who have far too little control over the actions of what should be their government. The frustration has serious consequences. Excluded from significant participation in governance, we feel little responsibility to give government the support it needs to meet its responsibilities. Further, we have little incentive to become politically knowledgeable when we are denied an empowered political role. As a result, we are unable to play even the limited political role we do have as voters in a rational manner. In particular, we are likely to be suspicious of change, preferring the familiar even if we find it alienating.[1] Unintentionally, we are an obstacle to the very political progress we want and need.

Negative feeling relating to the citizen-excluding nature of partyocracy is compounded by the performance of party government. Uncertain about their support, governments avoid hard decisions. Weak representation of citizens in government begets weak government. If we are fully aware of the character of the current representative system and see a viable alternative to it, will we tolerate it any longer?

The misrepresentation that characterizes the system starts with how the system itself is presented by the political terminology in common use. It continues with the malfunctioning of the formal and informal systems of representation that we now depend on to represent us to government.

Protecting Partyocracy with Rhetoric

The words we use to describe the existing representative system are confusing. Their choice, and the meaning assigned to them, is largely in the hands of the political establishment who lead our political discussion. Understandably, they describe "their" political system, including its representative aspects,

---

1   The defeated provincial referenda on electoral change are an example of this phenomenon. People want stronger representation in government but are uneasy when presented with an opportunity to get it.

in flattering system-supporting, but grossly misleading, terms.[2] Critics of the system must either use their terminology, unintentionally bolstering its democratic credentials, or resort to words that may seem off-putting, awkward, or unfamiliar but that honestly describe the system or features of it—words like *partyocracy*.

There will be frequent references in this chapter to the "representative" system while the basic argument presented is that, from a democratic perspective, its significant characteristic is its *un*representativeness. An accurate description of our system would be that it is one where citizens delegate their political powers and responsibilities to a party, particularly its leader, that is engaged with other parties in an often corrupting adversarial competition. From the perspective of citizens, the system requires they must trust one or other of the parties to represent them. When government is so vital to our well being and parties such discredited institutions, this is a recipe for popular political alienation.

Representation of citizens is absolutely not the base of our system nor can it be until citizens are organized to express their clear consent to or rejection of proposed public policies. The right to replace leadership must involve far more than the opportunity to change the governing party team every four years.

Citizen is a word that will be used as an alternative to *voter* or *person* to denote a legal status. Its general use in political discussion suggests, however, that we already enjoy the status of democratic citizen, i.e., are actively and responsibly engaged in governing our community and country. If we were to refer to ourselves as *subjects* of a party or its leader, a more accurate description of our political status, we would constantly be reminded of the need to press forward with democratic reform.

Parliamentary government, or *parliamentary democracy*, conjures up a positive, reassuring, but unrealistic image of elected MPs from across the country consulting, setting policy, and overseeing the administration

---

2   "Language determines, of course, how we think in trying to make sense of the world ... Thus, when people adopt the vocabulary of the powerful, they implicitly (and often unconsciously) find themselves unable to imagine any other way of thinking about issues." Neil Brooks, *Left vs. Right* (Ottawa: Canadian Centre for Policy Alternatives, 1995), 11. www.policyalternatives.ca

of government. That is what policy democracy based on constituency parliaments aims to achieve. It does not exist now. The terms *prime ministerial government* or *partyocracy* convey a more accurate picture of the central government. Again, using these descriptors would emphasize the need for reform.

The negative impact of outdated terminology was described, brilliantly, by Aneurin Bevan, a now-deceased British political figure:

> The student of politics must be on guard against the old words, for the words persist when the realities behind them have changed. It is inherent in our intellectual activity that we seek to imprison reality in our description of it. Soon, long before we realize it, it is we who become the prisoners of the description. From that point on, our ideas degenerate into a kind of folklore which we pass on to each other, fondly thinking we are still talking of the reality around us.
>
> … If this is not understood, we become symbol worshipers. The categories that were the tools we used in our intercourse with reality become hopelessly blunted. The social and political realities we are supposed to be grappling with change and reshape themselves independently of the collective impact of our ideas. We become the creature and no longer partner of social realities. As we fumble with outworn categories, our political vitality is sucked away and we stumble from one situation to another, without chart, without compass, and with the steering-wheel lashed to a course we are no longer following.[3]

The Formal and Informal Representative Systems

We are currently represented in politics in two quite different ways or modes: formal and informal. The right to elect a member of parliament to speak for us in the House of Commons in an open, regular, competitive election constitutes the *formal* system of representation. In this system, we have an equal input, one vote, although the forces determining how we exercise our franchise are quite unequal. The *informal* comprises the various means—

---

3   Aneurin Bevan cited in the **CCPA Monitor** (March 2009).

party membership, interest group lobbying, demonstrations, etc.—that we use to influence those in the government who have the formal responsibility for making public policy. Political parties play a minor role in the informal system but dominate the formal. The resources needed to influence policy-makers through the informal system are very unequally shared by citizens and organized interests.

The evolution of the formal (party) representative system. Elections leading to the delegation of our citizen rights and responsibilities to parties and their leaders are the foundation of the formal representative system. That relationship was established in the latter half of the 19th century. But when the Assembly of Upper Canada was created in 1791, the election by men of some wealth from among those standing for office was the method of choosing its members. With small constituencies, and with the elected part-time members of the Assembly spending most of their time making a living in their communities, it was natural to see them as able to represent their constituents in a general way on the policy and administrative issues coming before the Assembly.

It was not seen as desirable, nor was it practical, to instruct the elected members on what they were to say and how they were to vote. Representation by local leaders in the Assembly, and rule by British-appointed governors, was accepted as normal.

Initially, the successful candidates for Assembly membership linked up with others in the Assembly in loosely organized, shifting factions to promote their common interests. Later, political leaders, competing for office in the executive and for control of government patronage, realized the value of having an organized body of supporters they could depend on for backing. Under their leadership, these factions were to evolve into parties in the Assembly. The groups of local people interested in supporting the party and its candidates were organized into constituency organizations, branches of those parties.

At first, constituency party members assumed most of the responsibility for nominating candidates for the Assembly and organizing their election campaigns. Over time, however, the local associations came to rely heavily on the central party. If the party leader was popular, the qualities of his local candidates and their performance in the Assembly became much less important in determining electoral success.[4] Acceptance of support from the national party brought with it an obligation to loyally support the party team and its leader in the Assembly. These developments took place gradually over the decades prior to Confederation in 1867. With Confederation, the names of institutions changed to those we are familiar with today: "Assembly" to "House of Commons," etc.

With parties, elected members of the Assembly, and then of the House of Commons, became members of their party's caucus, that is, the party leader's support group and sounding board. The balance of pressures on the elected constituency representatives (MPs) emanating from party leaders and from their constituents became overwhelmingly skewed in favour of the former. Where they existed at all, the views of constituents were diverse and generally uninformed. Further, constituents lacked the kind of organization that would enable them to insist on their views being represented. The party leader, on the other hand, was in a position to exert tight control of the views and behaviour of the MP, because he possessed the power to advance or retard the MP's career and could claim, with more validity than any other, to speak for the public at large.

Our first post-Confederation prime minister suggested what was expected of supporters: it was not enough that they supported the PM when they agreed with his position. Sir John A. Macdonald reprimanded a senator taking that position, writing, "That is no satisfaction. Anybody may support me when I am right. What I want is a man that will support me when I am wrong."[5] Parties provided such men (and later, women).

In the early years, independent MPs were sometimes referred to as

4   This shift to the primacy of party leaders in the decision of local voters took place over an extended period. Contemporary research suggests that in recent elections "the local candidate was a decisive consideration for five percent of Canadian voters." André Blais, Elizabeth Gidengil, Agnieszka Dobrzynska, Neil Nevitte, Richard Nadeau, "Does the Local Candidate Matter? Effects in the Canadian Election of 2000," note, *Canadian Journal of Political Science* 36, 3, (July-August 2003), 659.
5   Exchange with Senator A. R. Dickey of Amherst, quoted by E. B. Biggar in "Anecdotal Life of Sir John A. Macdonald," 1891, cited in *Colombo's Canadian Quotations,* ed. J. R. Colombo (Edmonton, Alberta: Hurtig, 1974), 381. A modern PM would not be as candid but would also expect loyal support of his or her policies.

"loose fish," because their support could be caught by attractive bait. With the emergence of disciplined parties, these "fish" became "sheep." On important policy questions, their constituents became heavily dependent on a distant figure, the prime minister, or party leader in the case of the opposition, to represent them. Polling suggests that over the years we have reached the stage where the MP is not expected to play a significant personal role in representing the policy-related views of citizens. Before there was polling, that was probably the case as well.[6]

In rankings of the respect accorded to various occupations, MPs run close to last.[7] Part of the reason is that, elected to represent their constituents, they find they are expected to loyally follow the direction of their leader. That behaviour is an ill fit with what constituents expect from someone who has campaigned to represent them. In defensive mode, MPs argue that behind the scenes, in caucus and in private interactions with the policy czars in the cabinet and PMO, they forcibly represent their constituents' views. However, studies of how various political actors influence policy show that, finally, even if MPs do this, their actual impact on policy is slight—as many of their constituents suspect.[8]

Each of the emerging parties adopted a platform setting out the policies they proposed to enact if given the opportunity. Voters were assumed to endorse the platform when they voted for a party's candidate. The personal representation offered by MPs was significantly restricted by their

---

6   In one poll, 62.4 percent of those questioned believed that the MP should give top priority to the needs of constituents as opposed to 7.4 percent who thought passing laws should be his or her top priority. Gallup Omnibus Poll cited in Peter Dobell and Byron Berry, "Political Discontent in Canada," *Parliamentary Government*, 39 (January 1992), 9.

7   While their constituency role may enhance the position of the MP, the enhancement still leaves MPs close to the very bottom of surveys measuring the respect and trust enjoyed by various occupations. One, reporting nurses with a 72 percent trust rating, places MPs with 4 percent—just ahead of the bottom categories: car dealers and telemarketers. Source: Pollara, cited in the *Toronto Star* (May 5, 2001), R5.

8   The current impact of MPs on policy is suggested in a survey in which senior business executives and bureaucrats rated the influence of those participating in making policy. Only 7 percent of bureaucrats thought that MPs had moderate or great influence in the process, as compared to an 80 percent ranking for cabinet ministers. Public Policy Forum, *Bridging Two Solitudes: A Discussion Paper on Federal Government-Industry Relations* (Ottawa: 2000), 8. www.ppforum.ca.

commitment to their party's program and leadership. The commitment required the MP to suspend many of his or her personal convictions about what was best for constituents or country.

One of the most helpful pieces of research on representation and our political ills generally has been conducted by Samara, a public interest group based in Ottawa. Sixty-five recently retired parliamentarians from across the spectrum of parties were asked for their views on why parliament seemed dysfunctional to many. The result was a surprise to its sponsor. In a synopsis of the report they write: "While many commentators focus on problems with Parliament itself....the MPs had a different view. .... For the Members of Parliament we interviewed, it was often the way their own political parties manage themselves, their members and their work that drives the contemporary dysfunction facing Canadian politics. This observation was consistent across all parties."[9] The conclusion reached is particularly significant in explaining our MPs loss of their ability to represent their constituents effectively but the critique of parties from former party stalwarts has wide ramifications for all aspects of the party-based political system.

Over the years, we have become more realistic about the value of being able to vote for a platform coincident with casting a ballot for a party's candidate. Those platforms can only include commitments relating to a very few of the issues the governing party and its opponents will face during their time in office. Further, while it is important to voters to be able, for example, to shift the government to the left or right through their choice of party candidate, we have come to realize that once in office, party governments are far more likely to act in response to the pressures on them than they are to follow the platforms on which they have campaigned.

In many cases, party governments are forced to renege on their campaign promises. Emerging economic and social circumstances, along with competitive factors, may make it impossible, or unwise, to act as they promised. For this and other reasons, party-dominated elections fail to give citizens much feeling of empowerment. They simply have too little connection to the actual performance of party governments to be citizen-

---

9   Press release, "Former MPs cite their own parties as source of frustration," Ottawa: Samara, April 18, 2011, 1. samaracanada.com

empowering. The really significant benefit from voting is to have a "voice" in the choice of the prime minister who "rules" over us.

Perhaps sensing that claims for the citizen-empowering nature of the vote are overblown, there has been a decline in voter turnouts, and—fully as significant but less noticed—there has been a progressive weakening of the political organization behind voting.

In short, with the capture of constituency MPs by their parties, an important link of the citizen with the formation of public policy was lost. And now the parties themselves are becoming progressively weaker. Professor Thomas Axworthy writes:

...unlike almost any other professionals, politicians are part of a self-selected minority. They are drawn from the tiny percentage of voters who are politically active. In Canada, for example, there is general awareness that, like every democracy in the western world, turnout has been declining (from an average of 75 percent from 1945–1988 to 65 percent in the 2006 election; the all-time low was 61 percent in 2004.) But underneath the mass activity of voting, participation in other forms drops even more dramatically. Less than one Canadian in ten did anything to help a candidate, such as attending a rally or putting a sticker on their car during the Federal Election in 2000. Of the eight to ten percent of Canadians who were engaged more robustly in election campaigns, only about 1-2 percent were consistently active members of a party, placing Canada at the bottom of the list of Western democracies.[10]

Citizens are significantly disempowered as a result of "tiny" hierarchically organized parties commandeering their representatives.

The weak link between citizens and "rulers" is widely recognized, and attempts are made to overcome it with extensive government-sponsored consultation. But as we shall discuss, citizens are sceptical of the value of consultation that carries with it no authority, i.e., that may be ignored by decision makers.[11] The absence of strong input into policy from constituents means that, for parties, people are "merely" voters, a key element in their

10   Thomas Axworthy, "Everything Old is New Again" (Kingston: Queen's University, 2011). 19. www.queensu.ca/csd
11   See the discussion of this point in chapter 8.

success that must be mobilized on a four-year cycle and, between elections, managed carefully. There is a lot of work in Ottawa for political consultants hired, indirectly, by us to help the party in office and its rivals, to do this.

The lack of respect the party system engenders for the views of voters is illustrated by party support for the first-past-the-post electoral system. As we know, this system allows the election of a one-party majority government while the majority of citizens have cast ballots for other parties. Do the parties care about this gross misrepresentation?

In summary, during the course of the 19th century, hierarchically organized, "disciplined" parties came to monopolize the formal representation of citizens The top-down control of the parties precipitated a highly significant role reversal. While the disappearing independent members of the legislative assembly might have carried the views of constituents to the Assembly, the party MPs represented their party's policy positions to constituents. The significance of this reversal should be highlighted in flashing neon! It has had a profound impact on the responsiveness of our government to us and on the general quality of our political life.

The formal representative system that evolved in the 19th century, capped by the achievements of responsible government and Confederation, represented progress from the autocratic rule of British-appointed governors that preceded it. This was particularly the case for Canadian political elites who found themselves newly empowered. The prime minister inherited virtually all the powers of the governor, and these were enhanced by his control of the dominant party in the House of Commons.

At the time of Confederation, the ideal of democracy—rule by the people—was anathema to our political elites, a dangerous American idea. Sir John A. Macdonald, our first prime minister, and his principal opponent, George Brown, explicitly rejected democracy.[12] (Remarkably, virtually

---

12   Historian Bruce Hodgins summarizes the views of Sir John A. Macdonald and George Brown on democracy: "Like all conservative fathers of Confederation, Macdonald rejected both the word *democracy* and many of those attributes now considered essential for it. He rejected political equality, favoured privilege for the propertied and well off, and seemed more concerned about protecting the rights of the minority than providing for majority rule ... he rejected ... the need and wisdom of popular appeals on matters as vital as confederation. Such an appeal, he argued, would be the device of a tyrant, would subvert the principles of the British constitution, and would be an obvious

the same system and its distribution of power that satisfied men so firmly opposed to popular rule is, today, accepted by some, and described by most, as "democratic," i.e., as supporting popular rule.) Given our founding leaders' rejection of democracy, it is understandable that they did not see the political system as a democratic project "in progress"; had no interest in how citizen participation might be expanded in the future. Their values were soon to be challenged by popular movements promoting democracy.

The citizen response to partyocracy. The party monopoly on representation did not go unchallenged. Changing public attitudes eroded the support for partyocracy in the early years of the 20th century, and then that support was dramatically undercut as a result of World War I. As the war progressed, the total mobilization of the civilian population and the nation's resources became necessary. To rouse popular support for this, the war was characterized as a struggle for "democracy," understood by citizens as popular rule, against "autocracy." In conservative Canada, where democracy had been denounced by the establishment, this new rhetoric had far-reaching consequences. It legitimated people power in the eyes of many and raised expectations that the system would be adjusted to embrace it when the war ended. People would now assess the representative system and the governments it produced against their understanding of democracy and whether it was being realized.[13]

Civil and political unrest followed the Allied victory, as citizens waited for the wartime promises to be realized. The unrest was particularly pronounced on the prairies, where the reform ideas of the American progressive movement were influential. Citizens of the newly formed provincial societies rejected the elitist values of the Eastern Canadian establishment. The bitter 1919 Winnipeg general strike demonstrated the new militancy of the working

---

absurdity." (87) George Brown, the Liberal leader, was as opposed to democratic values as Macdonald. Brown, Hodgins writes, "Saw democracy as illiberal, as a threat to individualism and free institutions, as promoting the tyranny of the unreasoning majority." "Democracy and the Ontario Fathers of Confederation," in *Profiles of a Province*, ed. Edith G. Firth (Toronto: Ontario Historical Society, 1967), 85.

13   For a discussion of the impact of the changed wartime rhetoric, post–World War I, see David Laycock, *Populism and Democratic Thought in the Canadian Prairies, 1910 to 1945* (Toronto: University of Toronto Press, 1990).

class and the determination of the establishment to maintain "its" system despite the promises made in the heat of the war.

The election of provincial farmer-dominated governments, and the formation of the National Progressives in the 1920s, demonstrated the popular desire to break out of established power relationships. The new parties enthusiastically endorsed virtually all the current reform ideas that would upset elite rule: electoral reform, direct democracy (referenda, initiatives, and recall), delegate democracy/constituency representation and "group government." The proposal for direct democracy was a clear attack on party rule.[14] A fatal weakness in this outburst of reform zeal was the absence of an agreed-on practical model of democratic representation and government that would embrace the reformers' values and could substitute for the existing party-based system.

There were "progressive" developments in our politics before and after the wartime crisis, but these were not sufficient to meet the expectations and aspirations of many Canadians. In the latter part of the 19th century, the universal male franchise was established, followed, after the war, by the extension for women of the right to vote and to stand for office. Still later the voting age was lowered from 21 to 18, and there is talk now of lowering it still further. I will discuss that issue in a following chapter.

The rhetorical response to demands for democracy. The popular desire for more control of government was, to a large degree, dampened down by elites persuading enough people that democracy already existed with a change in the rhetoric describing the system. This response was not deliberate and planned, an elite conspiracy, but rather, resulted from the actions of many political leaders naturally seeking to ward off change that would threaten their dominance.

Representative democracy increasingly replaced *parliamentary government* in descriptions of our form of government. The concept of popular sovereignty was no longer denounced. Political elites stopped asserting that citizens should leave governing to them. Instead, they implied, in various ways and on different occasions, that citizens already played a significant role in

---

14   These ideas are considered more fully in chapters 8 and 10.

determining public policy—by penciling an X on a ballot after the name of one of the party candidates in the contest for control of the House of Commons.

The right to vote was portrayed as a significant means for citizens to express themselves on policy issues. That portrayal was based on the presumption that citizens could and would think their way through the cacophony of conflicting claims, charges, information, misinformation, exaggeration, and distortion that characterized adversarial party electoral politics, to a body of coherent, reasonable conclusions about their interests and those of the country. These conclusions would then be expressed in a simple X on a ballot. The decision of voters would "mandate" the actions a party government would take in their name. That the government could well be one that the majority of voters had refused to support was a "bother"— but not too serious, given the little importance assigned to the views of citizens.

The one X was, at various times, claimed to allow citizens to choose a constituency representative, governing party, and PM—and, at the same time, to endorse some policies and reject others, hold incumbents accountable, and direct incoming governments. The reality is far different. The vote can send only a confused message on these important matters, one that is subject to self-serving interpretations by politicians and others.

Many political scientists, who appeared on the scene in larger numbers in the post–World War II era, helped complete the finesse of passing off rule by party elites as *democracy* by redefining that term. In the modern period, democracy was, some said, a system where parties competed periodically for power and office in an open contest decided by voters, i.e., democracy was partyocracy.[15] People living in large states were to dismiss as impractical and idealistic the notions about democracy as "government by and for the people." Canadians should trust that the outcome of the competition of parties for office would provide adequate representation, while the government formed by the winning party would serve their interests. Citizens were not to be

---

15   See, for example, "Political democracy is, *in primis,* a method or procedure by which, through a competitive struggle for sanctioned authority, some people are chosen to lead the political community." Giovanni Sartori, *Democratic Theory* (Westport, Conn.: Greenwood Press, 1962), 124.

consulted in an organized way about their political needs and aspirations beyond what could be conveyed by that X on a ballot.

In the real world, elections are an exercise in frustration for those who try to send clear messages to our rulers. The more we want and need to direct how the big state wields its power, the more alienated we are by how little we can do this by voting. Most of those who choose to vote do so primarily as an exercise in good citizenship. Others are caught up in the drama of parties and politicians competing for power and want to participate in it.

The counter-attack on the reform movement launched in the early party of the 20th century was almost completely successful in stalling the adoption of more democratic institutions.

Dumbing Down of the Electorate

John Stuart Mill wrote, "The only sufficient incentive to mental exertion, in any but a few minds in a generation, is the prospect of some practical use to be made of its results."[16] The absence of much practical use for us to pay attention to politics means that we will be uninformed. [17] In that state we will be prone to making mistakes in the limited role we do have, i.e., in voting, and in our nervous, negative reaction to constructive changes in our political institutions. We are profoundly dissatisfied with politics-as-usual but apprehensive about making changes the implications of which we do not understand.

That we are uninformed is confirmed by social science research.

That the public is overwhelmingly ignorant when it comes to politics ... is a discovery that has been replicated unfailingly by

16   John Stuart Mill, three essays: *On Liberty; Representative Government; The Subjection of Women* (repr.,London: Oxford University Press, 1969), 181.
17   As Karen Evans, a prominent British educator, writes, "People do not become good citizens by accident, any more than they become good nurses, good engineers, good bus drivers or computer scientists... people not only have to learn to be good citizens, but the structures have to be there for them to exercise citizenship rights and responsibilities actively and fully. This applies throughout life and through work as well as social and community life." Cited in Anthony Barnett, "The Creation of Democracy," in *Reinventing Democracy,* eds. Paul Hirst and Sunil Khilnani (Oxford: Blackwell, 1996), 100.

political scientists; indeed, it is one of the strongest findings that have been produced by any social science—possibly the strongest.

Pollsters, pundits, journalists, and non-specialist scholars routinely attribute movements in public opinion to the effect of subtle philosophical and policy debates that are, in reality, the purview of small elites—debates of which the general public usually has not the slightest knowledge. Similarly, elections are consistently over-interpreted as "mandates" for philosophical convictions or policy positions of which most voters are only dimly aware.[18]

The research supporting this conclusion is predominantly American, but specifically Canadian studies confirm that we, too, are grossly uninformed about our politics.[19] This lack of political knowledge limits the value of public opinion polling, which might otherwise substitute for popular consultation.[20] On at least one issue, however, polling is substantive and deserving of respect. Canadians' support for constituency representation has been strong over a long period and expressed in support for the parties that

---

18   Jeffery Friedman, "Introduction: Public Ignorance and Democratic Theory," *Critical Review* 12, 4 (Fall 1998): 397-98.

19   A chapter in a survey of the state of citizenship in Canada summarizes the data on civic literacy as follows:,

—Significant numbers of Canadians do not know such simple facts as the names of the federal party leaders, the federal finance minister, or even their prime minister or premier.

—Even more Canadians are unaware of where the political parties stand on some of the issues of the day.

—Women, poorer Canadians, the young, and those with less formal schooling typically know less about politics.

—Election campaigns may cause the knowledge gaps to widen, unless there is intense media coverage of a party's position.

—Many Canadians are unfamiliar with basic ideological terminology and have problems placing even ideologically distinctive parties on the left-right spectrum. Elizabeth Gidengil, André Blais, Neil Nevitte, and Richard Nadeau, *Citizens* (Vancouver: UBC Press, 2004), 71. Also see Patrick Fournier, "The Uninformed Canadian Voter," in Joanna Everitt and Brenda O'Neill, eds. **Citizen Politics** (Don Mills, Ont.: Oxford University Press, 2002), 92–109.

20   This point is illustrated by a government-sponsored poll reporting that "almost half of respondents believe aboriginal people have an equal or better standard of living than the average citizen." Jack Aubry, "Canadians believe aboriginals living well," *Toronto Star* (July 8, 1996).

promise it, as well as in polls and in the major study of Canadian political opinion (the Spicer Commission).[21] Since this support is also consistent with the democratic values of Canadians and runs counter to the ideas of the political elites who dominate opinion formation, it can be taken as the authentic and firmly grounded view of most Canadians.

While social scientists produce factual evidence of low levels of civic literacy, politicians are more likely to praise our "natural smarts." To do otherwise would not win them many votes. Moreover, it would challenge one of the major myths underpinning the system. How strong could the popular mandate claimed by the governing party be if it were admitted that the voters issuing it have only a rudimentary understanding of their political interests? (Left aside for later consideration are the other egregious weaknesses in the mandate theory.) As well, it would follow from an acknowledgment of the state of our political awareness that our leaders should do something about it. Many would have ambivalent feelings about doing that.[22]

In my many years of teaching political science, I do not recall any politicians expressing interest in or concern for its expansion and improvement. They may be concerned about teaching science to girls, etc. but not about the political education of citizens. Public apathy and ignorance can be helpful to politicians. They provide an important justification for acting contrary to public opinion.

Of course, some Canadians resist the socializing impact of the system— they are likely to be among the readers of this book—take their role as citizens seriously, and inform themselves as fully as they can about public affairs. They constitute a tiny minority. Others, known to be "interested in politics," merely enjoy the spectacle of party competition, the melodrama of individual men and women, and teams of them, struggling for power.

"Not to worry," suggest some students of politics—despite the political ignorance of the public, the system appears to work well. They proceed to develop a number of speculative theories as to why this is the case: people

21   The "promising parties" are discussed in chapter 9.
22   As a British social theorist observed, "It is simpler to govern a society when most people are not interested in its government, and no politician or bureaucrat quite knows whether the people, if it took to having a mind of its own, would agree with him or not. It is therefore safest to let sleeping dogs lie." G. D. H. Cole, *Essays in Social Theory* (London: Oldbourne, 1962), 111.

find, early in life, the party that best reflects their interests and just follow its direction, or the direction of influential people, or a favourite media source, and so on.[23] Their argument is based on the premise that the system does work well. In a democracy, however, Canadians on the receiving end of politics are the ultimate judges of that. Overwhelmingly, citizens are highly critical of politicians and their governments.

At the beginning of the 20th century, Mill's thoughts on participation and political learning were extended by political theorist Mosei Ostrogorski, who wrote about the impact parties have on us as political beings: "The first problem... arises in democratic practice is the following: how to so organize political action as to develop spontaneous and regular impulse, to stimulate individual energies and not let them fall asleep. The party system offered its solution: let the citizens choose a party, let them enlist in it for good and all, let them give it full powers, and it will undertake to supply the required impetus. Put forward with every semblance of political piety, this solution found favour with the citizens and enabled them to sink, with an untroubled conscience, into their habitual apathy.... They raised political indifferentism to the level of a virtue, and this aloofness has combined with the ignorance of the masses to repress public spirit."[24]

Most of Ostrogorski's fears proved justified. The ignorance he anticipated is present. *Indifferentism* is not an option for most citizens, however. Government and politics are too intrusive to be ignored. Indifference has been replaced by anger, frustration, and cynicism. Public spirit is, however, repressed by a party system of representation that pits us against one another and, along with a competitive economic system built on consumerism, focuses our attention on narrow self-interest.

Most students of politics support wider citizen participation in political life and the experiential learning that would result. They recognize the social and economic damage, and the missed opportunities that result from uninformed, seemingly irrational decisions by voters. Parties and the media

---

23   Ilya Somin summarizes what she refers to as "shortcut theories," i.e., those that "predict that voters can cast informed votes without themselves possessing even minimal levels of political knowledge." Ilya Somin, "Voter ignorance and the democratic ideal" *Critical Review,* 12, 4 (Fall, 1998), 419–31.

24   M. Ostrogorski, *Democracy and the Organization of Political Parties* (1902: repr. Chicago: Quadrangle Books, 1964), 332–33.

are routinely urged to do more to raise the existing low levels of civic literacy. It is difficult to show, however, how an emphasis on public enlightenment would benefit parties in terms of voter support. Generally, parties and media behave as they do because they have learned from experience what works for them. Simply exhorting the parties to perform differently is unlikely to be successful. The system of rewards and punishments built into the system must be changed if more attention is to be paid to informing citizens.

The observation of Sir Ivor Jennings, a British political scientist, sums up the challenge citizen education poses to democratic reformers: "It is one of the difficulties of the extension of democracy that democracy cannot extend without education, and it is difficult for education to extend without democracy."[25] Policy democracy based on constituency parliaments would break into the circle Jennings describes by increasing education and democratic involvement simultaneously. Most of the education would be experiential, flowing from significant participation in setting public policy. Exclusive dependence on the media to interpret politics would be reduced by direct involvement in governance.

The Informal System of Representation

We are often seriously misrepresented in the formal, party-dominated representative system.[26] But those who have the necessary resources can ensure that they are heard, and perhaps heeded, by policy makers, by doing an "end run" around the formal system. The means they use to enhance their political clout are familiar: the membership wings of parties, interest groups, media, public demonstrations, and other forms of political activity.

---

25   Sir Ivor Jennings, *Party Politics: The Growth of Parties* (Cambridge: Cambridge University Press, 1961), 5.

26   As one study reports, a fundamental gap has emerged between the values of elites and the public they claim to represent: "The wide discrepancies between the public and the decision-makers on values and priorities suggest a chasm exists between those charged with governing our country and those being governed. Whether elites are correct in their beliefs or not, they are clearly disconnected from the views of the mass public; and this disconnection serves to underline the growing rift between the comfortable and insecure segments of Canadian society." Ekos Research Associates Inc., *Rethinking Government '94*, 13.

Parties. Perhaps parties should not even be mentioned as agencies of informal representation. At one time, people might have considered the extra-parliamentary wings of parties as vehicles to voice their political interests. Students and others were advised to be good citizens, join the party of their choice, and contribute to the political life of the country through them. At the same time, organized interests ensured that they had sympathetic people in the ranks of party members. Today, however, students and others are unlikely to get such advice, and policy advocates want direct access to those making policy. Working through weak and continuously shrinking party organizations is much too circuitous a route to influence government.

In a series on the "democratic deficit," *The Economist* explains the rise of interest groups and the decline of parties, asking, "Why should voters care about the broad sweep of policy promoted during elections by a party when other organizations will lobby all year round for their special interest?"[27] The answer is that citizens *should* care, because the broad sweep of policy is of great importance to the quality of life of everyone. However, when the citizen-excluding system makes it so difficult for busy individuals to influence what government does—broadly—they focus on important personal issues and use informal means of influencing policy relating to them. Those citizens who have issues, but no means to access policy makers, can only hope that their concerns are articulated through the formal system, i.e., by voting.

Interest groups. The legitimacy of lobbying MPs and governments, once questioned, is now accepted as necessary and legitimate. The growth of the lobbying industry has been rapid and in 2010 it was estimated that there were nearly five thousand lobbyists registered in Ottawa.[28] Some lobbyists have even been encouraged with government grants to represent their particular constituencies more actively in politics.[29] Government financing lobbies to lobby government! Does that suggest some weakness in the formal representative system?

---

27   "Empty vessels," *Economist* (July 22, 1999).
28   Thomas Axworthy and Julie Burch, "Closing the Implementation Gap," (Queen's University: Centre for the Study of Democracy, 2010), 10. www.queensu.ca/csd
29   The point is discussed more fully in chapter. 8.

The emergence of big, intrusive government has stimulated the demand and need to be heard by the many interests now affected by its policies. The approach government takes to listening is extremely important to the future of democracy, as two American political scientists suggest: "An expanded group process is fraught with implications for democratic governance.... To some, the cacophony of interest articulation is the fulfillment of the pluralist promise. To others ... with the clamour comes an increasingly divided and fragmented society, a paralysis in national policy-making, and a politics in which statesmanlike concern with the common good yields to the tunnel vision of the narrowly interested."[30]

Currently, as these academics suggest, there are two principal ways that liberal democracies accommodate the input of interest groups: pluralist and corporatist. Neither is found in pure form, but national political systems tend to emphasize one or the other.[31] Put simply, the *pluralist* mode is a free-for-all competition among groups for influence on policy-makers. The competition takes place in many venues, using a wide variety of means, ranging from chats in a golf club for the well connected to street demonstrations for those who do not have any more effective way of influencing policy-makers.

The pluralist model is demand-focused. Groups are preoccupied with receiving favourable treatment from government; offering support in return is not on the agenda of most. Demands must be continuous, or other competing interests might move into the political space occupied by the favoured group.

The *corporatist* mode has the opposite features. Stakeholders speaking for significant social interests are recognized by government as legitimate participants in making the public policy affecting them. They can count on being given a place in policy deliberations: governing parties are willing to share some control over policy with them. The inclusiveness and sharing are the price paid by the government for the support for, or more moderate opposition to, the policies finally adopted.

---

30   Kay Schlozman and John Tierney, "More of the Same: Washington Pressure Group Activity in a Decade of Change," *Journal of Politics* 45, 2 (1983). 372.

31   This discussion of *pluralism* and *corporatism* draws heavily on Arend Lijphart, *Patterns of Democracy: Government Forms and Performance in Thirty-Six Countries* (New Haven and London: Yale University Press, 1999), 173.

The democratic corporatist model encourages collaboration and cooperation, qualities consistent with democratic citizenship. Pluralism, on the other hand, encourages conflict and divisiveness. Our winner-take-all electoral system supports pluralism. The "victor" at the polls feels that it has won the right to govern unilaterally; it will consult with and heed others as suits its interests.

In his comparative study of government in 36 countries, Arend Lijphart found that Canada has the most pluralist interest group system and Norway the most corporatist of the governments studied.[32] Despite the research, I feel that this pluralist "honour" belongs to the United States. However, it is clear that pluralism predominates in Canada. As a result, demands on government exceed support for it by a wide margin.

One of the most frequently quoted observations in studies of partyocracies is that of political scientist Stein Rokkan, who wrote, "Votes count, but resources decide."[33] For us to accept a system where this is the case, where money and other resources decide policy, is for us to jettison the democratic ideal of political equality. But that jettisoning is what is occurring as the significance of the informal representative system grows at the expense of the formal. The trend can be reversed by bolstering the political clout citizens can exercise through new institutional arrangements in the formal system.

Corporations, in particular, have a major ongoing incentive to influence public policy, since they are strongly affected by it. Designated executives and hired lobbyists keep the corporations' views constantly before the relevant policy makers. Further, since the actions of the corporate sector have such an enormous impact on so many facets of life, governments cannot ignore its representations. Business leaders do not have to demonstrate in the street or even get their favoured parties elected to get their messages across.[34] This access does not, however, prevent them playing the pluralist

---

32   Ibid., 180.

33   Stein Rokkan, "1966 Norway: Numerical Democracy and Corporate Pluralism," in *Political Oppositions in Western Democracies,* ed. Robert A. Dahl (New Haven, Conn.: Yale University Press), 105.

34   Charles Lindblom makes a convincing case for the proposition that in a private-enterprise, market-oriented society the power of business makes it more than a "mere" interest group, i.e., that it is more realistically seen as a kind of alternative government. (170) He writes, "In any private enterprise system, a large category of major decisions

game and frequently complaining that their views are not being heard by government.

Citizens, generally, lack the organization needed to have a countervailing impact to that of market actors. We depend on the efforts of a few, organized in public interest groups and concerned with specific policies, to represent us in the interest-group arena, where so much policy is decided. Clear away their rhetoric, and most interests lobbying government are self-seeking— the approach encouraged by the competitive aspects of partyocracy and pluralism.

Policy makers need interaction with lobbyists and what they may provide, i.e., information expertise and an indication of the probable reaction of those affected by government policies. We should listen to them. However, to reconcile essential special-interest lobbying with true representative democracy we, as citizens, must be in a position to ensure that our general interests have appropriate weight in the policies finally adopted by government. We *would* be, when empowered constituency parliaments are in place. Lobbyists would then have to press their demands on empowered CPs as well as on senior levels of government. Citizens would have the opportunity to assess whether their demands were in the public interest.

I admire the relative few who devote time, energy, and money to public-interest groups. Their activity will always be valuable, no matter what changes we make in the political system. At the same time, I understand the majority who do not make much of a contribution. They can legitimately argue that they elect a government to "look after" the public sector and pay substantial taxes to support its activities. The ordinary citizen may have little time, energy, or resources left for lobbying government to fulfill its

---

is turned over to businessmen, both small and larger. They are taken off the agenda of government. Businessmen thus become a kind of public official and exercise what, on a broad view of their role, are public functions." *Politics and Markets* (New York: Basic Books, 1977), 172. It shows a remarkable lack of understanding of power relations in our system that, in a 1991 Gallup Poll, 48 percent of us thought that business ought to be more involved in public affairs and government policies. Only 15 percent thought that business was currently very involved. George Brett, "'Ma Bell,' top corporate citizen, poll says," *Toronto Star* (September 24, 1991).

responsibilities after they have fulfilled theirs to family, local communities, and employers.

Mass media. When we are not directly involved in political life, we must depend on the media to be our political eyes and ears. Editorial writers frequently present themselves as spokespersons for Canadians. We hope that on many issues the media will represent us to government and hold it accountable for us.

The media are also a significant force in setting the agenda of government. Issues the media focus on are likely to seize the attention of government— particularly if the government is managerial, i.e., has no firm agenda of its own. Conversely, those issues the media choose to ignore or downplay may be neglected.

While the mass media are in an exceptionally strong position to strengthen the informal representation of citizens, their ability to do that is compromised. Media owners, of course, have a basic agenda of their own which goes beyond the propagation of news: profitability and the promotion of ideological interests. To provide an audience to advertisers and profit to owners, most of the media must appeal to viewers and readers en masse. These business demands often interfere with, or take precedence over, serious, responsible journalism. For example, in a recession, media coverage of news shrinks along with its revenues from advertising, regardless of what is happening in the world. Parties are not primarily public service agencies, and neither are the media when they are corporate-owned.

Critiques of the media from a democratic perspective, i.e., of its horse-race, personality-focused, trivia-centred coverage are legion and need not be repeated here. There are, however, two features of the media that are particularly relevant to the policy democracy model. First, a symbiotic relationship exists between citizens and the media. If we were highly sophisticated politically, the media could publish more in-depth news and analysis without losing audience.

Second, it is difficult for government to bring about a restructuring of the media to make it a more effective educational-representative agency. Party government is the only agency with the power to do this, but it lacks the necessary citizen trust to win quarrels with the media's controlling interests. Royal Commissions on the media are set up and report concerns about their concentrated ownership and performance, but there is little or no follow-through on their recommendations. With the establishment of policy democracy, we would be in a position to take any action we deemed desirable to strengthen the media's contribution to our politics. I favour employee ownership for this extraordinarily powerful institution; it should not be treated as just another corporation.

Even without media restructuring, however, there are a wide range of diverse interests that do depend on the media for at least some informal representation. We would have still more citizen input to the media if there were empowered constituency parliaments demanding their attention.

One might hope that in supplementing the weak formal system, the informal system of representation would produce a stable, balanced political order. The formal system would represent the people as equal voters, and the informal would represent the same people, but organized around their particular interests. Combined the two systems would represent citizens adequately. But this is not the case, in both modes of representation but, particularly the informal. The resources available to those seeking representation weigh heavily in the outcome of competitive elections and in the competition of interest groups for influence on government. The ideal of "one person, one vote" must remain distant in partyocracy. With constituency parliaments in place we could come much closer to realizing that ideal.

Currently, as an atomized citizenry watch control of "their" government passing increasingly to organized interests, they feel powerless, resent their lowered political status, and withdraw support from government.

Conclusion

The formal representative system based on competitive elections and parties evolved in the 19th century, as the powers of a British governor were transferred to the prime minister and parliament. That system, progressive for its time, became firmly established, and adjusting it to meet the very different political challenges of following centuries has proven difficult. Those with the power to institute change were those committed to the status quo. Citizens, the ultimate power holders in a democracy, lacked organization, leadership, and a collective commitment to a particular institutional change that would have "encouraged" our leaders to be open to the development of more democratic representative institutions.

With essential adaptation to changing circumstances largely stymied, the formal representative system has become something of a political sideshow, dysfunctional but full of drama. This diverts attention from where most public policy is being determined, i.e., in the informal representative system where "resources decide." Persons and interests are forced to express themselves through this system, if they have the means, because it compensates for the weak formal system as a mode of gaining representation in the policy-making process.

The informal system, however, carries ever more demands on government from organized interests, without any accompanying increase in support that would enable the administration to meet them in an effective and timely manner. Citizens elect representatives to protect and advance their interests—but find that they respond primarily to pressure from organized interests with which their party identifies. Actions are taken by government in the name of citizens, which citizens feel no responsibility for and no obligation to support. To function, governments are increasingly forced to resort to compulsion and manipulation to gain what limited support they can.

In the last century, our interest in influencing the policies of ever-expanding government has increased dramatically. But few significant changes in the formal representative system, beyond dressing party-elite rule in democratic garb, have been made to accommodate this legitimate interest. A more significant response is long overdue.

With the policy democracy/constituency parliament model in place, both the formal and informal representative systems would be restructured to truly represent us. Key to the restructuring would be the ability of citizens, meeting with their MP, to learn about, deliberate on, and form a majority constituency view on some of the significant issues facing the country. The MP would be charged with the duty of representing this view in the House of Commons. Claims of parties and interests to be speaking for Canadians would no longer be credible unless they corresponded to the views of citizens emerging from a House of Commons composed of constituency representatives. Elections would be used only to choose representatives from among those vying for the positions in the junior and senior parliaments. Policy would be set in deliberations engaging members of the constituency parliaments with their MP and the MP in follow-up deliberations with colleagues in a vitalized House of Commons.

The strengthening of the formal representative system by the addition of empowered constituency parliaments would check the usurping of political power by organized interests functioning in the informal system. Political equality among citizens, difficult to establish, would be given a major boost. Citizens would take control of their government to a degree never before experienced in any liberal (electoral) democracy.

Prime Ministerial Misrule

The power of the system operates even over those who
are among its more powerful participants.

Michael Parenti

The most important condition of the emergence of good
leadership in modern industrial societies is, for the great mass of
human beings, direct responsibility through participation.

Arnold S. Kaufman

Leadership in the new politics can neither control a self-confident
electorate nor concede to it. It needs to find a new way, a new form of
politics that both listens and leads. We need to build a participatory
democracy in which self-confident citizens are fully engaged in the
political process, and in which politicians respect this engagement
and use it to fuel change; a democracy that understands the basic
principle of modern politics—the more empowered the citizen the more
powerful the leader. This is not an abdication of leadership, but rather
the opposite; it is facing and meeting the new leadership challenge.

Philip Gould

Introduction: The Source of Prime Ministerial Powers

We enjoy the dubious distinction of having the most powerful (autocratic) prime minister of any of the Western liberal democracies.[1] With that distinction comes, in intense form, a list of problems associated with the political domination of one man or woman.

Canadians did not choose to have an autocratic prime minister any more than we chose representation by parties. The historical development of Canadian political life led to prime ministerial dominance, and we were born into a political system in which it has long been institutionalized. We have already considered the unhealthy staying power of dysfunctional institutions.

With responsible government, the powers of a British-appointed governor were transferred to a prime minister sitting in, and responsible to, the Assembly. The executive power was "domesticated" and also increased because, elected and head of a party, the prime minister had more legitimacy than the governor. With the transfer, the governor became a virtual puppet of the prime minister (PM), who was told what to say and signed official documents as directed.[2]

The powers the prime minister inherited from the governor included appointing members of the Legislative Council (now Senate), the Executive Council (now Cabinet), and a wide range of other office-holders, including judges. He also assumed the right, within some limits, to set election dates. Before responsible government, the governor had a constitutional veto over legislation. The PM's domination of his colleagues gave him an implicit veto over all policy and administrative decisions. Apart from the private

---

1   In a comparative study of twenty-two "advanced" parliamentary systems, Canada stood first as having the most powerful PM. Eoin O'Malley, "The Power of Prime Ministers: Results of an Expert Survey," *International Political Science Review* 28, 1 (2007): 7-27..

2   In his study of the origins of Canadian politics, historian Gordon Stewart summarized how power was distributed after Confederation: "The premiers of the Union and the prime ministers after Confederation were able to take over the powers of the governors, as well as exercise the power due to their political weight and claim that Canada's monarchical constitution validated their comprehensive exploitation of the public service and manipulation of the electoral system." *The Origins of Canadian Politics* (Vancouver: University of British Columbia Press, 1986), 82.

members' bills that seldom passed, legislation could only be introduced by the government with the prime minister's approval.

The powers of the prime minister were buttressed by his or her party leadership, as Donald Savoie notes: "In Canada, winning candidates on the government side are aware that their party leader's performance in the election campaign explains in large measure why they themselves were successful. The objective of national political parties at election time is more to sell their leaders to the Canadian electorate than it is to sell their ideas or policies. Canadian elections invariably turn on the question of whom—which individual—will form the government. It should come as no surprise then, that if the leader is able to secure a majority mandate, the party is in the leader's debt, and not the other way around." [3]

Before responsible government, members of the public were expected to defer to the British-appointed governor and allow him to define the public interest. With the advent of it, the rulers became the prime minister and his cabinet, drawn from the elected House of Commons. They would now do the defining, influenced by the uninformed, deferential, and unorganized voters, to whom they had to appeal occasionally and others.

In the new political order, the Canadian party-dominated parliament, apart from some lingering vestiges of colonialism cleared away with the passage of the Statute of Westminster in 1931, was constitutionally sovereign. Of course, this was of enormous significance to those who were members of the House of Commons and to citizens generally. However, the extent that the changes benefited ordinary people largely depended then, as now, on whose interests the prime minister and his or her colleagues supported.

What should we call a political system in which the principal office holder, the prime minister, has a larger voice in determining the policies of government than millions of citizens, other members of the House of Commons, and his cabinet colleagues—"representative democracy" or "prime ministerial government?" Clearly, it is the latter, and a focus on prime ministerialism provides an important complementary perspective to our surveys of the representative systems in the preceding chapter.

The character of a particular polity, in addition to the historical factors

---

3   Donald J. Savoie, "The Rise of Court Government in Canada," *Canadian Journal of Political Science* 32, 4 (December 1999), 642.

giving rise to it, is a major factor in determining just how much power will reside in the office of prime minister (PMO). In Canada, both the formal and informal representative systems are highly adversarial. The prime minister must be powerful enough to lead his team effectively in a political world of warring parties and, often, hostile groups. For good reason, our governments are identified by the name of the PM, i.e., the Chrétien, Martin, or Harper government, as often as they are by the name of the party in office. The prime minister's aspirations, needs, and beliefs—personal and partisan—shape the style and policies of his or her government.

The role of the state has grown enormously since the 19th century, when prime ministers initially inherited the powers of governors. This growth has led to successive prime ministers expanding their office to maintain control.[4] The prime minister has become institutionalized, with a significant body of the government's most talented personnel supporting him or her from positions in the Prime Minister's Office (PMO) and Privy Council Office (PCO). They have a vested interest in maintaining the authority of their offices. With their assistance, the prime minister's span of control is, Savoie states, as extensive as the prime minister chooses.[5]

A prime minister, drawn from a society that subscribes to democratic values, may be uncomfortable with the powers that come with the office. However, he or she sits atop a house of cards and must question whether any card can be removed without bringing down partyocracy. Parties need a strong commanding officer if they are to be successful in the fierce competition for office. Any actions that would weaken the control of the PMO must be resisted.

In sum, governing in Canada involves a significant exercise of personal power. Confidence in and support for government is tied to the performance of one fallible human, elevated out of the ranks of ordinary mortals and

---

4   The PCO employed 209 people in 1969 but was staffed by approximately 1,100 in 2005. Canada, *Commission of Enquiry into the Sponsorship Program and Advertising Activities* (the Gomery Commission), *Restoring Accountability,* Phase 2 Report (Ottawa: Public Works and Government Services, 2005), 145. An additional 85 staff were employed in the Office of the Prime Minister. Source: e-mail from PMO to author, December 20, 2005.

5   See Donald J. Savoie, *Governing from the Centre* (Toronto: University of Toronto Press, 1999), 108.

subjected to the corrupting influence of great personal power. The cost of maintaining this limited autocracy is high, and it is steadily increasing.

The Impact of Prime Ministerialism on Policy and Administration

Personalized Policy. Democracy, rule by the many, is highly valued as a means of escaping the abuses of autocracy. In autocracies, the policy preferences, interests, idiosyncrasies, unpredictability—even the possible dementia and paranoia of the leader—determine how people are ruled. Partyocracy supports a significantly limited autocracy and milder versions of the same abuses and weaknesses. But, still, the retired MPs who were interviewed in the Samara study referred to previously found that: "The MPs said that decisions from the party leadership were often viewed as opaque, arbitrary and even unprofessional. Furthermore, those decisions often ran counter to the MPs' stated motivations for entering public life in the first place: the desire to practice politics differently."[6]

The most significant of the weaknesses in PM government is the control exercised by the office holder of the government's agenda. Savoie observes that, in prime ministerial government, only policy initiatives that particularly interest the prime minister are encouraged. Those that do move rapidly through the system, sometimes even bypassing the minister formally responsible for them.[7] Ministries that are not involved with the prime minister's issues are given to understand that they are to stick to business as usual, i.e., to tread water.[8] The policies on which the PM chooses to focus may or may not be consistent with those desired by the majority of citizens—or even of party colleagues.

Governing by "bolts of lightening" is how Savoie describes this style

---

6   Samara, a public interest group based in Ottawa. Press release summarizing views in "It's My Party": Parliamentary Dysfunction Reconsidered (Ottawa: Samara, April 2011), 2. samaracanada.com

7   For example, in l978, the prime minister (Trudeau) announced a drastic cut in government across-the-board spending without consulting the Minister of Finance or his deputy. See Christina McCall and Stephen Clarkson, *Trudeau and Our Times, Volume 2: The Heroic Delusion* (Toronto: McClelland and Stewart Inc., 1994), 130. A recent example of a prime minister (Harper) making profound changes in the relationship of Canada with Quebec without consultation are discussed in chapter 6.

8   Savoie, *Governing from the Centre*, 8.

of governance, suggesting surges of political energy and the damage that may accompany them.[9] The content, mode of implementation, and possible risks of policies "bolted" through are likely to be inadequately considered. Further, it is difficult to get an appropriate balance in government programs when it depends so heavily on the priorities of one person.

Tailoring the agenda of government to the PM's interests is one task of his or her advisors. A related challenge is protecting the PM while the agenda is implemented. In studies of the prime minister, scarcely any theme receives greater emphasis than the preoccupation of the cadre of politicians and bureaucrats surrounding the PM with guarding his or her image and authority.[10] To provide this, the PMO and PCO demand, in the PM's name, full disclosure and a large measure of control over initiatives being proposed in the ministries and agencies of government. Any one of these might provide the opposition with valuable ammunition that would tarnish the image of the leader, on whom the party depends to win elections.

The work of government should be coordinated by fully informed, high-level personnel. Excessive control, however, can reduce the benefits that should flow from ministers, senior bureaucrats, and parliamentarians working together to initiate or improve programs. Creative room in the system is appropriated by the prime minister and it is used, not used, or misused by him or her.

Examples are legion of how the particular interests and qualities of the PM affect policy and administration and of the harm that may result. The prime minister (Diefenbaker) is inept and emotionally unstable; "his" government reflects his qualities. Another prime minister (Trudeau) is particularly interested in constitutional questions; "his" government's agenda is skewed in that direction, at the expense of economic policy.

Prime Minister Mulroney reversed his and his party's position on the issue of free trade with the United States after his election.[11] He succeeded

9   Ibid., 359.
10   Ibid., 73.
11   Mulroney admits that his opposition to free trade was "a less-than-honest position for me to take." It was adopted, he writes, to distinguish his position from that of John Crosbie, who was a strong advocate of free trade and one of the persons contesting the party leadership with him. Brian Mulroney, *Memoirs: 1939-1993* (Toronto: McClelland and Stewart Ltd., 2007), 231. How often have the competitive aspects of partyoc-

in committing the country to what is, as a practical matter, an almost impossible-to-reverse agreement with the United States that has far-reaching implications for almost every aspect of Canadian life. At the time he did so, a slight majority of citizens opposed his action.[12]

In an interview long after he had left office, Mulroney reflected on the wisdom and courage that had characterized his leadership. Graham Fraser of the *Toronto Star* interviewed him in 2000 and reported, "Mulroney says he had no illusions about what he was proposing would be popular. You ask yourself, do you want to be popular now or do you want to be right in history? Do you want easy headlines now, or a better Canada in 10 years?"[13]

There is no suggestion, in that statement, that the values and policy preferences of millions of his fellow citizens were entitled to respect or that in a democracy our views might properly trump his, and prove to be wiser—even though individual Canadians would, on average, be much less informed than the PM.

We can hope that the prime minister will be checked where necessary in his or her exercise of power by the team of bureaucrats working with him. The superior talents of these officials cannot be guaranteed, however. Nor is the first minister obliged to heed their advice. The PM appoints them, and they serve at his or her pleasure. Not every prime minister will choose to be surrounded by the "best and brightest."

In addition to the ability to impose his or her personal views on policy, the prime minister, like the monarch of old, sets the general character of his or her administration—the grandiosity of Mulroney was followed by the seat warming of Chrétien. Ideally, that character would be positive and

---

racy led politicians to feel that they must twist the truth to succeed?

12   On public opinion at the time of the free-trade election (1988), see G. Bruce Doern and Brian Tomlin, *Faith and Fear* (Toronto: Stoddart, 1991), 238–39. The authors make an interesting comment on how Mulroney reached his decision to espouse free trade. They dismiss the significance of his economic liberalism and write, "Nor was it the power of the economic arguments put forward by the Macdonald Commission, the Economic Council of Canada, and others, that persuaded Mulroney, because he never received a comprehensive briefing from his trade officials on Canada-US free trade. Instead, the prime minister made an intuitive political judgment that this was a policy whose time had come." (273)

13   Graham Fraser, "Mulroney: A Legacy Revisited," *Toronto Star* (September 16, 2000).

consistent over at least one administration, perhaps over many, allowing individuals and interests interacting with government to plan their activities with assurance.

The prevailing mood and productivity of government is affected by developments in the (perhaps inseparable) personal and political lives of the leader. When, for example, then-Premier of Ontario William Davis conducted a lengthy internal debate about when he should retire, it was generally perceived that his administration shifted into neutral, and little got done. When he finally made the decision and would no longer be responsible for winning elections for his party, he unilaterally reversed the party's long-standing policy not to finance parochial high schools, citing his personal feeling that its denial was unjust. He left his colleagues to defend his decision in an election, which they lost.

On an even more personal level, one would like to think that the breakup of a premier or prime minister's marriage would remain strictly a private matter. When former Premier Harris's marriage broke up, however, observers felt that his administration entered a period of drift, and they speculated on the connection between the two. He asked that his privacy be respected, and to a large extent it was.[14] At the same time, however, it was clear that given his centrality in the system, what was happening in his private life had a serious negative impact on his leadership of the government. The breakup of Trudeau's marriage had a similarly negative impact on his governing.[15]

The course of government will always be affected by circumstances in the lives of those leading it. However, where the leadership is more collective and more democratic than is possible in adversarial partyocracy, the impact of the personal will be reduced significantly.

Loss of critical input. Another of the problems with prime ministerial policy-making is the potential loss of critical input to it. American political scientist Gabriel Almond writes, "Policy acquires strength to the extent that it is derived from competitive discussion in front of a critical audience capable

---

14   The issue is discussed by Richard Brennan, "Harris wants his private life to stay far from prying eyes," *Toronto Star,* March 11, 2000, A12; Kim Honey, "Where Public and Private Meet," *Globe and Mail,* December 4, 2001, A13.

15   See John English, *Just Watch Me* (Toronto: Alfred A. Knopf, 2009), 312.

of judgement and discrimination."[16] It is possible for a prime minister to find a critical audience for his or her ideas, but this need not happen. It is not required, made unavoidable. The institutions exist in which constructive criticism of his or her proposals should take place, but the ability of most to facilitate it has been subverted over time.

Cabinet. "Cabinet government," a phrase once much used to describe the system, has been replaced now in most contexts by "prime ministerial government," for good reason. While cabinet ministers have always been appointed and dismissed by the prime minister, at an earlier time it was thought that there was some substance to the notion that at the cabinet table the prime minister was only "first among equals." Collectively, those equals represented a broad cross-section of Canadians—some with a strong personal power base. Cabinet members could check a PM bent on following a personal agenda with which they disagreed. Further, the cabinet's involvement in developing public policy was seen as compensating somewhat for the weak representation on policy issues that backbench MPs provided constituents.

Cabinet government, however, continues to evolve—negatively, from a democratic perspective. Savoie provides convincing evidence that the cabinet has now been downgraded to little more than a focus group for the prime minister.[17] Yet, it is only cabinet members, with access to "secret" information, who could be informed enough to be fully capable of the "judgment and discrimination" that Almond deems essential to strengthen policy. With the downgrading of the cabinet, the views and values of the government will more than ever be those of the prime minister and those to whom he or she chooses to listen.

Caucus. Few have any illusions about the parliamentary caucus of the governing party compensating for the downgraded cabinet. Also governed by the rules of secrecy, the caucus is primarily the institution that allows the PM to organize his Commons support. Only secondarily, under special

---

16   Gabriel A. Almond, *The American People and Foreign Policy* (New York: Harcourt Brace, 1950), 145–46.
17   Savoie, *Governing from the Centre*, 260.

circumstances, does it become a critical audience representing citizens. Caucus secrecy is an essential feature of partyocracy, but it is an affront to us. MPs claim that they represent us in caucus—debates in the Commons are just for statements of party policy—but we can't see whether they actually do so.

As in cabinet, no votes are taken in caucus; the PM is not placed in the difficult position of clearly rejecting the views of his or her colleagues. In a case where the caucus is opposed to the course the prime minister is following, the PM can always remind its members that he or she is accountable to the party membership that chose him or her to lead the party, or to the voters, rather than to them. Short of occasional opportunities to vote, there is little opportunity for either cabinet or caucus to hold the PM accountable. Damaging policy decisions made by the prime minister cannot be reversed by removing the country's CEO—this would probably precipitate an election.

Parliament. A classic text used to educate a generation of post–World War II students of political science describes the role of the House of Commons in these words: "The fundamental importance of the House of Commons is ... derived from its essential representative character, the fact that it can speak, as no other body in the democracy can pretend to speak, for the people. It presents in condensed form the different interests, language groups, religions, classes, and occupations whose ideas and wishes it embodies (sometimes with approximate exactness, sometimes not). It serves as the people's forum and the highest political tribunal; it is, to use Mill's phrase, 'the nation's committee of grievances and its congress of opinions.'"[18]

What a wonderful ideal! With the policy democracy model, we would come much closer to realizing it. The politics of partyocracy, supporting prime ministerial government, distances us from it. Even the presence of the opposition parties does not normally make parliament an effective critical audience for, and a check on, the prime minister. Only occasionally, when a short-lived minority government is in place and the PM cannot assume that the Commons will support his or her initiatives, will the House of Commons

---

18   R. MacGregor Dawson, *The Government of Canada,* 5th ed., revised by Norman Ward (Toronto: University of Toronto Press, 1970), 305.

come alive as a significant force. Even then, however, prime ministers may successfully avoid subjecting their decisions to its scrutiny. For example, troops were committed to an enlarged anti-terrorist-reconstruction role in Afghanistan by one prime minister—without a parliamentary debate. The decision was renewed and extended by a second PM, who headed a minority government and resisted holding even an after-the-fact parliamentary debate on his action until he was sure of significant opposition support.

For at least a century, political activists have advocated more freedom for MPs from strict party discipline, so that they can assess policy, including its gaps, on behalf of the people. Party platforms frequently promise this. However, the promise is difficult, or impossible, for a governing party to fulfill within the confines of the system.

MPs require a strong constituency base, i.e., independence of party, if the ideal of parliament as a forum of the people is to become a reality. Only with this would they be able to provide a critical analysis of policy proposals originating from the executive.

Despite the many features that lead to its ridicule, the Senate has more freedom to critically examine and comment on what the government (PM) proposes than the Commons does. With its weak claim to democratic legitimacy, it is, however, even less able than the Commons to insist that the PM heed its views.

Abuse of Prime Ministerial Power

Patronage. It is no surprise to find that the prime minister (and, following his or her example), cabinet colleagues, and even government MPs cannot resist giving themselves an additional edge in a highly competitive system, by directing patronage to their constituents and supporters.[19] The PM and cabinet sometimes rationalize this behaviour by arguing that while they are occupied with running the country, some of their constituents feel neglected and deserve some extra consideration ("pork") as compensation.

---

19   Under attack, and ultimately forced out of his office for patronage abuses, Alfonso Gagliano, the Minister of Public Works in the Chrétien government, defended himself: "He's the boss," he said, referring to the prime minister. "I served the way he wanted me to serve." Cited in Margaret Wente, "Alfonso's Many, Many friends," *Globe and Mail* (January 12, 2002), A15.

Patronage is to the PM and ministers what performance-enhancing drugs are to Olympic athletes—unethical but irresistible.

Toronto Star reporter Graham Fraser describes the anticipation of voters in former Prime Minister Chrétien's riding: "In the past, it has been taken for granted, particularly in Eastern Canada, that having a senior minister as member of Parliament was the equivalent of having an industry in the riding. According to this reasoning, having a prime minister was like getting a mega-project. In 1993, people on the street and in the grocery stores hoped that having a prime minister as their MP would bring jobs to the riding, the way Brian Mulroney brought jobs to Baie Comeau and Sept-Iles with a federal prison and government support for an aluminum smelter."[20]

Ordinary MPs have few opportunities to indulge in dispensing patronage but fight for those that do come their way.[21] They must, however, largely content themselves with inferring that they are personally responsible for what may well be normal government expenditures in their ridings.

In relation to the overall operation of government, the dollar cost of ministerial patronage is modest: a prison, hospital, or highway in a less-than-optimal location; a friend of a minister with a contract or appointment that he or she would not otherwise have; a musical fountain in the middle of a river to remind voters in a former PM's riding that they produced a prime minister; a government program stretched to include benefits to a particular riding or ridings not entitled to them, and so on. But there are costs other than misspent dollars.

The media and opposition enjoy this form of patronage. It permits an attack on the hypocrisy of prime ministers and others who deny favouring their voters when outside their ridings, while proudly pointing to it when within. Like so many other forms of political behaviour in partyocracy that discredit politics and politicians, however, ministerial patronage continues because it pays. While it sows mistrust and scorn in the general population,

---

20   Graham Fraser, "Sending Money Home," *Toronto Star* (March 11, 2000).

21   When scandal touched the partisan administration of the government's job-creation fund, it was decided one day that decisions should be made on its distribution by civil servants without the local Liberal MP's input but, after the protest of MPs, their input was restored. Heather Scoffield, "Manley to Control $2-Billion in Liberal Reversal," the *Globe and Mail* (February 5, 2001), A1.

it gets votes from its beneficiaries.[22] It is hard to buy votes with only sound policy and administration, when most voters are too apolitical to assess either. Pictures can best reach people kept illiterate; voters can be bought by goodies. Partyocracy corrupts us, as it does politicians.

We put a prime minister and his cabinet colleagues in a conflict-of-interest situation when we expect them to simultaneously promote national *and* constituency interests. Removing the conflict is difficult in partyocracy but could be handled without difficulty in the policy democracy model. Recall that in that model, various means of replacing MPs who became cabinet ministers were suggested. With the adoption of one of these, a minister would be responsible to the Commons and participate in its deliberations but would have no vote. Cabinet members, including the PM, would be free to focus exclusively on the interests of the country at large. MPs, in turn, would concentrate on their important and much-expanded task of liaising with and representing their constituents.

A footnote to this discussion of ministerial patronage: in partyocracy, the PM is often the recipient of patronage from affluent Canadians. Premiers and prime ministers frequently benefit from trust funds set up to supplement their salaries. In some cases, money is raised and paid to already highly paid individuals in the private sector to entice them to assume political leadership. In others, the prime minister or premier finds his or her salary insufficient; the party and "friends" are asked to supplement it. The public relations value of a low taxpayer-paid salary is maintained, while a higher income is enjoyed. Normally, an attempt is made to keep the existence of these supplements secret. Despite this, however, they do come to the attention of the media and public.

The practice of accepting this money raises important questions. Is the integrity of the office-holder and the political process compromised?

---

22   Lloyd Axworthy, known in Ottawa as the "king of pork," was one of the few Liberals able to survive on the prairies in recent years. Perhaps his success should be attributed to his many fine qualities or to his outstanding performance as a minister—but one wonders. On his retirement from electoral politics, *Globe and Mail* columnist Jeffrey Simpson wrote, "Big Lloyd. That's what some of us used to call him, because it sometimes seemed as if the grass wouldn't grow in the city unless Big Lloyd agreed. Through his office poured millions upon millions of federal dollars for Winnipeg." Jeffrey Simpson, "Big Lloyd will not soon be forgotten," *Globe and Mail* (September 22, 2000).

The recipients, of course, deny that it is.[23] If, however, premiers and prime ministers feel they are above being influenced by gifts, why shouldn't MPs and even bureaucrats take the position that they are too?[24]

Compromised Leadership

A search for positive features of prime ministerial government, to offset its serious weaknesses, might lead to the potential of the powerful PM to use his or her bully pulpit to educate and lead. Since virtually every word and action that the PM utters or takes is regarded as newsworthy, he or she could play the role of the great teacher and unifier of a heterogeneous people. However, the prime minister in partyocracy is a highly partisan divisive figure—a party salesperson and commanding general—and fatally handicapped in playing those constructive and necessary leadership roles.

The style of leadership forced on the PM in partyocracy is virtually the antithesis of the democratic leadership people experience as members of most associations. His or her interactions with the public must be guarded, cautious, and carefully scripted by advisors. A misspoken word can commit a whole government; can destroy a carefully constructed public persona; can weaken the PM's hold on power. Only the utterances of heads of central banks are scrutinized as closely, and those by only a small segment of the community.

Prime ministers who attempt to use their office to inform and educate quickly learn its hazards. Pierre Trudeau came into politics from an academic background and proposed to dialogue with the Canadian public, on occasion playing the devil's advocate as he might in a university seminar. But the cost

---

23   During his career as Liberal leader and Premier of Quebec, Jean Charest received a "salary supplement" of $75,000 annually. In the midst of a scandal over breaches of the province's electoral finance law by the Liberals, he was finally forced to relinquish it. Rhéal Séguin, "Scandal-ridden Charest welcomes recess," *The Globe and Mail* (June 11, 2010), A7.

24   Bernard Lord, Premier of New Brunswick, admitted receiving $60,000 a year from benefactors and defended his action by stating that taking the money was deemed acceptable under the terms of the provincial conflict-of-interest legislation. Canadian Press, "Lord shrugs off ethics complaint, *Globe and Mail* (November 4, 2003). A9. What does this suggest about the adequacy of the conflict of interest legislation whose content was probably heavily influenced by the premier?

to his party of a single didactic question directed at a farm audience—"Why should I sell your wheat?"—was enormous. A statement in a speech where he referred to a failure of the free enterprise system to adjust to changing economic circumstances, producing stagflation, damaged his standing and his party's support among another group of Canadians.

Before our political leaders can candidly discuss public issues, in all their complexity, with their constituents, citizens will have to be more politically sophisticated than they are likely to be in our present political system, the competition for power less adversarial, and the means of communication between citizen and representatives organized differently. Only then will the prime minister's words and ideas be received as an important contribution to the public dialogue and not as perhaps threatening harbingers of autocratic government action. A prime minister uninvolved in a partisan power struggle, who is trusted and respected, could contribute significantly to the quality of Canadian politics.

Recruiting and Dismissing Prime Ministers

The almost dictatorial powers of the prime minister would be less damaging if consistently outstanding leaders could be recruited by the parties and expeditiously removed from office when colleagues deemed that desirable. The example of the corporate sector, in this instance, is helpful. Those CEOs who prove inept are often "golden-parachuted" out with dispatch.

Our problem in recruiting leadership talent starts with party constituency organizations that are often too weak to recruit the best talent to become MPs. Leaders, usually chosen from the limited talent pool the parties have mustered in the Commons, must then to be "sold" to us. The sales process usually involves extravagant claims for the qualities of the candidates. Having succeeded, in varying degrees, in promoting their leaders to themselves and to voters, party members then have great difficulty in admitting mistakes and expeditiously changing their leader when he or she fails to perform adequately. The difficulty is compounded by the feeling of some leaders that, having gone through a long struggle to get to the apex of power, the office is their personal possession for as long as they wish to hold it or until they are rejected by the voters.

The multiple lines of accountability of the prime minister enhance his or her hold on office. Election by the extra-parliamentary wing of the party, and by voters, allow prime ministers to argue that they are not primarily accountable to their Cabinet or House of Commons colleagues—the people in the best position to judge their performance. Further, removal of a reluctant-to-leave party leader, particularly if he or she is prime minister, is a difficult, party-divisive act that can damage the party's image with the voting public.

Prof. Denis Smith's study of the career of John Diefenbaker illustrates a number of the pitfalls in the recruitment/dismissal process.[25] When chosen, Diefenbaker was, perhaps, the best of a weak group of candidates for the leadership of the Progressive Conservative Party. He went on to become a flawed prime minister. Masses of Canadians, unengaged in political life, were largely unaware of how inadequate Diefenbaker's leadership was. Secrecy surrounding the PMO and cabinet, and general political passivity, protected the "queen bee." Insiders, however, were appalled at his performance and that of his government—in prime ministerial government the two are inseparably entwined. Swift remedial action was difficult, however, because many members of the party and its supporters had a large, unhealthy emotional investment in the leader. Smith cites Dalton Camp, the president of the membership wing of the party who led the revolt against Diefenbaker, as saying, "In the process of making a god of our leader, we made sheep of ourselves."[26] The bitter and protracted process of forcing Diefenbaker out of the leadership tore the Progressive Conservative Party apart and weakened its performance as government and as official opposition. The Diefenbaker case was unique only because it was so egregious.[27] Internecine warfare frequently distracts politicians from constructive activities.

In a more recent example of the sense of entitlement party leaders assume, Jean Chrétien, Mulroney's successor, was widely criticized in the

25   An account of Diefenbaker's life and political record is set out in Denis Smith. *Rogue Tory,* (Toronto: Macfarlane Walter and Ross, 1995), and of his record in office in Peyton V. Lyon, *Canada in World Affairs: 1961–1963* (Toronto: Oxford University Press, 1968.)
26   Smith, *Rogue Tory,* 513.
27   Prime Minister Chrétien's leave-taking was as tortuous as Diefenbaker's for party and country, but in different ways.

media as being a man lacking vision who, by overstaying his tenure in office, was denying the country more dynamic leadership. Many party members, and certainly most members of the public, felt he should have retired before he did.[28] The prime minister, however, held onto office, making it clear that he thought it was his right to do so.[29]

The parties are now torn between two models of choosing their "commanding general." A vote of the membership is the new approach, while a vote by convention delegates is the traditional model. The new approach represents a desperate effort to bolster declining party memberships. As an inducement to join for at least the duration of the leadership campaign, new members are offered the opportunity to participate in choosing the party leader. There is no reason to think that their participation in the process improves the quality of the outcome. It does, however, reduce the value of party membership to the "sustaining" members to have this key decision heavily influenced by "temporaries."

Electing the party leader by a general vote of the membership does nothing to strengthen the PM's accountability to those in the best position to judge his or her performance, i.e., cabinet and parliamentary colleagues and, next to them, the ongoing party membership. As is typical of efforts to reform institutions that are fundamentally obsolete, changes merely create new problems. In this case, the reform weakens the constituency organizations that critics of parties want to see playing a larger and more constructive role in political life.

In the policy democracy/constituency parliament model, members of the executive, including the prime minister, would be recruited by the members of the House of Commons, from within its membership or from outside. They would remain in office only as long as they enjoyed the confidence of members of the House of Commons, who would be in close touch with their constituents. Relatively little trauma would be involved in replacing office-holders found unsuitable for their posts.

---

28   "Seven in ten (68 percent) Canadians say that prime minister should step down—including 58 percent of Liberal supporters," News Release, Ipsos ASI. http://www.ipsos-na.com/news/pressrelease.cfm?id-1535&email-friend

29   Chrétien was subjected to a savage series of attacks by the leading political columnists of the country as he clung to office. See, as one of many examples, Jeffery Simpson, "Jean Chrétien's only agenda: 'I'm in charge here'" Globe and Mail (May 4, 2002).

Conclusion

Prime ministerial government, based on hierarchically organized parties, is an ersatz form of democracy. We are asked to trust our government to an individual office-holder—wielding far from absolute, but still astonishing political power—as a substitute for a government that truly represents us. This form of government is subject to all the strengths and weaknesses that must be expected when the program of the government and its administration reflect the strengths, weaknesses, interests, and temperament of the prime minister. His or her service to the polity is compromised by the corrupting influence of nearly unbridled power and the demands of party leadership.

The autocratic features of prime ministerial government are so completely at odds with the democratic values held by Canadians, and the prime minister so much a partisan figure, that he or she lacks the democratic authority required to provide effective, visionary, and unifying leadership. Further, the choice and retirement of party leaders by weak parties, normally moribund and with tiny memberships, does not ensure that we have the opportunity to choose the best and brightest to lead our government.

Prime ministerial domination poses a basic dilemma for all of us who see the need for strong, responsive government. To be effective, government must have more, not less, authority.[30] But an electoral choice among three or four competing party-chosen leaders, which cannot really mandate the victor, is insufficient to vest the First Minister with democratic legitimacy. To increase the authority of government without first requiring that it have a real popular mandate for its actions would be to strengthen our elected dictatorship, with all its abuses.

We are trapped in an unhealthy cycle. Despite the best efforts of the prime minister's handlers, inevitably the inflated pre-election expectations of him or her will be punctured. For too many, it will then be time to transfer their trust to someone new. Another cycle of naive expectation, followed by

---

30   Benjamin Barber, a strong advocate of participatory democracy, warns against confusing it with an absence of strong leadership. He writes, "In the end, bridling our leaders does not get us more democracy, just less leadership. It does not make for better citizenship; it only makes for worse government." Benjamin R. Barber, *A Passion for Democracy* (Princeton University Press, 1998), 126.

disappointment, is set in motion. When that cycle has run its course, and expectation is replaced by cynicism, more trust may be placed in private-sector actors, whose motivation is profit for shareholders, than in elected leaders.

We can escape this dilemma by adopting institutional arrangements that allow citizens to determine the policies that leaders, secure in the knowledge that they have public support, can then implement. Former Ontario Premier Bill Davis, quoting Bismarck, was fond of saying that politics is the "art of the possible." What is possible for a prime minister to accomplish today is directly related to whether he or she has a positive collaborative relationship with Canadians. Partyocracy does not facilitate this relationship—policy democracy based on constituency parliaments would.

Partyocracy: Courting Bankruptcy

A greatly expanded popular base of political participation is the
essential condition for public support of the government. This
is the modern problem of democratic government. The price of
support is participation. The choice is between participation and
propaganda, between democratic and dictatorial ways of changing
consent into support, because consent is no longer enough.

E. E. Schattschneider

The distinctive feature of a politically bankrupt regime is that
citizens are indifferent to it. An indifferent citizen is not up in arms
against authority; instead, he just shrugs his shoulders and turns
his back on government, using the sophistication of the city streets
or the wiles of a peasant to evade government's commands.

… An indifferent citizen will do what the government wishes if it is in his
interest to do so, or if government convincingly threatens punishment
for inaction. Civic indifference offers a cheap, easy, and safe alternative
to organized rebellion for individuals who no longer have a positive
allegiance to their regime, yet can see no satisfactory alternative.

A politically bankrupt government is not consigned to the dustbin of
history, like a regime overthrown by violence. Politicians remain in
office, but they are bereft of authority…. The weakness of government
will be welcomed by those who see its economic failings as the cause

of their personal troubles. Yet every citizen will suffer some loss, for a bankrupt government cannot maintain the education, health, pensions, and other services that citizens expect as the benefits of public policy.

Richard Rose and Guy Peters

Introduction

There is a huge void between us, our elected representatives, and the governments they form. It is not total—elections provide a link in the formal system and interest groups in the informal—but these links are too weak to create a strong working relationship between us and those elected to govern. A troubled *we-they* relationship exists; we need one that is collaborative if government is to respond to our needs and aspirations.

As government has grown enormously and its performance has become crucially important to our quality of life, we can no longer so exclusively entrust its management to elected party leaders. Their interests and ours too often clash. Party governments, lacking our support, are weak and unresponsive. Remarkably, we put more trust in corporations, the source of some of the challenges to government, than we do in government.[1]

The effects of the unsupportive relationship that exists between government and citizen can be illustrated by a few examples:

- With much fanfare, party government commits itself to ending child poverty and to the provisions of the Kyoto Accord on reducing the emission of greenhouse gases. Years later, child poverty and the discharge of greenhouse gases have increased. Buffeted by interest group pressures, and lacking a solid citizen base of support, government has been too fearful of the electoral consequences of effective action—increases in taxes and or regulation—to meet its commitments to us and to the international community. As a result, future generations will have to devote substantial resources to dealing with

---

1   A 1990 poll showed that Canadians (51 percent) saw big government as a larger threat to Canada in the future than either big business (21 percent) or big labour (17 percent). Gallup poll cited in the *Toronto Star* (September 10, 1990).

dysfunctional adults and our contribution to catastrophic global warming.

Scientists are already claiming that we have reached the tipping point at which we cannot reverse global warming.[2] We need to examine what it is in our political system that has resulted in the delay in meeting the challenges posed to government and correct it.

- Government hosts conferences of international leaders, such as the meetings of the G-8 and G-20 in 2010, at a cost of $1 billion, most of it for security. Some of us, feeling powerless in the formal system, exploit such conferences to express hostility to "our" representatives, those of other countries, and the global economic developments they are promoting.[3]

- We reject the opportunity to involve ourselves in public life as members of parties, the central institution of partyocracy. Parties are hollowed out, as membership declines and hostility and cynicism relating to how they perform the functions we rely on them to provide increases.

- Elected leaders have learned through recent experience with the defeated referendum on the 1992 constitutional accord that their leadership mandate is weak. Allowed to participate in a referendum, many citizens will vote against whatever position their leaders take. Our alienation from politics and politicians, and often our lack of comfort with issues we do not fully understand, both products of partyocracy, are at play.

- Provincial party governments, often ignoring public opposition, accept and promote casino gambling.[4] In so doing, they bow

---

2   Bill Graveland, "New study suggests climate change is irreversible, even with zero emissions," *Globe and Mail* (January 10, 2001), A6.

3   Steven Chase, "Canada's $1-Billion Summit," *Globe and Mail* (May 26, 2010), l; Six thousand police officers had to be mobilized to protect delegates at the Summit of the Americas in Quebec City in 2001from (some) Canadians who took to the streets to express themselves. Rhéal Séguin, "1000 extra police officers assigned…." *Globe and Mail* (March 28, 2001).

4   The conclusion of a 2004 poll on public attitudes on gambling was that "Most Canadians agree there is too much government-run gambling in the country and the boost in tax revenue is not worth the social cost…." Dennis Bueckert, "Social cost of gambling a

to pressure from interests wanting to profit from it; they get politically inexpensive revenue but display indifference to the social problems they are creating. The establishment of poorly funded agencies and programs to deal with these problems are scarcely redeeming.[5] Governments that feel too insecure to raise needed revenues in ways that do not damage lives are morally bankrupt, as is often observed.[6]

- We need to stage public extravaganzas, like the Olympics or an International Exposition, in order to get beyond party politics and to mobilize otherwise unavailable public support for government that it requires to build social housing, athletic amenities, and other needed public facilities.

- A former minister of finance suggests that since government cannot finance essential public services and facilities, this might be done through public or private partnerships.[7] The proposal is made despite the increased costs that private funding of the services would probably involve and the humbling of government forced to admit its inability to meet its responsibilities without appealing to the private sector for help. The capital exists in the community to provide the services, but the support for

---

concern, poll shows," *Globe and Mail* (December 23, 2004), A11.

5   A study by the *Toronto Star* notes that 450,000 people in Ontario are classed as moderate to severe problem gamblers. The government spends $37 million a year on gambling prevention, treatment, and research. Andrew Chung, "Millions in perks woo casino gamblers," *Toronto Star* (December 10, 2005), A1. The Ontario Lottery and Gaming Corporation website stresses the positive: 29,500 jobs, $21 billion generated for worthy causes since 1975. Ontario Lottery and Gaming Corporation (2005). http://OLG.ca. Tobacco industry publications make similar "redemptive" claims, touting the number of jobs the industry provides.

6   On the subject, columnist Thomas Walkom writes, "When a government encourages its citizens to gamble in order to produce revenue for its treasury, it is admitting defeat. It is saying that society is no longer able, in an open and democratic way, to tax itself for the services it wants. It is conceding that government has lost the moral authority to convince taxpayers that, if they want public goods such as roads and health care, they must be willing to pay for them." "Gambling on casinos a sign of desperation," *Toronto Star* (March 20, 1993), D5.

7   Michael Wilson, "The road to saving our services," *Globe and Mail* (March 8, 2004), A13.

government that would permit politicians to draw on it by raising taxes does not.

- We fail to vote: turnouts decline to historically low levels.[8] Concerned and thoughtful people suggest forcing people to cast ballots to boost the sagging claim of partyocracy to legitimacy. How relationships between citizens and leaders have changed! Not too long ago people were fighting for the right to vote and political elites were resisting. Now elites worry about poor electoral turnouts and what that says about their political system.

- The public service, reflecting the general decline in the status of the government, is increasingly seen by its employees as just another place to work and by citizens as just another of the public and private bureaucracies with which they must interact. Unionization and strikes have become features of the public service. Civil servants cannot trust party government to put fair treatment of them ahead of its partisan interests.

- Large numbers of citizens ignore the law and participate as producers, vendors, or users of illicit drugs, indifferent to the various costs their actions impose on our government and society and the governments of the other drug-producing countries. Suggesting to users that they should desist because their actions are not those of good citizens, are draining public resources better used elsewhere, and are stimulating crime and violence in the community, would invite derision.[9]

- The underground economy flourishes. Many trades people regularly offer those hiring them the option of paying cash. Affluent citizens seek out tax havens and search the tax code for loopholes. Tax evasion was estimated to amount to $22 billion in 1995; a tiny reduction in this amount, produced by stronger

---

8   See the discussion of electoral systems and voting in chapter 8.

9   Estimates are that 10 percent of the adult population smokes marijuana and the numbers are growing. Brian Laghi, "Advocates get puffed up over the use of marijuana," *Globe and Mail* (July 20, 2002), A10. The issue here is not whether or not the use of marijuana is damaging to the health of those smoking it but, rather, the level of disrespect for the law shown by its extensive use.

feelings of responsible citizenship, would pay for constituency parliaments many times over.[10]

In a polity where the political system minimizes empathetic relations between citizens, tax evaders cannot be expected to worry much about defrauding government and, indirectly, their fellow citizens. The whole taxation-regulatory edifice has to rely heavily on coercion.

The stark conclusions to be drawn from these few (of many) negative examples of citizen-government interaction are that government in partyocracy is incapable of inspiring the support it requires to perform essential functions well, and that it must limit what it could be doing to further the public interest if it could count on more support from citizens.

Authority-Support Deficit

Default position: coercion. Faced with an authority-support deficit, government must resort to a great deal of coercion and manipulation of citizens in order to function. Citizens will, however, only accept a certain level and type of coercion as the price they must pay for a well-ordered community. When the governing party exceeds that it is inviting defeat at the polls. This acceptable level declines as political alienation increases, setting in motion a politically destructive cycle. Hostile to whatever party is in office, people withhold support from it; government then functions

---

10   The astonishing extent of tax evasion is reported in a Tax Foundation study: "We have defined the underground economy for the purposes of our estimates in very broad terms—that is, in terms of both tax evasion in respect of legal activities and illegal activities as such. Given this definition, our estimates suggest that the Canadian underground economy grew steadily between the mid-1970s and the mid-1990s both in nominal terms and as a percentage of measured gross domestic product (GDP). To be specific, we estimate that it amounted to about 3.5 percent of measured GDP in 1976 and almost 16 percent of GDP in 1995." (236) "Even the most draconian tax policy changes could not recover more than a fraction of this amount. When we factor our estimate of the 'hard core' into these calculations, the recoverable portion of the tax gap in 1995 is about $22 billion—an amount equal to about 7.3 percent of tax liability in 1995 or approximately 2.8 percent of GDP." (231) David E. A. Giles and Lindsay M. Tedds, *Taxes and the Canadian Underground Economy,* Canadian Tax Paper, 106 (Toronto: Canadian Tax Foundation, 2002).

even less satisfactorily, causing still more hostility and loss of support until, finally, bankruptcy looms.[11]

From an economic perspective, too, coercion costs. A government resorting to it requires enforcers—police, army, courts, etc. These are expensive and none too effective in dealing with people who are hostile to government. For too many of those who are hostile, eluding laws and regulations is seen as justified.

Authority is the democratic alternative to coercion as a means of government mobilizing support. If government has authority, we willingly support it.

The sources of authority have differed through time. Kings no longer rule by divine right, i.e., drawing on God to support their claim to power. Currently, the level of respect for political institutions primarily determines their ability to vest politicians with authority. American political scientist David Easton writes, "… if the authorities are to be able to make decisions, to get them accepted as binding, and to put them into effect without the extensive use of coercion, solidarity must be developed not only around some set of authorities themselves, but around the major aspects of the system within which the authorities operate."[12]

Solidarity is a difficult term to associate in any way with a party system of representation and governance, since parties divide us, often artificially, as they compete for support. In surveys asking people to rank institutions in terms of their confidence in them, parties usually come close to last, and other political institutions rank poorly. Working within them, our political leaders must simultaneously try to unite us behind their administration while successfully waging an ongoing party war that divides us.

Twentieth-Century Challenges to Party Government

In the years when our party system was evolving, the demands placed on

---

11   An example of how this lack of trust hobbles government was revealed in a poll reporting on public opinion at the time the administration was launching a review of social services. The poll reported that the public believed there was waste in many social programs but did not trust government to reform them. Canadian Press, "Canadians think UI, welfare wasteful," *Globe and Mail* (March 7, 1994).

12   David Easton, *A Systems Analysis of Political Life* (New York: Wiley, 1965), 157-58.

government, and its need for citizen support, were exceptionally modest. The economy was resource-based: farming was the dominant activity. Extended families and private agencies provided support and security to many in need; others went without. Government took responsibility for only the few essential services required to support the economy and meet a modest number of social demands. It intruded little on the lives of citizens; it took almost nothing directly from them in taxes. Tariffs and other sources of income provided its revenues.

The large and powerful institutions able to challenge government—transnational corporations, professional organizations, trade unions, international institutions, and others—did not exist or did so only in rudimentary form. Free from their pressures, governments were in a better position to respond to the few demands of citizens, if they chose to do so. A rough balance existed between citizen demands on government and support for it. This was all to change in the 20th century, as government, of necessity, became large, ubiquitous, expensive, and intrusive. Demands exceeded supports by a wide margin.

Economic management. The 19th-century economic world gave way to one emphasizing manufacturing and services. An urban workforce emerged, its members more dependent on an employer and government programs for their economic security than on their own enterprise and extended families. The notion that this new economy could be self-regulating was destroyed by the Great Depression of the 1930s—except for those with an exceptionally high tolerance for human suffering. Governments responded to the widespread fear that the economy would relapse into a depressed state in the post–World War II period by assuming new responsibilities for its macro management.

As economic managers, political leaders were faced with the task of reconciling the interests of the organizations associated with the new economy, i.e., big business and big labour, in a way that would maintain high levels of economic growth and employment. The strategy free-enterprise party governments chose was to exercise some general control of the economy through monetary and fiscal policy, but to leave most decisions regarding the disposition of capital and the creation of jobs largely to market forces.

When, however, business activity cycled down, market actors—business and union leaders—were quick to blame government policies, often finding diametrically opposed weaknesses in them. We blamed government, too, even though we probably voted for parties committed to the free enterprise system that was largely responsible for the downturn.

To some extent, political leaders brought this criticism on themselves. Unable to resist claiming that their economic policies were responsible for good business conditions, they found it difficult to deny responsibility for the periodic market corrections.[13] Further, the dominant national governing parties could not blame the decisions of investors and consumers, etc., without inviting pressure to become more involved in managing the economy than they wanted to be. By assuming most of the responsibility for the level of economic activity, however, governments put their limited public support at risk.

While remaining generally committed to macro management of the economy, public officials were forced by social and economic developments, and our pressure, to intrude on corporate management in a host of ways. Through regulations related to environmental and consumer protection, workplace safety and health, union organization, non-discriminatory hiring and promotion practices—the list goes on—the state intervened in areas that were once seen as strictly the responsibility of private sector management. As a result, business was forced, if only as a matter of self-protection, to take an ever-larger critical interest in politics. Watching the involvement of government with business, some felt—with good reason—that their political clout, limited to start with, was being eroded.

Most business clearly benefits from the enlarged role of government in the economy.[14] An unregulated economy is not in the short- or long-term interests of most corporations or of their investors, as the 2008

13   In 1978, pollsters asked, "Who do you think has the primary responsibility for solving the unemployment situation?" Forty percent said the federal government; and 6 percent said private industry. "The Weekend Poll," *Weekend Magazine* (January 28, 1976).

14   As C. B. Macpherson wrote, "In capitalism, the state is increasingly pulled into the economy: to support it, to regulate it, sometimes to save it from itself, sometimes to save human beings from it." *The Rise and Fall of Economic Justice* (Oxford: Oxford University Press, 1985), 38.

collapse of financial markets illustrated yet again. With a party in office that supports the free enterprise system, and another committed to it waiting in the wings, plus the power emanating from control of much of the job market, the corporate sector has infinitely more to fear from government mismanagement than from hostile policies. That said, in a pluralist system, the various political participants, such as business, feel it is important not to let up their pressure on government for ever more "friendly" policies. Business-financed policy institutes mount steady pressure on government to reduce taxes and downsize the state establishment. In so doing, they promote the impression of government as a drag on the economy, rather than as a necessary and valued support for it. Government support for business is far from fully reciprocated.

The welfare state. The state has adopted an expanded and intrusive role in the social as well as the economic sector. As mentioned, many of the traditional sources of security for people were lost or weakened in the transition to a modern economy. Governments had two reasons to respond to the loss. As part of their macro economic strategy, they wanted to maintain consumer purchasing power during market downturns. In addition, as part of their commitment to serve their constituents, and to win votes, some party governments, belatedly, launched needed social programs. These returned to us some of the security lost with urbanization and the shift away from self-employment.

The slowly adopted parade of social programs started, in the 1920s, with skimpy pensions for age qualifying voters. The Great Depression of the 1930s stimulated the eventual launch of others. Unemployment Insurance (UI), now labelled as Employment Insurance (EI) followed—but only after the lengthy period of mass unemployment in the 1930s, ending with the outbreak of World War II, had permanently blighted many lives. In the prosperous post-war period, when personal incomes and government revenues grew rapidly, easing their introduction for politicians, other social programs followed. They were intrusive—on us, on business, on the professions, and on the jurisdiction of the provinces. The welfare state had arrived, and so had a higher level of political controversy.

Medicare. The most intrusive of these programs on citizens and health professionals, and the most challenging for governments, is medicare. Government-sponsored universal health care has been a boon to individual Canadians and to national unity. For many, it has replaced the parliamentary system as a source of pride when we compare our country to the United States. Appreciation should not, however, prevent us considering why such an obviously important public service was not introduced earlier. Why did neglect trump positive action for the first half of the 20th century? The Liberal Party first promised comprehensive health care in its 1919 election platform, recognizing both its public appeal and its feasibility. The party completed acting on its promise roughly a half century later, with the introduction of medicare in 1966.

Why did this half-century delay occur while the lives of millions continued to be blighted—arguably unnecessarily—by inadequately or completely untreated illnesses and high medical bills, at the same time that their incomes were often lost? Why didn't governments, supposedly representing citizens, override the strong opposition of the doctors—after they turned against the idea of government medical insurance—and the insurance industry and provide medicare earlier?

Part of the explanation lies in how the system offers citizens only difficult, limited choices at the polls. Our parents, many of whom wanted publicly financed health care, for most of the century, had the option of voting for a party in national elections that advocated it (CCF)—and some did. However, a voter for that party had to endorse all the other policies and leadership that comprised the party's total package, and most voters were unwilling to do this. Second, parties are free to act on their platforms or not, as they choose. That means, election over, parties have the freedom to respond to changing circumstances and pressures from other than voters, if they consider doing so to be in their interests. Citizens who voted for the Liberals because of their commitment to health care were unable to insist that their representatives adopt it when they were in office. Third, despite the Liberal Party's commitment to medicare, the commitment of some Liberals, ideologically opposed to government expansion into the field, was weak or non-existent. It was easy for opponents of medicare to convince them to delay acting.

It was only in 1966 that the balance of pressures led the Liberal Party's leaders to conclude that the benefit to the party from adopting medicare would exceed the cost of battling with its opponents.[15] The Saskatchewan government had broken the ice on the issue in 1962. With its second successive minority government, the Liberal Party now needed this popular program to turn its fortunes around.[16] Many or most Canadians had always needed it and, for at least half a century, it had been feasible for government to provide it.

Under the program finally launched, federal and provincial governments assumed responsibility for health care costs but veered away from interfering with the work of health professionals. Decisions relating to the health care of individuals were to remain a personal matter negotiated between them and caregivers. With the rapid escalation of health-care costs over time, however, party governments were forced to become much more deeply involved in health care than they had originally intended. Budgetary and political interests had to be protected. Taking on this expanded role set in motion an ongoing test of governments' managerial competence and its public support vis-à-vis entrenched interests. Many people question whether it has met the test. The struggle to maintain the public system continues on.

Its enlarged role in health care drew government into an interest in the prevention of illness and the health implications of the lifestyle of citizens. Administrations that once were largely uninterested in the personal behaviour of individual citizens now urge them to practice safe sex, stop smoking, eat lots of vegetables, avoid stress, reduce consumption of pharmaceuticals, exercise, and so on. They also displayed a new interest in supporting medical research.

None of former Prime Minister Trudeau's statements has been quoted as frequently and approvingly as his comment that "the state has no place in the bedrooms of the nation." The administration of health care brought the state

---

15   The "pressures" included the enlightened support of a man who was more a distinguished public servant than a party politician—Prime Minister Pearson.

16   The CCF in Saskatchewan also delayed the introduction of medicare. Elected to office in 1944, it only introduced medicare in 1962. The medical profession led a long and bitter strike against the action of the government when it was finally taken. Its members were not prepared to recognize the authority of the elected government to act on its commitment to voters.

into every room in the house. For the state to become so involved without arousing anxiety, people had to have trust and confidence in its policy-makers and managers. Neither of these is encouraged by the performance of warring politicians in partyocracy.[17]

The adoption of medicare forced a more *caring* or, depending on one's perspective, *paternalistic* role onto free-enterprise party governments. This was something that citizen pressure expressed through the representative system had been unable to do. It seems safe to assume that citizens welcomed most of this caring. Acting on their own, citizens would find it difficult to accomplish what effective public-health measures can for the quality of our health.

The government's new role in providing health care has proven troublesome, exposing how close to *support bankruptcy* party administrations are. Many of the changes in health-care delivery, required by governments and intended to reduce costs and increase effectiveness, are recognized as positive and overdue. That does not, however, lessen the intense strain they place on the relations of politicians with important and powerful parts of their constituency. The health-care system is commonly depicted as existing in a state of crisis. Professional groups that could at one time largely ignore government are now caught up in what is, for them, its uncomfortable grip.

Currently, politicians are crying "crisis" with renewed vigour, as health-care costs rise steeply with a fast-growing population of elderly citizens and more expensive medical procedures and pharmaceuticals.[18] Politically insecure parties, short on public trust, are afraid that raising taxes to finance these costs will weaken their competitive position, while cutting programs, instead, will do the same.

For those members of the public who are able to finance their own care,

17   Health care costs constitute a large part of government budgets and, when asked, citizens express little confidence in how these and other government expenditures are made. "Canadians believe third of taxes wasted: poll," *Toronto Star* (August 15, 1988).
18   The crisis rhetoric is challenged from within and outside government. See Heather Scoffield, "Medicare study challenges crisis scenario," *Globe and Mail* (April 15, 2004), A1; Thomas Walkom, "The system ain't broke," *Toronto Star* (November 20, 2004), J1.

a return to private-sector medicine has become increasingly attractive.[19] Governments are turning a blind eye to the number of private clinics opening up. More than one governing politician would happily get rid of the politically difficult set of responsibilities that government health care puts on them. Indeed, some are doing just that.[20]

The dispute over the relative merits of private and public health care would be eased if we were able to decide the level of care we wished and would pay for. Those prepared to pay more for a higher level could then do so. But as long as politicians establish the level of care, many of us feel we must resist the pressure to allow spending outside the public program, for fear that it will erode the program on which most of us depend.

The government's social programs are popular with most of us. They provide some security in a rapidly changing world of uncertainties that we often cannot deal with as individuals. It seems natural that a government that claims to be representative and responsive should provide and maintain these programs, without needing intense continuing pressure to do so. There is, however, a downside for party government even in introducing programs that are popular and needed.

For years, government was protected from serious assessment of its administrative abilities by the relatively low cost and simplicity of most of them. In 2004, 38.9 percent of the GDP (15.5 percent federal) was devoted to all outlays by the three levels of government.[21] Taxation without representation led to revolution south of the border. High taxation, with

---

19   "Canadians are increasingly giving serious consideration to privately run health care services.... There has been a slow and steady trend in consideration of private services." Stuart N. Soroka, *Canadian Perceptions of the Health Care System*, A report to the Health Council of Canada. (Toronto: Health Council of Canada, 2007). www.healthcouncilcanada.ca; Colin Campbell, "Sick and Tired of Waiting: According to a new survey, a majority of Canadians support private health insurance," *Maclean's* (November 28, 2005), 34.

20   The *Globe and Mail* columnist who monitors health care writes, "Today, there are more violations of the program criteria of the Canada Health Act than ever, but there is essentially no enforcement. The federal government—under the Conservatives as well as the Liberals—abdicated its responsibilities under the CHA." André Picard, "At 25 the Canada Health Act deserves better from our leaders," *Globe and Mail* (August 20, 2009), L6

21   Graham Rose, Department of Finance, re: Government outlays in relation to GDP, e-mail to the author (November 7, 2005).

little control over how it is spent, is contributing significantly to our political alienation.

With the welfare-state programs, millions of us, either as clients of programs or as providers, have became dependent on what governments do—or fail to do. We feel highly vulnerable, because we lack effective control over those decisions. Governments often seem willing to sacrifice our interests to meet objectives to which they assign higher priority. Sometimes they act capriciously, seemingly uninformed about or indifferent to the harm they are causing to citizens.

An example of this capriciousness: the Liberal government cut back on employment insurance during the recession of the nineties, when levels of "official" unemployment rose to over 12 percent. At the same time, it drew on the surplus in the unemployment insurance fund to help finance its deficit. What fire insurance company could retain the confidence of its clients if it reduced a homeowners' coverage when a fire broke out, despite holding a large reserve fund to meet just such emergencies? The law does not allow such behaviour in the private sector, but party governments are not similarly restrained. Our powerlessness and the *un*representative nature of the system are brought home to us in such situations.

New power centres. While the confidence of citizens in government and deference toward the governing elite has declined, the challenges facing government from new power centres have increased—dramatically. Political economist Robert Campbell writes,

> Developing appropriate policies in response to globalization is not simply a matter of replacing one group of government leaders with another "better" or more informed set. This heroic view of government is naïve and outdated, reflecting perhaps a view of what a government might have been capable of doing in a less complex world. Does anybody seriously believe that any political party in Canada has the imagination, intelligence, and capacity to devise—on its own—the appropriate range of policies to deal with globalization? The sooner this myth is shattered the better.
>
> ... Canada needs mechanisms that will avoid antagonistic and

defensive response to change, that ensure the representation and articulation of all interests.[22]

Amen!

While the corporate sector is the most significant power centre with which government must now contend, the 20th century featured the growth of other large organizations for which government policy is important, like the trade unions and professional associations. In their respective spheres, each of these is in a strong position to influence, perhaps dominate, the development of public policy relating to its concerns.[23] The sight of politicians catering to their often-indefensible demands raises questions of fairness and demeans government in the eyes of individual citizens.[24]

Aware that our voice, expressed through elections, is not likely to have much impact in relation to these heavyweights, various self-styled citizen lobbies have formed to provide at least some modest countervailing citizen influence on policy. Some have received government support. But, for a host of reasons, this improvised approach is problematic. It would be unnecessary in policy democracy.

New citizens. As will be discussed in more detail in later chapters, the performance of big, intrusive government in the late 20th century has been abysmal. That, alone, is sufficient to destroy our confidence in, and support

---

22   Robert Campbell, "Coping with globalization instead of just talking about it," *Policy Options* (December 1992): 18.

23   Their political clout increases as trust in government declines. A poll conducted by Ekos Research Associates for the Trudeau Foundation found that "just one in four Canadians trust the federal government to do what is right, while the majority believe politicians lose touch with the public soon after being elected." "Trust in federal government hits new low: poll," CTV news release (November 11, 2005). www.ctv.ca

24   Lee Iacocca, former CEO of Ford and then of Chrysler, describes how governments are manipulated: "I have played Spain versus France and England for so long I am tired of it. Ford, when I was there, and General Motors, Chrysler—all over the world—we pit Ohio against Michigan; we pit Canada against the United States; we get outright grants and subsidies in Spain and Mexico and Brazil—all kinds of grants. With my former employer (Ford), one of the last things I did was, on the threat of losing 2,000 jobs in Windsor, I got $73 million outright." Cited in Ontario, *Hansard* (October 22, 1980), R-1042. How is respect and support for government affected by this brazen corporate blackmail?

for, the political establishment, but there is more. Coincident with that performance, the political audience has become more critically aware and less tolerant of malfunctioning governments.

Traditionally, party politicians argued that they should monopolize the making of public policy, because they alone were in a position to know what was best for the country and its inhabitants. The expansion of education, communications, and personal wealth have eroded the validity of that claim. With these social changes, many of us have become less willing to defer to the judgement of the governing party elite, and we are more resentful of its refusal to open up a system claiming to be democratic to more participation by us. We are told that as citizens of a democracy we should participate, but we are not given opportunities to do so that seem significant to us.

Mandate Mythology

Only a valid claim to a popular mandate can vest government with sufficient democratic support or authority to function as citizens wish.[25] With such a mandate, government—party or non-party—could then proceed, in the name of the people, to offer dynamic, timely, and often controversial policies without fear of being punished by voters. Aware of the significance of the mandate, defenders of the present political system claim that partyocracy does, indeed, vest government with it. They tell us that by endorsing a particular party at the polls, we agree to or mandate its governance. It can then, acting with our consent, adopt and implement its policies. "Good" citizens should support the government as it does so.

Implicitly, this claim may have once been widely accepted. No longer. People are increasingly annoyed or angered when government claims that it is following the will of the people. Polling often suggests the reverse. The election of a new party to office does not establish that a majority of citizens has agreed to its program or, in most cases, even to it holding office. The unpopularity of the incumbents is likely to be the principal reason for the

---

25   "Mandate: The term (the general implication of which is 'command') is used in the theory of democratic politics in a special sense—to describe the things which electors have told their elected representatives to do." P. A. Bromhead in *Dictionary of the Social Sciences,* eds. Julius Gould and William L. Kolb (New York: The Free Press, 1964), 404.

new party's success not its policies. To hide the fact that "the emperor is wearing no clothes," some academics concerned with the ability of the system to function, but also with their professional integrity, struggle on the one hand to be honest and on the other to avoid undercutting the legitimacy of the governments produced by partyocracy.

David Cameron and Graham White, University of Toronto political scientists, wrestle with the mandate issue in their study of government transitions in Ontario, in the 1990s.[26] The province moved from Liberal to NDP to Progressive Conservative (Harris) governments in those years, as its voters engaged in the never-to-be more-than-moderately successful search for a satisfactory governing party. Cameron and White hold that the Harris government succeeded in obtaining a clear mandate from the voters because it issued a very specific, well-publicized program to voters, and it was elected following this with 45 percent of the popular vote—a high figure in a multi-party system. However, intellectual integrity forces them to qualify the conclusion that a clear mandate was issued and received. They write,

> [In] The 8 June 1995 Ontario election … the party running third was led by a conviction politician with clear, hard-edged policy commitments that had been laid out far in advance of the election. Vote for the Mike Harris Tories and you will get the policies contained in the Common Sense Revolution. Every one of them. The strong Conservative win, attracting an impressive 45 percent of the vote share in a three-party race, gave Mike Harris and his colleagues an unusually clear mandate to govern and to implement the policies they had campaigned on. The voting public had formed a very clear notion of what the Tories were proposing and, in voting for them, had no reason not to expect that this was what they would get.

This certainly was the Conservatives' preferred interpretation, but less clear-cut readings are also possible. In terms of a mandate, it could be argued that, aside from a few central hot-button issues such as welfare reform, the Harris victory was less an explicit acceptance

---

26   David R. Cameron and Graham White, *Cycling into Saigon: The Conservative Transition in Ontario* (Vancouver: UBC Press, 2000).

of the whole Common Sense Revolution—which few voters likely read and digested in its entirety—than a more inchoate search for change among many who were dissatisfied with the status quo. As in 1990, when the clear choice for those seeking change was the NDP, Harris's strong campaign established him as the voice of change. Moreover, the Common Sense Revolution is a less detailed road map to change than is sometimes imagined. For every precise commitment (a 30 percent cut in provincial income tax rate) there is a vaguely worded commitment—"rationalize the regional and municipal levels to avoid the overlap and duplication that now exists"—or a broad policy swath not addressed. (The document is entirely silent on environmental issues.)[27]

In Ontario, in 1995, there was as fulsome an attempt to get a "real" electoral mandate for a government's policies and approach as is ever likely to occur in Canadian politics. Yet, Cameron and White point out that even there the success of the attempt is questionable. Their questioning should go further. Only 45 percent of those who voted cast ballots for the Conservatives. From a *democratic* perspective, it would be appropriate for them to stress that most voters refused to give that party a general mandate to govern and, of course, did not mandate any of its specific policies.

The common phenomenon of a party getting into office principally because the alternatives are unacceptable, and its leader then claiming a mandate, was highlighted, too, in the 2000 federal election. An Ipsos-Reid poll conducted soon after the election found, in the words of a *Globe and Mail* report on it, that "Prime Minister Jean Chrétien won his third consecutive majority even though most Canadians disapproved of the way he was doing his job…." Asked "Do you agree or disagree: Jean Chrétien doesn't have what it takes anymore to lead the country?" Sixty-six percent agreed; 33 percent were opposed. On the further question, "Do you agree/disagree: The Liberals are arrogant and corrupt," 58 percent agreed, and 41 percent disagreed.[28] Rejected by the majority of citizens, a happy and smug

27   Ibid., 58.
28   Shawn McCarthy, "Public frowns on PM despite vote, poll finds," *Globe and Mail* (December 2, 2000), A4. Two years later, seven in ten poll respondents, including 58

winner in the party/electoral game returned to the prime minister's office to exercise his "mandate."

The claimed existence of a citizen-mandate is fraudulent. Even if we assume, contrary to evidence, that citizens are well informed and equipped to vote rationally, partyocracy does not allow us to clearly mandate a governing party or its policies. We need and deserve a system that does both.

Conclusion

Partyocracy evolved in the 19th century out of the need of rival elites for a system that allowed them to compete peacefully for the right to manage the public's business. In the 21st century, partyocracy is asked to produce governments able to perform a wide range of vital functions. "Genetically" programmed for one purpose, partyocracy is ill suited to perform others that are different and very challenging.

The attempt to pass off the 19th-century political system that institutionalized the rule of competing elites as "representative democracy" alienates 21st-century citizens. Many of us experience it as party and/or prime ministerial rule or misrule, not as democracy, As the challenges facing government and popular disillusionment with its performance grow, its support base shrinks.

To overcome the authority deficit, far more is needed by a government than a certificate stating that it won a competitive, party-dominated election. Full support for government will only come with a program that is developed collaboratively by citizens, their elected representatives, the political executive, and the bureaucracy.

Most of us support constituency representation, a mode that would allow us to escape from party domination and our powerlessness. We deserve the opportunity to formalize that choice. No citizen should be condemned to living with weak government when there is a strong, viable democratic alternative to it.

---

percent of Liberal supporters, said the Liberal prime minister should step down. Ipsos, May 31, 2002. www.ipsos.ca/

Partyocracy as Government

It is time to consider the possibility that if millions are disillusioned with
conventional politics, it is because conventional politics are disillusioning.

Michael Parenti

Sustainability has to be a choice, a choice of a global society that
thinks ahead and acts in unaccustomed harmony. Governments will
have to be restructured for such twenty-first-century problems.

Jeffrey Sachs

Canadians appear to distrust their political leaders, the political process
and political institutions. Parties themselves may be contributing
to the malaise of voters…. Whatever the cause, there is little doubt
that Canadian political parties are held in low public esteem, and
that their standing has declined steadily over the past decade.
They are under attack from citizens for failing to achieve a variety
of goals deemed important by significant groups within society.

Royal Commission on Electoral Reform and Party Financing

Introduction

Unaware of any better alternative, we accept party representation and
government as a necessary evil. I challenged the notion that parties are

inevitable or necessary by setting out an alternative to party representation: the policy democracy/constituency parliament model. Now is the time to examine the "evil," i.e., the damage party representation and government do to the quality of government and citizenship.

Most of us already recognize that party government is riddled with deeply unsatisfactory features. Criticizing the performance of government is almost as common and safe a topic of conversation as the weather—but government performance is something we could and should influence. It will strengthen and add urgency to the case for fundamental change to show that the most damaging of these features would not exist, or that their impact would be greatly reduced, if government were firmly rooted in the citizenry.

The general critique of the performance of our system in this and the following chapter is not an attack on our politicians and bureaucrats. My fundamental argument is that the rewards and punishments built into the institutional framework within which they function heavily influence, or control, the behaviour of both. A failure to respond to the demands of the system would simply mean that they would be replaced by others who would. To change undesirable behaviour, we must change the institutions that determine so much of it.

Two intimately connected features of partyocracy have a major impact on the performance of our political leaders and their governments: basing the acquisition of power on competitive party elections, and the authority deficit to which that leads.

Holding free and fair elections to decide in an orderly way who and then who and what party would govern was an advance of unparalleled significance when they were introduced. Electoral democracy brought numerous benefits: The peaceful management of elite competition for power is the most significant of these, but there are others. Party recruitment of candidates and their presentation of platforms have given voters a limited, manageable choice at the polls and a feeling of some empowerment. Parties, with the help of the electoral system, are usually able to form stable governments. As they do so, they are kept somewhat responsive to their constituents by the knowledge that voters have periodic opportunities to replace them. Elections are a safety valve for discontented citizens as they, inevitably, become fed up with the performance of the incumbent party. Finally, the contests inform voters on some issues, enabling them to cast a better-informed ballot.

Party-dominated elections perform all these essential functions, and others, but as is obvious to most of us, they do so inadequately. Our continuing dependence on elections as the sole formal link of citizens to government has a serious negative impact on the performance of government. As we have previously discussed, elections do not really mandate the policies party governments adopt and do not give governments the democratic authority they require to perform effectively. This cannot be fully acknowledged by most observers, only because they believe there is no alternative to electoral democracy. Prime ministers and their governments are frequently attacked for lack of will, courage, or imagination—when the focus should be on how elections and the fear of losing votes restrict their ability to take controversial but vitally important policy decisions in a timely fashion.

Parties, Elections, and the Performance of Government

Political Patronage. Government favouritism of various kinds, intended to curry support for the individuals and/or the party in office, is the most widely noticed abuse of power related to party/electoral politics. Parties are never confident that they have sufficient resources to guarantee success at the polls. As a result, the governing party, showing indifference to the public interest, often exploits the opportunities office-holding offers to build its support.

Traditional patronage. Familiar traditional patronage bestows quite specific unearned (except for party support, given or anticipated) government largesse on individuals and interests. It was once the driving force in party politics; the right contacts with the governing party still benefit many. Tendering for government contracts, supposedly open and competitive, often favours party insiders. Most of the government's legal and advertising business changes hands with a new governing party. Appointments to the boards of a wide range of public agencies go to government supporters. Party bagmen stand a good chance of being rewarded with an appointment to the Senate. If we collect news reports of traditional patronage, the files holding them will overflow quickly.

Policy patronage. Traditional patronage, easily understood and still significant was, however, supplanted in importance in the last century by what we may call policy patronage—policy favourable to particular interests that support the party in office. Its character is not so easily grasped. Indeed, it is not seen as patronage at all by those who believe that elections produce a significant policy mandate for government. To them, it may seem nonsensical to suggest that the governing party is dispensing patronage when it has successfully appealed to voters on those policies or on others like them. They may well ask, "If party government doesn't base its program on the mandate it claims to have, how is it to govern? Should it, perhaps, take actions it does not necessarily agree with just to respect the superficial views of citizens revealed in public opinion polls?"

If we set aside the myth that the election has mandated the policies of the governing party, however, we can see that public policy is often patronage that differs only in form from the traditional variant. It is the major abuse of the present political system and, at the same time, is an integral part of it. We deserve policies that reflect our interests, i.e., those endorsed by informed citizens uncontaminated by party interests.

Prof. John Meisel recognizes the importance of some forms of this "grander" patronage. He writes, "Patronage has changed from being localized, small potatoes to becoming colossal, Guinness Book of Records-sized pumpkins. Government decisions affecting the location of major industries (automobile production, aerospace, for instance, the quintessence of political culture (multiculturalism), or centre-periphery tensions (regional development), are made in response to their potential impact on voter support for the government party."[1]

We realize in a general way that party government moves to its own drummer, looking after supporters as it does so. It would become strikingly, intolerably obvious, however, if we had the means to deliberate and

---

1   John Meisel, "The Dysfunctions of Canadian Parties: An Exploratory Mapping," in *Democracy with Justice*, eds. Alain-G. Gagnon and A. Brian Tanguay (Ottawa: Carleton University Press, 1992), 419–20.

independently establish our interests. We could then compare the result of our informed deliberations with the policies adopted by government.[2]

Policy patronage has grown in significance in tandem with the expansion of government and with the impact of its policies on individuals and interests. The traditional form awards special privileges to relatively few, while policy patronage often affects the whole country and can have a lasting impact. This form of patronage cannot be eliminated within partyocracy, because the system is based on it. As long as it exists, however, many will not be able to see what government does as worthy of their support. A conservative/democrat would be able to support a "socialistic" policy if it were endorsed by his or her fellow citizens but not if the authority behind it was only that of a socialist party government.

Parties depend on their ability to distribute patronage, particularly policy patronage, in order to survive. It is their life-blood that enables them to attract support and monopolize politics despite citizens' hostility toward them.

The Impact of Party Elections on Rationality in Policy Making

Limited Experience: Policy Inconsistency. Experience is almost always needed to perform a challenging role well; representing and governing are not exceptions. But with a plurality electoral system, an incumbent party's defeat normally results in a completely different party team forming the executive and a large turnover in membership of the House of Commons. Significant numbers of inexperienced people are swept into office with each election, even when the same party remains in control. The newcomers may bring with them values and policies that differ, perhaps very significantly,

---

2   Academics have attempted to make this comparison. Polls are used to solicit the views of citizens, and these are compared to those of their "representatives" in government. Strong differences are revealed. But the polling reflects only the uninformed public's instant response to survey questions. It leaves open the argument that informed and responsible citizens might see that the policies adopted by government were appropriate and that representatives were really acting in the interests of those they represented. See, for example, François Petry and Matthew Mendelsohn, "Public Opinion and Policy Making in Canada 1994–2001," *Canadian Journal of Political Science, 37, 3* (September 2004): 505–29. The "rightness" of representation can only be determined if the represented have the means to determine and express their policy preferences.

from those of the departing government. Disruptive policy shifts that have little to do with the public interest often result.

A high point in turnover was reached in 1993 when 66 percent of the incoming parliament were new members.[3] This led political scientist David Docherty to comment, "Parliament seems to do a better job of losing talent than it does retaining it."[4] Membership turnover would be dramatically reduced in the policy democracy model because there would be little reason for voters to replace an MP who was working collegially with his or her constituency parliament.

The newly elected team and, in particular, its leader, must now usually unlearn *oppositionism* and acquire governing skills, on the job, in an environment that is unforgiving of error.[5] Many new members of cabinet will have no previous experience in that body, and those that have will probably find themselves in unfamiliar portfolios.

The problems with inexperience are compounded by the practice of frequently shifting cabinet members to new ministries to put a more politically acceptable face on the administration. That may suit the competitive interests of the prime minister's party, but it poses a further obstacle to ensuring consistent policy and leadership at the ministerial level and political control of the bureaucracy. Many ministers may never have time to master their departments and end up serving primarily as spokespersons for their officials or the prime minister.

The rapid turnover of ministers is more than matched by the merry-go-round experience of their deputies. A study of the public administration

---

3   David C. Docherty, *Mr. Smith Goes to Ottawa: Life in the House of Commons* (Vancouver: University of British Columbia Press), 52.

4   David C. Docherty, *Legislatures* (Vancouver: University of British Columbia Press, 2005), 63.

5   Former premier of Ontario, Bob Rae, comments, "There is probably no worse training in the world for becoming premier than spending a career in opposition. It is hard, if not impossible, for an opposition leader to meet and be briefed seriously by the bureaucracy on an ongoing basis. This is even truer for NDP leaders than for others. The suspicions are simply too great. The reluctance to share information is based on the natural apprehension that anything important will be immediately used to partisan advantage in question period." Bob Rae, *From Protest to Power* (Toronto: Penguin Books Canada Ltd., 1996), 130. The significance of the rapid turnover in MPs is discussed fully in Docherty, *Mr. Smith Goes to Ottawa*, 51–59.

finds that: "public sector employees feel that the excessive rotation of senior staff (31 percent have had three supervisors in three years)—is a major issue for performance improvement. With deputy ministers and assistant deputy ministers spending less than two years in their positions [a minimum of five years is deemed desirable] public servants are constantly readjusting to new management, which affects their ability to do their job."[6] Stability in political and administrative leadership (or effective management) appears to take second place to competitive party interests.

A professor in development at the London School of Economics highlights how politics, and excessive personnel turnover, interferes in the effectiveness of the Canadian International Development Agency: "... CIDA has been particularly vulnerable to meddling by politicians eager to pander to ethnic voters, corporate interests, and nationalist sentiment. ... The minister of international co-operation, responsible for CIDA, has traditionally been a comfortable resting spot for loyal mid-ranking politicians with little apparent interest or commitment to development issues. In the past 10 years, we have seen no fewer than six ministers come through the turnstiles at CIDA's office, most of whom haven't had a tenure exceeding two years.

"... Needless to say, the ebb and flow of political appointments to CIDA has not engendered a stable backdrop for effective development policy-making. As each minister reinvents priorities and programs to suit their pet interests, so does CIDA's effectiveness wane."[7] There is reason to believe that the experience of CIDA is gone through in slightly different form, in other government departments and agencies.

The turnover of parties in office leads to problems in addition to the loss of experienced legislators and members of the executive. The identification of a policy with one party may be enough to delay a new governing party acting on it for years. General sluggishness of the system is exacerbated by partisan considerations. For example, the Chrétien Liberals, as part of their opposition routine, denounced the preceding Mulroney government s decision to buy particular replacements for the armed forces ancient Sea

---

6   Thomas Axworthy and Julie Burch, "Closing the Implementation Gap," (Queen's University: Centre for the Study of Democracy, 2010), 5.

7   Nilima Gulrangi, "How politicization has been silently killing CIDA's effectiveness," *Globe and Mail* (June 5, 2009)

King helicopters. They then, as government, resisted making virtually the same decision for most of a decade. They did so even though there was wide agreement that the original decision was well grounded.

When the purchase was finally concluded, an extensive and expensive effort was made to make it appear as different as possible from that proposed by the Mulroney government years earlier.[8] Political face had to be saved. The cancellation cost the taxpayers millions, risked the lives of pilots asked to fly worn-out aircraft, and subjected the government to ridicule and anger. High-level bureaucrats must have wasted thousands of hours working through the issue with different administrations, their frustration with the political process increasing as they did so.

Authors of a report for the National Council of Welfare express frustration at how the governing parties abuse their freedom to shift policy about: "Once a program has been properly evaluated and shown to be effective, it should be immune from senseless changes by governments. This will be difficult, because governments in Canada have traditionally interpreted a clear victory at the polls as a mandate to change almost anything in sight."[9]

The changes may be sweeping as well as specific. The policies of economic nationalism of Trudeau in the 1970s gave way to the continentalism of Mulroney in the 1980s. The Harper government, favouring an emphasis on the military as a combat force, downplays the long Liberal tradition of Canadians as peacekeepers and this requires changes in military hardware

---

8   In a column reviewing the details of the helicopter purchase about-face, Jeffery Simpson writes, "The EH-101 was the chopper the military wanted. But the optics of choosing it, 11 years after Mr. Chrétien rejected it, were too awful even for the Martinites, who, as we know, cannot find anything good to say about their predecessors.
"So the rule of all politics, all the time, in defence-procurement matters continued to the last: the wrong helicopter chosen for reasons of political optics." "Damn it, it's still the wrong helicopter!" *Globe and Mail* (July 24, 2004), A15. Peter Newman claims that exercising the contract cancellation clause on the helicopters entered into by its predecessor cost the Chrétien government, i.e., us, $487 million. Peter Newman, "Restoring Fallen Kings," *Maclean's* (October 20, 2003), 44–45. Another high-profile Chrétien cancellation of a contract made by the preceding government—relating to the privatization of Pearson airport—also cost us millions. The millions that were lost as a result of these partisan decisions would easily support a system of constituency parliaments for several years.
9   National Council of Welfare, "Healthy Parents, Healthy Babies," (Ottawa: Minster of Public Works and Government Services Canada, 1997), 35.

and training. Were the changes sought by us or the result of pressure from the different set of interests backing each party, its competitive concerns, and its ideological mindset?

Many of the policy changes resulting from a change in governing party will be completely unrelated to the reasons for the defeat of the incumbents. Claiming to be acting in the public interest or—in this less deferential era when the public must be flattered—as mandated by it, the new party team will shift policy in many disruptive ways. Public investment of various kinds in policy X will be lost as the new government replaces it, arguably without good reason, with policy Y.

If we were to take the mandate theory seriously, policy shifts from one party government to another should be difficult to make. If policy X had really been mandated by us in an authoritative way in an election, the new governing party would not be able to change it without a different mandate from us. Otherwise, the change would be seen as a rejection of our preferred policy and votes lost. But, of course, that is nonsense. An election in which the policy was mentioned does not mean that citizens took ownership of it. Most issues for which a mandate is claimed were not mentioned at all.

The sweeping changes in party government are often presented positively, as "refreshing" politics and government with new policies and faces. If the existing system is maintained, then indeed, a regular opportunity to express hostility and fantasize again about how a change of party in office may set things right is a valuable system safeguard. The honeymoon a new party government typically enjoys with citizens is, however, increasingly short and expensive. We are progressively more sceptical about the promises made by the new team. Indeed, the "representative" system distorts the wishes of voters so grievously that many of those voting for the winning team—their choice of party primarily determined by a desire to defeat incumbents—may be fearful lest the new government does act on its promises.

The new government's changes in administration and policies are as likely to be disruptive, destructive, or annoying and expensive, as refreshing. It is one thing for the new owners of a house to alter it to make it their own, and quite another for a temporary tenant, i.e., a party, to do this to a country.

Our politics should be organized so that we can decide on the future direction of our country for ourselves rather than being forced to depend on the vagaries of party politics and the electoral system. Government that has our steady support and adjusts smoothly to our demands should replace disruptive cycles of hope and alienation.

Election timetable. The impact of the electoral timetable, fixed or flexible, is another of the features of electoral politics that negatively affects the rational development and implementation of public policy. Whether it is the best time from a public-interest perspective or not, controversial policies are, whenever possible, introduced early in a government's term, to allow citizens to become accustomed to them before they are asked to vote again. For example, good party generalship requires that attention-getting tax increases and cuts be staged so that increases are imposed early in a government's term in office and cuts made just prior to an election. Good economic management often requires a different ordering.[10]

Further, many vital policy initiatives, like additional government child care or action on climate change, will only produce most of their benefits in the long term. They are, therefore, less attractive to party government than policies producing a fast return. To use stock market parlance, party governments are day traders rather than value investors.

The actions of the Liberal government leading up to the 2000 federal election are a case in point. The election loomed, large tax cuts were announced, and more promised. Long-needed financing for crucially important programs, such as health care, was provided. Recovering support in the Maritime provinces was seen as crucial by the Liberals for winning re-election. The government announced large grants to the region and the partial restoration of the EI benefits, cut earlier, that were of particular importance to the area's many seasonal workers.[11] Uncharacteristically, the

---

10   The finance ministers of most liberal democracies would probably agree with the observation of a long-time Swedish finance minister, Kjell-Olof Feldt: "In economic policy, I've learned, when things are due to be done for economic reasons, it's very often too early for political reasons. The crisis is not manifest, not obvious. When the crisis is there, the things you have to do come at the wrong time." Cited in David Crane, "Sweden at the Crossroads," *Toronto Star* (May 16, 1993), A12.

11   The restoration still left EI benefits substantially reduced: "Only 38 percent of unemployed workers now [2005] receive benefits, down from over 75 percent in the

prime minister apologized for allowing the cuts to be made in the first instance.[12]

At one level, some people—political junkies—appreciate the manipulative skills of party operatives and enjoy the fun-and-games aspect of competitive electoral politics. At another, it disturbs many that important public business is so significantly affected by partisan manoeuvring. Those who do find the politics of partyocracy entertaining must be persuaded that its social cost is exorbitant.

Elections are needed to choose representatives. Used for more than that, i.e., to choose a governing party team and its agenda, they disrupt the rational development and implementation of public policy on a grand scale. Policy should be made in deliberative institutions—constituency and national parliaments—between elections. This would spare us the frustration of trying to express ourselves clearly on policy issues with an X after a name on a ballot. The silly claim that elections mandate party governments to adopt all their policies could be dropped.

Impact of Authority Deficit

As discussed previously, when the system does not vest the party in office with sufficient authority to meet its obligations, the usual behaviour of government is to dodge, finesse, delay meeting, and otherwise avoid going beyond its "line of credit" with us. To do otherwise would be to lose electoral support. At a time that governments need more authority to meet its challenges, however, what they do have is slipping away, leaving them ever more vulnerable to diverse pressures from organized interests.

Priorities. One consequence of this loss of authority is the inability of government to set and stick to priorities. Obviously, if government is to maximize its contribution to our well-being, the resources available to it must be devoted first to meeting our most important needs. An administration

---

early 1990s." Armine Yalnizyan, "Canada's poverty reduction progress slowed by decentralization," *CCPA Monitor* (November 2005), 10.
12   Shawn McCarthy, "Chrétien backtracks on EI rules," *Globe and Mail* (September 22, 2000).

that is all over the place—responding to the crisis of the day, its policies often conflicting and inconsistent—is failing us.

No government today would be without a high-level priorities and planning committee. The need for both is recognized. It is usually the case, however, that in spite of the work of these committees, party governments "run after events" rather than following even their own priorities. Authors of virtually every academic study of a particular policy area are struck by the tardy, ad hoc, confused, and often counterproductive policy development they uncover.[13]

The early Trudeau administrations were, for example, strongly committed to bringing rationality into setting policy. However, their elaborate planning and priorities exercises succeeded only in revealing how difficult it was to apply the priorities in the face of unanticipated social, economic, and political developments.[14] That said, however, if government were organized differently and had a more secure base of popular support, its ability to put first things first consistently would be enhanced. The absence of this base almost ensures that immediate pressures, the "squeaky wheels," will get government's attention and resources.

Child poverty and child care. The related issues of child care and child poverty provide a tragic illustration of party governments' inability to prioritize. I have chosen a social issue as an example, because it is the area

---

13   Economist Fred Lazar's assessment of the performance of government as it makes policy is typical of others': "The literature on public choice, regulatory capture, and interest group bargaining, and the political reality of the need to balance competing and divergent regional interests at the cabinet table in Ottawa, all suggest that good ideas get seriously distorted as they proceed through the decision-making process of the federal government. The policies that come out at the end of the process do not necessarily have much in common with the ideas that initiated the process ... I fully concur ... that 'stupidity, hubris, and bad luck' undoubtedly play a role in producing the policies that have failed to enhance our economic position and performance; but these factors alone cannot explain continual repetition of policy mistakes. There is a more serious failure in the process that produces these policies." *How Ottawa Rewards Mediocrity* (Toronto: University of Toronto, 1996), 28.

14   A major theme in the two-volume biography of P. E. Trudeau by Christina McCall and Stephen Clarkson is the struggle of Trudeau's cabinets to impose rationality on the process of making policy. *Trudeau and Our Times,* vols. 1 and 2 (Toronto: McClelland and Stewart Inc., 1990, 1994).

of policy where government is weakest. Economic interests are in a strong position to press their priorities on government. The public, and particularly economically disadvantaged members of it, are not.

This particular social issue is highlighted because there is close to universal agreement among party politicians and citizens on the high priority that should be given to the care of children. The evidence that careful nurturing in early years can forestall costly social problems later is abundant. In addition, the almost universally shared liberal value of equality of opportunity demands that all children experience similar high-quality care.

This wide consensus on the importance of care does not however extend to the state's role in providing it. Some people support the state helping parents finance daycare for their children if they choose to use the help provided them through allowances to families and tax breaks for that purpose. Others favour its direct provision by the state in a universal daycare program.

I will consider the ability of government to give sufficient priority to either form of care delivery to make a significant dent in the number of children living the poverty experience. If the importance of that objective is not reflected in timely government policy, despite the virtually unanimous support for it, something is seriously amiss with our version of representative democracy. The wealth needed to provide the very best child care in the world is available in Canada. There is no mystery about how to establish it.

Attacking the problem of child poverty through support to parents presents different problems than direct state provision of child care. The former requires government boosting the resources of families through allowances for children and hoping that it will be spent as intended. The latter approach to ending child poverty now is to provide as much equalizing support as possible to children "in the village." This can take many forms but the most important, certainly, is high-quality daycare. The issue of whether state funding is actually spent on children does not arise when it is spent this way.

The provision of public money, directly or indirectly for daycare allows many parents—who might otherwise be forced to stay at home -- to work, pay taxes, and significantly improve their family's financial situation.

The child-care issue is complicated, as are so many others, by the federal nature of Canada. (Our politics does not allow us to remove some of these complications and make the lines of accountability of governments to citizens clearer.) The national government has taxing powers that are superior to those of the provinces, which have jurisdiction over providing services to people. In the past, Ottawa has used its spending power to circumvent this barrier to offering programs directly to citizens by offering grants to the provinces if they participate in national social programs.

In the case of child care, under the terms of the Established Programs Financing Act (now lapsed and replaced with bloc grants the provinces are meant to spend on social programs) the federal government assumed half the cost of provincial programs directed at poor Canadians, including, of course, their children. In 1999, however, under pressure from provincial governments, primarily that of Quebec—which the national government chose not to resist or was too weak to do so—Ottawa (the prime minister?) committed itself to forgoing the use of its spending power to establish social programs without the agreement of the majority of the provinces. This has meant that the central government could not initiate a national child-care program to be administered by the provinces without their agreement.[15] At a time when Ottawa's social role was more important than ever to us, it was changed without our permission. Of course, that behaviour is normal in partyocracy.

The flawed record. The saga of child-care policy was set in motion by changes in the roles of women and government in the latter half of the 20th century. In a limited response to these, the government adopted a popular universal family-allowance program in 1945. A modest allowance was paid to mothers for each child in school up to age 18. The program marked a break from the notion that raising children, apart from the important exception of public schooling, was almost entirely the responsibility of parents. This quite tentative state commitment to the welfare of children was not followed up with other measures of support at that time. Of the program, Dennis Guest,

---

15   For a good summary of the distressing negotiations that failed to produce a national child care policy post-2000, see University of Toronto's Childcare Resource and Research Unit, "What is the state of early childhood education and childcare in 2007?" www.childcarecanada.org/ECEC/pdf/ECEC06/pfd

a professor of social policy, writes, "Despite the program's popularity, it was largely neglected by the federal government. Between 1945 and 1973 only one marginal increase in benefit was legislated, even though inflation had badly eroded the [value of the allowance].... The government's neglect of the family allowance program in postwar years appears to have been directly related to its lack of appreciation of the program's potential in terms of social equity and administrative consistency. In addition, the predicted postwar recession did not occur."[16]

The expected post-war economic crisis did not occur, easing the pressure on governments to increase the incomes of families. Neither the family allowance, discontinued in 1992, nor the child tax credit substituted for it, were sufficient to make a significant impact on child poverty levels or to ensure that child care was available to all who needed it. With fluctuations caused by changes in the levels in unemployment, poverty continued to blight the lives of approximately 15 percent of adults and their children.[17]

Arguably, the development of a comprehensive national child-care program was widely seen as a priority by social activists and many others no later than the early 1960s. However, while public interest in action by the national government increased significantly in the years after 1960, pressure on governments for it was not sufficient to prompt a response. The vital community concern for our children did not result in an appropriate policy response from our "representatives."

In 1989, however, a new factor strengthened the weakly represented public voice and that of the virtually unheard poor. The United Nations General Assembly adopted the Convention on the Rights of the Child. In the discussions leading up to its adoption, Canadians paying attention to such matters learned, or were reminded, that Canada stood 9th of 12 OECD countries in terms of the level of child poverty. We were also reminded that a high (expensive) level of child care was, demonstrably, not incompatible

---

16   Dennis Guest, "Family Allowance," *The Canadian Encyclopedia*. http://www.the-canadianencyclopedia.com.

17   Source: UNICEF, "Child Poverty in Rich Countries, 2005," Innocenti Report Card No. 6 (Florence, Italy: Innocenti Research Centre). www.unicef-icdc.org

with a buoyant economy [and] might even contribute to it.[18] It was, and is, affordable.[19]

The House of Commons reacted, unanimously endorsing a resolution to end child poverty in Canada by the year 2000. The resolution, standing alone, was a "motherhood" statement but important nonetheless as recognition of what the government ought to, and could, do. A plan to reach the objective in the time frame the Commons adopted might have been expected to follow its adoption, but it didn't. In the following year, the then-prime minister, Brian Mulroney, co-chaired the World Summit for Children sponsored by the United Nations. As intended, these UN activities brought considerable public and media attention to the plight of children living in poverty in Canada and elsewhere.

The years between 1989 and 2000 saw a change in governing party and a period of recession and deficit fighting followed by several years of booming government revenues. The recession should not have deflected

---

18   Source: UNICEF, "Child Poverty and Changes in Child Poverty in Rich Countries Since 1990," Innocenti Working Paper 2005-02 (Florence, Italy: Innocenti Research Centre, 2005), 12. www.unicef-icdc.org. An earlier report by UNICEF noted, importantly, "As for the argument that such an emphasis on relative incomes runs counter to the need for incentives, it can be argued that, whatever the intricacies of this long-running debate, nations such as Sweden, Norway, and Finland contrive to be among the most egalitarian and yet among the wealthiest countries in the world. The top six places in both child poverty league tables—relative and absolute—are occupied by the same northern European countries, all of which combine a high degree of economic development with a reasonable degree of equity." UNICEF, "Innocenti Report Card, Issue #1," (Florence, Italy: Innocenti Research Centre, 2000), 9. www.unicef-icdc.org

19   Citing Stats Canada survey of assets, debts, and wealth, the *CCPA Monitor*, vol. 9, 6 (November 2002), l, reports, "The wealthiest 10 percent of family units in Canada held 53 percent of the personal wealth, and the top 50 percent controlled an almost unbelievable 94.4 percent of the wealth. That left only 5.6 percent to be shared among the bottom 50 percent." In another report, Stats Canada, using new calculations, Market Basket Measure, found that 1 in 8 Canadians are poor, 13.1 percent, with a high of 23.4 percent in Newfoundland and a low of 11 percent in Ontario. Margaret Philp, "New yardstick places more people in poverty," *Globe and Mail* (May 27, 2003). Despairing at the failure to consider redistributing the tax burden, Neil Brooks, a Canadian tax expert, observes, "One of the great mysteries of Canadian politics is how a few rich people (and their spokespersons) can convince other Canadians that taxing the wealthy would risk bringing our civilization to an untimely end." "Death taxes: a fine part of the Robin Hood tradition," *Globe and Mail* (June 2, 2004), A24. Are "other Canadians" unconvinced, or powerless?

government from taking action on so vital a matter as the commitment to the country's children. However, social programs were cut, and child poverty increased during those years to 21 percent.[20] The governing party, seeking a way out of its financial difficulties, decreased its contributions to many of the provincial programs it had previously initiated. The provincial governing parties, in turn, dealt with the loss of federal support by cutting programs benefiting the politically weakest members of society. If we had been making those decisions ourselves, the limited evidence from polling suggests that the response would have been different.[21]

In most of the decade that should have seen substantial progress toward meeting the 2000 target, the public heard only expressions of concern about child poverty and excuses for inaction from elected representatives. Even after the battle against the deficit was clearly won, attacking child poverty was not restored as a government priority.

The role of Finance Minister Paul Martin in the fight against the deficit was important, indirectly, in shaping child-care policy. Ambitious and anxious to secure his succession to the leadership of his party, Martin, as finance minister, was determined to make a name for himself by slaying the deficit. The way he chose to do this damaged crucial social programs and violated the spirit of our international commitments to children.[22]

---

20   Campaign 2000, "Poverty Amidst Prosperity: Building a Canada for All Children," 2002 Report on Child Poverty, 1. www.campaign2000.ca

21   See Peeter Kopvillem, "Unemployed, without a safety net," CBC/Maclean's News Poll, *Maclean's* (December 21, 1995/Jan. 1, 1996), 21.

22   The commitment made by Canada on behalf of its citizens to the United Nations on the rights of children was insufficient to make it a constant operational priority of policy makers: "In adopting the World Declaration on the Survival, Development and Protection of Children ... world leaders promised something else of immense importance: that they would always put the best interests of children first—in good times and bad, whether in peace or in war, in prosperity or economic distress." United Nations, "We the Children: End-decade review of the follow-up to the World Summit for Children" (United Nations General Assembly, May 4, 2001), 8. unicef.org/specialsession/documentation/documents/a-s-27-3e.doc. Clearly the Canadian government, staffed by well-intentioned people, but functioning in partyocracy, was unable or unwilling to fulfil its commitment on this crucial matter. Giving up on the ability of party politicians to meet the recession with appropriate policies, respected journalist David Crane suggested that a non-partisan commission set the national agenda. "Non-partisan commission should set national agenda," *Toronto Star* (May 22, 1993), D2. A Commons

Supported by the prime minister, the finance minister had a virtually free hand in designing the government's anti-deficit policies. All the problems associated with PM rule were temporarily, in this policy area, associated with that of the finance minister.

It was not until the target date for ending child poverty had passed that a national child-care program was proposed. It would have particularly enriched the lives of children from poor families that could not afford quality daycare. The United Nations made further information on child poverty available in 2000, again noting Canada's continued low ranking on the national child-poverty scale.[23] This "prompting," plus domestic lobbying, put the issue of child poverty and child care back on at least the rhetorical priority list of the national government. In 2002, we find Prime Minister Chrétien, on the verge of retirement, repeating shop-worn sentiments in his reply to the Speech from the Throne: "We must put Canada's families and children first ... we will begin immediate consultations with our partners so as to be ready in the next budget to put in place a long term investment plan to enable Canada to turn the corner of child poverty and break the cycle of poverty and dependency for Canadian families."[24] Consultations were to begin over a decade after the parliamentary resolution! (Quebec, where the balance of interests and pressures are different, already had its own much-admired child-care program.)

Toronto Star columnist Carol Goar made the appropriate comment on the prime minister's self-congratulatory tone in announcing an increase in the National Child Benefit in that same year, 2002: "The National Child Benefit is not quite the social breakthrough that the prime minister portrays it to be. It is a '90s-style replacement for some of the safety nets that Brian Mulroney's Tories and Chrétien's Liberals slashed. The 46-year-old family allowance was eliminated in 1992. Then jobless benefits were pared. Then Ottawa's share of welfare was chopped. It is a bit disingenuous of Chrétien to congratulate himself for putting in place 'a new architecture for helping

---

composed of constituency representatives would constitute Mr. Crane's non-partisan commission and be democratic.

23   In 2000, the *Globe and Mail* reported, "UNICEF study just released showing Canada ranking 14th of 23 industrialized nations [on child poverty], in between Poland and Ireland," (June 13, 2000), A16.

24   Cited in Campaign 2000, Report, 4. www.campaign2000.ca

Canadian families and children' when he helped tear down a more generous scheme."[25]

Further, action on the consultations was conditional on provincial agreement, since the federal government had agreed to the limits set out in the Social Union Agreement on its autonomous use of the spending power. Policy-makers would know that provincial agreement would not be easy to reach. The federal government's actions in shifting the burden of social costs to the provinces to "slay the deficit" was fresh in the minds of provincial leaders.

When there was little follow-through on Chrétien's announcement, people promoting child welfare were again disappointed; their scepticism about the depth of the government's commitment to children was renewed. Ideally, their disappointment would have led to a consideration of the institutional factors leading politicians to act with such indifference on such an important issue, but it didn't.

In 2005, with the former finance minister (Martin) now heading a minority government and reacting to a new set of political imperatives, and a new minister of social development (Ken Dryden), negotiations with the provinces for a national daycare program finally got underway. When they did not produce an agreement, the federal government made agreements with some provinces to fund provincial child-care programs and significantly extend the number of daycare places for poor children.

The agreements did not contribute to national unity as a comprehensive national child care program—perhaps explicitly modelled on Quebec's— would have. Further, the agreements with some of the provinces fell considerably short of breaking "the cycle of poverty and dependency for Canadians families," but they were significant..

The long-delayed and faltering effort to further child care was, however, to meet yet another obstacle. An election intervened before the provincial daycare programs, initiated by Ottawa, were firmly established. As promised in its election campaign, the Conservative minority government elected in 2006 terminated the recently negotiated Liberal programs. An annual child allowance of $1,200 to parents for each child under age six was substituted

---

25   Carol Goar, *Toronto Star* (October 5, 2002).

for it. In addition, the government's first budget provided $250 million per year to support the creation of new child-care spaces.

The centrepiece of the Conservative program, the child allowance, was welcomed by some as giving parents choice in the form of child care they preferred, although there could be no assurance that their choice would be quality daycare or any child care at all. Others criticized it as an inadequate substitute for a high-quality child-care system that would be of particular benefit to the children of poor parents. The negative impact of the Conservative government's decision on the number of daycare spaces being opened up in Canada was pronounced.[26]

In summary, the dynamics of partyocracy, of the unrepresentative system, frustrated the public interest in and support for early child care. Over a forty-year period, proponents of child care, including the United Nations, had to push the government from outside parliament to act on what our politicians declared was a primary concern for them. At the conclusion of that period, nobody could say that the challenge had been met. Indeed, citing Statistics Canada figures, in 2007, Campaign 2000 reported that 18 years after the all-party resolution in the House of Commons, the child poverty rate was exactly the same.[27] Further, the shortage in the number of the daycare places continued to present a problem.

The record of those working within the framework of the political system on the care of children is an example of a tragic pattern of behaviour forced on MPs—good people—many of whom would like to represent us differently in Ottawa. In the case of daycare, public input into the system through both representative systems was too weak to overcome (a) other pressures from competitors for government resources, (b) the inhibiting pressures of party competition when matters relating to taxes are involved, and (c) the ideology of the governing party.

Think—as just one more of many additional examples of delay and neglect

26   Sue Bailey, "Regulated child-care spaces way down, report says," *Globe and Mail* (April 11, 2008), A9. In her full report published on the web site of the University of Toronto, Childcare Resource and Research Unit, Ms. Bailey notes that the Conservatives cancelled the $250,000 budget of the Unit. www.action.web.ca/home/crru/rscs_crru_full.shml?=115655&AA_EX_Session=e80943

27   Campaign 2000, Report card on child and family poverty, 2007. www.campaign2000.ca/rc/

of priority concerns—of those dying on waiting lists for organ transplants, while governments talk endlessly about establishing an effective national system for harvesting these organs. The deaths occur without policy-makers showing any sense of urgency about dealing with the situation.[28] Men and women, most of whom would rush to the assistance of an injured person on the street, as MPs view deaths resulting from their policies with apparent equanimity.

Normal feelings of humanity, of empathy of citizen for citizen, are frustrated by party government. Politicians become inured to suffering that does not pose a significant political threat to them and that is usually distant from their direct experience. It often takes a personal family tragedy to activate one of them, and then they are surprised at how difficult it is to rouse their fellow MPs or Canadians. A conversation with or appeal to Canadians who are not organized to accommodate either is difficult.

When parties monopolize political life, we are often as unanchored and uncertain about our priorities as our governments. Kept ill informed, free of responsibility for public policy, and dependent on battling parties for policy guidance, we are unable to get a clear fix on our interests. If they were focused, priority issues could be dealt with, each in turn, rather than many issues being nursed along inadequately by successive generations.

One party government or another claims credit for the social achievements that do occur. There is both justice and hypocrisy in the claim. *Justice*, since the public has been largely excluded from finally designing and implementing programs—they are party-government achievements. *Hypocrisy*, in that the self-congratulatory politicians have often had to be pressured for years by groups lobbying on our behalf before they fulfilled, in part, what many might

---

28   A report commissioned by Canadian governments finds, "After ten years of deliberations by various lobby groups, professional associations, and governments, the shortage of organs and tissues remains an ongoing concern for Canadians in need of organ and tissue transplants. National donation rates lag behind countries which a decade ago had similar rates to Canada. Canada now has the dubious honour of having one of the lowest donation rates among developed countries … many individuals with end-stage organ failure will die without the opportunity of an enhanced quality of life." Canada, "A Report from the National Coordinating Committee for Organ and Tissue Donation and Transplantation to the Federal/Provincial/Territorial Advisory Committee on Health Services," (Health Canada: Ottawa, April, 24, 2006), 1. www.hc-sc.gc.ca/dhp-mps/pubs/biolog/summary-sommaire_e.html.

consider basic responsibilities. The politicians may even be claiming credit for dealing with a problem or crisis that would never have arisen had they been responsive to public needs at an earlier time. Meeting the challenges of climate change will provide many instances of this.

All the evidence points to the validity of economist Fred Lazar's conclusion about party government's ability, as presently organized, to prioritize: "There is good reason to be sceptical about the ability of the federal government to implement and stick with the right mix of policies. The political need to balance competing and divergent interests always subjects the policy-making process to political whims and short-term expediency."[29]

Crisis Management

Crisis management is the style of governance supported by our politics, i.e., one where government lacks a solid base of citizen support. That lack, in turn, is largely the product of the socially divisive party competition on which the system is based. Spokespersons for each party are continuously telling voters that the other parties and their leaders are untrustworthy or devious or misguided or all three. The voters are then required to trust one of these "unworthies" with governing.

In this unsupportive environment, party government must avoid getting ahead of public opinion, if it is to survive. With the public excluded from significant political engagement and people preoccupied with their private concerns, that opinion may run very far indeed behind the need for action. It is often necessary to put off difficult decisions until conditions, real or contrived, convince even the politically tuned-out voters that a crisis is forcing the government's hand.[30] The politically engaged may be aware of problems and demand action earlier, but that is not enough to make it "safe" for party government to proceed.

Government procrastination can be very costly. By the time it does

29   Lazar, *How Ottawa Rewards Mediocrity,* 125.
30   "Crisis" has been defined as: (1) A crucial turning point in an affair or a series of events and (2) a critical moment. *Funk and Wagnall, Standard Desk Dictionary,* (New York: Funk and Wagnall Inc., 1977), 151.

act, problems that it might have anticipated and headed off may have caused a great deal of damage, sometimes irreparable damage—lost lives, environmental degradation, etc.

There are exceptions to this general pattern of procrastination. As we have noted, public policy is the product of a number of interacting pressures: the policy predilections of the prime minister and his or her party; the point in his or her career when policy decisions must be made; the strength of various lobbies, including those claiming to speak for us; circumstances (war, recession, threat to national unity), etc. One or some of these may combine and lead the governing party to take electoral risks by moving well ahead of public opinion. Examples would be the Progressive Conservatives' action on free trade and the Liberals' on bilingualism. However, these instances are a departure from the general pattern of behaviour, i.e., of citizens having to pressure government to provide even basic services, like adequate child and health care, if they promise to be controversial.

A crisis, real or contrived, is valuable to politicians as a means of mobilizing support and diverting attention from the policy failures that have led to the need to act. "Now is not the time for assigning blame; we must all pull together," is a familiar message. Debate about alternatives to the policy the governing party is proposing is stifled. "No time for that. Immediate action is called for." Additionally, crises offer opportunities for dramatic leadership to politicians searching for a positive profile. The critical moments they exploit to get this profile may well be the result of their own or their party's previous failures. In the stampede for action, the public is unlikely to notice that this is the case.

When crisis rhetoric is overused, as is the case today, it loses some of its impact. Before it will be taken seriously, there must be overwhelming insistence that there really is a crisis, or the crisis must hit home in some direct, personal way. The former is illustrated by the debt-deficit crisis of the 1980s and early '90s. In that period, there was widespread agreement among members of the political elite that public spending and revenues were seriously unbalanced. But while the politically engaged were easily made aware of the perceived problem, the general public was not. It took most of a decade, during which the problem worsened, and a sustained barrage of crisis messages from successive Progressive Conservative and Liberal governments and the media, to move public/voter opinion to accept that action was essential. Only then did party government feel it was politically safe, advantageous even, to act.

In the real world, there is scarcely ever only one way to accomplish an objective but crisis talk pushes them off the agenda. In the case of the debt-deficit crisis, a group of economists and others on the left produced carefully researched alternative budgets that, they believed, would put the government's financial house in order.[31] At the same time, their proposals would have taken the burden of achieving this result off the most economically vulnerable and politically weak members of society. The social safety net would have remained in place when it was most needed, i.e., during a recession. Those who were the primary beneficiaries of a market system, would, under their proposals, have been expected to pay a larger share of the cost of the periodic economic downturns that characterize it.

It is unlikely that many citizens understood the full implications of the cuts or of those alternatives. The absence of an appropriate institutional setting in which citizens and politicians could collaboratively work out a solution to the financial crisis, and share responsibility for its implementation, made alternatives to the government's program merely interesting.

The debt-deficit crisis was dealt with in a remarkably short time for what was presented as a fundamental challenge to the fiscal integrity of the country. The Liberal government found itself with a surplus in 1997, which it could spend in a variety of ways. In Canada's competitive system, the governing party would be politically inept if it did not make these choices with a view to strengthening its support base. It seems clear, for example, that in deciding to spend the surplus on tax cuts and debt reduction before restoring full financial support to previously reduced social programs, the Liberal Party-government was expressing the ideological predispositions of its dominant leaders, catering to its significant supporters and, perhaps most importantly, seeking to blunt the tax-cutting appeal of the right-wing party that was its major competition. It was not representing citizens.[32]

---

31   See Canadian Centre for Policy Alternatives, "Alternative Federal Budget." www. policyalternatives.ca/index.cfm?act=main&call=BOE2A12E

32   Citing the results of a *Globe and Mail*/Angus Reid poll, Edward Greenspon concluded, "If Canadians were writing this month's federal budget, their top priorities

The management of the crisis was successful from the perspective of the governing Liberals. That party won the 1997 election with 38 percent of the popular vote and a slim majority of seats in the House of Commons. The victory was repeated in 2000. Some Canadians were untouched by the crisis-inspired cutbacks, felt no responsibility for the impact of the policies and, with limited empathy for their fellow citizens who were hurt, were impressed by the finance minister's "accomplishment."

From the perspective of many economically marginalized groups, the accomplishment needed qualification, however. When the deep cuts were finally made, they had to be much more drastic and disruptive to meet the government's fiscal objectives than would have been the case if the rising deficit had been effectively attacked five to ten years earlier. The reduction in spending, or tax increase, might then have been phased in more gradually and less hurtfully to some already-disadvantaged Canadians.

By the time the government acted decisively, the economy was beginning to turn around and generate more tax revenues. With the benefit of hindsight, some of the dislocation that resulted from cuts that damaged public services and disrupted lives might have been avoided. The cuts forced advocates of a high quality of people services to devote years of effort to simply recovering lost ground.

The crisis approach forestalled a full and informative public discussion of how the crisis had evolved and how to avoid similar disruptions in the future. Yet, such a discussion on this and other economic issues is essential if the role of the political system in contributing to this sort of crisis is to be more widely understood. The entire episode gave Canadians less rather than more reason to have confidence in government.

An interesting example of the costs of crisis management in a different area of policy, health care, is provided by Bob Rae. Some time after leaving the office of premier of Ontario, he advocated in a presentation to the Romanow commission on health care that the constant state of crisis be met by dedicated funding. Rae, a strong supporter of party government, proposed that the strategic concerns of the governing party must be taken out of policymaking relating to health. In doing so, he raised the question of whether party interest

---

would be precisely the opposite of that of the Chrétien government." "How we'd spend our federal surplus," _Globe and Mail_ (February 7, 1998).

should be taken out of just this one policy area or all policy, through the adoption of a different form of representation. Rae said,

> Governments are going to have to address the issue of dedicated funding.... Such a system would help create a stable and predictable level of funding.... I believe we should be very clearly looking at making sure that this system [health care] is protected from the whims of political and partisan changes.... I think Canadians are deeply resentful of the fact that a system, which they think belongs to them, has been treated as a kind of political football by their respective federal and provincial governments.... Everybody wants to be there to cut a ribbon and everybody wants to take credit for the new MRI machine, but nobody is prepared to take credit for the fact that we've had incredible inconsistency in funding over the last decade.
>
> ... Funding instability means that hospitals never know until well into their financial year how much money they can expect to receive. And as the ripple effect spreads, professions such as nurses get shafted with massive layoffs.... You have funding which varies from day to day; it varies from year to year...."[33]

Global warming. Global warming stands on its own as a crisis of historic proportions that party governments, lacking the support they need, are ill equipped to confront. The Canadian government, acting on our behalf, agreed to the Kyoto Accord, committing Canada to a substantial reduction in greenhouse gases by the year 2008. Policy makers recognized the crisis and the need to act quickly and decisively. However, political realities—the desire of party governments to maintain their hold on office—then took over. Four years after the signing of the agreement, an examination of the government's performance concluded that, "It has yet to move past restating the problem until it sounds like an answer."[34] The production of greenhouse gases continued to rise, not decline.[35]

---

33   Theresa Boyle, "'Dedicated taxes' urged to cure health care woes," *Toronto Star* (June 1, 2002), A10. Mr. Rae was out of office when he made these comments. He showed no interest in designated spending while he was premier.

34   Tom Spears, "Promises, Promises," *Ottawa Citizen* (November 24, 2001), B1.

35   In an extended report, the *Toronto Star*, citing climate experts, confirms that Can-

Prime ministers Chrétien and Martin bequeathed the problem of meeting the Accord's targets to their successor in office (Harper), rather than run the political risks of taking the action they had previously agreed was needed. Harper denounced the Accord's targets as unreachable but was unwilling to bear the political costs of formally withdrawing from it. Denying the urgency of the challenge, he allowed partisan interests to dictate policy, as had the Liberals before him. The Harper government sends our representatives abroad to lecture the international community on the need for action on global warming. At the same time, that community, looking at our record and positions on the issue, sees us as a major block to progress.[36]

The challenge that the oil sands be developed in an environmentally friendly way, or not at all, is one that national parties cannot meet. Many Albertans share concerns about the development, but most have been so conditioned to see Ottawa as the enemy that they are completely unwilling to accept the national government acting for the national and global interest on the project. The Alberta government, with its electoral interest in instant prosperity and subject to enormous pressure from the oil industry, cannot be expected to meet the responsibilities that fall to the national administration.

Unity of purpose is required in the face of the global challenge, while divisive partisanship rules. Canada stands second to last among industrialized countries in responding to the global warming challenge.[37] Perhaps UN Secretary General Ban Ki-moon had Canada in mind when he warned, "Our foot is stuck on the accelerator and we are heading toward an abyss…. Climate change could spell widespread economic disaster."[38]

---

ada has fallen behind rather than progressed toward meeting its Kyoto goals but, also, accuses governing politicians of misleading the public with statistics that are not supported by their own experts. Further, the report quotes a climate expert as stating, "Canada is the only country [of those signing the Accord] which has thrown up its hands and surrendered, saying it can't meet its Kyoto target six years before the fund deadline." Peter Calami, "Emissions reality check," *Toronto Star* (May 27, 2006), F1, 3.

36   A typical news report reads, "The Harper government urged the global community to step up efforts to fight and adapt to climate change—in the midst of criticism that Canada was the one blocking progress on the international stage." Mike De Souza, "Feds urge climate action at UN summit," *Vancouver Sun* (December 12, 2008), B1.

37   Martin Mittelstaedt, "Canada lands second-last in climate-change ranking," *Globe and Mail* (July 3, 2008), A4.

38   Cited in Robert Matas, "Vancouver 2010," *Globe and Mail* (September 5, 2009), S3.

A similar show of weakness and indifference to the well-being of others is found with respect to the export of asbestos. While its use is illegal in Canada, governments lobby to keep it on the international market.[39] They do this to avoid damaging their electoral position in Quebec.[40] Asbestos mining there employs an insignificant number of workers while generating significant health hazards at home and, particularly, abroad. Still, the industry is regarded as politically untouchable.[41] We are not hypocrites, but guilt by association with weak party governments makes us seem to be.

Think of how different policy development might have been if Kyoto had been submitted to constituency parliaments for approval before being ratified by the House of Commons—there is every indication that it would have been approved locally. Raising the awareness level of CP members and their neighbours on issues is an important feature of the proposal for constituency parliaments. Even without their impact, however, citizen opinion on this issue appears to have run far ahead of that of government.

With an organized citizenry behind it, government would have been able to proceed with the policies needed to meet the targets it had accepted on our behalf without fear of electoral repercussions. Instead, the Harper government continues to dither, as it tries to preserve its base of support while, at the same time, finding a responsible response to the global crisis.

Robert Dahl, a distinguished American political scientist, observes that in partyocracies (he uses the term *polyarchies*), "the making of government decisions is not a majestic march of great majorities united upon certain matters of basic policy. It is the steady appeasement of relatively small groups."[42] That pattern of behaviour, common to Canada, too, is intolerable and not inevitable. The people *can* be organized into politics with great majorities making decisions in a responsible manner. Indeed, if we do

---

39   See "Asbestos exporter Canada blocks UN Convention on dangerous chemicals," *CCPA Monitor* (May, 2008), 33.

40   It is promising that more and more groups in Quebec itself are speaking out against the continuation of mining and sale abroad of asbestos. See Martin Mittelstaedt, "Quebec officials dare to speak out against asbestos," *Globe and Mail* (December 2, 2009), A10.

41   "Canada, Hazardous hypocrisy," *Economist* (October 25, 2008), 49.

42   Robert A. Dahl, *A Preface to Democratic Theory* (Chicago and London: University of Toronto Press, 1956), 146.

not restructure our political institutions to allow that to happen, strong democratic voices are pessimistic about us maintaining the democratic progress made to date.[43]

In summary, the crisis-management characteristic of making policy in partyocracy is a desperate, costly, and progressively less-effective approach to mobilizing public support. "Wolf" is cried too often, in too many different contexts, to have the desired impact. Constantly lambasting the public with talk of crises, real and contrived, debases the quality of public discussion and lowers still further our confidence in the ability of government to manage the public's business.

Most politicians extensively engaged with social and economic issues are, personally, at least as far-sighted as most of their critics and are anxious to serve their constituents and country. Their foot-dragging behaviour is not a reflection of a lack of commitment to the public interest. It is a product of those two features of partyocracy mentioned at the beginning of the chapter, i.e., the need of our leaders to win a popularity contest every four or five years and their lack of democratic, citizen-based authority between contests. For politicians in partyocracy, "The future whispers, the present shouts."[44] That need not be the case if citizens are allowed to share responsibility for making public policy.

Delegation

Many of the weaknesses in party government considered thus far are concealed by delegation. Limits on the time and attention span of politicians and bureaucrats, and the need to bring specialized knowledge into public administration, justify delegating some policy making and administration to so-called independent agencies.[45] In too many cases, however, particularly

---

43   The distinguished political economist Robert Heilbroner writes, "... candour compels me to suggest that the passage through the gauntlet ahead may be possible only under government capable of rallying obedience far more effectively than would be possible in a democratic setting. If the issue for mankind is survival, such governments may be unavoidable, even necessary." *An Inquiry into the Human Prospect* (New York: W. W. Norton and Company, Inc., 1975), 110.

44   Robert Kennedy Jr. quoted in *Maclean's* (August 7, 2000), 7.

45   "So-called" because the government usually appoints the members of the agency boards, finances them, and writes their terms of reference.

sensitive policy and administrative areas are placed at arm's length from government for unacceptable reasons. This may be done to placate special interests unwilling to accept the authority of party government; because political leaders do not trust themselves to make decisions relating to certain significant policies without letting partisan considerations interfere; and to avoid responsibility for controversial actions.

Two policy areas where Canadian politicians recognize that low levels of public trust and competence require them to delegate are of particular significance: monetary policy and policy relating to the protection of individual rights. They will be considered as examples of the wider delegation phenomenon. The controversy over unrepresentative party governments committing the country to global trade agreements that then inhibit their ability to respond to their constituents' demands will only be footnoted.

The Bank of Canada. Financial interests, and probably many politically attentive citizens, would be alarmed if the party in office were to set monetary policy. (Interest rates would likely fall prior to each election, regardless of the state of the economy!) To reassure them and remove the temptation of the governing party to meddle, monetary policy is entrusted to a largely independent central bank. The Bank of Canada is given wide discretionary powers in setting interest rates and, in so doing, makes a major contribution to the macro management of the economy.

A conservative approach to monetary policy that places a high value on controlling inflation may be desirable in some circumstances. When it causes an economic slowdown and unemployment, however, it is highly unpopular with voters. It is helpful, then, for the governing party to be able to blame the Bank. Raising taxes might sometimes be a better way of dealing with inflationary pressures than counting on the Bank to curtail credit. However, the government would have to bear the responsibility for that and suffer any negative electoral fallout.

The danger of delegating to the Bank was illustrated when a post–World War II government was forced to remove, by not reappointing, a governor whose fixation on low inflation was held responsible for compounding the seriousness of a recession. The government took advantage of a particularly propitious political moment to retire the governor and avoid politically costly controversy—the kind of moment that would not normally be available.[46] At the same time, it protected itself and its successors against a repeat of the Bank following a course widely regarded as aberrant. New legislation allowed the minister of finance to give written direction to the Bank.[47] It is unlikely that such overt, high-risk intervention in the Bank's policies will be taken, but the government's authority ensures a closer collaboration between itself and the Bank.

The collaboration still does not ensure, however, that the Bank's policies will be what representatives of the people might endorse. The government appoints a governor and board of directors of the Bank, who they hope will have the confidence of those in the financial world, giving them a special place in making economic policy. However, the Bank's interest-rate policies affect us all, particularly the economically marginalized who need the job opportunities that low interest rates may open up, and the rich who have wealth to protect from inflation. Only the latter are represented directly on the board of the Bank. The bias of the system toward the interests of the affluent is shown in this representation of interests, as it is through all the institutional arrangements in partyocracy.

We will have taken a major step forward politically when the management of monetary policy can, with confidence in the result, be transferred from a bank that is only very indirectly accountable to the public, to parliament, where it can be openly debated and decided. The Bank could still play an important advisory and administrative role. We will never reach that state as long as we rely on parties to govern.

The Charter of Rights and Freedoms. The role of the courts must feature prominently in a discussion of party government's tendency to avoid its

---

46   The defeat of the extremely unpopular Mulroney government allowed the incoming Liberals the freedom to both end the reign of John Crow as Governor of the Bank of Canada and cover their policy reversal from opponents of NAFTA in opposition to strong supporters in office. "Canadians didn't seem to care about anything other than the fact that he [Chrétien] wasn't named Brian Mulroney," write Edward Greenspon and Anthony Wilson-Smith, in *Double Vision: The Inside Story of the Liberals in Power* (Toronto: Doubleday Canada, 1996), 103. For the discussion the government's relations with the governor of the Bank, see 67–71.

47   See Bank of Canada Act, R.S.cB-2, S14 (l)(2)(3). www.laws.justice.ca/en/B-2/220710.html.

responsibilities and accountability through delegation. Pre-Charter, we were told that elections allowed us to hold governments accountable for their "misdemeanours," including violations of our rights. The courts played a role, too, but it was of secondary significance. Parliamentarians, led first by John Diefenbaker and then by Pierre Trudeau, finally implicitly acknowledged that this system-supporting rhetoric exaggerated the protection elections afforded us in an era of big government.[48]

Parliament and the provincial legislatures, except for that of Quebec, agreed in 1982 to the Charter of Rights and Freedoms that, they realized, would grant increased powers to the courts in the rights area. Resisting the fuller grant of sovereignty to the people, political leaders were prepared to share it with the unelected courts. Most citizens, apparently feeling that their rights vis-à-vis government would be better protected in the courts than by party governments, joined the elite in supporting the Charter's adoption.

The courts make public policy and interpret the meaning of charter language as they decide cases. As is the case with the Bank, however, the power of the court to make policy is not absolute. There is one clause in the Charter of Rights and Freedoms that gives government some leeway in imposing laws that might otherwise be interpreted as infringing on rights "demonstrably justified in a free and democratic society" (Section 1). A second, the "notwithstanding" clause (Section 33), allows government to override the Charter. That clause was adopted as the price of getting some provinces, unwilling to give the court the final word on rights issues, to agree to the Charter.

The override/notwithstanding clause has not been used by the federal government and seldom by the provinces. It may be that the federal government found itself in broad agreement with the court's interpretations of the Charter and had little inclination to apply the notwithstanding provision. Even if this is not the case, there are important reasons for the central government to resist resorting to the provision. If it were used even occasionally, the value of the Charter as an instrument that protects our rights against the state would be

---

48   Bill C-60, "The Recognition and Protection of Human Rights and Fundamental Freedoms," was introduced by the Diefenbaker government in 1958 and gained Royal Assent in 1960. Its scope was limited to human rights violations of the federal government.

undermined. Further, it would be more difficult for the government to avoid responsibility for making controversial policies now taken by the court, such as that relating to same-sex marriage, if recourse to the override provision were to have become acceptable through use.

While students of politics realized that the Charter would strengthen an unelected and unaccountable policy-making body, most Canadians were focused on its rights guarantees. Now, however, even many who view the Supreme Court positively, in its current, arguably non-partisan character, are troubled that in a democracy so much policy-making power has been transferred from parliament to judges.

Many critics of the courts' post-Charter assertiveness attribute it to power-hungry judges, judges pursuing their own agenda, etc. The real problem, however, is unrepresentative government—government out of touch with its constituents and prone to delegating to avoid outrunning its limited support. As law professor Allan Hutchinson writes,

> Democracy is in trouble. The twin foundations of democracy—popular participation and political accountability—are going the way of the polar ice caps; what now passes for democratic dialogue is an elite conversation between the judicial and executive branches of government, with the contribution of ordinary Canadians conspicuously lacking.

He continues, arguing that asking whether courts can or should invade the political domain is to miss a more important point:

> The neglected issue is not the politicization of the judiciary but the democratic failure of the executive and legislative branches in fulfilling their constitutional responsibilities and mandate[49]

The value of the Court as a trusted safeguard for our rights depends heavily on its non-partisan character. However, even while appointments to it are not yet the bitterly partisan issues they are in the United States,

---

49   Allan Hutchinson, "Do we want judges with more muscle?" *Globe and Mail* (November 13, 2003), A27.

concerns are being expressed about their politicization, and these will probably intensify.[50]

Prime Minister Harper suggested in his 2006 campaign for office that the existing court is Liberal in character. With that perception, he rationalized making partisan appointments to balance its composition.[51] It appears that the politicization of the court—now that its Charter decisions are so significant—is virtually inevitable, unless we have a change of political system or take the appointment of judges completely away from elected politicians.[52] If politicization, or greater politicization, does occur, the benefits seen in shifting some policy from a party-dominated parliament to a non-partisan court that we would feel was trustworthy would be lost.

Canadians support the Charter, but they also believe it is the responsibility of Parliament, rather than the courts, to make public policy.[53] This is the case even though Parliament is held in low esteem while trust in the Court

---

50   Court appointments in Canada are not subject to approval by a partisan House of Commons, and this reduces some of the controversy over them.

51   See Gloria Galloway, "Harper warns of activist judges," *Globe and Mail* (January 19, 2006), A1, A5. The appointment of David Brown, a lawyer noted for representing "Christian family-value positions," to the Ontario Supreme Court is seen by some observers as the start of a more active party struggle for control of the courts. See John Ibbitson, "Stacking the courts: fair play?" *Globe and Mail* (September 22, 2006), A4. Subsequent to the appointment of Brown, Mr. Harper stated in the Commons that he wanted the selection of judges to reflect the government's law and order policy. This comment, taken as evidence of his desire to shape court-made policy through the appointment process, created a stir in the Commons and media, as did the Conservative party's changes in the composition of the committee advising the government on appointments. www2.parl.gc.ca/HousePublications/Publication.aspx?Language=E&Mode=1&Parl. Campbell Clark, "Harper brushes off judicial critics on appointments," *Globe and Mail* (February 22, 2007), A5.

52   The adoption of the Charter, and enhanced policy-making role of the Supreme Court as its interpreter, is one of many steps in the Americanization of Canadian politics. Where there is no strong domestic vision of how the parliamentary system and democracy should evolve in Canada, it is inevitable that reformers will be drawn to the model next door for inspiration. The fact that the system in the United States is even less successful in serving the needs of its constituents will not stop our tendency to emulate it when new ideas are needed, unless we develop our own political model.

53   Seven in ten (71 percent) agree in one poll that parliament, not the courts, should make laws in Canada. Source: http://www/ipsos-na.com/news/pressrelease.cfm?id=187

is high.[54] This ambivalence suggests that we are not prepared to give up on the ideal of parliament as a forum of the nation—and sovereign—although in its present party-dominated form it disillusions us. We deserve a parliament we can trust, so that policy now made by the Bank and the courts can be brought back to it. To establish that trust, MPs must truly represent their constituents in the House of Commons.

With a Commons revitalized in that way, a charter of rights would still be valuable. It would then serve as legal reinforcement for solid citizen respect for political and minority rights rather than, as is sometimes the case now, the first line of defence for them.

Delegation to international agencies. The upward delegation of policy responsibility, particularly on trade but also on the environment, etc., must be added to those areas of the public business that are being increasingly placed beyond our control. This delegation, too, is taking place at a time when we are demanding more control of public policy.[55] Excluded from participation in the deliberations leading up to those agreements, many people question whose interests are being advanced by government.

The delegation of authority to international agencies, is often defended on the grounds that, since they are agreed to by governments representing us, they are democratically legitimate.[56] This line of reasoning

---

54   "The survey record over time ... has consistently demonstrated the same pattern: the public puts more of its faith in the courts than in Parliament by a margin of about two to one." Data cited in Jerome H. Black and Bruce M. Hicks, "Strengthening Canadian Democracy: The Views of Parliamentary Candidates," *IRPP Policy Matters* 7, 2, (March 2006), 38. www.irpp.org. A slightly more recent report shows the public as even more trusting of the courts (78 percent) than of politicians (14 percent). Dene Moore, "Judges trump politicians in poll," *Globe and Mail* (March 20, 2006), A4.

55   Donald Savoie notes that the nation-state is "leaking away at the edges" and gives examples of the upward flow of sovereignty over trade issues: the International Monetary Fund, the World Bank, the European Union, the Group of Seven Industrialized Nations, the General Agreement on Tariffs and Trade, and regional trade agreements, such as the Canada-US Free Trade Agreement and the North American Free Trade Agreement. He also notes the strong pressure being generated to harmonize a wide variety of laws and policies between nations. Donald Savoie, "Reforming Civil Service Reforms," *IRPP Policy Options* (April 1994), 4–5.

56   This line of reasoning was used by Donald Johnson when he was head of the

is unconvincing to those who are aware that our governments are not acting on a clear policy mandate from us at any time, including when they enter into these agreements. Since such agreements are likely to increase in number and scope, it is important that the governments signing them are truly representative democracies if they are not to provoke progressively more anger and frustration among political activists.

Checking Party in Party Government

Governments recognize that they must do more than delegate responsibilities to reassure special interests and citizens that party concerns will not intrude on sensitive areas of policy. They increasingly surround themselves with agencies intended to bolster their resistance to the temptation to pursue partisan advantage at the expense of the public interest. With the passage of the Accountability Act of 2006, the proliferation of such bodies has continued.[57] *Globe and Mail* columnist Jeffrey Simpson writes,

> You want more bureaucracy in Ottawa? You'll love the Conservatives' Accountability Act. Therein you will find the following new offices: a Commissioner of Lobbying, a Parliamentary Budget Officer, a Public Appointments Commission, a Procurement Auditor, a Public Sector Integrity Commissioner, a Director of Public Prosecutions.
>
> We're not done yet. New powers, which mean more money and people, will flow to the Access of Information Commissioner, the Auditor General of Canada, the Chief Electoral Officer, and the

World Trade Organization. But as a candidate for the Liberal leadership and former member of the Canadian cabinet, he had an entirely different view of the legitimacy of the Canadian government as spokesperson for Canadians—one shared by many Canadians when they are thinking in critical mode. He wrote, "The imposition of party discipline in the House of Commons has eroded the value of the institution. It has turned intelligent, vigorous, creative members into eunuchs. It has depreciated the value of the standing committees. It has permitted cabinet to arrogate all meaningful policy development. Worse, it has permitted the Prime Minister's Office to emasculate even cabinet." Donald Johnston, *Up the Hill* (Montreal: Optimum Publishing International, 1986), 263. If Canada's agreement to global trade arrangements is, essentially, the agreement of only a prime minister whose mandate is dubious or non-existent, how much democratic legitimacy does it have?

57   Canada, Bill C-2, Federal Accountability Act, (S.C. 2006, c9).

Ethics Commissioner, whose job expands to become the Conflict of Interest and Ethics Commissioner.[58]

Relying on these outside checks is another "patch-up" job and, like others intended to keep the system minimally functional. Their recommendations are, however, too easily ignored when they conflict with the interests of the governing party to really check party government effectively.[59] Politicians, wearing their party hats, act in ways that make external checks on their behaviour necessary. Then, wearing their responsible leader hats, they appoint numerous agencies to check themselves. Completing the circle and back to wearing their party hats, they subvert the checks.[60]

At what point do we say *enough?* When a host of agencies is needed to steer the government toward the public interest and away from that of party—and even they are often ineffective—surely it is time for a new, non-party base for government. This new institutional base must be one that rewards a strong commitment from both politicians and bureaucrats to our interests, as *we* define them after appropriate deliberation. The policy democracy/constituency parliament model would provide such a base. Responsibility for policy that is now delegated to courts, banks, and other agencies could be brought back to a Commons that truly represented us. We could dispense with almost all the expensive and ineffective watch-dog agencies intended to make party government honest and accountable.

A judiciary continuing to enjoy a large measure of independence would,

---

58   Jeffrey Simpson, "Accountability Act: Overkill in Action," *Globe and Mail* (April 12, 2006), A17.

59   Berlin cites Jeffery Simpson's characterization of the reception of the Information Commissioner's annual report: "The report becomes the opposition's plaything of the moment.... Ministers do their best with feigned concern to assure Parliament that they are indeed taking the commissioner's suggestions seriously, all the while knowing that this fury of denunciation from across the aisle will pass like a summer storm." David Berlin, "A Love Affair with Secrecy," *The Walrus* (November 2004), 37.

60   Shortly after the Parliamentary Budget Officer was established to provide parliament—and through it, us—more reliable financial information than the party-influenced data released by the government, the government sought to clip his or her wings. It required that the officer clear all reports with the government before release. Michael Warren, "Why is Kevin Page [the Budget Officer] left twisting in the wind," *Globe and Mail* (June 29, 2009), A11; Steven Chase, "Stimulus impact months away, Canadians told [by Budget Officer]," *Globe and Mail* (July 9, 2009), A8.

most assuredly, always be needed. But at the same time, the public might have sufficient confidence in its judgement of the community's interests to call on its government to use Section 33, the notwithstanding clause, when it disagreed with the policy the Court was making through its interpretation of the Charter.

Lost Opportunities

In this chapter on the weaknesses of government by party, I have strongly inferred that, with government by representatives of the organized citizenry Canadians could achieve great things—achievements that are impossible even to consider as long as we struggle with the existing dysfunctional political system. The belief that we could, and that it is vitally important to us and others that we open the door to these achievements is, however, a major reason why I think citizens should rally behind the policy democracy model. I do not want to leave any impression that adopting the model is merely important as a way to eliminate the abuses and weaknesses in partyocracy, important as that is.

I offer only this inference, rather than a full discussion of possibilities, for two reasons. First, a discussion of what might be accomplished by a government that *belonged* to us would require a book in itself, if not a shelf of books! Second, considering what I think we Canadians might do if empowered and directing our government would sidetrack discussion of the policy democracy model. Some opponents of adopting the model would, I think, devote their attention to the hopes for what might be accomplished in a more democratic Canada to avoid directly criticizing the policy democracy model. We should hold the focus on the issue of adopting policy democracy/constituency parliaments while at the same drawing personal inspiration from our ideas about what the adoption of that model might make possible.

Conclusion

The dynamics of partyocracy make it extremely difficult for our governors to be responsive, effective, and efficient. The keystone of our politics—the periodic election of leaders in competitive party contests—brings with it a set of pressures on the gladiators that are, on balance, inimical to good government today. Abolishing elections is unthinkable, but our heavy reliance on them to represent the views of citizens on public policy and to vest government with authority, which they can do in only a limited, ambiguous manner, is a major source of political weakness. A pencilled *X* after the name of a candidate on a ballot is a crude and limited form of expression, best used *only* to choose between candidates for office.

Policy democracy based on constituency parliaments would fundamentally change the dysfunctional dynamics of partyocracy. Deliberation in constituency and national parliaments would set policy and the "deliberants" would appoint the executive leadership of the country to oversee its implementation. When a constituency elected an MP that members of its constituency parliament could respect and collaborate with, his or her re-election would be close to automatic. Sudden turnovers in the ranks of parliamentarians bringing in large numbers of inexperienced people, would be a thing of the past. The government's agenda, developed collaboratively by citizens, their leaders, and civil servants, would not be subject to sudden disruptive shifts, i.e., to the *stop-go* phenomenon now caused by changes in the leadership of governing party and, to a lesser extent, the leaders of the opposition parties.

Restraints on rational policymaking enforced by the electoral timetable would be eliminated. Further, with more stability in the membership of the Commons and the executive, opportunities would exist to move beyond meeting the latest government crisis. Consideration could be given to the now-latent range of long-term possibilities for community action that would enrich our lives.

Now unrestricted by a citizen-defined set of interests, the party in office follows its own agenda, which favours its supporters and furthers its competitive interests. Traditional and, most important, *policy* patronage is dispensed as a matter of course. Our confidence in and support for whatever party is in office is eroded by its adoption of policies that we have not agreed to (mandated) and by its unedifying partisan manoeuvring both during and between elections.

The policies of the opposition parties are similarly biased toward the interests of their supporters and heavily influenced by their determination to bring down the government. These parties, too, engaged in their ongoing struggle for power, are supposed, as a kind of a by-product of their struggles, to represent us.

Elections frequently replace one party government claiming to speak for all the people with another that has differing policies and leadership but makes the same unwarranted claim. The changes in governing party have a disruptive impact on the rational, consistent development and implementation of policy. With a mandate that is 99 percent myth, and a great deal of freedom for the new PM to act on his or her personal policy preferences, a largely, or totally, inexperienced team sets out to govern. Handicapped by inexperience and subject to strong pressures from organized interests, the team's likelihood of earning our respect and support are slight.

The lack of that support deprives party government of the democratic authority that would allow it to act decisively on critically important issues without losing votes. The party's response to these issues is now characterized by foot-dragging and vacillation, as it struggles to avoid weakening its already inadequate base of support. Both weaknesses are displayed in the inability of party government to stay with even the issue to which it has assigned the very highest importance, i.e., child care. The same negative features characterize the government's approach to global warming. It is surprising that while many criticize the government's inaction on environmental issues they do not turn their attention to the features of the system that encourage that inaction.

Further, the electoral vulnerability of the governing party forces it to adopt a crisis management, manipulative style. Action is delayed on emerging problems to allow us to become aware of its necessity and then—to forestall strong opposition from vested interests—is only taken tentatively. Social and economic issues are nursed along or ignored altogether while enormous damage is inflicted. Political foresight and preventive action are uncommon.

Party governors, conscious of the mistrust their performance engenders and implicitly admitting that it is too often justified, seek to compensate by delegating sensitive responsibilities to agencies like the courts and central bank and establishing watch-dog agencies to monitor their performance. Those delegations, intended to build confidence, do highlight the malfunctioning of the system that make them necessary. Further, each delegation brings with it a new set of problems. Short-cuts around the dysfunctional system are unable to compensate for its fundamental weaknesses.

A new system of representation and governance is needed to replace one that has become operationally obsolescent and that conflicts with the democratic values now held by citizens. Properly organized, the mode of representation favoured by the majority of citizens—constituency representation—would be free of the most debilitating aspects of partyocracy. Policy democracy would open the door wide to participation by those of us willing to accept a share of responsibility for our own governance. We would, for the first time, be able to define our interests clearly and vest governments with the democratic authority/support needed to respond to them, uninhibited by competitive considerations.

The informal learning that would accompany increased citizen participation in government would result in early recognition of emerging problems and support for dealing with them. Delay, crisis management, manipulation of public opinion—all the techniques now needed to make necessary or desirable action politically possible—would no longer be required. Policy would develop as we recognized our needs in a rapidly changing social and economic world. Our vision would be considerably longer than that of party politicians now transfixed by thoughts of the next election. All the resources that now must be poured into correcting situations that have been allowed to get out of hand by weak government could be saved and made available to citizens to further their own personal interests, or to allocate to social purposes, as they decided.

Government has grown, while our ability to direct its work has remained static. We are still forced to beg, beseech, wheedle, pressure, and shame elected representatives in the hope of persuading them to heed significant social needs. We should be able to meet with *our* representative to deliberate and decide on the policy direction we want *our* government to follow. Our MP would then pool our ideas with those of others also represented in the House of Commons.

Perfection in government would not be achieved with the adoption of the policy democracy/constituency parliament model. The model would bring with it new problems with which the next generation would have to grapple.

It would, however, deal infinitely more effectively with today's issues. The quality of our lives and that of our children's would be enhanced.

Sound advice on how to meet our current political difficulties is flowing to citizens and their governments from many sources; action on it is urgently required. One of many such sources is a report commissioned by the government of New Brunswick that concludes,

> We must strengthen the public voice. In a democracy, the most powerful voice belongs to the people. The stronger and clearer it is, the harder for leaders to resist it—or to control it. Public engagement could produce greater clarity, order, coherence, and authority in that voice. Ideally, this will take us beyond the narrow, confrontational politics of the 20th century and toward a new, more deliberative, form of democracy.
>
> *Report to the Government of New Brunswick from the New Brunswick Public Engagement Initiative, 2008*

Party Administration: Neutral and Professional?

Loyalty, let there be no mincing of words, is often interpreted as a code word for those who go along, get along! It can be contorted by the self-serving into an admonition to public officials not to exhibit moral courage; not to criticize or speak up; not to report misdeeds for appearing disloyal—the unforgivable corporate sin.

Annual Report of Information Commissioner, 1997–1998

Canada's political institutions are in shambles. There is evidence of this everywhere—in the Senate, which few Canadians now take seriously; in the House of Commons, whose operations a number of its members are trying to reform before the House slips into irrelevance; in the Cabinet, which has recently been described as a "focus group rather than a decision-making body"; in the Supreme Court, which now is subject to the kind of bashing until recently reserved for politicians and bureaucrats; and in the national civil service, which still remains plagued by morale problems.

Donald Savoie

Introduction

The damaging impact of party extends into the farthest reaches of the bureaucracy. The damage is recognized, and attempts are made to minimize it while, at the same time, maintaining party control, the source of the damage. In our highly adversarial system, the governing party cannot resist exploiting the administration for any advantage it can as it struggles to hold onto office.

Party government needs a bureaucracy that supports its interests, but so do we. If we are to be responsible citizens, rather than merely members of an alienated political audience, we will need the help of the "public" service. Its members are government insiders and our neighbours who share our concerns and aspirations. Given appropriate institutional arrangements, public servants would be in a unique position to collaborate in the development and administration of public policy with constituency parliament members and MPs. Currently, however, their primary loyalty is to the governing party's leaders. They stand between the civil servant and us. Public servants are even legally enjoined from unauthorized conversation with us about their work, although basically, they are supposed to be working for us.[61]

Canadians need to be clear about the corrosive influence of party government on the administration: it is a powerful part of the case for a change to policy democracy based on constituency parliaments.

A Neutral, Professional Bureaucracy?

Attempts to limit party exploitation of the bureaucracy started early in the 20th century. Governments recognized that it was intolerable that after the defeat of a party at the polls, inexperienced recruits who supported the new governing party would replace experienced bureaucrats. The recognition of the need to put an end to that staff turnover was far from a general recognition of the negative impact of party on the administration,

---

61   As a condition of employment, civil servants are required to swear as follows: "I, ———, solemnly and sincerely swear (or affirm) that I will faithfully and honestly fulfill the duties that devolve on me by reason of my employment in the public service and that I will not, without due authority in that behalf, disclose or make known any matter that comes to my knowledge by reason of such employment. (In the case where an oath is taken, add "So help me God") Canada, "Public Service Employment Act," R. S., c.P-32, Sch, III section 23.

however. The government was motivated in acting on the turnover problem by its competitive interests as well as by concern for the public interest.

New parties, challenging the established Grits and Tories, were winning votes by criticizing patronage appointments to the civil service. The media delighted in news of the higher-profile and more egregious of them. Further, MPs and ministers found operating employment agencies fraught. Disputes over who should control what appointments divided colleagues. For every appreciative appointee, there were some partisans, perhaps many, who were passed over and disgruntled.

In response to these difficulties, in 1918, appointments to a permanent civil service, apart from certain exempt positions, were placed in the hands of a non-partisan Civil Service Commission—renamed, in 1967, with expanded functions, as the Public Service Commission. Merit, not party service, was established as the criterion for appointment to most positions. From that point forward, it became customary to refer to the bureaucracy as *neutral* and *professional*. The terms were reassuring, suggesting that the public service would administer the policies of the governing party with a high level of competency and not allow the purely political interests of the governing party to intrude on their doing so.

Only part of that objective was achieved. The quality of hires was improved, and the turnover of staff with changes in governing party was largely eliminated. However, party governments, with a hands-on management style and an ever-present interest in improving their competitive position, remained engaged in the administration of policy through the political ministers and their deputies. Deputy ministers, the highest ranking bureaucrats, were excluded from the new hiring rules and appointed by the PM.

The deputy ministers, as professors David Cameron and Graham White observe, function "...at the nexus between politics and administration."[62] Assuming that partyocracy is democracy and that the ruling party has a substantive democratic mandate, these political scientists conclude that government leaders are entitled to work with senior bureaucrats who share their aims. They write,

---

62   David R. Cameron and Graham White, *Cycling into Saigon: The Conservative Transition in Ontario* (Vancouver: UBC Press, 2000), 44.

The most senior positions in the public service are Order-in-Council appointments (that is to say, direct Cabinet decisions) and in that respect indistinguishable from other patronage appointments a prime minister or premier is entitled to make ... deputy ministers hold office at the pleasure of their political "masters," and can be dismissed at any time, with or without cause. There is good reason for this arrangement. A minister and deputy minister exist in a state of mutually dependent professional intimacy; neither can do his or her job properly without the other's assistance and support. While it is formally the responsibility of the minister to give political direction to the deputy and the department, it is the task of the deputy to offer advice to the minister. It would be a grave error to believe that this advice has only to do with the implementation of political decisions or with the administration of the department over which the two preside. One of the most common responses of deputy ministers, when asked to identify their most crucial responsibility, is "to keep my minister out of trouble." A deputy not equipped with highly sensitive political antennae will not last long.[1]

Deputies are not to identify themselves with the governing party formally, but they are to implement policies reflecting its views and values. In a recent study of the Canadian and Ontario bureaucracies, over half of the respondent civil servants stated that they believed their organizations suffered from undue political influence.[2]

The neutrality of the deputy ministers, especially, but also of regular appointees to the civil service, is of a very special kind. It is more accurately described as "job-related partisanship." That terminology would not present the relationship of civil servants to government in as attractive a light as the word *neutral*, but it would be more accurate.

Disagreeing, Cameron and White write:

Although bureaucrats understand that they work for the government

---

1   Ibid., 44–45.

2   Thomas S. Axworthy and Julie Burch, "Closing the Implementation Gap" (Kingston: Canadian Centre for the Study of Democracy, Queen's University, 2010), 10. www.queensu.ca/csd

rather than the governing party, the political reality, which is also well understood by bureaucrats, is that the interests of the two are inextricably bound together and that their political masters are less inclined to make that distinction than they are.

… Civil servants … conceive loyalty to be bound up with professional and conscientious service to the government of the day—loyalty to the office as much as to the transitory officeholder. Loyalty is to the state and to the political actors in the system only insofar as they are the authorized representatives of the state.[3]

If the interests of the political minister and his or her deputy are "inextricably" linked, and the dominant minister is a party combatant, how neutral can that deputy be in the party struggle to gain and maintain power? The limit placed on loyalty in the Cameron and White's formulation—"only insofar as they are the authorized representatives of the state"—is legalistic and bypasses questions about the legitimacy of the state when it is in the hands of a party—almost always enjoying less than majority support. When we clear away all the verbiage, it is clear that the "neutral" bureaucracy is, in reality, forced to be significantly partisan.

When they are not defending the present political system, political leaders frequently make it clear that they do not see the bureaucracy as neutral. The former premier of Ontario accused the bureaucracy he inherited as remaining loyal to his predecessor in office. It was, he wrote, "determined to wait us out, and in true passive-aggressive fashion, resist change…."[4] Stephen Harper, campaigning as leader of the opposition in the 2006 general election, wanted to reassure voters that, as PM, he would not act rashly. To do so, he stated that he would be checked by the Liberals in the bureaucracy, on the Supreme Court, and in the Senate.

In office, Harper was particularly bitter about what he perceived to be the resistance of the Department of Foreign Affairs to support his government's policies. The issue of competing loyalties faced by members of that department's bureaucracy is suggested in a letter to the editor defending

---

3   Cameron and White, *Cycling into Saigon*, 54.
4   Bob Rae, *From Protest to Power* (Toronto: Penguin Books Canada Ltd., 1996), 217.

the Department: "Pity Canada's diplomatic corps (Top Bureaucrats Take Aim At Ottawa's Diplomats, June 29). On the one hand, it is obligated to promote the policies of the government of the day; on the other, it is saddled with a government whose foreign policy is so incompetent, diplomats must cringe with embarrassment when asked to present Canada to the world with such a foolish face.

"Under Prime Minister Stephen Harper, Canada has needlessly antagonised China, become a sycophant to the U.S. and Israel in the Middle East, and forgotten Africa.

"Canada's diplomatic corps is in a difficult situation: Follow its own expertise and try to minimize the damage caused to Canada's standing in the world by Mr. Harper and his advisers, or do what the government wants and facilitate Canada's decline in the eyes of the international community."[5]

It stretches credibility to believe that a civil servant can think he or she is serving the public interest in being loyal to the government, when the perception of the public interest changes with a change in the governing party. And, of course, until the public has the means to define the public interest anyone or any party can claim to represent it.

The *professionalism* of the bureaucracy is only somewhat less questionable than its neutrality. A truly professional civil servant is one who is committed to fulfilling his or her responsibilities, whether modest or major, as set out in government policy, with integrity and competence. The professional in our civil service is required to act on the assumption that the government's policies are legitimate, even though they are suffused with the values of party. More than that, however, this professional is often required to go beyond this system-imposed duty and bend his or her views to suit the partisan interests of a minister, or the government, or both.[6]

The notion that "a diplomat is someone sent abroad to lie for his or her

5   Letter, Shaun Narine, Dept. of Political Science, St. Thomas University, Fredericton, *Globe and Mail* (June 30, 2007).
6   Professionals expect to be respected and free of partisan management. The Harper government, it is reported, "... muzzled its scientists, ordering them to refer all media queries to Ottawa where communications officers will help them respond with "approved lines." Margaret Munro, "Muzzle placed on federal scientists," *Vancouver Sun* (February 1, 2008), A1.

country" is repugnant to most citizens. Sending professional civil servants out to protect party-government is no less ugly. (Supposedly, they are only explaining government policy.) In addition to corrupting the integrity of the individuals concerned, it breeds cynicism and destroys the value of their expertise which, untainted by party interests, would be more valuable in the public discussion of issues.

The claim that the reformed bureaucracy is neutral and professional is only another of the myths promulgated to improve the image of partyocracy. Professionalism, like neutrality, is compromised by the demands of loyalty to whatever party is in office. The claim itself is, however, a form of recognition that having such a bureaucracy is important.

The organized citizenry must authoritatively define its interest before one can expect a full-out commitment from civil servants to their work, i.e., work for their fellow citizens. Until then, painful as it may be, we have to recognize that the civil service is an extension of a party government.

Whistle-Blowers

Some civil servants, unable to completely accept the loyalty norms of the system, feel forced to resort to whistle-blowing, or going public, to protest various forms of improper behaviour within government. In most cases, they do so after failing to gain satisfaction from internal grievance procedures. These government employees face their bureaucratic and political superiors with a dilemma. On the one hand, the superiors may admire the whistle-blower's commitment to the public interest. On the other, they are threatened by his or her challenge to their control which must be maintained in an adversarial environment. The dilemma is obvious in party-government's response to the whistle-blower issue.

Most politicians give verbal support to the idea of protecting civil servants who go public with significant issues that have not been resolved internally. Despite the rhetoric, however, a pretext is often found for dismissing whistle-blowers or forcing their resignation by subjecting them to intolerable treatment in the workplace. Historically, whistle-blowers have had to turn to the courts for protection.[7]

---

7   An example of court intervention, in a 2000 case: a federal court upheld the rights

It was only very recently that a unique set of circumstances—a retiring Liberal prime minister anxious to rehabilitate his reputation in the face of major scandals—opened the door to reforms in how whistle-blowers were treated by government. The first attempts of Liberal governments to provide them with protection were deemed too weak, and a new Conservative government extended the protection and encouragement of whistle-blowers further in its Accountability Act.[8] Despite the additional safeguards, however, whistle-blowers are still likely to be rare. They know that the risks involved in speaking out are unlikely to disappear just because words are on paper. A change in political culture is needed before the whistle-blower will be protected.

Whistle-blowing is only needed because of the conflicting loyalties of civil servants. Many feel "in their bones" that they should be loyal to citizens but the system, based on the myth that the government has a real popular mandate to govern, dictates otherwise. The governing party can enforce its demand for loyalty in a myriad of ways, while citizens are not organized to back up their interests. Members of the House of Commons, supposedly representing us, should act for us—but party interests interfere with their ability to do so.

Regulation: Delayed and Corrupted

The regulation of individual and institutional behaviour is one of the most vital functions of modern government. If it is not done well, lives—often large numbers of them—are put at risk, and the smooth flow of commerce may be disrupted. Party government, in collaboration with many interests, including its bureaucracy, is responsible for establishing a regulatory framework of legislation and rules. The bureaucracy is charged with administering them

of two Health Canada scientists to speak out on drug safety matters, after they had exhausted internal appeal procedures. A spokesperson for the Council of Canadians, one of several interveners in the case, interpreted the decision to mean that "civil servants' responsibility for public safety supersedes their responsibility to their employer." Caroline Alphonso, "Supporters hail ruling for public whistle-blowers," *Globe and Mail* (September 18, 2000). Regardless of the judicial opinion, the party government employer continues to insist that the employee's first loyalty be to it.

8   Bill C-2, Federal Accountability Act, 2006, which incorporated the Public Servants Disclosure Protection Act Amendments, Sections 194–225. www.parl.gc.ca.

neutrally. Party government, however, intrudes on the work of its regulators in two ways. First, fearful of electoral consequences, it fails to adopt timely and effective regulatory policy. Second, it then interferes, for partisan reasons, in their effective administration.

Regulation presents the governing party with serious challenges, because support for government is limited. This often puts it in a weak position vis-à-vis those interests it needs to regulate. Further, in our pluralist and adversarial version of partyocracy, it is accepted as legitimate for each organized interest to battle party government when it feels its interests are threatened by its regulations. This is not seen as hostile to the interests of citizens, or as undemocratic behaviour, because the government has only a weak claim to be acting on a mandate from us. The interests who oppose regulation often have the resources, including the general hostility to government, to do so forcefully. Frequently, at least behind the scenes, the opposition parties will take up the interest groups' cause to weaken their governing opponent.

Even when regulatory action is taken, there is often a further evasion of responsibilities. Government sends implicit or even explicit messages of various kinds to the civil servants charged with enforcing regulations, suggesting that they should proceed *gently*—effectively gutting the regulations.[9] Alternatively, the government may simply hire too few enforcers to regulate properly and let the bureaucrats take responsibility for the failures that result.

Weak enforcement brings government into disrespect and may lead at some point to the eruption of politically damaging situations. With elections changing the governing party there is, however, a reasonable chance that those actually responsible for the regulatory crises can avoid having to deal with the fallout from them. It is a calculation the system encourages. When the damage from global warming reaches a peak several years from now, who

---

9   A news report cites the Sierra Legal Defence Fund statement, "The province rarely prosecutes repeat offenders of the pollution laws, often exempts companies from its clean-water rules, and asks businesses to comply voluntarily with regulations." Martin Mittelstaedt, "Few Ontario polluters charged, study says," *Globe and Mail* (November 5, 2001). Environmental groups insist that "voluntary compliance" is not effective, but it does work for the incumbent party, or it would not be relied on. Few citizens are offered the option of self-policing!

will be interested in looking back and assigning blame to parties that failed to act on the challenge in a timely fashion?

Regulatory failures are common and, sometimes, disastrous. In a short article, Mitchell Anderson, a staff scientist with the Sierra Legal Defence Fund, provides an example of one of the worst, in a brief account of the tragic destruction of the cod fishery on the east coast. He writes, in part,

> With 40,000 jobs lost in Newfoundland and $4 billion spent in federal aid, one would hope that Canada's painful experience with the now-vanished cod stocks would make the Department of Fisheries and Oceans question its policies. Yet, the DFO continues to indiscriminately license dragger boats. Draggers tow large, weighted nets across the ocean floor, scooping up whatever is in their path…. The huge year-round catching capacity of many of these boats, coupled with the latest in sonar equipment, means few fish stocks are safe.
>
> In Newfoundland, hook-and-line-fishermen predicted the decimation of the cod stocks by dragger boats years before it happened. When the DFO refused to heed their warnings, these same fishermen took the federal government to court in 1989 in an ultimately unsuccessful court action to prevent draggers from finishing off the last of the cod.
>
> …By 1992, the once abundant cod had been "managed" into near extinction. A belated moratorium on all commercial cod fishing was brought in—too late. A fishery that for more than 400 years had sustained hundreds of small coast communities was undone in a few short decades by destructive technology and government incompetence.
>
> …So why do Canadians have to go to the trouble of filing lawsuits against their own government to ensure that it does its job? Why does the DFO continue to favour destructive methods of fishing over more sustainable hook-and-line fish boats that employ far more people, waste less fish, and don't damage the ocean floor?[10]

---

10   Mitchell Anderson, "The cod's gone, yet those draggers remain," *Globe and Mail* (April 30, 2003), Op-ed page.

The explanation for this and other regulatory disasters is found in the system of rewards and punishments meted out in partyocracy. In the short term, the governing parties won votes that they would not have received had they regulated properly. The short rather than the long term is what matters to politicians, for whom elections are never far away.

I doubt whether the fisheries' bureaucracy would have let this tragedy occur if it had had a mandate from citizens, organized in constituency parliaments, to implement timely and effective conservation measures—or, put differently, if that bureaucracy had not been required to support the electoral interests of its political masters.

The regulation of the tobacco industry provides a spectacular example of social and economically costly regulatory failure over many years. The "neutral" and "professional" bureaucracy has been forced to be complicit in this failure.

Approximately forty years ago, the Surgeon General of the United States identified tobacco as a serious health hazard. His conclusion has been confirmed repeatedly since and now is accepted by the tobacco industry itself, after it had publicly denied for years what the evidence in its files showed.[11] The denials by our fellow citizens in corporate positions provide a classic example of how the weak citizenship encouraged by the political system is easily trumped by private interests, even those that cause illness and premature deaths.

Currently, the government claims that smoking results in 45,000 of those deaths every year. A leading oncologist asserts that, "Overall, about 30 percent of cancer mortality is from smoking. There's no drug, there's no operation, there's no concept that will get rid of 30 percent of cancers in one swat. In my view, that [the end of smoking] must be the greatest breakthrough in cancer medicine that has ever occurred and ever will occur."[12]

The health-care system is said to be in crisis due to the rising costs of caring for the sick, a population to which the tobacco industry makes a huge contribution. At the same time, industry spokespersons continue to advance

---

11   Barrie McKenna and John Saunders, "Philip Morris admits cigarette smoking is a health hazard," *Globe and Mail* (October 14, 1999).

12   Sheryl Ubelacker, "Despite medical progress, lung cancer a dreaded disease," *Globe and Mail* (August 2, 2005), A13.

the most callous rationalizations to promote their industry's interests. Their product is legal, industry spokespersons point out, transferring moral responsibility for its sale to government.[13] They then lobby successfully to make sure that the cloak of legality remains.

The Tobacco Manufacturers' Council, in an extensive study, draws the attention of Canadians to what they allege is the large positive impact of their industry on the Canadian economy. Scarcely a word in the lengthy report refers to the human costs the industry imposes.[14] In other studies it has sponsored, the industry claims to actually reduce the costs to the health care system by preventing consumers of their product reaching an advanced age when their medical expenses could be expected to be high.[15] Murderers might justify their crimes in the same way.

The tobacco industry has long had one of the best-financed and most effective lobbying organizations in the country. Before the tightening of regulations against tobacco promotion, its dollars purchased support in all corners, from publications carrying its advertising to sports and cultural event sponsorship.

In addition, the industry has special political "assists." It provides jobs in a part of the country that is politically sensitive, i.e., Quebec, where the national government is especially fearful of antagonizing any voters.[16] Further, the industry is able to exploit the prevailing anti-government feeling, which translates into hostility toward any actions that can be presented as paternalistic or as restricting individual liberties. Some politicians may

---

13   John Wildgust, "Bashing Big Tobacco's a nasty habit," *Globe and Mail* (September 17, 2002), A17.

14   Peat Marwick Associates, *Economic Impact of the Tobacco Industry in Canada* (Montreal: Canadian Tobacco Manufacturers' Council, 1979). One of the many estimates of the costs of smoking finds that each package of cigarettes sold costs the economy more than $11 in medical care and lost productivity. André Picard, "Cigarette smokers costly to economy, data show," *Globe and Mail* (April 13, 2003), A14. The pain and sorrow associated with the tobacco-caused illnesses is not factored into this assessment.

15   "Smokers' deaths save money, tobacco firm says," *Globe and Mail* (July 18, 2001).

16   The political sensitivity of (weak) Ottawa to Quebec leads to failures to impose national regulations on Quebec in areas such as health care. Gloria Galloway, "Quebec escaped sanctions over Canada Health Act Violations, report says," *Globe and Mail* (February 21, 2008), A4.

even rationalize the function of the industry, and all the costs it imposes on society, by focusing on the tax revenues it generates.

The central aspect of governments' anti-smoking campaigns is deterring young people from starting to smoke. The industry still makes every conceivable effort to thwart this effort while trumpeting, sanctimoniously, that it shares the administration's concerns.[17] In what appears to be a game without end, the government imposes regulations tardily, and the industry devises imaginative ways to evade them.[18]

It is disappointing, but understandable given the norms supported by partyocracy, that far from being ashamed of their association with this killer-industry,[19] executives representing it brazenly use the courts and appeals based on the Charter of Rights and Freedoms to fight off restrictions on their promotions.[20] At the same time that the industry appeals to the law

---

17   For an expression of industry "concern" about youths smoking, see Wildgust, "Bashing Big Tobacco's a nasty habit," A 17. For one example of numerous media accounts, based on confidential industry files stressing the importance of targeting youth, see Mark MacKinnon, "Tobacco sales target was youth," *Globe and Mail* (May 29, 2000), A1, A7 .

18   For example, a news report states, "Imperial Tobacco Ltd. unveiled two new subsidiaries yesterday, as the domestic industry's biggest player attempts to carve out a marketing plan that stays within the boundaries of Ottawa's new anti-tobacco legislation. Montreal-based Imperial said it has created one subsidiary, Channel 2, to conduct product displays in bars, sporting events, and other entertainment events directed at adults. Canada's largest cigarette maker has also created a wholly owned unit, Rumbling Walls Events, to promote other companies' products through its own magazines and websites, and organize events where cigarettes could be displayed." Simon Tuck, "Tobacco giant creates new marketing arms," *Globe and Mail* (October 2, 2003), B5.

19   They can and do, of course, argue that tobacco is a legal product and imply if it were not they wouldn't be involved with producing and marketing it. And there is the age-old rationalization: if we did not work for the industry, someone else would.

20   Reporting on a tobacco industry challenge to limits on its promotions, a report notes, "The companies say the law infringes on their right to freedom of expression. In 1995, the Supreme Court of Canada agreed with a similar argument and overturned earlier tobacco legislation." Tu Thanh Ha, "Tobacco ads target teens, lawyer says," *Globe and Mail* (January 15, 2002), A9. Considering the use of the Charter by corporations, Professor Allan Hutchinson, observes, "The right to advertise is more about commerce than people. To confer constitutional status on large corporations makes a mockery of any understanding of the Charter as a bulwark for ordinary Canadians against the abuse of power and inequality." Allan C. Hutchinson, "Tobacco ruling no triumph for free speech," *Toronto Star* (July 29, 1991), A13.

for protection, it violates the law when it interferes with the operations of its business. Two tobacco companies have pled guilty to criminal charges involving the large-scale smuggling of their products, exported to the United States and then brought back into Canada and sold on the black market to avoid Canadian taxes.[21] They were fined $600 million—chump-change in relation to what they made by breaking the law, according to a former tobacco company executive.[22] If this record were not distressing enough, a tobacco company spokesperson defended the settlement, inferring that our government was complicit in the illegality.[23] She is probably right: the media frequently reported on the illegal activity.

As domestic tobacco consumption falls off gradually, assuring some Canadians longer and healthier lives, the industry turns to developing its foreign markets to maintain its profits.[24] The modest financial aid the government directs to developing countries is offset, in part, by slick Western advertising promoting the "joys" of smoking.

While Prime Minister Chrétien and Premier McGuinty of Ontario included a tobacco industry sales representative on their teams making commercial visits to China, Canadian representatives to the World Health Organization pressed for international restrictions on tobacco distribution.[25]

---

21   For an account of the tobacco companies' smuggling operations, see Victor Malarek, "Tobacco company had natives smuggle," *Globe and Mail* (July 12, 2003).

22   Timothy Appleby, "Big Tobacco hit with $1-billion penalty," *Globe and Mail* (August 1, 2008), A1.

23   She is quoted in the press as stating "both the government and Imperial knew what was going on, that the shipments were going down into the US and that they were imported back into Canada through whatever means…." William Marsden, "Ottawa caved in to big tobacco, former Imasco executive says," *Vancouver Sun* (September 6, 2008).

24   In an article describing the lobbying of the tobacco industry, the claim is made that despite the decline in smoking, the industry has successfully manipulated the tax/political system to ensure steadily rising profits. Aaron Freeman, "When money meets politics," *Maclean's* (April 10, 2000), 66–69.

25   Linda Waverley Brigden, "Big Tobacco's Next Target," the **Globe and Mail** (November 8, 2000), A17. Geoffrey York, "Ontario Premier, tobacco growers courting China," *Globe and Mail* (November 7, 2000), A4. Spokespersons for the World Lung Foundation estimate that the number of smoking-related deaths will double by 2030 and attribute this increase to the effective promotion of smoking in developing countries. Wendell Roelf, "Doubling of tobacco deaths expected by 2030," *Vancouver Sun* (November 10, 2007), A12. How much of the value of Western foreign aid is offset by

With the absence of firmly based priorities, inconsistencies like this in party government policies are the norm.[26]

The story of government regulation of the tobacco industry is "softly, softly," despite the huge number of lives put at risk. As recently as 2002, newspapers carried a full-page announcement from Health Canada that set out the destructive impact that the industry is having on Canadians; congratulated itself on having a plan to deal with the tobacco menace; and in a few vague phrases, asked for public support.[27] The "plan," whatever it was, was just a little overdue.

The more rapid and effective regulation of this health-destroying product—which surely would have been the course followed by a bureaucracy free of party intervention but acting on a mandate from us—would have resulted in hundreds of thousands of Canadians who would still be with their families and thousands more who would be in better health. Further, wealth spent on tobacco would be redirected to other, less harmful, purposes. People employed in the industry would be working in others instead, free of the burden of guilt they should have now; respect and support for demonstrably caring government would be enhanced; relations with foreign countries would not be contaminated by our government putting dollar exports above respect for the health of their people.

The failure to regulate the tobacco industry effectively in a timely fashion is symptomatic of the wide problem the government faces as it struggles to withstand various pressures. Employees leaving the Health Protection Branch of the federal government suggest that drug companies successfully pressure the government to have new prescription drugs put on the market before adequate testing is done.[28] We are told that professionals, who might

---

the promotion of smoking by Western companies? Millions are spent to deter smoking in the developing nations, while Canadian governments facilitate its promotion. Christine Kearney, "Billionaires give $375 million to battle tobacco use," *Vancouver Sun* (July 24, 2008), A12.

26   Note another inconsistency: The Investment Board of the Canada Pension Plan is allowed to, and does, invest in the tobacco industry, whose sales the government is trying to curtail. Peter Gillespie, "CPP is investing in bombs, tobacco, and corporate criminals," *CCPA Monitor* (February 2006), 15.

27   Canada, Health Canada, "Over 45,000 Canadians die each year from smoking," *Toronto Star* (January 26, 2002), A23.

28   Braving the risk of retribution, a steady stream of Health Canada scientists com-

expect to be able to report on their work openly and stand behind it, are to be "assisted" in their reporting. The Harper government, it is reported, "muzzled its scientists, ordering them to refer all media queries to Ottawa, where communications officers will help them respond with 'approved lines.'"[29]

What will probably be seen as the greatest regulatory failure of this century, one that is just now being recognized, belatedly relates to the exploitation of Alberta's tar sands. National and provincial environmental protection laws have been evaded with the collusion of federal and provincial governments anxious to strengthen their respective competitive positions with Western voters. There is no other word for the damaging environmental consequences than *horrendous*.[30]

In addition to those consequences, it is hard to measure the damage done to the good reputation, built up over many years, of our country abroad.

Even where those to be regulated indicate not just willingness but a desire for stronger environmental or other forms of regulation, party government may be discouraged from acting because the political system stands in the way of converting that willingness into voting support.[31] General demands

plain of pressure to approve drugs without what they believe is adequate testing. See, for example, Helen Branswell, "Fast approvals outweigh drug safety, report says," *Globe and Mail* (April 21, 2009). When Health Canada established its Canada's Natural Health Products Expert Advisory Committee, 6 of its 13 members were natural-health practitioners or supplement merchants, raising questions about their objectivity. See Mike Jacobson, "Natural, Effective, and Safe," *Nutrition Action Healthletter* 30, 9 (November 2003), 2.

29   Margaret Munro, "Muzzle placed on federal scientists," *Vancouver Sun* (February 1, 2008), A1.

30   For a succinct summary of the "horrendous" environmental consequences, see Christopher Hatch and Matt Price, "Canada's Toxic Tar Sands" (Toronto: Environmental Defence, 2008). www.environmentaldefence.ca/reports/pdf/TarSands_The Report. For a more extensive award-winning treatment of the subject, see William Marsden, *Stupid to the Last Drop: How Alberta Is Bringing Environmental Armageddon to Canada (and Doesn't Seem to Care)* (Toronto: Alfred A. Knopf, 2007).

31   Ninety-one percent of Canadians indicate they are prepared to make lifestyle and behaviour changes to reduce their own climate-changing emissions. Peter O'Neil, "Canadians strongly back sacrifices to fight climate change: poll," *Vancouver Sun* (November 7, 2007), A4. In a policy democracy, those views would be forcefully represented in a House of Commons empowered to direct the executive to develop an adequate response to them.

for regulation may be met by intense opposition when they are translated into specific controls.

Government is criticized at home and abroad, for example, when our support for more environmental protection is not matched by support for a particular policy, like a carbon tax. However, the official opposition is always present to tell us that the specific policy is the wrong one—even though its members may not believe it—inferring that some easier solution is available. Soft but ineffective solutions to hard problems are made to seem attractive.

The governing party cannot know what the voters' response to particular actions will be, so caution is the safest course. Further, partisanship guarantees that many citizens will reject the specific policies adopted simply because they oppose the party sponsoring them. The longer the government allows the crisis to deepen, the more political acceptance there will be for regulation when it is finally adopted—but great damage may well have resulted from the delay.

The record of provincial governments in the regulatory field is at least as flawed as that of the federal government—as one would expect with both governments handicapped by the same political system. Reports of elder abuse in poorly regulated nursing homes; children placed in poorly supervised foster homes; lax food and water inspection, etc., are regularly featured in the press.[32]

Essential regulations, established after a long struggle, are far from

---

32   Typical of the regulatory failure, meat inspection in Ontario is found to be scandalously lax. Inspectors explain why to the media investigating lapses: "The province's Ministry of Agriculture and Food 'has a wonderful habit of looking the other way.... They don't want any trouble; the inspectors are told to make it work. [Ministry officials] haven't been doing their job for years.'" As is typical in the closed environment of government, where civil servants are expected to be party government loyalists, the inspectors being quoted asked not to be identified, for fear of reprisals. Paul Waldie, "Aylmer warnings ignored, inspectors say," *Globe and Mail* (September 3, 2003). Coincidentally, a major problem with the safety of meat processed by Maple Leaf Foods and sold in Canada surfaced at the same time that the federal government's intentions to cut back on its food safety inspections became known, thanks to a leak from the federal bureaucracy. Paula Simons, "Cutting corners on meat inspection, Reductions to the Canadian Food Inspection Agency raise questions about the safety of the country's food supply," *Globe and Mail* (July 21, 2008), A7. The "leaker" was fired. Kathryn May, "Scientist fired for circulating document," *Times Colonist* (July 9, 2008), A9.

secure. One party government functioning without a real mandate may undo the work of many predecessors. Demolition is much easier and quicker than construction.[33] We will often have forgotten the very good reason the regulations were adopted initially and their repeal is, superficially, attractive. Interests that found regulation onerous will welcome the deregulation, and it will take time for us to become fully aware of the consequences of what has been done and react at the polls.

On an almost daily basis, regulatory failures resulting in human tragedies of various kinds are exposed and investigated. "This must never happen again," is familiar rhetoric that emerges from the investigations. But it does, routinely, when the systemic causes are not recognized and corrected. They seldom are because too often the investigators take the system as fixed. Shallowly rooted party governments, always needing support and with upcoming elections to win, are in a weak position to protect the interests of citizens, and civil servants are forced to respect party interests.

The record of governments would be even worse if various citizen lobbies did not pressure governments to fulfill their responsibilities. In most cases, however, they lack means to mobilize sufficient support for government to offset its fear of losing votes by regulating effectively.

Citizens would have a critical, constructive interest in government and all its policies, especially its regulatory policies, if democratic citizenship were fostered in appropriately designed constituency institutions. In a sense, all those policies would *belong* to us and we could be expected to back *our* government in implementing them. Citizens from across the country would be in a position to insist that regulation furthering the national interest be adopted. Opposition to regulation from provincially based special interests,

---

33   The report of the provincial auditor of Ontario in 2001, after six years of neo-Conservative government in the province, is a horror story. It tells, for example, of the grossly inadequate testing of the safety of food bound for consumers and notes that the government has cut inspectors from 103 in 1995 to 8 in 2000. Theresa Boyle, "Food safety branded 'critical,'" *Toronto Star* (November 30, 2001), A1, A6. The cumulative effect of warnings like that of the auditor plus numerous accounts of damage caused by lax provincial regulation undoubtedly contributed to the decision by voters to defeat the government in 2003. But installing a new party government does not ensure that the problems identified will be corrected. These will persist until the political system is such that government can act without fear of losing our support, because it is acting as directed by us.

such as tobacco interests headquartered in Quebec and the oil companies in Alberta, could be smartly overcome. Further, with citizenship strengthened, individuals in their personal, social, and business lives would be more likely to comply voluntarily with regulations without requiring heavy-handed government prosecutions. Finally, it would be unnecessary to protect whistle-blowers when there was a free exchange of information between bureaucrats and citizens on most issues.

Accountability. The final difficulty with the relationship of political ministers and the bureaucracy that I want to raise is the existing uncertainty about lines of accountability. These now give rise to problems in the administration and make it difficult for us—mere voters—to sort out who is responsible for which actions.

Theoretically, political ministers are accountable to the Commons for the performance of their departments. The deputy minister, the senior bureaucrat in each, is accountable to a minister. Theory and practice have separated, however, as governments and their bureaucracies have grown enormously. The size of departments has made it unreasonable to hold ministers accountable for all the actions taken within them. Increasingly, accountability, as well as responsibility, for controversial actions and policy has shifted informally from the minister to the bureaucrat most directly involved, i.e., the deputy minister. However, it is unreasonable, too, to hold the civil servant accountable, because if the bureaucrat had been managing without partisan interference from a minister, he or she might have acted quite differently. With the current difficulty of holding either minister or deputy accountable, there is a void in the chain of accountability.[34] As Thomas Axworthy and Julie Burch note in their survey of the bureaucracy, "Ministers publicly blame officials for mistakes and officials have had to learn public relations skills in order to survive."[35]

The question of whom is to be held accountable is not just academic.

---

34   The dilemma facing civil servants is summarized in a British study of the bureaucracy: "The civil service finds itself serving ministers and sometimes regulating them; it is impartial and yet accountable to those ministers. Discharging these often conflicting roles successfully in parallel is not possible." Ed Straw, *The Dead Generalist: Reforming the civil service and public services* (London: Demos, 2004), 9.

35   Axworthy and Burch, "Closing the Implementation Gap," 20.

The scandal over the administration of federal government advertising in Quebec highlighted the confusion and led to the establishment of the Gomery Commission to study the circumstances that led to the improper disbursement of funds. The Gomery hearings heard conflicting claims, as politicians and bureaucrats blamed one another for the malfeasance that had occurred. Citizens were left confused about whether the failing was bureaucratic or party political—or a mix of both.

To resolve the confusion, the Gomery Commission reiterated some of the recommendations of post–World War II studies of the organization of the federal government.[36] He also recommended a more independent status for deputy ministers in his final report.[37] This status would be achieved by removing the power of appointing deputies from the PMO, and providing the right for a deputy disagreeing with directions from his political minster to ask that the disagreement be recorded.[38] The deputy would be accountable for the management of his or her department, except where following the written the instructions of the minister; then it would be the minister who would be held accountable. Another much-needed blow would be struck against party control of the administration. Although foreign to Canada, this organization of accountability is followed in some other parliamentary democracies.[39]

The PM of a party government (Harper) again rejected recommendations that it adopt these best administrative practices.[40] The rejection was rationalized as being in the public interest, as such matters usually are. It seems more likely, however, that it was taken to preserve the governing

36   These are mentioned in Ned Franks, "It's right to hold deputy ministers to account," *Globe and Mail* (February 13, 2006), A15.

37   Canada, Commission of Inquiry into the Sponsorship Program and Advertising Activities (the Gomery Commission), *Restoring Accountability, Recommendations* (Ottawa: Minister of Public Works and Government Services, 2006), 83–107.

38   Ibid., 101.

39   The United Kingdom and New Zealand have recently reorganized their systems to give their bureaucracies more autonomy. Judge Gomery's recommendations would clearly have brought Canadian practice into line with many other parliamentary democracies. See Peter Aucoin, "An Agenda for Public Management," *Policy Options* (March 1996), 40–44.

40   Gloria Galloway and Campbell Clark, "Harper dismisses key Gomery proposals," *Globe and Mail* (December 21, 2006), A5.

party's ability to intervene in the administration to promote its partisan interests without having to advertise the intervention by issuing written instructions.

Most senior members of the bureaucracy also support the status quo, despite the confusion surrounding lines of accountability.[41] It may sometimes be convenient to have political ministers standing between them and the House of Commons, taking some of the criticism when it is the bureaucracy that has earned it. Neither party government nor senior bureaucrats are prepared to put the public interest ahead of their own—another example of the need for us to intervene authoritatively in making changes in government.

Conclusion

Over the past century, politicians have made some efforts to limit party influences on the bureaucracy in the interest of improving the quality of government. Those efforts have, however, been limited by the desire of the governing party to retain its ability to insist that the bureaucracy support its partisan interests as it administers government policy.

Hiring by merit was introduced, but it was compromised by the need of the governing party to have people that it could trust to be sympathetic to its partisan needs in the top echelons of the bureaucracy. Party government, as a show of its commitment to integrity and openness, adopted whistle-blower legislation. But it is party government's tight restrictions on the flow of information between civil servants and the outside world that makes it necessary for bureaucrats to blow the whistle in the first place. There has been no move to modify the oath sworn by civil servants not to engage in unauthorized discussion of their work with fellow citizens. Despite repeated recommendations that the government clarify the ambiguities in the accountability of ministers vis-à-vis senior bureaucrats, it has refused to act.

The rhetoric surrounding the bureaucracy—"public service," "neutral," and "professional"—continues to indicate what should be, rather than what

---

41   The deputies' support for the status quo is confirmed in a study of the role of deputy ministers. See the Hon. Gordon F. Osbaldeston, *Keeping Deputy Ministers Accountable* (Toronto: McGraw-Hill Ryerson, 1989) 6.

is. In partyocracy, the civil service must move to the drumbeat of the current governing party. Its interests and strategic needs suffuse the program the bureaucracy must administer and are injected into how it is implemented.

The weak to non-existent mandate that partyocracy bestows on government does not allow its acceptance as government 'of the people' and its bureaucratic arm as, truly, a public service. If, however, government were managed by political leaders consulting closely with their constituents, the partisan environment which now gives rise to many of the problems with and for the bureaucracy would be fundamentally altered. The walls that defensive politicians have erected around the bureaucracy, and the programs and institutions they manage, would come tumbling down as citizens became more directly involved in administration.

The isolation of citizens from civil servants would be replaced by interaction; bureaucrats as officials and as citizens would be expected to share their knowledge and advice fully with members of constituency parliaments. Good government would be enhanced as these servants, aware of boondoggles, dishonesty, and waste of resources, could alert the public, and that empowered public could act to protect its interests. Civil servants, on the other hand, would benefit from direct feedback from those they are paid to serve.

The strict hierarchy and lines of control in the bureaucracy—necessary when it is one aspect of a fighting party machine—could be relaxed. The initiative and creativity of all 454,000 federal employees could be welcomed, at work as well as in their communities.[42]

The federal government is the country's largest employer; its personnel are spread across the country. Removed from party control and responsible to a parliament truly representative of Canadians, civil servants could make a significantly larger contribution to our public life.[43] At the same time,

---

42   As of 2006 the numbers of employees in the various categories of federal employees were: federal employees 180,000; federal agencies 60,000; parliamentary officers and administrators 20,000; Canadian Forces and RCMP 106,000; federal business enterprises 88,000. en.wikipedia.org/wiki/public_service_of_Canada

43   Commenting on the current state of the bureaucracy, Axworthy and Burch state: "Surveys of public sector employees reveal a moderately dissatisfied and unmotivated work force with midline optimism for the future. This will not suffice going forward. Canada needs a creative, risk-taking, globally informed public service. To achieve it,

the quality of their working lives would be improved. We need a public service whose work is uncompromised by party, and it needs us to direct and support it.

*****

The existing political system can be thought of as an old and battered ship whose days of good service have long passed. A significant part of its crew must now devote its time and energies to keeping it afloat. Its hull, rusting through in many places, is patched, but still more leaks appear as its metal hull deteriorates steadily. The ship can only limp along, bearing a limited cargo toward an uncertain destination. That destination shifts with crew changes; weather that can easily blow the ancient tub off course; and frequent stops for repair. Traversing familiar routes poses dangers; striking out on new ones is beyond consideration. The decrepit nature of the ship poses risks to the crew and all others dependent on its performance.

Discussion of the ship's future by its owners is focused on how it is to be maintained and their investment preserved. Conspicuously absent is consideration of whether it is time—or past time—to design and operate a new vessel, in the interest of those dependent on its service. This is primarily because the ships' "customers" have not organized and insisted that the "owners"build a modern replacement ship, one that can provide vastly superior service—a model for such a ship is now available and perhaps it will stimulate an irresistible customer demand for it.

---

the public service must attract talented young people and create a work environment stimulating and effective enough to retain them." Axworthy and Burch, "Closing the Implementation Gap," 29.

7

Parties: Agents of National Disunity

The party system, importantly conditioned by the electoral system,
exacerbates the very cleavages it is credited with healing.

Alan Cairns

At certain periods of Canada's history the party system performed
only indifferently as a national unifier. ... the party functions of
structuring the vote, mobilizing the mass public, recruiting leaders,
and organizing the government were accompanied by the dysfunction
of widening the gap between regions and attenuating national unity. ...
there is a need to explore new or modified ways of carrying out some
of the tasks parties have assumed within Canada's political system.

John Meisel

The danger of adversary politics... is that it encourages persistent
irresponsible competition and too much oversimplification.... Where
conflict does not exist, adversary politics manufactures it; where
genuine conflict is present, adversary politics exacerbates it, and
yet may frustrate its resolution; and where the clash of opinions and
interests is many-sided and complex, adversary politics offers little
hope of creating that basis of consensus which is indispensable if
there is to be effective political authority. These are the difficulties
to which a particular style of politics has given rise. They are

likely to be overcome only through changes in the ground rules of political life, which would change the adversary mould itself.

Nevil Johnson

Introduction

The political integrity of Canada is not assured; the administration's ability to serve its citizens is severely compromised as a result. Too often, when considering policy, the central government has to ask, "Will this threaten national unity?" rather than, "Is this in the best interests of the majority of citizens whom we were elected to serve?" The task of preserving Canada has been aggravated by the politics of partyocracy, which often reward divisive party tactics with votes while penalizing parties that attempt to rise above regional and provincial appeals.

The linguistic divide separating French and English speakers continues to cause serious tensions among us. The population outside the ranks of those two founding groups is heterogeneous and becoming more so, presenting new challenges to our social cohesiveness. Further, Canada is a federal state with provinces grouped in regions that have some distinctive interests. These tend to be emphasized in our competitive party politics at the expense of the common concerns of Canadians.

Our constitutional arrangements add to the divisive pressures in the country. Responsibilities and powers are not clearly divided between the provinces and the national government. Interpretation of their constitutional distribution at first favoured the development of a clearly dominant role for the central government. That changed with the outcome of provincial challenges taken to the Privy Council at Westminster. Ambiguity replaced clarity, opening the door to continuous struggles over powers between the provinces and Ottawa; buck-passing between the two levels and delays in implementing needed public policy; public confusion over which government to hold accountable for various actions and non-actions; and, importantly, the formation of parties that exploited provincial and regional grievances.

Each province has its own unique history and is led by its own team of power-seeking party politicians, who frequently undermine the national government. Currently, one province (Quebec) poses a threat to the physical integrity of the country. Another such threat looms in the West.[44] Adjusting to these threats seriously restricts the ability of the national government to govern in ways that would strengthen national unity.

In addition to these internal divisions, in virtually every respect Canada is subject to pressure from its imperial neighbour.[45] It is difficult to develop and maintain a common, meaningful value system to underpin the politics of the country in the face of that pressure. With no strong counter vision to guide us, we are drawn to the US model—even more dysfunctional than our own—when we consider changes in our institutions. If Canada is to survive as an independent country, our political institutions must actively encourage national unity.

The Motivation of Parties

Winning, or seeming likely to win power or influence, is key to the survival of any serious party and must be its first consideration—strengthening national unity can only be secondary.

In a limited way, individual parties do aggregate, pulling some people together, around certain issues and leaders, as each builds a base of support. But these parties also disaggregate, pitting Quebecers against the rest of us, East against West, ethnic voters against the establishment, partisans of one party against others, etc. Party leaders are not indifferent to the need

---

44   In a speech to the Canadian Bar Association, Peter Lougheed, former premier of Alberta, is quoted as predicting a ferocious federal-provincial clash over environmental issues related to the development of the Athabasca oil sands that will "cause significant stress to Canadian unity." Kirk Makin, "Clash over oil sands inevitable: Lougheed," *Globe and Mail* (August 14, 2007).

45   Polling consistently reports public doubts about the ability of the country to survive as an independent country. Asked "Do you believe that Canada will be an independent country 25 years from now?" 30 percent responded "Certainly," 42 percent "Probably." Here are more results from the same poll: "Considering various areas such as economy, culture, international politics, and national security, would you say Canada is independent from the United States?" "Very independent" 11 percent; "Somewhat independent" 45 percent; "Not very independent" 30 percent; "Not at all independent" 10 percent." Maclean's-L'actualité poll, *Maclean's* (September 9, 2002), 38.

to build national unity, but they are not service organizations, as we noted previously. Their primary interest is, and must be, in winning votes. In a heterogeneous country like Canada this has led almost all of them to adopt nationally divisive strategies. The Greens are the notable exception.

In competing, parties must adapt to the first-past-the-post electoral system; to a multiparty system; and to the level of civic literacy of the electorate. None of these encourages the major parties to adopt a nationally aggregative strategy. The winner-take-all electoral system, with several parties competing, puts enormous pressure on each to use whatever strategies will win votes, and those are ones that appeal to voters in areas of strength, even though that approach may be nationally divisive.

The political literacy of the electorate is such that it encourages party manipulation of voters and demagoguery. Vote-getting myths—generally related to hostile treatment by the national administration—are easily propagated and can have far-reaching consequences in terms of national unity.[46] In short, the common interests of citizens in different parts of Canada are obscured by the divisive strategies forced on the parties by the system of incentives built into the system.

In the pages that follow, I consider the divisive behaviour of our parties in some detail. The behaviour will be familiar, but we need to recognize its inevitability in the existing political system. Exhorting parties to act differently is futile if it is not in their interests to do so. Citizens do not want the country to break up, but parties may manoeuvre us into a position where it does.[47] They are already responsible for the increasing Balkanization of the country that inhibits effective national government.

---

46   Columnist Jeffrey Simpson often devotes columns to debunking political myths while, at the same time, bemoaning the hopelessness of doing so. In one he writes, "As we know, however, myths do not die, and the existence of a 'fiscal imbalance' has become a myth in Quebec. Myths do not fade away like old soldiers. They have a life of their own. They are propagated widely, believed almost universally and uncritically, drive political actors, and cannot apparently be dislodged from the minds of the news media and general public." Jeffery Simpson, "The fiscal imbalance myth refuses to die," *Globe and Mail* (February 9, 2007), A17. The quality of public life in Canada would be vastly improved by the death of a number of pernicious myths. Some would be buried when serious discussions of public questions in constituency parliaments raised the level of political sophistication.

47   Recent polling in Quebec finds that "About a third of Quebecers (32 percent) be-

National Disunity: The Party Contribution

Until the early years of the 20th century, a two-party system, composed of the Liberal and Conservative parties, dominated Canadian politics. Provincial branches of the same parties did likewise in their respective jurisdictions. The two parties, each appealing to voters in all parts of Canada, were agents of national unity. Their hegemony was not to last, however. The two-party system gave way to one that was multi-party, as sections of the country, aided by ambitious politicians, were persuaded that representation by these catch-all parties was inadequate. Parties based in certain provinces were organized to give voice to the feelings of local people that they were being neglected in Ottawa. It became difficult or impossible for either of the "national" parties to aggregate effectively across the whole country while these newcomers corralled significant segments of the vote with their anti-Ottawa stance. They were forced to adopt defensive strategies, concentrating their appeal where their support was strongest.

The national Liberal and Conservative parties were forced, over time, to change their organizational structures as well as their appeals to voters. Provincial wings of the national parties separated from their national organizations so that they could compete more successfully with provincially based parties. This parting significantly weakened the positive linkage parties provided between provinces and the national government. The separation occurred in several provinces but posed a particular threat to national unity when it occurred in Quebec. There the separation left the federal Liberals with only a very uncertain ally in the provincial Liberal Party. That party often found electoral success in echoing many of the anti-Ottawa positions of the separatist party.[1]

---

lieve that Quebec has enough sovereignty and should remain part of Canada, 28 percent think that Quebec should separate from Canada, and 30 percent say that while Quebec needs greater sovereignty, it should still remain part of Canada." Press Release, *Angus Reid Strategies* (Montreal, June 9, 2009). These opinions could change quite suddenly, given the ability of separatist parties to portray actions by the national or provincial governments as hostile to Quebec.

1   The most recent of these are summarized by William Johnson in "The Bloc's silent partner," *Globe and Mail* (August 17, 2010), 11.

Quebec. Some tension between centre and periphery is expected in any federation. In Canada, however, it is exacerbated by parties appealing to provincial or regional interests to the point where it threatens national unity. Parties based in Quebec and Western Canada—the latter represented here by Alberta—are the major source of the tension, but Ottawa cannot count on support and cooperation from any provincial administration or region.[2]

The ability of the two major parties to further the integration of Quebec Francophones into the Canadian polity, never easy, met sharp reverses shortly after Confederation. Difficult relations between the governing Conservative Party and Quebec Francophones, intensified by the hanging of Louis Riel, were compounded by a Conservative government imposing conscription on the province during the First World War.[3] After that, historian George Perlin writes, "Conservative defeat in Quebec became self-perpetuating. Left in control of an English Protestant majority, which remained persistently insensitive to French-Canadian opinion, the party continued to make decisions that offended French-Canadian voters and permitted Quebec to become a Liberal Party stronghold."[4]

Giving up on Quebec, the Tories tilted their appeal to English-speaking Canada, where they had more hope of winning seats. People harbouring strong anti-French, anti-Quebec feelings gravitated to the party.

The weakness of the Conservatives in Quebec left an opposition vacuum. It was filled, first, by the nationalist Union Nationale (UN) party and then, in the late 1960s, principally by the separatist Parti Québécois (PQ). If the Quebec voter was dissatisfied with the provincial Liberal government, he or she had little choice but to vote for one that would foster Quebec nationalism and isolation (the UN) or, after the demise of that party, one that advocated the separation of the province from Canada (the PQ). Both promoted and

2   Polling has shown that regional discontent is general and, surprisingly, given the federal support to that region, is particularly strong in Atlantic Canada. Centre for Research and Information on Canada, *Opinion Canada* 5, 17 (May 8, 2003), 2.
3   "The 1917 conscription crisis witnessed the collapse of the party system as a vehicle of political integration across the linguistic divide." Roger Gibbins, *Conflict and Unity* (Toronto: Methuen, 1988), 295.
4   George C. Perlin, "The Progressive Conservative Party," in *Party Politics in Canada*, 4th ed., ed. Hugh G. Thorburn, (Scarborough, Ont.: Prentice-Hall, 1979), 161.

capitalized on the alienation of the province from Ottawa. It was more in the interest of the national Liberal Party seeking votes in the province to make deals with political elites in Quebec than it was to challenge the popular beliefs and myths that were the basis of that alienation.

During the long period that the Liberal Party dominated Quebec's representation in Ottawa, the party integrated the federalist segment of Quebec's political elite into the national administration. At the same time, however, it sought votes among the general Francophone population by promoting the notion that only it stood between French-speaking Quebecers and a vaguely threatening Anglophone majority in the country, represented by the Conservative Party.

For a period extending to the 1960s, it was in the strategic interest of successive national Liberal governments to maintain an uneasy truce with the provincial governments of Quebec. In an arrangement dubbed "consociationalism" by political scientists, elites at both levels of government avoided conflict with one another.[5] Ottawa stayed out of provincial politics, and in return, provincial politicians tolerated the dominance of the national Liberals in Quebec federal politics. Liberal MPs from Quebec adopted a low-profile role in Ottawa. An informal political division of the country on linguistic lines evolved, with the Quebec government representing Francophones and the national government belonging to the English-speaking majority in the country. Citizens in each of the "two solitudes" passively accepted agreements made by their leaders.

This meant that for a long period, the national Liberals abandoned Quebec citizens to the despotic provincial Union Nationale regime of Maurice Duplessis. It held office for most of the period from 1936 to 1959, except for the war years when the provincial Liberals formed a government. During those years, English dominance of business in the province went unchallenged by Duplessis.

The hold on office of the national Liberal Party, and its ability to make deals with Quebec's political elites, weakened gradually in the post–World

---

5   For a discussion of consociationalism, see S. J. R. Noel, "Political Parties and Elite Accommodation: Interpretations of Canadian Federalism," in *Canadian Federalism: Myth or Reality?* 2nd ed., ed. J. Peter Meekison (Toronto: Methuen, 1971), 121-42.

War II period, breaking conclusively in 1959.[6] Premier Maurice Duplessis died in office that year and with him the reactionary politics he had practiced. For personal and party advantage, Duplessis had used his power to reward friends and punish enemies to an extent unprecedented in 20th-century Canadian politics. A voting public subjected to his demagoguery, bribery, and bullying kept him in office. Duplessis remains only the most flagrant of many examples of the danger in assuming that voters "dumbed-down" in partyocracy will choose enlightened leadership.

The impact of the Quiet Revolution. No Quebec political leader was interested in continuing Duplessis' style of leadership. Most, released from the grip of his party machine, were determined to press forward with the long-delayed modernization of the province. Elitist consociational politics could not function in the dynamic new citizen-engaging political environment of Liberal Premier Jean Lesage's Quiet Revolution. The new provincial leadership adopted a demanding strategy in dealing with Ottawa and the country at large, pressing for a better deal including expanded jurisdiction for the province.

In hindsight, consociationalism, while of short-term advantage to the parties engaged in it, was an unhealthy holding action insofar as the unity of the country was concerned. It relied on a weak commitment to Canada from Quebec federalists. They organized Quebecers into supporting the national Liberals on the basis that it furthered the interests of the province for them to

---

6   The national Liberal Party, in particular, prided itself on playing the role of national unifier. But, as Matthew Mendelsohn observes, "The Liberal Party since 1968 has satisfied its own ends by continuing to win elections but has stopped serving the broader public function that it used to fulfill. Because of the Liberals' refusal to find accommodation with some of the most important movements for change in the country—Western devolutionists, populists, and Quebec nationalists—they now actually exacerbate rather than moderate regional and linguistic differences." Matthew Mendelsohn, "Healing Social, Political, and Regional Divisions," in *Memos to the Prime Minister,* ed. Harvey Schachter (Toronto: John Wiley and Sons, 2001), 12. Mendelsohn implies that the Liberals could have found "accommodations" with the various interests he mentions. They would have done so if they could and still win elections—their "must" priority. The argument here is that the Liberal unifying role declined sharply long before 1968. For years prior to that date it was based on *consociationalism.* This was only a politically expedient way of avoiding overt conflict in the short term while winning elections, not a strategy for building a deep sense of common interest among citizens.

hold a largely "watching brief" in successive Liberal governments. When the federalists were no longer willing to perform that limited function, national politicians were confronted with a Francophone population whose links to the federal administration, i.e., to Canada, were shallow.

The federal government's response to the new Quebec. In the 1958 federal election, prior to the end of the Duplessis era, the Progressive Conservatives (PCs), led by John Diefenbaker and informally supported by the Duplessis machine, scored a major breakthrough in winning 50 of Quebec's 75 seats. As a government, however, the PCs failed to secure their position in the province. It fell, primarily, to the national Liberals, in office from 1963 to 1984 (led by Lester Pearson and Pierre Trudeau) with only one short break, to recognize the politically dynamic "new" Quebec. Both did so. This was now a good competitive strategy, since the Liberal Party could no longer rely on a reactionary political elite in the province to allow the federal vote to go to it almost by default. Of course, too, as talk of separation intensified in Quebec, the prime ministers felt a strong obligation and interest in doing what they could to hold the country together.

Many outside Quebec were unhappy about the attention paid to the demands of that province. The consociational model, so strategically valuable to the Liberals, had not encouraged much thought about the aspirations of Francophones among Anglophones outside Quebec. Partyocracy allowed little room for ordinary citizens to respond, even if such aspirations did happen to intrude on their consciousness. With the end of the peace achieved through consociationalism, and with talk of separation, many turned to the Liberal Party of Pearson and Trudeau. It was seen as the best political vehicle to hold the country together, given the Liberal Party's history of support in Quebec. Ironically, the party that had contributed to creating the divide between Quebec and the rest of the country in its pursuit of votes was now rewarded as the party best able to deal with the emerging national-unity crisis.

With the breakup of the country a distinct possibility, the PC party, in opposition, could no longer afford even covert appeals to anti-French feeling in the country. Three of its leaders—Stanfield, Clark (briefly), and Campbell (even more briefly)—all adopted a conciliatory approach to Quebec. The party became more acceptable in the province as a result. The preferred position the Liberals enjoyed in Quebec ended in 1984, with the election of the Progressive Conservatives, led by Brian Mulroney. In Mulroney, for the first time, the Conservatives had a Quebecker to lead them. Mulroney led the national response to Quebec's ongoing threat to national unity until his retirement in 1993.

While the federal parties adapted their policies to the new demands of Quebec, in that province the Lesage Liberals were faced with opposition from a revived Union Nationale, lost office to it from 1966 to 1970, and then returned to office. From 1968, following a merging of separatist movements, the main opposition to the Liberals was to come from the Parti Québécois (PQ). The PQ significantly ratcheted up the tension in Canada-Quebec relations by advocating "Sovereignty Association," interpreted in the rest of Canada, and by many Quebecers, as separation. The PQ governed the province in the years 1976–85 and 1994–2003, with the provincial Liberals in office in the intervening years.

As the provincial government, the PQ was able to use the resources of the province to put a consistently negative, nationally divisive interpretation on Ottawa's treatment of the province. At the same time, of course, it stressed the benefits it anticipated coming from independence. The PQ submitted the first of two referenda on sovereignty association to Quebec voters in 1980. Roughly 60 percent of those voting cast "no" ballots, but 50 percent of Francophones voted in favour of sovereignty.

Although arrived at democratically, the decision of the majority of Quebecers did not end the agitation of the PQ for separatism. The threat it posed continued to be useful in getting the attention of the federal government. Further, while the PQ had established its reputation as a progressive governing body, it could not give up its "foundation policy" without a serious loss of appeal to the ideologues in the party—as well as a loss of face.

The "no" vote was taken by the PQ as simply a bump on the road to some degree of sovereignty. But if—perhaps by taking advantage of a temporary crisis of some kind—the "yes" side had won, Quebec separatists almost certainly would have interpreted it as a definitive expression of the will of Quebecers and acted on it. A refusal by the rest of Canada and by

Ottawa to accept the verdict would have been exploited by the PQ to build its support and increase the likelihood of ultimate separation.

After the referendum, policy and administration in Ottawa continued to be filtered through consideration of how the separatists might interpret and exploit the government's actions. The national government still could not assume a strong national leadership role without feeding separatist forces in Quebec. Initiatives beneficial to Canadians, including Quebecers, might be interpreted as an attack on provincial rights or a power grab by Ottawa. The nationally divisive pressure by Quebec parties for a still further devolution of power to the province prompted similar demands from most of the other provinces.

Constitutional politics and Quebec. Early in his administration, Prime Minister Trudeau, recognized the Quebec government's dissatisfaction with existing constitutional arrangements and opened negotiations on changes with the provinces. A series of unsuccessful talks with provincial leaders occurred during the 1970s. Few Canadians outside the ranks of "professional observers" paid much attention to them. That was to change.

In the course of the 1980 referendum campaign in Quebec, Trudeau implied a readiness to amend the founding document. His statement was widely interpreted by Quebec's politicians as a commitment to accept some of the provincial government's constitutional demands. Later, Trudeau insisted that he was referring to pressing his own agenda for change.

Trudeau's commitment and his awareness, as a leader coming to the end of his time in office, that he would not have another opportunity to change the Constitution, led him to further negotiations with the provinces in the early 1980s. Determined to reach an agreement, Trudeau "motivated" the provinces to reach agreement with the threat of a national referendum on the federal government's proposal to add a Charter of Rights and Freedoms and a formula for amending the constitution.[7] Of the leaders who claimed to represent their province's people, only the separatist Premier of Quebec seemed confident that he could carry his constituency with him in voting no on the threatened referendum.

---

7   See David Milne, *The New Canadian Constitution* (Toronto: James Lorimer and Co.), 146–47.

Parti Québécois premier, René Lévesque, participating with the other premiers in the negotiations, was party to an informal agreement among them to present a united front to the federal negotiators. The final compromises that led to an agreement were, however, negotiated in an overnight session in his absence. Presented with a fait accompli, Lévesque refused to sign on to the agreement, claiming that his fellow premiers had betrayed him. As a result, the adoption of the 1982 package of changes was agreed to by all the provinces except Quebec.

The other premiers denied that Lévesque had been deliberately excluded from the final negotiations. He had gone to bed while they continued talking informally into the night. In addition, they argued that Lévesque himself had already broken their agreement to act collectively by his unilateral expression of willingness to accept Trudeau's challenge to hold a referendum on the Charter.

Political scientist David Milne suggests that Lévesque was looking for a pretext to walk away from the agreement. "Quebecers had empowered the government to pursue federalism only. Success at the bargaining table would undermine the Parti Québécois' argument that federalism does not work, set back the independence movement, and imperil the government's position with its party base. Therefore, its fundamental political interest lay in continuing federal-provincial conflict, in goading the federal government into more arrogant displays of unilateralism, and in preserving a bloc of provincial opposition."[8] The "betrayal" of Quebec during the "night of the long knives" was added to the Parti Québécois's list of examples of the intolerable treatment of Quebec in Canada.

The most high-profile part of the constitutional package, the Charter of Rights and Freedoms was, and continues to be, supported by the overwhelming majority of Canadians, including Quebecers.[9] Who was the Premier of Quebec representing when he refused on behalf of his province to accept it? Trudeau claimed that the reforms fulfilled the commitment

---

8   Ibid., 155.
9   A poll reports that 91 percent of Quebecers support the Charter and 7 out of 10 believe the Supreme Court when it declares a law unconstitutional because it conflicts with the Charter. Centre for Research and Information on Canada (CRIC), "The Charter: dividing or uniting Canadians?" (April 2002), 4. www.ccu-cuc.ca

he had made to Quebec during the referendum debate. His Quebec critics disagreed, continuing to accuse him of betraying his fellow Quebecers.

Despite the significance of the constitutional package for the lives of Canadians, following tradition, it was finally negotiated and agreed to by only a few politicians—nine of the premiers and, acting for the government of Canada, the Minister of Justice. The "closed" negotiating process, which seemed to have gone on interminably, failed to alert the public, or indeed many legislators, to the full impact the Charter would have on the relationship of citizens with the government and courts.

The Constitution adopted in 1867 focused on the division of powers between levels of government. With the addition of the Charter, it also asserted the rights of individual Canadians vis-à-vis government. The role of the courts was greatly increased: limits were placed on the sovereignty of parliament. Overall, the adoption of the Charter and the patriation of the Constitution were unifying. However, separatist party charges that it represented a betrayal of Quebec sullied what should have been a proud moment for all Canadians, including Quebecers. Further, the nation-building impact of the adoption was much more modest than it might have been, because citizens had not been engaged in the process leading to its adoption.

The anti-Quebec interpretation the Parti Québécois put on "the night of the long knives" was, unhelpfully, validated for some Quebecers by the national Progressive Conservatives. When he became leader of that party, Brian Mulroney realized that his major challenge as he pursued office was to break the Liberal Party's stranglehold on Quebec. His strategic interest in enlisting Quebec voters and, perhaps, a conviction that he was fostering Canadian unity, led Mulroney to express sympathy for the view that Quebec had, indeed, been betrayed in the 1982 negotiations.[10] This position helped him persuade a number of "soft" separatists to become PC candidates in

---

10   William Johnson comments, "He [Mulroney] depicted it [the 1982 signing] as Quebec left alone, isolated, humiliated, traumatized, mocked, and ostracized. Quebec was left outside the Constitution of Canada. 'The Constitution is not worth the paper it's written on,' he maintained. Quebec was isolated when, in fact, the whole operation was driven by Quebec's most respected representative, Pierre Trudeau, with 70 Quebec MPs, and all for Quebec reasons." "Attack of the killer Meech," *Globe and Mail* (June 21, 2000).

the 1984 federal election.[11] In that election, the Progressive Conservatives succeeded in winning 58 out of the 75 federal seats in Quebec and a majority position in the House of Commons. Accepting the separatist's interpretation of the 1982 events had apparently contributed to the party's success. Both the separatists and Progressive Conservatives managed to profit electorally from the nationally divisive interpretation they put on the constitutional developments.

As prime minister, Mulroney set about righting what he had identified as the injury to Quebec. As a step in this process, he appointed Lucien Bouchard, a dynamic Quebec nationalist and friend, to the position of Canadian ambassador to France. Bouchard had been chair of the 1980 pro-independence referendum campaign. Then, in 1988, Mulroney brought Bouchard back from France and appointed him to his cabinet, where he served as minister of the environment until he resigned in 1990.

At roughly the same time as he appointed Bouchard to the cabinet, Mulroney relaunched constitutional negotiations with the provinces, aiming primarily at reconciling Quebec to the 1982 reform package. Some thought it was a mistake to reopen the constitutional issue, since time appeared to be healing the wounds—created by and serving some parties' interests—of the 1982 negotiations.

In two rounds of constitutional negotiations leading up to the Meech Lake Accord and then the Charlottetown Accord, the Mulroney government attempted to reconcile the now-Liberal government of Quebec to accepting an amended constitution. Mulroney had, of course, helped to make this reconciliation necessary. Now he hoped to undo that damage and strengthen his position in the country at large with his initiatives. Reflecting back on Meech in 2000, journalist William Johnson wrote, "Meech was the consummation of Brian Mulroney's Faustian bargain with the ultranationalists. It gave him power, twice. Now the country still pays the forfeit."[12]

Many process and content factors account for the defeat of Mulroney's major constitutional initiatives. The Meech Lake Accord was reached by the

---

11   On this point, see Peter H. Russell, *Constitutional Odyssey: Can Canadians Be a Sovereign People?* (Toronto: University of Toronto Press, 1992), 133.

12   Johnson, "Attack of the killer Meech."

premiers and the federal government but required the approval of provincial legislatures. There was almost no public input to the negotiations, and many citizens were not prepared for changes in the extremely sensitive area of Quebec-Canada relations. The lack of trust in those elected to represent them surfaced in intense public suspicion and hostility. Meech was an exercise in elitist politics in an era when, at least at the constitutional level, many saw this political style as unacceptable.

Partisan politics and other features of partyocracy further complicated the approval process. The acceptance of Meech by the premiers was not repeated in all of their legislatures. Many Liberals opposed it. Undoubtedly, some were unwilling to give Mulroney a constitutional victory regardless of the merits of the accord. Former Liberal Prime Minister Trudeau came roaring out of retirement to denounce the agreement and, later, the Charlottetown Accord. Supporters of both accords downplayed the importance of his interventions at the time they were made. However, the failure of elites to educate Canadians by sharing power with them was coming home to roost.

In partyocracy, the public reaction to policy initiatives depends heavily on the leaders associated with them, rather than with their substance, with which most citizens will have only a superficial knowledge. Although leadership issues were not the only ones involved, in the influence contest between the retired and seemingly principled Trudeau and the in-office and seemingly manipulative partisan, Mulroney, Trudeau won.[13] The Meech Lake Accord failed to win approval in two legislatures. Its defeat was followed later by the rejection of the Charlottetown Accord in a national referendum.

---

13   Trudeau's and Mulroney's positions on Meech and Charlottetown may have been heavily influenced by their conflicting personal/partisan feelings. Trudeau's views were put down to personal pique by his long-time bureaucratic advisor, Gordon Robertson. He believes Trudeau was determined that Mulroney would not succeed where he had failed, while Mulroney was motivated, it seems, by a desire to highlight his superior negotiating skills. See Gordon Robertson, *Memoirs of a Very Civil Servant* (Toronto: University of Toronto Press, 2000), 338–39. Democracy is intended to overwhelm the personal feelings of one or a group of leaders with the wisdom of the collective. Partyocracy empowers a party leader and makes the polity heavily dependent on his or her judgment.

In the course of Mr. Mulroney's last-minute negotiations with the premiers to make the Meech Lake Accord more acceptable, his recruitment of Quebec soft separatists as candidates returned to haunt him—and us. Angered by the proceedings, or perhaps just seeing an opportunity to strike out on his own in the party power game—or a mix of both—Lucien Bouchard resigned from the cabinet and the PC party, taking five colleagues from Quebec with him. The Bloc Québécois party was launched.

Formal ties between the national and provincial wings of the Liberal and Conservative parties had long since been severed. Now a provincial separatist party had links with an Ottawa "cousin," also committed to dismantling the country. The Bloc gave Quebec separatists a strong voice in the House of Commons and a cadre of tax-supported MPs to bolster the separatist position back home. Further, with changes in electoral law relating to party finances, the campaigns of the BQ would be partially financed by Canadians outside Quebec.[14]

With the collapse of the Tory vote following the 1993 election, the Bloc became the Official Opposition in Ottawa. It did this exclusively on the strength of its Quebec vote—49.3 percent and 54 of 75 seats. Weak feelings of national citizenship; all the years of Ottawa-bashing by Quebec's provincial parties; and the resentment felt as a result of the role played by the national parties in the province (collaboration with Duplessis, etc.) made the success of the Bloc possible.

Mulroney responded to the intense controversy the Meech Lake Accord aroused, and its final rejection, by appointing the Citizens' Forum on Canada's Future (the Spicer Commission).[15] The Commission was widely seen as a move to let the public vent its hostility to the citizen-excluding procedures followed in negotiating Meech and, more generally, toward elitist politics. The Commission consulted exceptionally widely and issued a report confirming the resentment we were feeling toward party representation. Canadians expressed the desire to be more responsible, engaged citizens. It was not a new message or one to which the politicians were prepared to

---

14   See the discussion of this point in chapter 9.
15   Canada, *Citizens' Forum on Canada's Future* (Ottawa: Minister of Supply and Services Canada, 1991). For the Commission's terms of reference, see appendix A, 149–51.

respond, except by increased informal, i.e., non-binding, consultation. The report of the Spicer Commission was buried quickly.

The Meech experience suggested that government must utilize a different strategy if it was to get its second (and more ambitious) attempt to amend the constitution adopted. Prior to the meetings that finalized the Charlottetown Accord, consultations were conducted across the country. The wide range of views expressed by citizens, some well informed, were left to the government to collate and act on, if it chose to do so. But they could easily be set aside, since those expressing them had no claim to be representative of the wider population. Academics noted the significant disconnect between the views expressed by citizens in the consultation exercise and those acted on by those negotiating the Accord—a disconnect characteristic of a system lacking formal agencies directly linking citizens and their representatives.[16]

Not wanting a repeat of the defeat of the Meech Lake Accord, the country's leaders decided, in an unprecedented move, to submit the Charlottetown Accord to a national referendum. Three provinces had already passed legislation requiring a referendum before they could ratify the Accord. The inability of elected representatives in partyocracy to act with democratic authority on so important a matter was recognized.

The recognition was belated and should be extended to other major policy decisions, but through a better means than a referendum. Some of these policies, such as the adoption of free trade with the United States, also have a tremendously significant impact on the lives of Canadians.

The Charlottetown Accord was long, complex, confusing, and incomplete. Despite the overwhelming support of elites for it, the Accord

---

16   Political scientist Matthew Mendelsohn responded to the suggestion that the negative vote on the Charlottetown Accord was a citizen rather than a system failure: "The Charlottetown Accord did not fail because 'mass input/legitimization ... (ensures that) constitutionalism will not succeed'; it failed, in part, because mass publics lacked sites for integrative bargaining, which permitted opposition to be more easily mobilized, because the public sensed no ownership of the document" (255–56) and "New public sites for managing the inevitable conflicts of interest and values are necessary in an era when citizens refuse to defer to elites on constitutional questions" (258). "Public Brokerage: Constitutional Reform and the Accommodation of Mass Publics," *Canadian Journal of Political Science*, 33, 2 (June 2000).

was defeated by a politically alienated citizenry, the majority of whom were unprepared to trust the judgment of their elected party representatives. As long as we are kept at arm's length from political engagement and responsibility, and uninformed, there will be a strong tendency for us to vote "no" to any fundamental political change that has not been approved in deliberations in which we are included. It is the rational response of people who are unsure of what is going on and do not want to jeopardize what they have, however unsatisfactory it may be.

The Progressive Conservative Party, led by Mulroney's successor, Kim Campbell, was able to win only two seats in the 1993 election; the Liberals then resumed responsibility for the Quebec/national unity file. Catering to separatist forces in Quebec had proven beneficial electorally to the PCs— but only in the short term. The party's success was at the expense of the country: the separatist position was strengthened during the two terms of a Progressive Conservative government that strove to bring Quebec into the constitution.

In 1995, a second Quebec referendum on separation was defeated, this time by a hair's breadth—50.6 percent of voters said no and 49.42 percent yes. Only 54,288 votes separated the two sides.[17] If half of those had voted differently, the separatists would have been victorious. Midway through

---

17   Polling shows dramatically how dangerous it is to rely on voting on such matters. It can only produce an ambiguous message from citizens that is subject to self-serving interpretation by politicians. A *Toronto Star* poll reported on the motivations of those who voted in the 1995 referendum on Quebec separatism: "One year after the 1995 vote, pollsters found that of the 49.4 percent of Quebecers who voted Yes, almost half said they did so to spur negotiations between Quebec and Ottawa on a new partnership, not to separate.

"But not all of the 50.6 percent who voted "No" did so out of a conviction that Quebec should remain part of Canada. More than a third (37 percent) said they did so out of fear of the economic consequences of sovereignty.

"An overwhelming 81 percent of Quebecers want to reconcile with other Canadians and put the national unity issue behind them, federally commissioned polls say." The polls were conducted in May, July, and October of 1996, a year after the 1995 vote. *Toronto Star* (February 26, 1997). A more recent poll puts the percentage of Quebecers saying it is time to move on issues other than sovereignty at 84 percent. *Globe and Mail/Le Devoir*/Leger Marketing poll cited in Richard Mackie, "Quebecers want ADQ—they think," the *Globe and Mail* (June 1, 2002), A10. The 84 percent will not get their wish as long as a major party relies on the issue of separation as its raison d'être.

a campaign that was going badly, Lucien Bouchard, with his personal charisma, was called on to rescue it from then-Premier Jacques Parizeau.

Leadership qualities played a crucial role in determining the vote on a question that required careful consideration of a wide range of factors.[18] Voters, dumbed-down by the system, were ill-prepared to engage with the issue in that way. Following the referendum, Bouchard replaced Parizeau as premier of Quebec. After leaving that post and returning to private life, Bouchard has become increasing critical of his former colleagues in the PQ, dismissing sovereignty as nothing more than a dream that won't be achieved any time soon.[19] Sovereignty, the issue which had distracted Canadian politicians for years was, one assumes, no longer consistent with Mr. Bouchard's interests and ambitions.

After the defeat of the second referendum, the PQ remained committed to separatism and to another referendum "when winning conditions exist." Neither Bouchard nor Bernard Landry, who replaced him in 2001, deemed these conditions present during their tenures in office. In the 2005 contest to replace Landry as leader of the PQ, André Boisclair, who was successful, promised to hold another referendum "as soon as possible" after receiving a mandate to do so in his first election.[20]

Following the close result of the 1995 referendum, and recognizing the possibility of another vote soon, the federal government responded with two actions. First, it launched an extensive public relations/advertising campaign in Quebec—the "sponsorship program"—to raise the positive profile of the national administration, kept low during the years of consociational politics. The program backfired seriously. Many Quebecers resented it as a crude attempt to manipulate the loyalties of the people of the province. When it was revealed that the funds spent had been mishandled—with some going into the hands of Liberal insiders, the Quebec Liberal Party, and even

18   On Bouchard's impact on the referendum outcome, see Pierre Martin and Richard Nadeau, "Understanding Opinion Formation on Quebec Sovereignty," in *Citizen Politics,* Joanna Everitt and Brenda O'Neill, eds.(Toronto: Oxford University Press, 2002), 153.

19   Rhéal Séguin, "Bouchard says PQ on cusp of 'radicalism'", the *Globe and Mail* (February 17, 2010), A9.

20   Rhéal Séguin, "Boisclair crushes PQ rivals," *Globe and Mail* (November 16, 2005), A1.

the PQ—there was further outrage. The federal Liberal government and party were discredited in Quebec and in the rest of the country.[21] Its role as unifying agency was weakened still further.

Mr. Justice Gomery was appointed to investigate the misallocation of funds and to report.[22] Canadians unwilling to reward the behaviour of the Liberal government, as revealed in the Gomery hearings, turned to the principal opposition party in the 2006 election. The Harper Conservatives were the lucky beneficiaries and were able to form a minority government. Naturally, its leader claimed a mandate for all his policies.

In partyocracy, if the political "orchestra" is playing jarringly off-key, the audience can only hope that a change to an eager alternative conductor sitting in the audience will improve the performance. It is a big gamble and one the policy democracy/constituency parliament model would not force on voters.

Perhaps the ill-fated Liberal advertising campaign would not have been necessary had federal party governments, chasing short-term electoral support, not lowered their profile in Quebec by allowing the province to opt out of citizen-supportive, national programs.[23] In doing so, it was acceding to demands by separatists and nationalists with no interest in a strong Canada. Further, the advertising campaign would not have been so disastrous had Liberal officials not used it as a way of rewarding unsavoury supporters in the province, who seized on it to line their pockets.

There are no institutional arrangements in place in partyocracy to facilitate a serious dialogue between opinion leaders in the constituencies and constituency representatives in the national government. The kind

---

21   In the middle of the Gomery enquiry, in a poll conducted for the *Globe and Mail* and *Le Devoir* by Léger Marketing, a repeat of the 1995 referendum question, was supported by 54 percent of Quebecers. Seventy-six percent of Quebecers reported feeling betrayed by the former prime minister and the Liberal Party of Canada following that vote. Rhéal Séguin, "54% in Quebec back sovereignty," *Globe and Mail* (April 27, 2005), A1.

22   Justice John Gomery, Phase 1, Report, "Who is Responsible?" (Ottawa: Minister of Public Works and Government Services, 2005).

23   The opting-out has undoubtedly contributed to the primary identification of Quebec citizens with the province (51%) rather than with Canada (35%). Source: poll conducted for the Association of Canadian Studies by Environics Research Group/ Focus Canada, (May 24, 2003). www/erg.environics.net.

of communications the Liberal Party used to try to fill the vacuum their absence creates proved counterproductive.

The second action stemming from the 1995 referendum was the adoption of the Clarity Act by parliament. Its contents reflected the advice received from a federal reference to the Supreme Court on the legality of a unilateral provincial declaration of independence.[24] The Court stated that such unilateralism would not be legal and set out the process that should be followed in the event a majority of citizens in the province endorsed succession. The Act, reflecting the Court's advice, among other provisions would involve Ottawa in reviewing the question submitted to voters. It would also require the federal government to negotiate separation with Quebec as a prelude to negotiations with the provinces, also parties to the secession process. The size of a "yes" majority required needed to start the negotiations on Quebec secession is left open in the Act.

It is important that voters in Quebec know in advance of a vote on separation what the position of the federal government would be in the event of a "yes" vote. The Clarity Act, adopted unilaterally by Ottawa, was intended to provide that. The statute was, however, promptly rejected by the Quebec government.[25] Since its adoption, there have been several statements by national politicians endorsing the position that 50 percent plus one would be sufficient to allow Quebec to withdraw from the federation. These undercut the national position, set out in the Clarity Act and the constitution, which

---

24   Canada, The Clarity Act, 2000, c.26 The principal provisions of the Act are: the House of Commons should determine whether the question on the referendum put to Quebec voters would clearly allow them to express their will on the issue of becoming an independent state. In considering whether there has been a clear expression of the will of Quebecers to leave Canada, the government of Canada should consider (a) the size of the majority that cast its vote for the secessionist option, (b) the percentage of eligible voters who cast ballots, and (c) any other matters or circumstances it considers to be relevant. If the voting requirement is met, then the procedure set out in the Constitution for its amendment, i.e., negotiations with the governments of Canada and the other provinces, would be required.

25   Quebec, Bill 99 (2000, Chapter 46) "An act respecting the exercise of the fundamental rights and prerogatives of the Québec people and the Québec state." (Québec Official Publisher) www.canlii.org/gc/laws/indexhtml pdf

provide that extensive negotiations with federal and provincial governments would be needed before separation could take place.[26]

The official position of the PQ is that a unilateral declaration of national sovereignty would be declared immediately following a "yes" vote, and a law would be passed "declaring that only the government of Quebec may raise taxes from the Quebec population."[27] In short, there can be no assurance that the conditions set out in the Clarity Act would be accepted by Quebec as legitimate.[28] The probability is that they would not be.

The province is no stranger to violence related to separation; every community has elements in it ready to use politics or religion, or both, to rationalize resorting to it. The inability of partyocracy to vest decisions of the national government and courts with more than weak democratic legitimacy enhances the possibility that violence and extra legal means might be used in any future struggle over Quebec independence.[29]

The current (2010) situation. The party search for votes in Quebec, too often at the expense of Canadian unity, goes on. The Liberal Party of Quebec, led by a former national progressive conservative, Jean Charest, won the election in 2003 and the two subsequent contests, eliminating the chance of another referendum for several years, at least. Charest's approach of working steadily toward more autonomy for Quebec within Canada, is seen by some, however, as, "death [for the country] by a thousand cuts."[30] Each cut would

---

26   William Johnson, "Still speaking with forked tongues," *Globe and Mail* (August 20, 2008), A13.

27   Paul Wells, "My, what big teeth you have," *Maclean's* (November 28, 2005), 25.

28   Polling reveals that 50 percent of Quebecers think that 50 percent plus one is a sufficiently large vote for Quebec to leave Canada. Brian Laghi, "Quebec still torn on future in Canada," *Globe and Mail* (October. 22, 2005), A12.

29   A constant argument of the separatists is that Canada will be better off without Quebec and vice versa. A comforting thought, but a country split into two sections with an independent country in between, and facing many challenges, will be difficult to hold together. See Gloria Galloway, "Canada better off without Quebec, Duceppe says," *Globe and Mail* (November 13, 2004), A8.

30   The varying degrees of commitment of Quebec party leaders to separation from Canada, and the Harper government response to them, is summarized by William Johnson, "The autonomist's threat: death by a thousand cuts," *Globe and Mail* (March 31, 2007), A25.

make a move to complete separation less threatening to Quebecers and easier for them to accept.

In 2006, the newly reformulated Conservative Party—a merger of the Alliance and Progressive Conservatives—led by Stephen Harper, defeated the short-lived national minority Liberal government and formed its own minority administration. In office, with the expectation that supporting Charest would be reciprocated in a federal election, Prime Minister Harper, formerly critical of federal Liberal concessions to Quebec, himself adopted a variety of concessions intended to bolster the position of the Quebec Liberals. [31]

Politically engaged Albertans did not attack Harper's change of position. Perhaps they were reluctant to weaken one of their own while he was in office and able to ensure that public policy important to Alberta's politicians, i.e., development of the tar sands, was supported.

Harper worked closely with the Quebec Liberals in their struggle to gain sufficient support to win the province's 2007 election against the separatists. [32] It was correctly anticipated, however, that even with that support, Charest would, at best, be returned in a minority position. The surprise in the election was that the runner-up party was not the PQ but the autonomy-supporting Action Démocratique du Quebec (ADQ), led by Mario Dumont. The PQ suffered a serious defeat, and the position of its sister, the federal Bloc Québécois, was weakened. The PQ and ADQ, in opposition to the Liberal minority government in Quebec, will continue to exploit every possible opportunity to drive wedges between Quebec and Canada and will pressure the Quebec Liberals to do so as well.

Before and after the Quebec election, Prime Minister Harper took actions that reflected a continued commitment to his decentralist views. For example, in November of 2006, the BQ introduced a motion asking that the House recognize the Québécois as a "nation." The PM, without consulting his

---

31   Author and columnist, Lawrence Martin, compares Harper's attempt to "buy" Quebec's support for Canada and for his Conservative party to the earlier attempt of Mulroney. "Shades of Mulroney: Harper rolls the dice in Quebec," *Globe and Mail* (March 24, 2007), A25.

32   The artificiality of many partisan divisions is suggested by the fact that the Liberal Premier of Quebec was, prior to his election to that post, a prominent federal Progressive Conservative and, in 2007, was a close political ally of the leader of the (new) national Conservative party.

cabinet, announced that he would ask the House to endorse the motion with the words "within a united Canada" added, so that it read, "That this House recognize that the Québécois form a nation within a united Canada." Harper's intergovernmental affairs minister resigned to protest the lack of consultation. The majority of members of all parties voted for the motion. No party could afford to have it on record that it had voted against the resolution when it next campaigned in Quebec. Harper's action was seen as clever politics designed, among other partisan objectives, to confuse the Liberal Party leadership contest then in progress. As is commonplace in partyocracy, the views of Canadians—77 percent of those living outside Quebec were opposed—went unrepresented.[33]

After the Quebec election, Harper followed up the recognition, in Quebec, with a speech in French, wherein he is reported to have said, "a re-elected Conservative government would lead a Canada that is 'strong, united, and free, with a Quebec [that is] autonomous and proud.'" Later, a representative for the party confirmed the worst suspicions of some, stating, "The recognition of the Quebec nation within Canada allows us to think that we can put some meat around it, and that a majority government is more able to do a number of things, while being respectful of all of the provinces."[34]

The *Globe and Mail* commented editorially on these developments: "To raise constitutional change at this time is to put party-building [in Quebec] ahead of nation-building."[35] The observation is certainly appropriate, but parties have nearly always proved willing to compromise their commitment to nation-building in their quest for voting support. Why should one

---

33   Immediately after the action of the Commons, a Leger Marketing survey found 77 percent of Canadians outside Quebec opposed to it. Canadian Press, "Quebec-as-nation support low: poll," *Peterborough Examiner* (November 29, 2006), A6. But in commenting on the action of his government, PM Harper stated, "I think tonight was an historic night; Canadians across the country said 'yes' to Quebec, 'yes' to Quebecers, and Quebecers said 'yes' to Canada." Transcript, CBC news (November 27, 2006). Politicians can claim to speak for Canadians, because citizens have no means to speak for themselves—the House of Commons elected to do so is disabled by party control of MPs.
34   Daniel Leblanc, "Tories plan to bolster Quebec in Constitution," *Globe and Mail* (April 2, 2008), 1.
35   Editorial, "A Dangerous message to Quebec," *Globe and Mail* (April 3, 2008). A12.

expect Stephen Harper, struggling to turn a minority government into a majority, to do otherwise? He is as much a captive of partyocracy and the competitive strategies it imposes as his predecessors. The only possible difference with Harper is that his action may be dictated not only by his party's competitive interests but also by his personal vision of Canada as an even more decentralized federation.

One of Canada's most respected journalists, Jeffrey Simpson, is in no doubt about where these developments are leading: "This prime minister now argues that people should build their own "nations" or provinces, even to the point of autonomy, and that through this building-block process Canada can be strengthened.

"He is implicitly, therefore, rejecting any idea that Canada might be something more than the sum of its parts. Canada, therefore, becomes a political entity assembled by provincialists, nationalists, and autonomists who grant what they wish to a limited federal superstructure but keep the important powers for their localities."[36]

To shift Canada from a federation to a confederation of semi-autonomous "states" topped by a limited central government without a specific mandate— and when turning back would be virtually impossible—would be an extreme abuse of prime ministerial power. It would also be an act of incredible personal arrogance—the kind of behaviour that partyocracy, supporting prime ministerial government, encourages.

When the Quebec Liberals finally lose office to the PQ or some other party, it is difficult to predict how much further the province's government will push for sovereignty or autonomy. "Conditions" will determine that; in the meantime, politics in Canada will continue to be played out against the party-maintained threat Quebec poses to the integrity of Canada.[37]

Since 1867, getting on to a century and a half, Quebec has been a province in the Canadian federation. The province has been difficult to integrate into the new federation because of its history and cultural differences. Even so, that period should have been more than enough to solidify the relationship

---

36   Jeffrey Simpson, "Harper fishes for votes in Quebec with Canada's future," *Globe and Mail* (May 2, 2007), A23.
37   Rhéal Séguin, "Parti Québécois reneges on promise of referendum," *Globe and Mail* (September 9, 2002), A4.

of the people of the province with Canada. Separatists are prepared to admit that during that extended period the cultural rights of Francophone citizens within Quebec were respected. The most serious abuse of Quebecers, if there was any at all, came not from the national government, or the English-speaking majority outside Quebec, but from the Duplessis government elected by Quebecers.

Something, however, has blocked the creation of a strong Canadian citizenship embracing both linguistic groups. Parties, national and provincial, found success in Quebec by exaggerating and exploiting the fears of assimilation and domination common to the Francophone majority in Quebec who live as a minority in Canada. Outside Quebec, the Conservatives and other parties tended to cast Francophone Quebec as a threat to the values and interests of English-speaking citizens. There were votes, but not many, in stressing the common interests of citizens on both sides of the borders of Quebec.

When Ottawa's political elites were confronted by the growing threat to the federation posed by Quebec separatists, the leaders of the three national parties were forced to move Quebec-Ottawa relations almost to the top of their concerns. Virtually every effort made within partyocracy to reconcile Quebec to continued membership in the federation has, however, been counterproductive. When Ottawa has given preferential treatment to Quebec to dampen down separatist forces, it has convinced Quebec provincial politicians of the value of maintaining the threat of separation. When the national government has interacted with Quebec on constitutional issues, Quebec separatists have sought, and inevitably found, issues that it could exploit to stoke separatist fires. There is now a dangerous feeling of inevitability about the eventual collapse of the country.

The collapse, if it comes, will be very much a product of the political system; in general, Quebecers and other Canadians have positive feelings about the country and each other. The Maclean's year-end poll in 2003 reports, "The national unity issue, that perennial buzzword for the Canadian psychodrama of the past 40 years, has all but dropped off the radar. Only 2 percent of Quebecers (and virtually no one elsewhere in Canada) consider it a major issue now. Too bad for those few hard-nosed separatists who cringe at the spectre of federal intervention, but Quebecers are far more inclined than other Canadians to urge Ottawa to focus on improving social programs."[38]

Those "few hard-nosed separatists" will continue to interpret every attempt of Ottawa to strengthen national social programs, which are desired by Quebecers, as an attack on the province. Outside party politics, separation is of little concern in Quebec but inside, it looms large.[39] Separatism is too valuable as a vote-getter for some of the province's party power brokers to allow Quebecers to forget it when they act politically.

It is not unheard of for unrepresentative politicians plying their trade in a partyocracy to manoeuvre citizens into accepting a breakup of their country that the people do not want.[40] In the case of some countries, a division may be deemed positive. But separation is not desired by Canadians on either side of the linguistic divide.

It is now more than 10 years after the narrow victory of the "no" forces in the second referendum on separatism. The anniversary was marked by numerous assessments of progress in stemming the tide of separatism. The virtually unanimous verdict: none.[41] Clearly, the strategies followed in attempting to counter the threat of Quebec leaving the federation have not been effective; they have, however, been the strategies dictated by partyocracy. That system should be replaced with one that gives politicians in and outside Quebec the incentive to build national unity. Involving Quebec constituency leaders directly in making national policy as elected members of constituency parliaments could accomplish that.

---

38   Benoit Aubin, "Canada, Oui," *Maclean's* year-end poll, *Maclean's* (December 29, 2003), 38.

39   The current (2008) leader of the PQ, Pauline Marois, while admitting the sovereignty has lost "effervescence," promises to revitalize it with a new manifesto for sovereignty and, if her party is elected, to govern Quebec as a nation, not a province. Rhéal Séguin, "Sovereignty not dead, Marois says," *Globe and Mail* (May 18, 2008), A10.

40   People in both sections of Czechoslovakia were opposed when their politicians, without a referendum, severed the country in 1993. The result of the severance has been generally positive, unlike others, i.e., Ireland, India.

41   See, as examples, Jeffrey Simpson, "Why There'll Be Another Referendum in Quebec," *Globe and Mail* (Oct 28, 2005). A29; Martin Partriquin, "Little Resolved Decade After Vote," *Toronto Star* (October 29, 2005); ... Laghi, "Quebec Still Torn on Future," *Globe and Mail* (October 22, 2005), A1.

Western Canada. It is not just the dynamics of party politics in Quebec that disrupts nation building. Alberta, and to some extent the West, makes a contribution as well. Parties in that region too are caught up in a political system that encourages, or even requires, them to adopt a grievance strategy vis-à-vis Ottawa in order to succeed.

The West was opened for settlement, and provinces established, in the latter half of the 19th and early years of the 20th century. This development was seen in the East as offering a new source of raw materials and a market for the products of its manufacturers. The perception, understandably, fuelled resentment among Albertans, and they wanted their views represented in the House of Commons. This was difficult in the existing system.

The Liberal and Conservative MPs who they elected went to the House of Commons and joined the caucuses of their respective parties. In the caucuses, where issues were discussed behind closed doors, they were outnumbered by Eastern MPs. MPs emerging from caucus sessions were subject to party discipline and obliged to defend their party's positions on policy. Westerners were hard to convince that their interests were being given fair consideration.

The Alberta wing of the Liberal Party governed the province in its earliest years. Tainted by its association with the national Eastern-dominated party, however, it was soon a casualty. Most voters turned to parties that promised stronger support for provincial interests, as their politicians defined them, in the House of Commons. The provincial wings of the national parties were seen by many as unsuitable spokespersons for these interests, until later, when they established formal independence of their national namesakes— and, even then, many still doubted.

The pattern of electing federal and provincial representatives from provincially based parties for long periods started in Alberta in 1921. The United Farmers of Alberta (UFA) "party" was elected provincially; a large contingent of national Progressive party candidates, which included UFA MPs, was sent to Ottawa. The pattern held, but with the demise of these agrarian parties in the 1920s and '30s, Social Credit became the principal party vehicle, representing Albertans both provincially and federally. After the demise of Social Credit, Reform/Alliance, assumed the mantle of champion of Alberta interests in Ottawa in 1987. The CCF (later NDP) played a similar representational role in Saskatchewan from the time of its organization in the early 1930s.

Even with the advantage the first-past-the-post electoral system gives parties with concentrated voter support, the provincial parties were not able to entirely drive out the national Liberal and Progressive Conservative parties. Both elected some federal members in Alberta during most of the 20th century. The provincial Progressive Conservatives have governed the province from 1971 forward.

A new party with limited resources must attract support by articulating easily raised or existing concerns. Leaders of such parties can, without much difficulty, convince potential voters who are in a minority nationally and possess some distinctive economic, social, or cultural interests, that the majority-dominated government does not treat them fairly. Once a culture of grievance is well established—and at one time Albertans did have substantial grievances with the national administration—it can be appealed to (and strengthened) without much risk of antagonizing many of the province's voters.

While the parties based in the Western provinces had extensive policy platforms, their appeal to voters in national elections was based largely on their identification with their province. They campaigned on, and usually exaggerated, past and current grievances with Ottawa, promising to raise them in the House of Commons.

In our electoral politics, a minority that is geographically concentrated is faced with a dilemma as it seeks to maximize its influence in the Commons. Should its members seek representation through the dominant national party or parties—or support a provincially based party whose MPs are freer to voice the province's demands on, and grievances with, the national administration in the House of Commons, but who are not part of the governing team? Alberta's voters behaved as one would expect, trying one strategy and then the other, depending on a variety of factors. The appeal of supporting provincial protest parties was, however, the stronger of the two options.

With provincial and national Alberta politicians overwhelmingly critical of the government in Ottawa, the national government's case for its policies was only weakly heard. The Liberal and Conservative MPs who did manage to be elected in Alberta were more likely to express some sympathy with the prevailing sense that Westerners were being treated unfairly in the federation than they were to challenge it.

In 1987, Preston Manning launched the West's most recent "protest" party, the Reform party, in Alberta. The party regrouped as the Alliance party and then merged with the Progressive Conservatives in 2003 to become part of the new "Conservative Party" under a Western leader, Stephen Harper. In the final regrouping under Harper the party lost its interest in democratic reform

In his autobiography, Manning provides a good example of the interpretation the protest parties put on national policy. He wrote: "I waited through the Trudeau years, which many Western Canadians regard as the political equivalent of the Dark Ages. It was as though Ottawa were a foreign country and Liberal ministers were representatives of a foreign power. It was not just that the National Energy Program transferred $100 billion worth of wealth from the West to Ottawa and consuming provinces; it was that this outrage was presented as being in our own best interests by federal politicians and bureaucrats who claimed to understand those interests better than we did."[42]

When Ottawa's negotiations with Alberta on the National Energy Program (NEP) were completed, the premier of the province, speaking in Ottawa, called it a "balanced agreement"—an assessment he and his colleagues did not often, if ever, express back in Alberta.[43] The agreement was too valuable a weapon—easily understood by a mass audience and feeding into established suspicions—for provincial politicians not to use it against their adversaries. On the other hand, policies related to the development of Alberta's oil resources that were inconsistent with the image of a hostile Ottawa were given little attention. There was, and is now, scarcely a mention of the National Oil Policy (NOP) that preceded the NEP.

The huge new oil strike in Leduc in 1947 launched Alberta's petroleum industry into the big time. Initially, however, because Alberta petroleum

---

42   Preston Manning, *Think Big* (Toronto: McClelland and Stewart, 2002), 24.
43   The reference to the "balanced agreement" is cited (180) in the account of the background to, and negotiation of the NEP, contained in Christina McCall and Stephen Clarkson, *Trudeau and Our Times* (Toronto: McClelland and Stewart, 1994), 162–86.

was high-priced compared to imports, it was shut out of Eastern Canadian markets. To make the industry viable despite its high costs, the federal government adopted the NOP in 1960. The oil market west of the Ottawa Valley line was reserved for Western Canadian petroleum. Consumers in Ontario west were required to pay higher-than world-market prices for the province's oil, prices that included royalties for the Alberta government.

This transfer of wealth from east to west continued until 1973, when the dramatic rise in world oil prices made the policy obsolete. From that point on, Alberta's oil revenues soared. To restrain costs to consumers, the National Energy Policy (NEP) was adopted by Ottawa. However, during the period that this policy was in force, prices still tripled in two years and quadrupled in five.[44] Alberta and its petroleum industry were able to cash in on the world price boom at the expense of consumers, but not to the extent that they would have if the NEP had not been in force. This exchange of support between areas of Canada should have strengthened national ties. Instead, interpreted by politicians capitalizing on grievance, it merely added to the hostility of many Albertans toward Ottawa.

The significance of citizen identification is illustrated in such cases. The identification of Albertans with their province, emphasized by its party politicians, made it difficult for people to react as Canadians willing to consider the common good.

Once again, a major clash over petroleum is shaping up between Ottawa and Alberta. This time it is over the development and regulation of the Athabasca tar sands. Unfortunately, it must be settled against the backdrop of a century of suspicion of Ottawa, fed by parties seeking support from Alberta voters. That backdrop, plus the weak sense of citizenship inculcated by partyocracy, will make it difficult for Albertans to consider the impact of the sands development on the rest of Canada, and beyond, or to accept with understanding and good will national intervention to protect the environmental interests we all share.

For years, policy-makers in Ottawa have had to bend policy to avoid losing support in Quebec. The same bending is now being seen in relation to petroleum policy. The interests of all Canadians have to be compromised for

44   Bill Longstaff, "Alberta's oil riches created by OPEC, not by politicians or CEOs," *CCPA Monitor* (February 2005), 13.

electoral success in the West. Our country, its constructive global citizenship once a source of pride, now has the worst record of the G8 nations on adopting measures to deal with climate change.[45]

Nor can we expect this to change in the short term. Mr. Harper's base of support is Alberta; he is ideologically opposed to a strong national government; he has been notably unwilling to take global warming as seriously as most of the world's leaders and scientists do.[46] Anxious to make an electoral breakthrough in the West, neither of the two major opposition parties is taking a strong stand challenging the petroleum development policies of the Alberta government in the national and international interest.

Despite the concessions to Alberta from a national government headed by an Albertan, the pattern of attacking Ottawa goes on from the government's "friends" in the province. On the concession side, Jeffrey Simpson observes that the government has been so deferential to Alberta opinion that, "Mr. Harper hasn't spoken a single 'home truth' to his fellow Albertans. In spite of the care exercised to not offend Albertans," however, Simpson notes that the Conservative government of the province has "…sent out 'talking points' to [its] MLA's listing a series of grievances with the Harper government. MLAs were told to discuss these grievances with their constituents…."[47] The politically useful sense of grievance must be kept alive even when the province's representatives dominate Ottawa.

---

45   According to the 2009 rankings in the Climate Scorecard issued by the World Widelife Federation and Allianz SE insurance. The rankings prompted this comment from columnist Jeffrey Simpson: "Climate change is not an issue that Mr. Harper feels passionately about, or at least reckons carries any political advantage." *Globe and Mail* (July 8, 09), A13. With prime ministerial government, if the PM does not care, we can do little to get appropriate action.

46   Working as a lobbyist in Alberta prior to a return to politics, Stephen Harper was the prime mover behind the "Firewall" letter sent to the then-premier of Alberta and circulated. In it Harper and colleagues expressed bitter resentment toward the national parties and their governments. The letter called for Alberta to cut all possible ties to the national government, citing Quebec as the model that should be followed. With its wealth, the letter argued, Alberta could afford to go it alone and should act promptly to prevent an economic slowdown which might tempt the national government to force a greater sharing of Alberta's wealth with the rest of Canada. Stephen Harper et al., "An open letter to Ralph Klein," *National Post* (January 24, 2001).

47   Jeffrey Simpson, "Family feud reflects an old instinct in one-party Alberta," *Globe*

The distorted view of the national government's treatment of Albertans is, of course, not limited to the one example of the petroleum industry. Most Albertans still believe that on many policy matters the interests of the province are ignored by Ottawa and, more generally, that the dominant Eastern establishment does not "respect" the people of the province. Citizens, kept uninformed and lacking in a sense of responsibility for the country at large by the dynamics of partyocracy, are in a weak position to resist their party leaders' constant "Ottawa does not care, doesn't understand, and is unfair to us" rhetoric.

Facts do little to abate a political culture of victimization and grievance, because in partyocracy citizens are not encouraged to face them. As Eddie Goldenberg, the long-time advisor to Jean Chrétien, wrote commenting on the constants in Canadian politics, "The West will continue to want in,[to be a force in Ottawa] even when it is in."[48]

Alberta joins Quebec in limiting popular support for the national administration and constantly pressing for a decentralization of powers to the provincial governments. At the same time, arguably, the national administration is already too weak to serve Canadians well. Professor John Meisel writes, with academic understatement, "There is a good deal of evidence ... that suggests that the extensive diffusion of power in Canada and the growing relative strength in the provinces have made the development of policies required to deal with emerging problems extraordinarily difficult and that the party system is not particularly well suited to coping with the new challenges."[49]

The exploitation of division and grievance by competing parties has succeeded in frustrating what we might expect the integrative impact of social and economic changes in Canada to be. Roger Gibbins, an Alberta-based political scientist, writes,

Regional differences within the Canadian society appear to be

---

and Mail (June 10, 2009).

48   Eddie Goldenberg, The Way It Works (Toronto: McClelland and Stewart Ltd., 2006), 389.

49   John Meisel, "The Dysfunctions of Canadian Parties: An Exploratory Mapping," in Democracy with Justice, eds. Alain-G. Gagnon and A. Brian Tanguay (Ottawa: Carleton University Press, 1992), 422–23.

waning at the same time that they are waxing within the political system ... the argument that regionalism within the political system reflects regional division within the underlying society has become less tenable over time.

Just as the Quiet Revolution led Quebec into the mainstream of Canadian life while at the same time increasing political conflict between Quebec and the broader Canadian community, so too has the regional homogenization of Canada in the wake of technological and industrial change been associated with increased regional conflict. The implication that one can draw from this is that the primary roots of regional conflict are to be found in the nature of the political system itself and that regional variations in social characteristics are of secondary importance.[50] While there are pronounced variations in the distribution of natural resources and the nature of economic activity, even here it can be argued that the study of regional conflict is primarily a study of political cause and effect.[51]

Gibbins is right in suggesting that politics is the significant source of regional alienation (taking Quebec as a "region"). It must be met with an appropriate political response, as indeed, he urges. But the actual response

50   In a recent comparison of the views of easterners and westerners, a group of Canadian academics concluded that "Support for right-wing positions tends to be higher in the West, but more striking is just how modest these differences are." They continue, "There is one issue where regional differences are really substantial: people's perceptions about how their province is treated by the federal government. In the West, 53 percent of respondents told us that their particular province is treated worse than other provinces. In Ontario, only 12 percent feel their province was treated worse." They noted a substantial difference in the position of Albertans on gun control but attribute this more to the rural-urban split than to differences in the values of Easterners and citizens of western Canada. André Blais, Neil Nevitte, Elizabeth Gidengil, and Richard Nadeau, "What is it that divides us?" *Globe and Mail* (December 18, 2000), A17. Similar findings on feeling neglected by Ottawa are expressed in a poll of British Columbians. See Caroline Alphonso, "BC feeling neglected, poll finds," *Globe and Mail* (February 24, 2001).
51   Gibbins, *Conflict and Unity*, 82. Mildred Schwartz also takes issue with the idea that, on the basis of Canadian experience, social and economic developments will reduce the impact of regionalism in politics. Mildred A. Schwartz, *Politics and Territory* (Montreal and London: McGill-Queen's University Press, 1974), 307. A different mode of representation holds out the hope of doing so, however.

of the party system to the challenge of political integration in recent years has been the launching of two new parties—Reform/Alliance/Conservative and the Bloc Québécois—both basing their appeal primarily on the exploitation of real and imagined grievances with the national administration. This suggests that as long as Canadians continue to rely on the party system to represent them, unproductive regional conflict and the further fragmentation of the country are likely.

Outside the realm of electoral politics, the identification of the majority of Canadians, excluding Quebecers, continues to be first with Canada and then with their province.[52] That is changing, however, particularly in western Canada.[53] With fluctuations after events like the winter Olympics in Vancouver, this decline is likely to continue as long as the present political system remains in place. We get caught up in this struggle between politicians at the two levels of government, often setting aside other interests that are much more relevant to our well-being, when we vote in general elections.[54] This course is leading us to weak central institutions that fail us.

---

52   Mildred Schwartz concludes, "Where one lives has been a principal determinant of how one views the federal government. When we examine the relation with party ties, we find that they have some impact, but quite secondary to that of region." Schwartz, *Politics and Territory*, 298. Conflicting and supporting views of the Schwartz position are found in Harold D. Clarke, Jon H. Pammett, and Marianne C. Stewart, "The Forest for the Trees: Regional (Dis)Similarities in Canadian Political Culture," (69) and William Cross, "The Increasing Importance of Region to Canadian Election Campaigns," (116–28) both in *Regionalism and Party Politics in Canada*, eds. Lisa Young and Keith Archer (Don Mills, Ont.: Oxford University Press, 2002).

53   In 2003, 53 percent (down from 63 percent in 1997) of Albertans told pollsters that they felt "more a citizen of Canada" than of Alberta (46 percent—up from 29 percent in 1997). The same study found that the number of Western Canadians who felt that "they get few benefits [from Canada] and should go it alone," had risen to 40 percent from 35 percent in 2000. The authors of the poll comment, "Since 1997, national attachment has diminished across the country, and there is a growing identification with the provinces. This is particularly apparent in Alberta, where between 1997 and 2003 there has been a 17-point increase in attachment to the province. If current trends continue, Albertans may become more attached to their province than Quebecers are to their own." Poll conducted for the Association of Canadian Studies by Environics Research Group/Focus Canada (May 24, 2003). www/erg.environics.net. The decline continues: A national poll conducted by CROP in 2006 found voters increasingly detached from common touchstones of national identity … just 61 percent felt "very proud" to be Canadian, way down from the 80 percent who felt that way when CROP asked back in 1985 … The parties' lack of vision may reflect a broader dearth of nationalistic fire." John Geddes, "Nobody loves Canada," *Maclean's* (January 23, 2006), 23.

54   In a landmark article on regional conflict in Canada, Richard Simeon pointed out

Pierre Trudeau reminded Canadians that, "Choosing to have feeble federal institutions would be to condemn ourselves to collective weakness in a world that will not be kind to nations divided against themselves."[55] Our status in the world must be of concern to us. In addition, however, we must consider the impact of weak national institutions on the ability of government to serve our everyday needs, from health care to protection of the environment. We need the support of the national government and it, in turn, needs ours if it is to function well.

Party-Led Unifying Strategies

A divisive election over, the governing party or parties must turn to the task of mobilizing public support for its administration. A suggestion for how this mobilization might be accomplished is found in the report of the Task Force on National Unity. It reported finding "A widespread frustration among our fellow citizens with the aimlessness and lack of common purpose that characterizes much of Canadian public life, and a strong desire to commit oneself to some projects and purposes which are held in common among large groups of citizens."[56]

The commitment to great national accomplishments requires leadership that party PMs have difficulty providing. Pierre Trudeau tried to enlist the commitment of Canadians for his vision of a country equally the home of Anglophones and Francophones. Prime Minister Pearson had set the stage.

---

that disadvantaged citizens face a choice among competing explanations for their status: "A poor New Brunswick logger may explain his poverty by saying he is disadvantaged because he is a New Brunswicker, or because he speaks French, or because loggers everywhere always get a poor deal." The choice, Simeon argues, will have important consequences for which axis of political conflict—regional, linguistic, or class—will come to the fore. To date, the first two choices available to Simeon's logger have prevailed and so have pre-empted political conflict based more on class than on regional or ethnic lines." Cited in Gibbins, *Conflict and Unity*, 159. The party capturing this regional vote will often endorse policies hurtful to the class interests of the citizens voting for it. A conspiracy to keep class interests out of politics does not exist, but allowing politics to be based on the concerns of politicians at both levels of government, rather than those of citizens, has that effect.

55   Pierre Elliott Trudeau, cited in Allan Gregg, "Quebec's Final Victory," *The Walrus* (February 2005), 51.

56   Canada, Task Force on National Unity, *A Future Together: Observations and Recommendations* (Ottawa: Task Force on Canadian Unity, 1979), 114.

Responding sympathetically to dramatic developments in Quebec in the 1960s, i.e., to the Quiet Revolution, Pearson signalled the readiness of the national Liberals to open a new era in the relations of English- and French-speaking Canadians, and in the governments of Ottawa and Quebec. The crisis that the Liberal Party had contributed to by its years of politicking in Quebec had now to be dealt with by the Liberals.

Support for official bilingualism was expressed in the report of the Royal Commission on Bilingualism and Biculturalism ("Bi and Bi") that Pearson commissioned to guide government policy in relations with Quebecers and to prepare public opinion to accept it.[57] The report certainly influenced the thinking of the political class in Canada. There must be considerable doubt, however, about whether it had much impact on the vast majority of Canadians. Few would be aware of the Commission's existence: the political restiveness in Quebec was remote from the lives and interests of most. Royal commissions as educative/mobilizing institutions are no substitute for a well-organized consultative system embracing elected representatives and their constituents.

When he replaced Pearson, Trudeau vigorously followed up on the recommendations of the Royal Commission providing, in particular, for recognition of the French language in federal government operations. At the time he did so, the need for action by the federal government to counter the growing separatist sentiment in Quebec was obvious. All parties in the House of Commons supported the adoption of the Official Languages Act of 1969.[58] The Act represented a substantive and symbolic step toward breaking down linguistic barriers and encouraging Canadians to adopt a vision of citizenship that embraced cultural duality—clearly a project that called for a commitment from Canadians.

Of the party unanimity that greeted the Act in the Commons, Professor Gibbins commented, "The surprising thing about opposition to bilingualism is that it failed to find a champion within the party system."[59] This was not really surprising. Party leaders could not afford to alienate Francophones

57   Canada, Report of the Royal Commission on Bilingualism and Biculturalism (Ottawa: Queen's Printer, 1967).
58   Canada, Official Languages Act, adopted 1969, revised 1985. RS, 1985, c.31 (4th supplement).
59   Gibbins, *Conflict and Unity*, 72.

by a high-profile act that would be used against their parties in Quebec for years. The same strategic logic was undoubtedly at play when the Harper Conservative government later sprang its legislation recognizing Quebec as a nation within Canada on the House of Commons. It, too, received unanimous party support.[60]

Undoubtedly, too, the cross-party support of official bilingualism, and of Quebec as a nation within Canada, was a reflection of our political leaders' concern for Canada. There comes a point where parties that may have contributed to the divisive forces in the country as they pursued their electoral interests are forced to modify their course or face the possible disintegration of the polity that supports them.

In the ridings, a different set of pressures was at work on party members and citizens than on MPs in the nation's capital. Referring to House support for the languages act and, later, for the Meech Lake Accord, John Meisel notes, "Both instances of opposition support for the government caused serious dissension within the opposition parties."[61] The dissension was also found among members of the public.

One might expect MPs voting for the Act to be a major force in mobilizing public support for it. However, the political interests, particularly of opposition MPs, discouraged any such effort. Faced with considerable hostility to the government's language policies—and no appropriate forum where they could meet with representative constituents, keep them "up to speed" on national unity issues, and solicit their active support—MPs were poorly equipped to enlist citizen support.

Opposition MPs could rationalize their failure to support in their constituencies what they had voted for in the Commons by thinking that it was up to the governing party to deal with any public hostility to its legislation. The cross-party backing for the languages act in the Commons could not disguise the fact that the program was a Liberal Party initiative intended, among other objectives, to bolster the strength of the party in

60   This was only one of a series of "accommodations" to Quebec seen as intended to bolster the position of the Quebec Liberal Party in an upcoming election. Others included a major boost in equalization payments to the province and establishing a formal role for Quebec in UNESCO. News release, PMO (May 05, 2006). www.pm.pc.gc.ca
61   Meisel, "The Dysfunctions of Canadian Parties," 427n7.

Quebec. For their part, government MPs might see it as in their best electoral interests to avoid discussing and defending the controversial legislation where possible. Citizens could reasonably take the position that it was the responsibility of politicians who insisted on monopolizing political power to sort out the difficulties facing the country.

The enthusiasm of supporters of Trudeau's vision, and there were many, was expressed in a number of ways, particularly by French-immersion programs launched in schools across the country. It was countered, however, by the resentment of others who saw the new language policies as a unjustified sop to Quebec; a vote-buying exercise of the Liberals; a needless expense; part of a conspiracy of the "French" to dominate the country; a menacing example of social engineering; and so on.

There is a significant gap between the worldviews of citizens and politicians in partyocracy, attributable to their differing roles in the polity. Citizens are preoccupied with the personal, and politicians with affairs of their party and the country. This gap exacts a particularly high price on government initiatives whose success requires active citizen support. People cannot be forced to take an enlightened interest in the culture of a significant minority and to welcome its contribution to the always-evolving national culture. Visions imposed from on high sit poorly with people whose sense of deference is weakening. Imposition, however, is the style demanded by a system that concentrates power in one political office.

It seemed a reasonable expectation that the Bi and Bi program would result in greater social cohesion and, in particular, generate increased support for the national government among Francophones. There is scant, if any, evidence that it did so, however. Support for separation was higher in the 1995 Quebec referendum on separatism than it was in the 1980 vote. Admittedly, it could have been still higher had the program not been adopted. Of its impact on English-speaking Canadians, veteran political observer the late Dalton Camp, offered this view:

> The persistence and growing pervasiveness of bilingualism had alienated English Canadians from their federal government, turning them inwards to more familiar, compatible, and nearer political jurisdictions in the provinces .... The government of Canada had

lost its constituency; furthermore, it had lost public sympathy and support for the idea of federalism, and public endorsement would await only the national leader or the party promising less of it. "Strong central government" had become as opprobrious a phrase to English Canadians as it had always been to Québécois.

... A majority in a democratic society must be led; it will not be driven for long.[62]

And,

... Bilingualism has been a noble experiment, wretchedly conducted.[63]

The "wretchedness" was inevitable. If the language policies had been fully considered at the local level in constituency parliaments, and only adopted by parliament if they had first been endorsed there, citizens would have had a stronger emotional commitment to their success.

It is realistic to assume that the language policies would have been adopted following local review. Constituency parliament members would share their MPs' feelings of responsibility for the fate of the nation; would be privy to the same information as MPs; would probably come to the same conclusion as almost all of them did about the desirability of Francophones having a fuller role in Canada; and would approve the bilingualism program as a means of achieving that objective.

Of course, the decision at the individual constituency parliament level would have been far from unanimous. The hostility to Francophones and to Quebec would have been represented, expressed, and responded to— as it should be when it exists in the community. Political learning would take place, however, as relations between Canada's founding groups were discussed intensively—locally.

With the support of politically active citizens in communities across the country, a securely based program, not contaminated by association with a particular party, could have moved ahead with broad participation. Its success in promoting social cohesiveness could not be guaranteed, but

62   Dalton Camp, *Points of Departure* (Ottawa: Deneau and Greenberg Publishers Ltd., 1979), 122.
63   Ibid., 118.

would be more likely. At the very least, it would not have compounded the alienation of many citizens from the national government. Trudeau left the country more divided than it was when he took office and, while he certainly cannot be held totally responsible for this, his major attempt at visionary leadership contributed. Public support now comes at a price, i.e., participation in developing and implementing the vision. Democratic participation, in turn, requires institutional means that do not now exist.

Unifying projects. An extension of the notion that the country needs visionary leadership to strengthen its unity is the idea that divisions could be overcome through collaborative effort and accomplishment on national projects. The connection to government, to Canada, would be weaker if it were not for such programs and activities as universal health care and peacekeeping. Other, similarly significant undertakings would, it is argued, bring Canadians together.

John Godfrey, a Liberal MP, and Rob McLean, authors of *The Canada We Want,* are two of those who argued the case for strengthening unity by building together.[64] The fact that Godfrey was a Liberal leadership hopeful at the time his book was published, undoubtedly influenced his choice of the six projects that he and his co-author believed could strengthen national unity.[65] There is an obvious omission from their short list. The authors do not mention the project with the greatest potential of all to unite Canadians—as we create it and after as it functions—a more inclusive, responsive, and democratic political system.

Conclusion

In the now-distant past, two dominant Canadian parties, each seeking votes across the country, contributed to a unified polity by institutionalizing the competition of political elites. They brought order to political life at the same

---

64   John Godfrey and Rob McLean, *The Canada We Want* (Toronto: Stoddart, 1999).
65   Ibid. The national projects mentioned are developmental health, children, new energy systems, educational new media, Y2K.

time that they organized the electorate into rival factions. For its time, party/electoral democracy was a giant political step forward.

The two parties would, of course, have preferred to maintain their political monopoly. Their wishful thinking, and that of many others for them, is reflected in the label that was attached to them, i.e., "catch-all" parties. The country was, however, too large and diverse for two parties to catch all. Inevitably, in office nationally, each of the parties adopted policies that alienated parts of the country. New parties were organized to represent people and interests in those parts; to offer ideological alternatives to the two established parties; to provide ambitious politicians with political careers outside the dominant two parties. It was difficult for these new parties to break into a system dominated by the two well-established parties enjoying a base of loyal voters, backed by elites, and benefiting from the first-past-the-post electoral system. They were forced to find ways to appeal to voters kept ill-informed and politically unsophisticated. In virtually every case where the new party was seriously interested in attaining power, it found its route to at least some success in exaggerating and exploiting existing regional and provincial grievances with the central government. These grievances can always be found or conjured up in a large and diverse country. They are compounded when provincial governments exist that are disposed to exploit the grievances to further their struggle for more power or to divert attention from local controversies.

Class politics, in which parties appealed to segments of the population on the basis of their common interests, would not divide us along geographical lines. That, however, was not to be the dominant style of politics in a country where strong provincial governments were able to shape politics around their concerns. Appeals in the provinces, based on grievance with Ottawa, offended the fewest voters and are welcomed by many. The success of these new competitors forced each of the national parties to adapt their strategies to meet their competition, and these adaptations tended to accentuate divisions in the country, too.

Experience in the nation's capital, leading to a heightened sense of the national interest, may moderate the views of party MPs who launched careers exploiting regional grievances. However, they tend to back away from the difficult task of sharing their revised outlook with constituents. The existing system does not provide a forum in which elected representatives can—absent the rancour of competitive party politics—share their increased understanding of the needs of the country with constituency influentials. Citizens are more likely to think that their MPs have sold out if they moderate their views than they are to change their views along with those of their parliamentarians.

Adversarial activities of people, interests, and regions competing for power and advantage will always be a part of democratic politics. They are not the problem. The problem is centring politics on adversarialism, on providing no institutional alternative to competitive politics that would enable us to establish a balance between unifying and divisive forces.[66]

French- and English-speaking Canadians—Easterners and Westerners— have lived side by side, but never together in a deep national citizenship, for over 200 years. Many, if not most, circumstances have been highly favourable to their gradual coming together as citizens in a cohesive community: a rich, undeveloped land able to support a high standard of living; only minor foreign incursions on our soil and in far off in Europe to disturb the peace; a generally friendly, or even supportive, attitude of the majority of English-speaking Canadians to the Francophone minority; a vast array of interests common to men and women, of whatever language, place, or residence. That these positive features have not secured the integrity of the nation is due to many factors, but our dependence on party representation, and their divisive strategies for winning votes, is the most significant by far.

Pragmatic Canadians want governments whose policies support good

---

66   An American political scientist sets out the challenge: "The national polity poses at its most difficult the problem that arises even in small groups when they try to move back and forth between unitary and adversary modes. We cajole and coerce ourselves into unselfish behaviour in ways that are often fragile and prone to slippage. We find it hard to dip in and out of the adversary mode without being tainted by it—hard to be selfish now and selfless ten minutes later. We can reach common interest with others in part by making their good our own, yet a too-frequent recourse to adversary procedures undermines the habits of thought and feeling that induce such behaviour.

"The subversive effect of adversary procedure on unitary feeling makes it essential that the necessary dominance of adversary democracy in national politics not set the pattern of behaviour for the nation as a whole." Jane J. Mansbridge, *Beyond Adversary Democracy* (New York: Basic Books, 1980), 298.

lives for themselves and their children. In the present political world dominated by parties, we find superimposed on that desire party issues shaped by their competition for power. During election campaigns, citizens normally unengaged in politics, and therefore uninformed, are persuaded to adopt parties issues as their own. As is often the case, however, these issues are nationally divisive; they damage the ensuing government's ability to respond to their constituents' needs and may threaten the country's very existence.

National unity requires that we refocus our politics from the issues that concern competing politicians at both levels of government to those that are meaningful to our quality of life. To do this, we must first have the institutional means of deliberating together and, second, of insisting that governments follow our agenda.

The aura of uncertainty that hangs over Canada's future causes us less distress, less questioning of the system than it might—only because we are socialized to leave worrying about political matters to politicians, and we feel powerless to do anything to rectify the divisions that threaten Canada's existence. We continue to depend on parties to avert or deal with crises of national unity but the competitive demands placed on parties makes it impossible for them to do other than create and exploit division.

Strengthening the nation of Canada requires the adoption of a mode of representation that strongly links citizens with the national government. The mode that will do that has long been desired by Canadians on both sides of the linguistic divide.

Patching Partyocracy:
Delaying True Representative Democracy

Oratory and symbolic action are a substitute for serious change.

J. K. Galbraith

Parliament is Canada's most important national institution. It is the only
forum in which all Canadians, through their elected representatives,
have a voice in the governance of the nation. Parliament should be
an expression of our highest ideals and deepest values, our greatest
hopes and grandest dreams for the future of our children. Our
government believes these ideals can only be achieved if Parliament
truly reflects the character and aspirations of the Canadian people.

Speech from the Throne, November 19, 2008

These suggestions [giving MPs more independence] never go beyond
the suggestion stage for good reason: our system of parliamentary and
responsible government has evolved over centuries; reforms such as
these, introduced piecemeal, could undermine the entire structure.

The key to revitalizing democracy must rest on two foundations: giving
citizens and their leaders a more intimate understanding of one another
by bringing the two into closer proximity; and providing real evidence
that citizens' efforts to affect the system can actually bear fruit.

Allan Gregg

Introduction: Setting the Reform Agenda

Why policy democracy based on constituency parliaments? Why assign the highest priority to implementing a model of representation most Canadians have never heard of? Surely it would be better to pursue one or more of the proposals already "out there" and enjoying some support.

Currently there is, again, some interest in electoral reform. Perhaps it's time has finally come. Consultation is a word on the lips of every politician and senior bureaucrat. The resistance of traditional parliamentarians to adding the devices of direct democracy—the initiative, referendum, and recall—to the political system has shown cracks. All party leaders promise parliamentary reform. Major parties are now largely financed from the public treasury, and more financial support for the smaller parties is proposed.[67] A consensus of sorts exists, as it has since July 2, 1867, on the need to do something about the Senate. In addition, there are other proposals for reform already percolating among citizens and politicians. Why not focus reform efforts on one or a series of these? Isn't incremental reform of the existing system the best way to proceed?

The justification for asking reformers to put aside their current projects in favour of constituency representation is its significance. It is the reform the Canadian people overwhelmingly support. Others reforms would patch an obsolete system but leave intact the basic power relationships that make partyocracy dysfunctional. Party prime ministers and their colleagues, driven by competitive considerations, would continue to decide public policy. Citizens would still be relegated to the role of members of an increasingly critical and unsupportive "audience" and occasional electorate. Indeed, when they are examined closely, it is clear that most of the proposals presented as democratic reforms would, if adopted, only strengthen the ability of party government to manage citizens. They would contribute little or nothing toward creating a close working relationship between citizens, their elected representatives, the governments supported by those representatives, and the civil servants working for them. Whether they do

---

67   At the time of writing it appears certain that the annual allowance to each party made on the basis of its national vote will be phased out.

support that relationship must be the test of whether a proposed reform is significant enough to warrant our commitment to it.

The establishment of constituency parliaments is an unfamiliar idea only because elites are able to exploit their domination of public discussion and suppress, by ignoring, reforms that might seriously weaken their position. Existing institutions are made to seem immutable, and proposals for significant reform, if heard at all, to sound foreign, threatening, and unrealistic. That approach is effective with the many who consider politics an unfamiliar realm into which they are reluctant to venture.

Once explained, however, the policy democracy model should not sound foreign. The majority of Canadians already endorse the idea of constituency representation. Once the linkage is made clear between the means (constituency parliaments) and the end (constituency representation), strong support for policy democracy should emerge. The social media will help spread the word. After our preferred mode of representation is in place, we will be in a position to decide for ourselves what, and when, further reforms are needed.

It is ironic that some progressive political activists may be as difficult to convince that fundamental political change in our political institutions is necessary as some conservative politicians and citizens. Preoccupied with fighting pressing policy battles—the latest "crisis"—they are often impatient with suggestions that they spread their energies wider and thinner by also looking at the institutions producing what they deem misguided policies or neglecting to produce needed policies. Further, members of groups organized around a problem sometimes develop a stake in its continuance, becoming indifferent to striking at its source. We must avoid that kind of entrapment in the status quo.

Despite the overwhelming support for fundamental change, actually bringing it about will, as in the past, be achieved by a minority who resist being co-opted by the system. That is no cause for despair, however. In the past, peaceful change has been forced on reluctant elites by determined minorities seizing propitious opportunities to do so. Absolute monarchs gave up their powers to parliaments; against resistance parliaments expanded the electorate first to include all men and then women; now, again against opposition, referenda seem on the way to replacing the approval of constitutional deals by "eleven men in suits"; and so on.

The fundamentals of a political system cannot be changed often without creating instability. Occasionally, however, citizens have the right to choose how they are represented. That right should be exercised now when our democratic aspirations coincide so clearly with government's need for our constructive engagement.

In assessing the adequacy of the reforms currently on offer, I will argue that (a) while they are presented as democratic, most would actually strengthen the existing citizen-exclusive system that is the root cause of our alienation from government, (b) politicians in partyocracy are often pressured by competitive considerations to subvert the reforms they do finally adopt, leaving the system fundamentally unchanged, and (c) the adoption of constituency representation supported by local parliaments would make other current proposals for change largely, or totally, redundant.

Alternatives to Policy Democracy/Constituency Parliaments

A new electoral system. Currently, as we cast about for some means of propping up partyocracy, many people focus on changing the electoral system to some variant of proportional representation (PR). The existing first-past-the-post, or plurality electoral system, is obviously a grossly undemocratic method of choosing constituency representatives and governments. It has made the election of one-party governments, claiming a popular mandate on the strength of a minority of the popular vote, the norm for Canada. The monopolization of power by one party has, in turn, encouraged a particularly adversarial style of politics.

With PR, and the new norm of minority and coalition governments it would almost certainly produce, there would be positive and negative developments. The misrepresentation of the voters' party preferences, leading to the wasted-vote feeling, would be addressed. Responsibility for governing would be shared more widely among the parties. Policy, the product of inter-party negotiations, would be more solidly based and less likely to be jettisoned by a new government. That said, however, it must also be noted that minority and coalition governments elected by PR systems present their own difficulties.

Assessing proportional representation is complicated, because there are so many variants of it, each with its own strengths and weaknesses. It is generally agreed, however, that most versions would strengthen the control of central party offices over the choice of candidates. Where the party places the individual candidate on the list it submits to the voters has a major impact on his or her chances of election. In addition, the relationship between voters and elected representatives would be more impersonal, as voters cast a ballot for a party list rather than for an individual. These developments would occur at a time when the public already finds party control of MPs objectionable.

Further, PR is advocated as a means of ensuring that power in the Commons is proportional to votes received, but it can only guarantee that seats won will be proportional. In forming the coalition governments likely to result from the adoption of PR, small parties may be key to the dominant party having a working majority. In that position, these parties, or party, will enjoy power in the government disproportionate to support in the country.

In addition, it is often argued that voters will lose the ability to mandate or hold parties to their election commitments with PR, since the dominant party will have to negotiate a program with other parties if it is to govern.[68]

---

68   The Norwegian government, elected by PR, has recently sponsored a study of democracy in that country. A commentator on the study writes, "Elections are by proportional representation and with easy access to representation for small parties. The result is a *Storting* [parliament] of seven or eight parties, without stable recognizable majorities and oppositions, and shifting minority governments. The Norwegian experience is that this is a form of disorder that voters dislike. Perpetual negotiations are seen to be governance without direction. Voters decide the composition of the Storting but find that they are without direct influence in the formation of governments. On several occasions they have had to swallow the humiliation of seeing parties which they have punished with defeat in the election go on to win cabinet power." The main report is "Norway, Power and Democracy" (Norwegian Official Reports 2003:19 in Norwegian only) 2004. Cited in Stein Ringen, "Where Now, Democracy?" (2003), 8. www.sv.ulo. Polling in 2007 reveals a strong voter preference among Canadians for minority government over majority (53–37 percent). James Wallace, "Voters want minority government: poll," *Peterborough Examiner,* citing an SES Research/Osprey Media poll (February 7, 2007). These views may have changed over the last three years when our parties have adjusted so poorly to their minority situation.

This may not be a significant problem, however, since even one-party governments seldom follow through rigorously on their election promises. Often they shouldn't, because their mandate is dubious, and the social, economic, and competitive political worlds to which they must adjust policy are in constant flux. Further, a new governing party, cut off from advice from the bureaucracy while in opposition, will have drawn up its program in isolation from all the relevant information that it should be considering. Commitments made in an election campaign may be bad policy, or may become so soon afterward.

Beyond those problems, there are other major reasons for urging that the zeal for electoral reform be redirected to an infinitely more significant "democratic" reform, i.e., one that changes our relationship to other political players. The most important of these is that PR might pose a serious threat to the already precarious unity of our country. In an ideal world, we could adopt the most democratic electoral system known, confident that any negative consequences flowing from that action could be managed. In Canada, however, national unity is so fragile that the impact a PR electoral system might have on the ability of the national administration to hold the country together, let alone govern effectively, must be an important consideration.

In 2008, we had a Liberal Party that some observers believe had given up attempting to be a truly national party, competing with a governing Conservative Party led by someone (Harper) opposed to the national government performing any but the most essential functions of a central administration.[1] The second-largest opposition party was committed to the separation of Quebec from the federation. In addition, the NDP was weak, and it did not have as strong a national orientation as it had once had. Its successes had been at the provincial level.

With that situation, it appears that PR could scarcely do more damage to national unity than the existing first-past-the-post (plurality) system that has contributed to this constellation of parties. It is likely, however, that some new parties would be encouraged to enter the system by PR, since even a relatively small number of votes would result in the election of MPs.

1   On the role of the Liberal Party, see Matthew Mendelsohn, "Healing Social, Political and Regional Divisions," in *Memos to the Prime Minister,* ed. Harvey Schachter (Toronto: John Wiley and Sons, 2001), 12.

New parties would be aided, too, by the recently adopted party/election finance regime and by the increasing fluidity of party loyalties.[2] It seems likely that, in order to become established, at least some of these new parties would exploit and exacerbate regional/provincial grievances with Ottawa, weakening the national administration. The Green party, with an appeal to all Canadians, is likely to continue to be the exception to this unity-destructive pattern of new party behaviour.

The report of the Law Commission of Canada, supporting PR, states: "Admittedly, the size and number of regional parties could possibly increase under a mixed member proportional system. It is at least arguable, however, that it is better to have these regionalist parties represented in Parliament with a handful of seats among them than to rely on an electoral system that systematically discriminates against minor parties. The latter option seems to be a formula for voter discontent and alienation."[3]

The PR option may, however, be a formula for even more of both.

The Commission argues that, under its preferred PR formula, the anticipated new regional parties would be unlikely to gain enough seats to threaten the stability of the national administration.[4] Even if the Commission is right, however, the number of seats these new parties would have is not the only issue their existence would raise. If the burning of a Quebec flag by a few rabble-rousers in a small Ontario town can feed the fires of separatism, what would the political fallout be from an overtly anti-Francophone party led in the Commons by a ranting Ian Paisley? Or by spokespersons from an extreme "Alberta First" party, interpreting, as Quebec separatists now do, every possible action by Ottawa as hostile to the interests of the people of their province? The rhetoric of such parties would not be tempered by the hope of taking office nationally.[5]

---

2   Polls show that very strong identification with a federal party has fallen from 30 percent in 1965 to 18 percent in 2000. Source is Matthew Mendelsohn, "Canadian public opinion on representative democracy," Canadian Centre for Management Development, 2002. (Queen's University, Kingston, Ont.: Canadian Opinion Research Archive). www.queensu.ca/cora/

3   Canada, Law Commission of Canada, Voting Counts: *Electoral Reform for Canada* (Ottawa: Minister of Public Works and Government Services, 2004), 145.

4   Ibid., 14.

5   While supporters of such views would find their way into constituency parliaments,

With the threat of referenda on separatism hanging over their heads, and the desire to gain votes in Quebec, politicians in all parties now in the House of Commons have been cautious in avoiding any rhetoric that would give ammunition to separatist forces. The leadership of the established parties have the authority (and have used it) to nullify the nomination of any radical Francophobes who might have been elected to the Commons and stirred up animosities between French- and English-speaking Canadians. The leaders of small parties that might emerge with PR cannot be trusted to follow their example.

Assuming that an exacerbation of ethnic and linguistic tensions by PR could be avoided, the country would still be left with additional parties that would likely press for a decentralization of powers to their provincial bases. The federal government could be forced to act even more as an uninspired broker of competing regional and provincial interests; it could be even more difficult to give Canada unifying national leadership.

Discussion of the impact of PR on national unity must be speculative, but it is certain that its adoption would delay Canada's moving forward with incomparably more urgent democratic reform. The run-up to the adoption of a different national electoral system could go on for many more years. Quebec has been debating the issue since the election of the first PQ government in 1976. British Columbians have voted on the issue twice, and Prince Edward Island and Ontario have all had recent referenda on electoral reform—designed, successfully, by governing parties to make their passage difficult.[6] (See discussion of the British Columbia case, below.)

Citizens using PR to elect governments are unhappy with that system. Citizens using first-past-the-post are even more unhappy. Dissatisfaction

their ideas would probably be overridden there by others with a more socially constructive perspective before they could do much damage.

6   The referenda in Prince Edward Island and Ontario gave citizens the opportunity to endorse the Mixed Member Proportional electoral system recommended by commissions in each province. Large majorities, in the province and in constituencies, were required: 60 percent of voters in the province and endorsement in 60 percent of the ridings for the referenda to carry. The results in Prince Edward Island were "yes" 34.6 percent; "no" 63.58 percent, and 2 of 27 electoral districts voted "yes." www.election-spei.ca/plebiscites/pr/results/display/index.php. In Ontario, 36.9 percent said "yes"; 63.10 percent said "no" and 5 of 102 ridings voted "yes." www.elections.on.ca

with both systems suggests that we should look past elections, whatever the rules governing them, if our alienation from governments is to be turned into support. PR is yesterday's reform, adopted by most liberal democracies, and first advocated by western Canadian reformers early in the 20th century.

Electoral reform should be set aside because it fails to meet the significance test set out above. And, as we discussed previously, it would not be necessary if the policy democracy model were in place. Elections would then only choose a constituency representative, not a governing party and PM. There would be no pretence that elections mandated policies or leaders. For the limited function of choosing a constituency MP, the present electoral system would be appropriate.

Electoral reform in British Columbia. Electoral reform in British Columbia has raised a question that warrants a digression into provincial politics: Can the weaknesses in partyocracy be overcome by delegating sensitive issues to ad hoc, randomly chosen bodies of citizens? Is this sort of "end run" around the formal system of representation and governance on some issues the answer to the weaknesses in partyocracy? Some British Columbians, and others, have come to believe that it is based on the impressive work of the British Columbia Citizens' Assembly on Electoral Reform.

Pressed by reformers, Liberal leader Gordon Campbell promised to consider changing the electoral system as he campaigned, successfully, for his first term in office in 2001. He followed up on his promise, appointing Gordon Gibson, a prominent and creative BC political figure, to make recommendations to his government on how to fulfill the commitment. Gibson's recommendations were adopted: the Citizens' Assembly on Electoral Reform was organized, its 160 members (politicians excluded) chosen at random from British Columbia's electoral constituencies. Assembly members were charged with the responsibility of studying electoral reform and making recommendations to the government. If they recommended changes, as proved to be the case, the voters were to decide on whether to adopt them in a referendum. To pass, the referendum required a double majority: 60 percent of the votes cast and majority support in 60 percent of the ridings in the province. If it were adopted, the new system was to be used for the first time in the 2009 election.[7]

After extensive study over a lengthy period, the Citizen's Assembly overwhelmingly (146–7) endorsed change from a plurality to a single transferable vote (STV) system. The referendum on its proposal almost passed, with a 57.69 percent "yes" vote and with 77 of 79 electoral districts supporting the change.[8] In view of the high threshold required for passage, and the closeness of the vote, the premier agreed to resubmit the issue to the voters at the 2009 election. By the time that vote was held, enthusiasm for change to an STV system had fallen dramatically and it was defeated again.[9] The BC initiative aroused wide interest.[10] It was copied in several other provinces, and their commissions recommended a change in their plurality electoral systems, too.

Despite the final rejection of the British Columbia Assembly's recommendations, the procedure it followed was widely seen as having demonstrated the ability of ordinary citizens, given adequate resources of time and information, to reach a sound decision on a quite complex issue of public policy. Some were convinced that the use of the process should be extended. Gordon Gibson, for example, argued that citizen assemblies could be used to break logjams in other areas of public policy where politicians are "inherently conflicted," such as Senate reform.[11] Gibson seemed to visualize, as have others, a series of citizen groups (juries) empowered to

---

7   The full account of the Citizens' Assembly, its history, organization, and recommendations, are to be found on its website: www.citizensassembly.bc.ca. For an academic study of the process leading up to the referendum, see Mark E. Warren and Hilary Pearse, eds., *Designing Deliberative Democracy* (New York: Cambridge University Press, 2008).

8   www.electionsbc.ca

9   Ibid. 39.08 percent of those voting and 7 of 85 constituencies supported a change in the electoral system. Voter turnout at the election was 51%.

10   For just one of many of the extensive and enthusiastic media reports, see Daniel Girard, "Democracy, from the ground up," *Toronto Star* (January 3, 2004), H3.

11   Showing justifiable pride in the unique process he helped set in motion, Gibson goes further, stating that, "It [the citizen assembly idea] could, in due course, become one of Canada's gifts to the democratic world." Gordon Gibson, "British Columbia, birthplace of a new kind of democracy," *Globe and Mail* (November 1, 2004), A13.

decide individual policies that politicians cannot deal with effectively—a kind of parallel set of institutions to the legislature or parliament.

This approach would have many of the weaknesses of referenda—discussed later—as policy instruments. It also raises a fundamental question: instead of a parallel, and cumbersome, policy-making process, why not make the legislature a truly democratic popular forum composed of members responsible to their constituents? Then, clothed in democratic legitimacy, it could deal effectively with all the challenges facing country or province. Further, individual policies would be considered in the broad context of all the issues facing government, rather than in isolation, as would be the case with juries studying individual issues.

Encouraging voting

Currently, the dysfunctional electoral system is the major focus of political reform. The related decline in voter turnout is, however, perceived as the more immediate threat to the legitimacy of the political system. The decline is common to many liberal democracies, but as a study reports, "Few Western democracies have experienced as steady and as significant a drop in turnout over the last 15 years as has Canada."[12]

Supporters of partyocracy have long insisted that as long as we can choose our leaders in open elections, democracy exists. This limited view of democracy, and inflated significance of the vote, has become increasingly hard to maintain. Even with elections, citizens feel powerless. Political columnist Richard Gwyn captures our mood when he writes, "Our democracy isn't doomed. But our current version of it has become stale, listless, and empty of passion, even of relevance. Maybe those who don't bother to vote are making the most relevant political statement of all."[13]

The political elite's response to the decline in voting and loss of legitimacy for the system is to turn to the management of citizens. Previous generations of ruling elites, protecting their interests, resisted extending

---

12   Canada, Centre for Research and Information on Canada, "Voter Participation in Canada: Is Canadian Democracy in Crisis?" (Montreal, October 2001). http//www. cric.ca.

13   Richard Gwyn, "No Wonder Democracy is in trouble," *Toronto Star* (May 26, 2002), A15.

voting rights to citizens. Now their interests call for the reverse, mobilizing citizens to cast ballots. Political leaders have come to recognize that, as a class, they have little to fear from voters and much to gain from citizens voting and legitimating the system that empowers them.

Government-supported and independent research has been directed at determining the causes of non-voting and turning up ideas that will reverse current trends.[14] Compulsory voting is one such idea, with Australia cited as an instructive example of its successful use.[15] Voter turnout there ranks close to the highest among the liberal democracies.

In his text on Australian government, L. F. Crisp observes that when the compulsory voting system was adopted in 1924, with all-party support, the parties "welcomed the relief which compulsion gave them from mounting electioneering costs." In addition, he observes, some felt that, "Compulsory voting could have the beneficial effects of educating and interesting in the processes and principles of government those who had hitherto been indifferent."[16] On the actual result, however, Crisp concludes, "Parties no longer have to worry about "getting the vote out"; it is enough that they concentrate their expenditures on "selling" their baits to the unattached voters during the last stages of the election campaign and that their worker be on hand outside polling booths to give oral and printed advice on how to vote. This has almost certainly made parties lazy between elections about trying to convert voters to their particular philosophy and programme, so essential a preparation for getting voters to turn out on polling day under conditions of voluntary voting. Compulsion may in this way actually have discouraged political educational efforts by the parties."[17]

Compulsory voting is one simple way of preventing citizens questioning the significance of the ballot to them. However, the Canadian public is

14   See, for example, Jon Pammett and Lawrence LeDuc, "Explaining the Turnout Decline in Canadian Federal Elections in the Millennium," *Choices,* 6, 6 (Institute for Research on Public Policy, September 2000). www.irpp.org.
15   Jeffery Simpson, for example, urges that, "The right to vote ... should be attached to the responsibility to vote," *Globe and Mail* (February 1, 2002), A15.
16   L. F. Crisp, *The Parliamentary Government of the Commonwealth of Australia* (London: Longmans, 1961), 66.
17   Ibid., 67.

overwhelmingly opposed to it.[18] It is a non-starter, cluttering up the reform agenda—one of many diversions from consideration of significant, citizen-empowering change.

Socializing young people early into voting is also advocated as a way to boost the number of voters. Mock elections, in which young people participate, paralleling the real thing, have now been staged in some jurisdictions. Co-sponsored by Elections Canada and Student Vote 2004, an effort was made to have such elections take place in all the high schools of the country.[19] The purpose was to develop an "appetite" for voting and to allay any fears young people might have about participating in the formal balloting procedure. In addition, it has been suggested that the voting age be lowered to 16.[20] Is it desirable to strengthen a malfunctioning system by training students to participate in it?

The union economist and columnist, Jim Stanford suggests paying voters in his submission to a *Globe and Mail* feature on getting more people involved in politics. He may not have intended to be taken seriously.[21]

One of the messages being sent by low electoral turnouts to our political elites is important, i.e., the right to vote in party elections, whether organized around our existing electoral system or around PR, no longer meets even the minimum participatory aspirations of many. That message demands a democratic response, not a cover-up.

Consultation. Electoral reform is the most significant defensive response

---

18   Canadians (73 percent in 2000) rejected the proposition that failure to vote should be punished by a small fine. Paul Howe and David Northrup, "The Views of Canadians," *Policy Matters* 1, 5 (Montreal: Institute for Research on Public Policy, July 2000), 28. www.irpp.org.

19   Details of the plan and other initiatives aimed at young voters are described in Elections Canada press release, "Elections Canada and Student Vote 2004 ..." (March 4, 2004). www.elections.ca/content.asp?section=med&document=mar0404=&dir=pr e&lan=e.

20   See, for example, Prof. Henry Milner, "Sweet 16 and ready to vote?" *Globe and Mail* (August 23, 2003), A19, and Columnist Roy MacGregor, "At 16, teens are considered mature enough to drive, marry and work—so why not vote?" *Globe and Mail* (March 4, 2003), A2. The NDP advocated lowering the voting age to 16 in its 2004 election platform. New Democratic Party, "New Energy: A Positive Choice," 40. www. ndp.ca.

21   Jim Stanford, "Pay for Votes," *Globe and Mail* (April 29, 2011), A6.

of elites to our demands for a more significant voice in political life.[22] The first response, actually implemented, is non-binding consultations on some issues. Since there has been considerable experience with this mode of bringing citizens into the system, its effectiveness in bridging the gap between citizens, elected representatives, and government can be determined.

The story of consultation as a semi-institutionalized aspect of government-citizen relations begins with the intense (angry) pressure from political activists in the 1960s. Although the vast majority of people remained in the system-prescribed role of "audience," vociferous minorities protested a range of government policies and the exclusive process by which all policy was made.

Political leaders might have seized on the restiveness as a welcome opportunity to restart the long-stalled movement to a fuller form of democracy. Some of us hoped this would happen when Prime Minister Trudeau endorsed participatory democracy in the 1968 election. However, he and other political leaders had no plan in hand to guide the democratic development of the system. For years, the establishment had accepted the comfortable notion that democracy already existed, instead of seeing it as an ideal to be worked toward continuously. For them, the demands for more participation were simply an unwelcome challenge to the status quo that had to be finessed. They responded with three major political changes intended to do that: different political rhetoric; expanded consultation, which included government intervention in the interest-group arena; and addressing secrecy in government.

The rhetorical adjustment. At one time, pressed to heed public opinion, MPs would wrap themselves in the protective blanket of what they chose to see as constituting the parliamentary system. They claimed that they alone were burdened with the responsibility for setting public policy. It would be irresponsible for them to abdicate this responsibility to curry popularity. This position came to be seen as self-serving and unacceptable by many. In response, MPs adjusted their rhetoric. On every occasion where it was at all plausible, and some where it was not, they claimed to be acting at the behest

---

22   "Defensive" in the sense that it can be used to damp down demands for change without affecting elite control of public policy and administration.

of the people. "The people of Canada want us to," or "demand that we," became standard phrases used to introduce or defend policy. No longer was there an emphasis on parliamentary sovereignty or a disparaging of popular sovereignty.

The expression of deference to our views was safe. In the absence of any organized means to deliberate among ourselves, we cannot decide what we really do want. It was impossible to contradict with evidence the politicians' claims that they were responding to us—other than with polls. These could be dismissed as reflecting opinion that is often fickle, uninformed, and easily manipulated. If this were not enough, political leaders could fall back on comments like, "Wait a few years, and when they look back, citizens will see that we were right in our perception of the public interest and thank us for acting as we did." I would add, "or not"!

Expanding consultation. Politicians needed some substance to back up their suggestion that they were following the direction of citizens. For politicians at all levels, and for bureaucrats with responsibility for developing policy, it became de rigueur on high-profile issues to solicit public input in some form. In an address to subordinates, the then-clerk of the Privy Council and secretary to the Cabinet noted that 300 public consultation exercises were at that moment being conducted by the public service.[23] Hundreds more were being conducted at other levels of government.

A variety of consultative/public-relations devices were used in reaching out to citizens: polling; focus groups; hearings of traveling and stationary parliamentary committees; mail questionnaires; town-hall meetings; radio phone-in shows; constituency office activities; etc. Premiers now use public meetings, where they invite citizen input as one of their consultative tools. Anything but organizing the public so that it can study and speak its mind on issues independently and authoritatively. The public's ambivalence toward the premiers' show of deference to its views is reflected in a journalist's comment on Ontario Premier McGuinty's 2004 consultation exercise: "It's poppycock, of course. Most of us don't have anything particularly original to say about how the province should be run.... A sceptical view, perhaps,

23   Jocelyne Bourgon, "Notes for an address to the Association of Professional Executives of the Public Service of Canada Symposium," (Ottawa, May 27, 1998), 3. Mimeo.

but Mr. McGuinty will be fighting even more intense scepticism that his dialogue process is simply cover for him to do what he wants to do.... All this said, the state of democracy in Canada is unhealthy enough that we should not turn our backs on an invitation to talk to our leaders.... Yes, voters told Mr. McGuinty last October [in the election] what they wanted, but if he wants to hear it again, let's tell him."[24]

The assertion that the previous election allowed voters to tell the premier what they wanted him to hear is an example of the usual misrepresentation/ exaggeration of what elections actually permit us to say. Where the system is organized around the principle that citizens delegate their political responsibilities to parties, it cannot then be expected that we will be motivated to learn enough to contribute significantly to most ad hoc political consultations or that we will be socialized into participating in them.

Interest groups do have substantive ideas to offer on the issues of concern to them, however.[25] Those representing powerful groups exploit the public consultation process when it furthers their objectives. Most of them would already have made their views known to policy-makers in other venues, as well. Allowing special interest and other groups to have an even louder voice— overwhelming whatever the "silent majority" might want to express—is scarcely what is required to bolster our confidence in the policy-making process.[26] The

---

24   Murray Campbell, "Premier's consultations innovative poppycock," *Globe and Mail* (January 28, 2004), A7. For an account of the Quebec Premier's similar venture, see Rhéal Séguin, "Charest moves to appease angry voters," *Globe and Mail* (February 9, 2004), A4.

25   On "public" hearings, political columnist John Ibbitson observes, "Anyone who has been condemned to sit through one quickly learns public hearings offer no real opportunities for citizens to offer their opinions. Instead, interest group representatives representing business, labour and social movements hog the microphone, competing to see which can be more strident and humourless." "Welcome to a new era of liberal democracy," *Globe and Mail* (January 12, 2004).

26   Some political leaders recognize the problem. Speaking to public servants, the then-Treasury Board President Marcel Massé is quoted as warning, "Governments are paying too much attention to special interest groups and risk losing touch with ordinary Canadians in shaping policies and services ... public servants must find new ways to 'define' the public interest rather than letting powerful special-interest groups dominate the policy-making agenda." Kathryn May, "Interest groups too powerful," *Ottawa Citizen* (May 29, 1988), A1.

usual claims of most organized interests that they speak for us are not to be taken seriously.[27]

The consultative opportunities now offered by party-government are of considerable defensive value to it—and to individual politicians.[28] The advertising associated with the government's solicitation of citizen input makes the government appear willing to listen. The individual politician benefits from a higher profile, secured through such activities as chairing town-hall meetings and circulating the fatuous questionnaires—incorporating solicitations for money—they routinely send to voters. Most important, faced with the almost-automatic accusation of those who dislike a government policy, i.e., that it has been adopted without proper consultation, administration spokespersons can usually ream off a list of opportunities people and interests have had to be heard.

These benefits accrue to politicians generally, and to party-government in particular, with little or no loss of control over policy. The consultative activity does not interfere with party-government's freedom of action or with individual MPs carrying on as dutiful party representatives in the Commons and outside, as their career interests dictate.

Benefits to us from this "democratic reform" are hard to find, however. Most of the "consultation" is intended to strengthen the system's weak democratic credentials rather than to provide us with more political influence. It does not do much of either. Political scientist Matthew Mendelsohn

---

27   The lobbying against gun control is an excellent example of how unrepresentative the views the government hears through its consultative process can be. That lobby has been the largest, loudest and, perhaps, the most persistent the country has seen in recent years. Yet, according to polls, most citizens support gun control, even in Alberta, where protests have been loudest. An Environics Research Group poll conducted in 2003 found that, nationally, 74 percent of Canadians supported the government's gun-control legislation. In Alberta the figure was 60 percent. www.erg.environics.net/news/default.asp?aID=513.

28   An academic study of government consultations sums up the process: "On major policy issues, the standard template of public consultation is deployed, complete with all the problems that have come to be associated with it—government controls the agenda and who is invited; information flows in one direction; and the process is episodic and ad hoc. In sum, there is a need for significant reform to produce effective means of engaging citizens." Susan D. Phillips and Michael Orsini. Executive Summary "Mapping the Links: Citizen Involvement in Policy Processes." CPRN Discussion Paper No. F.21. (Ottawa: Canadian Policy Research Networks, April 2002), iii. www.cprn.com.

dismissively refers to the consultations as offering opportunities for "public venting" and, for politicians, to "tell and sell."[29] Citizens tell pollsters that they find "the consultative techniques largely unrepresentative and ineffective," or worse.[30] While consultation is a booming (and expensive to taxpayers) political industry, the level of political alienation continues to rise.

Managing public voices. The new emphasis on consultation has had the effect of legitimating lobbying—once seen as interfering with the MP's contemplation of the public interest. Rapid growth in the government-relations industry has given rise to concern by government about balance in the representation of group interests. If policy is to be made (informally) in the interest-group arena rather than in parliament, where it is formally ratified, then the public interest must be represented in that arena. To somewhat offset the risk that it would not be heard, three strategies were adopted. First, government gave aid to some poorly resourced groups that claimed to speak for the public interest in particular policy areas. Second, it sought to regulate interest groups by registering them and placing some limits on their activities. Supposedly, bringing interest group activities out into the open would limit improprieties. Third, as will be discussed further in the next chapter, it restricted the election-related spending of powerful interests. Here we will consider only the first element of this three-pronged approach.

Financial grants and organizing assistance were distributed, at the discretion of government, to a range of community agencies and organizations that would otherwise have been largely or totally mute politically. Spokespersons for the poor, handicapped, battered women, native Canadians, environmentalists, ethnic groups, and a wide range of others, were able to promote their issues more forcefully with this financial assistance.

---

29   The phrase is Matthew Mendelsohn's, "Public Brokerage: Constitutional Reform and the Accommodation of Mass Publics," *Canadian Journal of Political Science, 33*, 2 (June 2000), 264.
30   Ekos Research Associates, Inc., *Rethinking Government '94: An Overview and Synthesis* (Ottawa, 1995), 7.

Like other reforms sponsored from within partyocracy, this action of government seems democratic—a balancing of interest-group representations to government. Also like them, however, it is fraught with problems. First, the encouragement of a fuller spectrum of interests in the political arena only adds legitimacy to the policy outputs of group interactions for pluralists. They celebrate the competition of self-interested groups for favourable public policy—a competition that informally pits Canadians against one another, with government responding to the "winner" of the competition.

Democrats, on the other hand, would emphasize the political equality of all citizens and celebrate their working collaboratively through government. Government stimulation of interest-group activity does little to create this political process.

In addition, any idea that this government intervention in the interest-group system might establish fairness among competitors is unrealistic. How could government decide what amount of aid to give groups representing battered women and other social and economic casualties to put them on a fair competitive footing with, for example, business groups seeking the same government dollars?

Further, as is the case with all decisions of party government, the allocation of support to groups is influenced by partisan considerations. Doling out grants offers a particularly good opportunity to reward or to punish. In the budgets of modern governments, the amounts dispensed to groups are little more than petty cash, but they may be their life-blood to the public-interest groups receiving them. Most recipients of government largesse insist that they are not compromised by the state aid they receive, but of course, many are.[31] They are vulnerable to party government deciding at any time to quiet them by withdrawing support. The integrity of civil society is breached, as government manipulates its elements.

The final reason why democrats must have reservations about government management of the public voice through grants is that the

---

31   "There is mounting evidence that voluntary organizations involved in public-service contracting, either alone or in partnerships, curtail their advocacy activities for fear of jeopardizing their contracts or other funding .... If their main point of invited contact is with the officials who oversee their contracts, voluntary organizations are likely to be quite cautious about speaking frankly about any problems they are experiencing in the realm of service delivery." Phillips and Michael Orsini, "Mapping the Links," 20.

allocation of support to groups will itself be the product of lobbying. The most vulnerable elements in society—those that most need help, such as children in poor or abusive families and dysfunctional mental patients living in the community—are in a weak position to compete for their share of government assistance.

Despite these unsatisfactory features of government intervention in the interest-group system, it appears that public lobbies are more effectively represented in the group arena than before the grants were made. However, when public-interest groups, backed by government grants, fight their way into the policy-making process, they provoke a counter-attack. Any powerfully entrenched groups that may feel under threat from these new forces will significantly escalate their lobbying to protect themselves. At the end of the day, more interests are scrapping over public resources of various kinds, and the dominance of the previously entrenched groups may be strengthened. That scenario has been identified by US researchers; it is difficult to see why their conclusions are not applicable to Canada.[32] In addition, the public is even more disillusioned by a politics that seem to be dominated by "gimme" groups.

Wider representation in the interest-group arena does not automatically translate into more citizen impact on public policy. For those in power, grants given to "cause groups" may be conscience money, a substitute for substantive action, or it may be intended to defuse particularly aggressive behaviour to which the government has no intention of responding.

Cause groups are more likely to get attention and support from members of the public if they have the resources to publicize their work; government subsidies may help them get this. Still, it is an uphill battle for many groups, because they must draw this support from a population socialized into a shallow form of citizenship. It is a tribute to a few people that they resist the system and live as "democratic citizens," but their numbers are usually far from sufficient to force governments to act in a timely, effective way.[33]

---

32   Kay Lehman Schlozman and John Tierney, *Organized Interests in American Democracy* (New York: Harper and Row, 1986), 387–88.
33   Generally, researchers studying volunteerism in its various forms find it in a decline that seems unlikely to be reversed. For a discussion of their findings, see Roy MacGregor, "In a sceptical, urbanized country, volunteers are an endangered species," *Globe and Mail* (April 2, 2004), A2. One academic study found, in 1997, that 8 percent of the

The attempt to balance the representation of interests through government grants may actually further damage the relationship of citizens with their government. The interactions of interest groups with government in a pluralist democracy are almost universally adversarial. Interest groups are largely *demand* organizations. Operating on the principle that "the squeaky wheel gets the grease," most organized interests squeak continuously. Placing unreasonable demands on the government is their typical bargaining strategy. When these cannot be met fully, members of the groups are likely to feel aggrieved. For them, mobilizing the support government needs to meet its responsibilities is somebody else's business. Since flimsy party organizations cannot do the mobilization, there often is no "somebody else."

Dilemmas abound as politicians strive to increase, manage, and control groups functioning in the informal representative system. Most of them cannot be resolved within partyocracy. In the policy democracy/ constituency parliament model, however, public interest—cause groups— would have an easily accessible point of entry into the political process, where their representations would be heard. If corporate lobbying were to be effective, it would also have to include appeals for support from constituency parliaments composed of informed and empowered citizens. Members of those parliaments would be in a position to apply a real public-interest test to all appeals.

The lobbying itself might be less self-interested when corporation executives and all other lobbyists are encouraged by the new system of representation to assume personal and institutional citizenship responsibilities. A more equitable balancing of private and public interests would partially replace the imbalance in favour of the rich and powerful that exists in the present informal system of representation.

Further, with citizen empowerment, government intervention in civil

---

adult population provided almost half of all volunteer time and charitable giving and 25 percent of all civic participation. Paul B. Reed and L. Kevin Selbee, "Patterns of Citizen Participation and the Civic Core in Canada," Paper presented at the 29th ARNOVA annual conference (New Orleans, Louisiana, November 16–18, 2000), 2. Mimeo. People concerned about reversing the non-participatory trend might look to an "engaging" political system as a means of encouraging citizens to become more involved in their communities.

society would not be necessary or justified. Limits on the political activities of charities, corporations, unions, and others could be removed when citizens, as an important participant in the policy-making process, are in a position to assess their claims on the government. The several bureaucracies supporting and regulating group and party activities could be dismantled and tax dollars supporting them freed up for other purposes.

Access to information. The privacy screen that covers government information was an ill fit with the new emphasis on consultation. How could any of those consulted contribute significantly without access to all relevant information? The declining trust in government also forced the issue to the fore. Secrecy allowed government ineptitude and corruption to go unchecked, and it was suspected even where there might be none. To strengthen their trust, Canadians needed assurance that government was not hiding important information. A commitment to transparency was added to the rhetoric of all parties and politicians.

The culture of secrecy in government was inherited from autocracies that preceded our system and then maintained by party governments in the new system.[34] Control of information was much too valuable a source of competitive advantage for the governing party to surrender it voluntarily, and for a long time, there was no external force that could require it to be relinquished. The public was deferential and unorganized; the opposition was compromised by its loyalty to the system from which it hoped, in its turn in office, to benefit. The courts were not the countervailing power to government that they became post-Charter.

The content of files is only one form of information traditionally kept secret. Even if most of them are opened, the administration retains a great deal of control over the dissemination of information. However, access to the files became the focus of reformers in the tumultuous 1960s. The value to the governing party of its information monopoly waned when the freedom of

---

34   The *culture of secrecy* phrase is used repeatedly in the annual reports of the Information Commissioner to describe the current belief system of authorities in Ottawa—two decades after the passage of the Access to Information Act. See, for example, Canada, *Annual Report Information Commissioner 2001-2002* (Ottawa: Minister of Public Works and Government Services Canada 2001), 14. infocom.gc.ca/menu-e.asp

information cause was taken up by a few academics and outspoken members of the public, their voices amplified by a media anxious to get access to information about the public's business.[35] Suppressing information was losing credibility and support for government and, more generally, the political process. Reformers' calls for more openness were reinforced by the knowledge, in some circles, of the use, or recent adoption in other partyocracies, of freedom-of-information legislation.[36] Their skies had not fallen.

After much study and discussion, the government of the soon-to-retire Pierre Trudeau[37] passed the Access to Information Act of 1982.[38] A statement of purpose introducing the statute sent out a strong message: when the inevitable conflict between differing interpretations on the amount of secrecy allowed by the Act occurs, openness should be favoured. Decisions not to disclose information should be independently reviewed.[39] With significant exceptions, most information relating to the activities of government was to be available to those requesting it.

The Act's provisions set out the procedure governing requests for

35   In particular, Professor Donald Rowat campaigned vigorously on the issue of open government. See Donald C. Rowat, ed., *The right to know: Essays on government publicity and public access to information* (Ottawa: Department of Political Science, Carleton University, 1980).

36   When Trudeau finally acted, twelve other countries had already enacted "modern" legislation. David Berlin, "A Love Affair with Secrecy," *The Walrus* (November 2004), 35.

37   At this point in his career, Mr. Trudeau had already announced his retirement once and was certainly not intending to lead the party in a new election. Was he, therefore, willing to give up some measure of control over information knowing that it would not present him with political difficulties? Some certainly thought his action was motivated by partisanship: "Ottawa insiders contended that the notoriously private Prime Minister Trudeau had finally agreed to the adoption of the Access Act only to undermine his Progressive Conservative successor." David Berlin, "A Love Affair with Secrecy," 35. If this was the case, it would be consistent with the behaviour of other premiers and prime ministers who, close to leaving office, endorsed reforms that would make life difficult for successors.

38   Canada, Access to Information Act, R. S. 1985, c. A-1, S. 2(1) www.scc-csc.gc.ca/information/index_e/asp

39   The statement of purpose included in the Act reads, in part, "Necessary exceptions to the right of access should be limited and specific and that decisions on the disclosure of government information should be reviewed independently of government." Canada, Access to Information Act, R.S. 1985, c. A-1, S. 2(1) www.scc-csc.gc.ca/information/index_e/asp

information and the—now routinely ignored—time allowed for responses. Crown corporations were exempt from the Act originally, and there were justifiable restrictions on access to information on such matters as criminal investigations. An additional exemption, that of all cabinet documents, was justified as necessary to maintain partyocracy.[42]

The records of cabinet are protected by statute for 20 years, and those of caucus meetings continue to be protected indefinitely, by convention. [40] The exempted "cabinet confidences" are deemed "discussion papers the purpose of which is to present background explanations, analyses of problems, or policy options to Council [cabinet] for consideration by Council in making decisions."[41] Other matters, such as the agendas of cabinet meetings, policy-related communications between ministers, and draft legislation, are also included under the rubric of cabinet confidences.[42] Then, in the section of the Act that immediately follows, the exclusion of discussion papers is lifted in two circumstances: "If the decisions to which the discussion papers relate have been made public or, where the decisions have not been made public, if four years have passed since the decisions were made."[43] Commenting on these exclusions, an Information Commissioner wrote, "It's one giant loophole."[44]

While it benefits governing party elites to have the continuing secrecy of cabinet confidences legitimized by the Access Act, the suppression of this information has a significant impact on our ability to participate effectively in the development of public policy. Access to cabinet documents would alert us to when our input to policy development would be most relevant and to the arguments it must address. Without this information, individuals and some interest groups, must try to influence decisions after the government has firmly committed itself to them, i.e., too late.[45] Well-connected lobbies,

40   Canada, Access to Information Act, R.S. 1985, S69 (3)(a) www.scc-csc.gc.ca/information/index_e/asp
41   Ibid, S69 (1)(b).
42   Canada, Access to Information Act, R.S., c. A-1, s. 69(1); 1992, c.1, s.144(F). www.parl.gc.ca/Publications/LOP-e.htm.
43   Ibid, s. 69(3).
44   Campbell Clark, "Access requests bogged down by PM's officials," *Globe and Mail* (December 24, 2007), A1, A4.
45   As a British academic notes, "A government, elected perhaps by less than 40 percent

staffed by professionals paid to keep informed on government intentions, are less handicapped than citizens. For them, making a living, raising a family, etc. leave little time for monitoring possible cabinet deliberations.

With cabinet operations cloaked in secrecy, there is less to disturb any illusions that the prime minister is more than a mere mortal; less support for the notion that it is not in the general interest to delegate so much control of government to him or her. Further, when members of the government act, it is easier to believe that they are doing so based on convincing information and advice that is not available to us.[46]

Thinking within the boundaries imposed by the existing political system, not even parliamentary reformers considered that the public might have the right to know what was being said in those key representative bodies, cabinet and caucus. Access would have disrupted the system. But shouldn't a system that requires keeping key policy-related information and advice from its citizens be disrupted and replaced by one that is almost fully transparent?

Perhaps the caucus can be seen as concerned with party business and, therefore, within a party's rights to keep discussions in that body under wraps. But the division between party and public business is largely artificial. Since MPs, silent in the Commons, often assert that they vigorously represent their constituents in caucus, their constituents are entitled to the substantiating evidence openness might provide.[47]

The Office of the Information Commissioner, reporting to parliament,

---

of the popular vote, can make radical changes against the wishes of the majority—or even before the majority's views have been heard or allowed to crystallize." Vernon Bogdoran, *The People and the Party System,* (Cambridge: Cambridge University Press, 1981), 70.

46   Think of how a whole generation of those Americans even modestly attentive to politics was forced, with the publication of the Watergate tapes, to come to terms with the uncomfortable reality of what really happened in the Oval Office during one president's term of office. Full access to cabinet deliberations might give Canadians even more confidence than they already have that with their input policy would be better than when left entirely to "professionals."

47   When being interviewed away from their constituents, MPs tell a different story. "Backbench MPs report that when working in caucus, they are rarely able to convince the governing party to introduce new initiatives, and even less successful in persuading it to change its declared course of intended action. Phillips and Orsini, "Mapping the Links," 3.

was established to review the government's compliance with the Access to Information Act. Complaints about the government's action or inaction on requests for information were first to be considered by the Information Commissioner and, if not resolved, could be referred to the federal court for an authoritative decision—a procedure that has often been necessary.

Even when reforms are sponsored by the political and bureaucratic leaders of the government, proper implementation of them is difficult when they run counter to that leadership's competitive interests. It is naïve to think that the government respects its own laws universally. In the case of access to information, government leaders acknowledge the desirability of transparency in principle and law. At the same time, they struggle to maintain as much of the competitive advantage control of information gives them as they can. The Harper government has proven to be one of the most secrecy-minded of modern administrations, even though it is legally bound by the Access to Information Act and has stressed its commitment to transparency in its winning election campaigns.

In the interest of their political masters, and their own, officials in the PMO and PCO have engaged in an ongoing struggle with successive information commissioners to give the language pertaining to cabinet confidences the widest possible interpretation. In his 1999–2000 report, in advance of Mr. Harper becoming PM and emphasizing the control of information, the commissioner wrote,

> The Privy Council Office (PCO) decided to resist and challenge almost all of the Commissioner's investigative powers. To this end, officials of the PCO have ignored orders for the production of records; failed to fully comply with such orders (in one case, non-compliance persisted until after two Federal Court judges had ordered PCO to comply); withheld records claimed to be privileged (with the full knowledge that privileges do not apply during the Commissioner's investigations); and refused to answer questions under oath. Most astoundingly, PCO developed the theory that the provision in the Access Act which gives the Commissioner the power to enforce his investigatory orders is unconstitutional.[48]

---

48   Information Commissioner, Annual Report 1999–2000, 9. www.infocom.gc.ca/

The Commissioner returns to this resistance in his next (2001–02) annual report:

> It is a fact that the Clerk of the Privy Council insists on the broadest possible interpretation of the scope of cabinet secrecy. As well, the prime minister is personally committed to insulating his office and offices of ministers from the Act's coverage and from the Information Commissioner's investigative jurisdiction. These "hostilities" at the top stand in the way of the good-faith efforts, at more junior levels, to get on with a cultural change to open government.[49]

The direct challenges to the Act mounted by senior members of the political establishment may not be as important as their quiet sabotage of it. Information cannot be pried out of government and responsibility for actions clearly assigned, if records are not kept. David Berlin cites the Information Commissioner as stating that, with the adoption of the Act, "government record keeping started slipping as officials became adept at finessing ministerial guidelines."[50] This has continued to the point that now, Berlin writes, "The attitude has truly become, 'Why write it when you can speak it? Why speak it if you can nod? Why nod when you can wink?'"[51]

The culture of secrecy the Commissioner identifies is the product of the intense competition between parties and indifference to the interests of citizens who want to share in governing.[52] It continues because we are too weakly represented in the system to insist on access to almost full information.

---

menu-e.asp.
49   Information Commissioner, Annual Report 2001–2002, 15. www.infocom.gc.ca/menu-e.asp.
50   Berlin, "A Love Affair with Secrecy," 35.
51   Ibid., 37
52   The Gomery inquiry into the sponsorship program in Quebec provided a journalist with a good example of this sabotage. "The sponsorship program was practically a 'black op,' managed directly out of the office of then-public works minister Alfonso Gagliano. Written notes were discouraged, most staff members were kept deliberately in the dark, and when Mr. Gagliano knew he was about to be punted out of the department, there was a general purge of whatever notations or instructions that did exist." John Ibbitson, "Heartbeat of democracy grows faint amid the noise," Globe and Mail (October 22, 2004), A4.

The adoption of the Access to Information Act, with its exceptions, may be one of those reforms that, as an unintended consequence, compounds the problem it was intended to help solve. The objective of reformers who pressed for openness was to improve the performance, image, and level of public support of government. Investigative journalism has certainly been stimulated by the Act. The public is now more aware than ever of the abuses of power, partisan distortion of policies, and blunders of party-government. While it was inevitable that these exposures would produce an increase in alienation, one could reasonably think that this would be temporary—replaced in a short time by greater trust in government as politicians cleaned up their acts in response to the new regime of transparency. However, with the continuing competitive pressures still shaping the behaviour of governing politicians, it appears that they will simply have to give more thought to hiding improper actions from the prying eyes of the media and public.

Despite the strong legislative exhortation to openness, and the narrowly worded exemptions set out in the Act, it is administered all too often as a secrecy statute. Frequently, the test used by officials is, "If in doubt, keep it secret"—a test that has been rejected by the Federal Court. As well, there are only halting efforts being made to put information into the public domain on a proactive basis.[53] By example and instruction, political leaders maintain the bureaucrat's commitment to the traditional culture of secrecy. Government leaders will fight to retain as much control of information as they can, for as long as they can, while a political system that gives a competitive advantage to a secretive governing party remains in place.[54]

Full access information would accompany policy democracy automatically. With constituency parliaments in place, approximately 24,000 local leaders across the country would be directly involved in making public policy. To govern effectively, political leaders and bureaucrats,

---

53   Information Commissioner, Annual Report 2000–2001, 19. www.infocom.gc.ca/menu-e.asp

54   Agreeing with a report that access to information is in decline in Canada, the current (2011) Information Commissioner writes, "Only about 16 percent of the 35,000 requests filed last year resulted in full disclosure of information, compared with 40 percent a decade ago…." Dean Beeby, "Canada hits bottom on global FOI rating," *Globe and Mail* (January 10, 2011), A7.

now preoccupied with defending themselves and their government from opposition attacks and general criticism, would have to earn the support of a parliament representing these local leaders. The empowered constituency parliamentarians would not tolerate important information being withheld from them and "their" MP. In these circumstances, an access to information act and the bureaucracy required to administer it might not be necessary.

Direct democracy. The adoption and widespread use of the devices of direct democracy—the initiative, referendum, and recall—appear, superficially, to have a much stronger potential for empowering citizens than any other reform, including the establishment of constituency parliaments. They could give all citizens—as voters on referenda and as signers of recall and initiative petitions—multiple occasions to wield real power.[55] They are already in very limited use in all three levels of our government, and there is foreign experience with them.[56]

When the issue of adopting the initiative and recall was put to voters in British Columbia in 1996, there was overwhelming support for the proposal (see discussion below). Should, then, pressing for wider dependence on direct democracy be a major, or perhaps *the* major focus of reform? Or should citizens be empowered through constituency parliaments, and then decide for themselves whether the devices of direct democracy have any place in what would then be *their* system?

As with proportional representation (PR), support for the incorporation of the institutions of direct democracy into the Canadian system has come in waves, dating back to the turn of the century. At that time, the progressive movement in the United States succeeded in having them adopted in many of

---

55   Support for the democratic aspirations of citizens has led some academics to seek ways of integrating direct democracy with the system responsibly. See, for example, Matthew Mendelsohn and Andrew Parkin, "Introducing Direct Democracy in Canada," *Choices,* Strengthening Canadian Democracy, IRRP 7, 5 (June, 2001). www.irpp.org; J. Patrick Boyer, *Direct Democracy in Canada and the people's mandate: referendums and a more democratic Canada* (Toronto: Dundurn Press, 1992).

56   For a summary of this experience, see Lawrence LeDuc, *The Politics of Direct Democracy: referendums in global perspective* (Peterborough, Ont.: Broadview Press, 2003).

the western states, but not nationally to break the hold of corporate interests on state governments. Reformers in Canada followed their lead with much less success. Provincial farm parties and elements of the National Progressives campaigned in the 1920s, promising measures of direct democracy at both levels of government. The parties proved unenthusiastic about following through on their promises, however, even when, as provincial governments, they could have done so.[57]

That direct democracy has resurfaced now as a significant issue in Canadian politics is attributable to several developments. Political leaders, forced to give up their rigid adherence to the doctrine of parliamentary sovereignty, find it more difficult to dismiss the public's demands that it decide high-profile issues directly. The erosion of the authority of government has led to broad acceptance by us and our leaders that at least significant constitutional changes must be endorsed by citizens in referenda. Their approval by a party-dominated parliament, and similarly dominated provincial legislatures, are not sufficient to establish citizen consent. The system purporting to be "representative" is not representing.

Developments in the party system, as well as in the constitutional debates, raised the saliency of direct democracy again. Politically ambitious Westerners, seeking to become a greater force in federal politics, were inspired by the earlier success, albeit temporary and limited, of the national Progressive party and provincial farm parties in promoting direct democracy. Organized in the Reform party in 1987 they, too, appealed to voters on regional grievances coupled with promises of democratic reforms. In the case of the Reform party, a right-wing social and economic agenda was also part of the party's package, however.

The commitment to direct democracy continued when Reform reorganized to become the Alliance party. However, it disappeared with the merger of the Alliance and the "old" Progressive Conservative Party into the "new" Conservative Party led by Stephen Harper.

A further contemporary push behind direct democracy is the discovery of its utility by right-wing groups and governments. The political right,

---

57   The experience of the farm parties with direct democracy is discussed more extensively in chapter 9.

once fearful of mob rule is, on the basis of a hundred years of experience with electoral democracy—and only a little less with a universal franchise—now confident of its ability to mobilize the public to advance or protect its interests. It has the resources to do so.

Experience with direct democracy again illustrates the difficulty of integrating supposedly citizen-empowering reforms into a system where party elites are entrusted with managing their application. At the national level, this experience is limited to the use of the referendum.[58] The first of these was held on the issue of prohibition in 1898. The Liberal government of the day was in control of deciding to put the question of prohibition to a vote, choosing its wording, and determining when the vote would be held. Further, it was protected by a safety net in the event that citizens came up with the answer it did not want. Constitutionally, the monarch, i.e., the Governor General or provincial Lieutenant-Governor, acting on the advice of the prime minister or premier had (and still has) the final word on legislation. The people's verdict on an issue cannot be legally binding, therefore. The government may, however, make it politically binding by promising not to use its right to advise the Governor General to reject the result of a vote.

With its referendum on prohibition, the Liberal government was not renouncing the principle of parliamentary sovereignty, not taking a first significant step in the direction of involving Canadians more fully in making the laws under which they would live. For the government, the referendum was merely a useful management device. The intense battle between the pro- and anti-prohibition forces in and outside the parliamentary wing of the Liberal Party put the party in a position where its electoral prospects would be damaged no matter which side it supported. Party strategists decided it was best to finesse the situation, at least temporarily, by referring the issue to the people. The people made the "wrong" decision, and it was set aside.[59]

---

58   A discussion of referenda at federal and provincial levels of government is found in Lawrence LeDuc, "Consulting the People: The Canadian Experience with Referendums" In *Citizen Politics,* eds. Joanna Everitt and Brenda O'Neill (Don Mills, Ont.: Oxford University Press, 2002), 247–67.

59   Voters were asked, "Are you in favour of the passing of an act prohibiting the importations, manufacture, or sale of spirits, wine, ale, beer, and all other liquors for use

The next resort to a national popular consultation was the referendum/plebiscite on conscription, held in 1942 by the wartime Liberal government of Mackenzie King. King had promised Quebecers that conscription would not be imposed as it had been during the First World War. It was the kind of irresponsible promise that success in electoral politics encourages in power-seeking politicians. How could King know when the promise was made how the war would evolve, and what recruitment policy would be needed to meet Canada's responsibilities? Again, a party leader in a difficult situation resorted to a referendum/plebiscite to finesse a difficulty. The overwhelming vote that King knew would be cast for conscription would help persuade Quebecers that he really had no option but to modify his position somewhat—but that the Liberal Party was still their special party friend in Ottawa.

The third national referendum—on the Charlottetown constitutional accord—was again adopted to deal with a particularly difficult political situation. This time the challenge was to the constitutional status quo, and to the mode of representation normally adopted by our political elite when it negotiated constitutional change, rather than to a particular party government.

The provincial premiers and the prime minister recognized that to overcome their "authority deficit" they needed direct citizen approval of the Charlottetown Accord. And with three provincial governments (Quebec, Alberta, and British Columbia) already required by provincial statutes to submit constitutional changes to a vote, a national referendum on the constitutional package was accepted as the appropriate way to get this approval. The prime minister and all provincial premiers, plus the majority of members of the political establishment, supported the Accord; the result should have been a foregone conclusion—if the political leaders' claims to represent their constituents had much substance.

In his study of the use of referenda in Canada, Lawrence LeDuc observes that, "In referendums, as in elections, the messengers often matter as much

as beverage." With a 44 percent turnout, 51 percent voted "yes" and 49 percent "no."
www.Canadian-politics.com/CPWiki/tiki-index.php?page=Prohibition

as the message."[60] With this being the case, a referendum can seldom be a serious public consultation on an issue. LeDuc concludes, "The three federal referendums that have taken place over our history have singularly failed to resolve the particular political problem that each was intended to address."[61] His assessment must raise doubt that referenda can compensate for the inability of an unrepresentative parliament to make decisions on major issues that will be unchallenged.

The provinces also provide egregious examples of how the devices of direct democracy are abused by elites in the absence of an organized citizenry able to ensure that their utilization is "honest," rather than manipulative. If the objective of direct democracy is merely to bolster partyocracy, its usefulness is still dubious. On the basis of his study of direct democracy in the United States, Matthew Mendelsohn concludes, "Data indicate that no growth in political efficacy accompanies the introduction or expansion of direct democracy. Citizens in those states that use initiative do not feel more efficacious, while the introduction of initiative processes in some states has not produced an increase in regime support."[62]

The devices of direct democracy have been embraced to deflect hostility to partyocracy; to permit a release of some of the pressure building up for radical change in the system; and to improve its "optics." In the competitive struggle between parties, the devices have proven useful in enabling the governing party to get out of politically difficult situations; to force its values on, or merely to embarrass, its successor in office;[63] and to attempt

60   LeDuc, "Consulting the People," 259.
61   Ibid., 247. Canadian support for referenda, even on constitutional issues, is far from universal. A poll asking whether changes to the constitution should be referred to a referendum found 23 percent responding "always"; 42.5 percent "sometimes"; 15.5 percent "rarely"; 9.9 percent "never." Institute for Research on Public Policy (IRPP), April 2000. (Queen's University, Kingston: Canadian Opinion Research Archive). www.queensu.ca/cora/
62   Matthew Mendelsohn, "Introducing Deliberative Direct Democracy in Canada: Learning from the American Experience," *American Review of Canadian Studies* 26, 3 (1997), 451.
63   I am thinking here of the decision of an outgoing Social Credit government in British Columbia in 1991 to hold a referendum on adopting the initiative and recall, the result of which forced the incoming NDP government to accept them reluctantly. Its reluctance was reflected in its decision to make it difficult for citizens to use the initiative

to legitimate constitutional policy where it is clear that party government's authority, or that of parliament or legislatures, is no longer adequate to do so.

The strengthening of the representative system envisaged in the policy democracy/constituency parliament model would make the adoption of the devices of direct democracy, like the other reforms considered in this chapter, almost completely redundant. Why would we need the initiative? With elected constituency parliaments in place, we could use them to insist that elected representatives introduce citizen-sought-after legislation. A legislature that truly represented us would be responsive to initiatives taken by constituency parliaments.

Again, with a House of Commons that did represent the people, what purpose would be served by referenda? Each vote of parliament could, honestly, be seen as a popular referendum. The only purpose of a popular vote on an issue would be to give added strength to a policy decision of fundamental importance to the country or, perhaps, to resolve jurisdictional disputes between levels of government. A constituency parliament might also want to conduct a referendum locally to confirm its judgement on an issue.

Finally, would the recall be needed where an MP was chairperson of, and worked closely with, the members of his or her constituency parliament? It is hard to see an MP continuing in office if a local parliament representing the people in the constituency were to express a lack of confidence in him or her. If the voters were to find they had made a mistake in their choice of MP, it could be corrected without resorting to a cumbersome, time- and attention-consuming recall procedure. I am assuming that those constituency parliament members enjoy the respect and confidence of the citizens who elected them. If that is not the case, the MP might successfully resist their attempt to remove him or her from office.

Far from enhancing the quality of our political life in partyocracy, the

---

and recall.
One result of this is to tie up citizens unhappy with the performance of a government, or a member of same, in nearly impossible-to-win campaigns. It has proven to be a useful device to neutralize public discontent.

more extensive use of the devices of direct democracy in the hands of elites would impact negatively on it. A higher level of democracy is to be found in making parliament *our* representative body. But that can't be achieved within the framework of partyocracy.

Reform in House of Commons. Virtually everyone, including most MPs, recognizes that many changes in parliament are long overdue. The mythology that has supported a party-prime minister-dominated parliament, i.e., that it represents the people and is acting on a mandate received from us, has lost its ability to mobilize popular support for government.[64] Canada acquired (briefly) a new prime minister at the end of 2003 who empathized, rhetorically at least, with the dissatisfaction surrounding parliament. As almost the first item of business for his government, Prime Minister Martin produced a series of proposals attacking what he had earlier identified as the "democratic deficit."[65] I will focus on those intended to attack that deficit by enhancing the role of our representatives in the Commons. Although it is not included in his proposals, I will also include a glance at the issue of Senate reform. It, too, is important for what it suggests about the dynamics of institutional change when we are excluded from the process.

The political environment was exceptionally favourable when Prime Minister Martin launched his parliamentary reforms. His Liberal government had replaced one that was scandal-ridden and led by a particularly bullying prime minister, Jean Chrétien. In the short time before a looming election, Martin faced the challenge of disassociating himself from that government and its leader. He acknowledged the pent-up frustration of the caucus he

64   Occasionally, polls ask us to indicate the respect or trust we have for members of various occupations or professions. It is virtually always the case that politicians are placed last or almost last in the rankings, and by a wide margin when compared to, say, business executives. Yet, these politicians are the people expected to lead the country. See, for example, Jane Armstrong et al., "Respect for Professions," *Globe and Mail* (November 10, 1998). It is consistent with this ranking that trust in politicians and their arena of combat, the House of Commons, is also low and declining. See data summarized in Centre for Research and Information on Canada, the CRIC Papers, "Voter Participation in Canada: Is Canadian Democracy in Crisis?" (October. 2001), 16. www.cric.ca
65   Canada, Privy Council Office, "Ethics, Responsibility, Accountability," An Action Plan for Democratic Reform (Ottawa: 2004) www.pco-bcp.gc.ca/

inherited with a package of reforms enhancing their status; he intended to rebuild team solidarity and enthusiasm for the upcoming campaign. It could also erode the opposition's ownership of an attractive issue.[66]

Speaking shortly before taking the reins of party leader and PM, Mr. Martin set out his vision of the role of parliament and of how to reach it. Both were widely applauded by democratic and parliamentary reformers alike, but not by the Official Opposition.[67] On the role of the House of Commons, Martin stated, "The House of Commons is where, first and foremost, the public will must be heard, articulated, and exercised; where Canada's response to dramatic changes must be shaped; and where our strategy for ensuring that it benefits Canadians must be forged. The House of Commons is where the country takes control of its destiny; and better than any other institution, it's the place where, as a people, we can set a common agenda."[68]

Martin has a vision almost identical to that presented in this book but without a model for achieving it.

On the means needed to allow the Commons to play this role, Martin said, "Under our system of representative government, there should be a direct line that runs from the people to their representatives—their members of Parliament—and through them to the executive. The problem is that over time that line has become obscured."[69]

That "direct line" between citizen and elected representative Mr. Martin refers to has not "become obscured." It was disrupted when parties took

---

66   The opposition was criticized for not welcoming the reform proposals: "No sooner had Prime Minister Paul Martin's government tabled reforms that might revolutionize and invigorate parliamentary life than, as if on autopilot, opposition spokesmen rose to denounce them as inadequate and inspired by partisanship. It was to weep." Jeffrey Simpson, "Four assassins stalk Martin's reforms," the *Globe and Mail* (February 5, 2004), A21.
67   "These latest Liberal proposals for a revitalized Parliament should be seen for what they are, a divisive action on behalf of Paul Martin and his crowd, eager to score political points against their own leader." Stephen Harper and Chuck Strahl, "Unleash our political process," the *Globe and Mail* (August 10, 2002), A15.
68   Paul Martin, Speech on Democratic Reform to students at Osgood Law School, October 22, 2002. Mimeo.
69   Ibid.

control of elected constituency representatives (MPs) over a century ago. Many MPs want to speak for their constituents, but they do not yet seem to recognize that a precursor to doing this must be to provide citizens with the means needed to form an informed constituency viewpoint.

To allow more free votes, the Martin government proposed a three-line classification of legislation. MPs were to vote as they chose on legislation designated as one- or two-line votes. Under this arrangement, the government stated, "Members will have much greater freedom to voice their views and those of their constituents." It was anticipated that this arrangement would require ministers to lobby MPs to persuade them to support their bills.[70] As they lobbied, the MPs could put forward the views of their constituents on the legislation.[71]

In a significant footnote to its proposal, the government stated, "The government will invite all parties to join in this initiative [freeing MPs from strict party discipline] so that all members of Parliament can represent the views of Canadians and to allow for parliamentary coalitions to be built across party lines. The government believes that a system based on consensus building will enhance respect for Parliament and strengthen Canadian democracy."[72]

In those few words, the government recognized (a) the damage that the prevailing highly adversarial model of party representation inflicts on the

---

70   It is generally agreed that MPs, almost as much as their constituents, need more clout in making policy. Both would get it in policy democracy. The current situation is suggested in a survey in which senior business executives and bureaucrats rated the influence of those participating in making policy. Only 7 percent of bureaucrats thought that MPs had moderate or great influence in the process, as compared to an 80% ranking for cabinet ministers.(8) The same survey found that neither government nor business felt understood by the other.(5) Public Policy Forum, "Bridging Two Solitudes, A Discussion Paper on Federal Government-Industry Relations" (Ottawa:2000). www.ppforum.ca. Bringing corporate CEOs into government as citizens, through constituency parliaments, might increase the level of government-corporate understanding somewhat.

71   Commons procedures would be changed so that MPs would not be presented with a government bill written in stone on second reading but, rather, a document open to development. This is a change also envisaged in the policy democracy/constituency parliament model presented in chapter l.

72   Canada, Privy Council Office, "Ethics, Responsibility, Accountability," 4.

functioning of parliament, and (b) that independent voting by government MPs would require that opposition MPs also vote independently. The incumbent government could not survive in office with its team "undisciplined" and the opposition ready to do battle as a united force. The survival instincts of MPs on the government side would cause them to close ranks on almost all issues, regardless of any formal offer of freedom implied by the designation of a bill as first or second line.

There is no question that, in theory, MPs both overwhelmingly support more free votes and see their absence as contributing significantly to the decline of parliament.[73] But how likely was it that the cooperation needed for the Liberal initiative to allow more free votes would be forthcoming from their party adversaries?

Other proposals of the prime minister, such as allowing MPs to review appointments made by him; a strengthening of Commons committees; an expanded opportunity for private members' bills to be considered; etc., could only be of indirect significance to empowering citizens as long as those MPs continued to represent parties first and what they guessed to be the informed views of constituents secondarily.

A questioning of the institutional arrangements that underpin adversarial party politics should logically have followed the government's endorsement of a "system based on consensus building." At the very least, Mr. Martin might have endorsed PR or some other more significant institutional change. Instead, he seemed to expect the opposition parties to respond positively to his appeal while the structures that rewarded their intense partisanship remained in place![74] His proposals were either insincere, merely election fodder, or incredibly naïve.

---

73   "On the public record, MPs have been almost unanimous in arguing for a relaxation of party discipline and more free votes. Most recently, a consultative study undertaken by the Library of Parliament under the direction of parliamentarians found that MPs overwhelmingly believe that the institution "has lost its way," placing the blame squarely on "strongly enforced party discipline." Jerome H. Black and Bruce M. Hicks, "Strengthening Canadian Democracy: The Views of Parliamentary Candidates," *IRPP Policy Matters* 7, 2 (March 2006), 34. www.irpp.org.

74   In Ontario, in 1992, the new premier, Bob Rae, asked the opposition for a limited truce and a more collegial approach. On his appeal being greeted with cynical amusement, he stated, "I'm prepared to admit that I am paying a fair price for having been

In only a matter of weeks after the government announced the details of its plan to attack the democratic deficit, to the cautious applause of even some jaded veteran Ottawa observers, the verdict was in. "The democratic-deficit-reduction initiative is dead, killed by the realities of electoral politics," wrote Hugh Winsor, a *Globe and Mail* political analyst."[75] His conclusion was supported by a lengthy list of old-style partisan actions taken by the new Martin government. A columnist for the *Toronto Star*, Carol Goar, reached a similar conclusion, noting that while the Liberals wanted better communication with voters, they had still to figure out how to make it happen.[76] The difficulty for the party was that making it happen would risk its raison d'être, i.e., doing people's thinking and speaking for them. Partyocracy is organized around that party role, not around listening to and acting as directed by the citizenry.

The Harper government replaced that of Paul Martin. Leading a minority government, and seemingly unwilling to trust his colleagues in this tight competitive position, Prime Minister Harper has imposed unprecedented controls on them, increasing the existing democratic deficit significantly. In 2007, the Conservatives legislated fixed election dates. It was widely expected that with the date fixed, governments, particularly minority governments, would govern the country with less partisan manoeuvring; the reduction in the discretionary powers of the prime minister was welcomed. It was little noted, however, that a provision in the section of the Canada Elections Act fixing the election date specifically empowered the Governor General—who

---

a particularly difficult and tendentious leader of the opposition .... Politics is a tough business. People have to be prepared to live with it. Everybody who goes into public life knows it's going to be tough. All kinds of allegations get made, many and most of which are completely unfounded." Richard Mackie, "Rae tastes his own medicine," *Globe and Mail* (April 22, 1992). Why does Rae assume that, "People have to be prepared to live with it"? He is expressing another version of the "parties are inevitable" argument. For him, it seems, the system with its egregious weaknesses must simply be accepted, the possibility of democratic development ignored. In directing his request to the opposition, did he really think that traditional behaviour could be changed with a verbal request that was not backed by institutional change?

75   Hugh Winsor, "When politics wins out over principle," *Globe and Mail* (May 10, 2004), A4.

76   Carol Goar, "Consultation is fine in theory, rather less so in fact," *Toronto Star* (February 10, 1994), A19.

virtually always must act on the advice of the prime minister—to dissolve parliament and call an early election at his or her discretion. Governor-General Michaelle Jean did this at the prime minister's request in 2008.[77] The reform proved ephemeral. These actions by Prime Minister Harper illustrate the futility of depending on party governments for "honest" reform.

In summary, since Prime Minister Martin's proposals were consistent with the way Canadians, including the political establishment, believe parliament should function; there should have been little difficulty in implementing them successfully. That was not the case. The democratically minded people who move into the political realm feel they must live by the dictates of partyocracy, just as the business executive is the slave of market rules. Politicians can, however, change their rules. Until they do, they must use the weapons at their disposal to further the interests of their party. This includes supporting a hierarchical form of organization in the parliamentary wing of the party and exploiting every opportunity it has to gain competitive advantage from holding office.

Instead of investing thought and energy on parliamentary reforms that MPs could make themselves if they were not so strongly tied to their system, reform-minded citizens should pursue their own preferred reform, i.e., establishing constituency representation. Policy democracy/constituency parliaments would put in place that direct line between constituents and their elected representative in the House of Commons that Mr. Martin, correctly, deemed essential for it to function democratically.

Powerful encouragement for a successful change in the mode of representation is found in a study of the attitudes of MPs toward their representational role. Prof. David Docherty writes,

> When asked whose direction is more important to deciding how to vote on an issue in the House of Commons, their leader and party, or their constituents, MPs from more recent parliaments tend to

---

77   Section 56.1(1) of the Canada Elections Act reads, "Nothing in this section [fixing election dates] affects the powers of the Governor General, including the power to dissolve Parliament at the Governor General's discretion." The Governor General, of course, acts as directed by the prime minister in almost every circumstance. www.elections.ca/home.asp

side with voters. A survey of MPs in the last Mulroney government found that only 30 percent of members would place district ahead of party and leader, compared to 59 percent of rookie MPs in the first Chrétien government. Yet ... this change has not been reflected in parliamentary practices. Members of the public are just or more cynical about the motives and abilities of members to represent them today as they were fifteen or twenty years ago. Members of parliament, at their most basic level, believe they are providing as close to delegate style of representation as the Westminster system allows. The public, however, is not buying. If there is a gap between the public and the men and women whom the public elect, it is likely to be found in this area.[78]

If citizens campaign vigorously for a different mode of representation, they may find a surprising number of allies among party MPs.

Senate reform. A senate composed of prime ministerial appointees serving until age 75, and possessing formal powers roughly equal to those of an elected Commons, is a startling anachronism to find in a 21st-century political system claiming to be democratic. At least its membership is not hereditary! The existence of the Senate is more tolerable to us and MPs because its members, aware of their lack of democratic legitimacy, are restrained in the use of their constitutional authority.

It is almost literally the case that as the ink dried on the signatures to the British North America Act in 1867, it became clear that the Senate was not going to perform its intended function. Since then, reconstructing the Senate has been a kind of extended make-work project for people interested in political institutions in Canada. It is yet another example of how, in the absence of pressure from an organized citizenry, our institutions have become outdated.[79] Especially, it is an example of the confusion that characterizes

---

78   David Docherty, "Citizens and Legislators: Different Views on Representation," in *Value Change and Governance in Canada,* ed. Neil Nevitte (Toronto: University of Toronto Press, 2002), 174.

79   Polling in 2004 revealed that 24 percent of Canadians wanted the Senate left as is, 39 percent supported reforming it, and 29 percent favoured abolition. Canada, Centre

efforts to improve the system incrementally when there is no clearly defined model to guide us.

The Senate is not merely an amusing anachronism useful to prime ministers wishing to reward party bagmen or retire MPs. Significant harm is done to the public's perception of politics by leaving this institution in existence. The occasional footnote about the good work the Senate does—most of it easily assignable to some equally or better qualified body—only minimally offsets the ongoing ridicule to which the Senate is subject.

The PMO's 2004 paper on parliamentary reform does not mention the Senate. While frequently expressing support for Senate reform elsewhere, however, Martin insisted that it must be considered as part of general negotiations on the constitution.[80] That would have been the above-board way of proceeding, but the Harper government has chosen a different approach.[81] The prime minister first refused to fill vacancies, except where the provinces have elected senators that he could appoint. Then, urgently in need of Senate support, he did make some appointments intending, to return to his original plan of only appointing elected senators if he were returned to power with a majority government as he was in 2011.

Brian Mulroney created a precedent for such appointments, by acceding to Alberta's demand that he appoint Stan Waters, an elected Alberta senator-in-waiting to the Senate in 1990. Prime Minster Harper followed his example with the appointment of Bert Brown in 2007. It is a remarkable example of the power that partyocracy bestows on the PM that Mulroney, followed by Harper, can initiate a practice that, if continued, would fundamentally change the parliamentary system by significantly adding power and legitimacy to the Senate by electing its members. He could do this without consulting citizens, members of the House of Commons, or the provinces. It is probable that most of us are unaware of the significant impact that the prime minister's proposed changes in the Senate could have on the

---

for Research and Information on Canada, "Portraits of Canada," January 2004, 8. www.cric.ca. Earlier polls showed majority support for an elected senate.

80   For a report on one of these occasions, see Brian Laghi and Katherine Harding, "PM vetoes Alberta's Senate proposal," *Globe and Mail* (November. 18, 2004), A4.

81   For a critique of the PM's approach to "reforming" the Senate, see William Thorsell, "End run to an Americanized Senate," *Globe and Mail* (May 1, 2010), A19.

functioning of our government. Those who are aware might well have felt helpless to check the prime minister if they disagreed with his unilateral "amendment" of the constitutional distribution of powers.

A senate completely composed of provincially elected members—the direction in which the country is being moved by first Prime Minister Mulroney and now Prime Minister Harper—would vest the Senate with powers similar to those of the House of Commons—think of the American Senate. It could be even more powerful than that body, since its members would have tenure until the age of 75 under present regulations and could serve in the cabinet. (It is proposed to limit senators to an eight-year term.)

Further, a senate composed of members elected in provincial constituencies might strengthen the hand of the central government vis-à-vis the provinces. Senators with an interest in the central government would compete with premiers as spokespersons for their provinces. That might be desirable, but it could be at the cost of consigning the central government to American-style "gridlock." We could find ourselves with two democratically empowered chambers on parliament hill, wrestling over policy issues, each claiming to represent the same citizens.

It is almost certain that those senators who were elected would be chosen in party contests—the pattern adopted in the "advisory" Senate elections already conducted by the Alberta government. To win, the candidate for the Senate seat would need a party's backing. Elections to both the Commons and to the Senate would be party dominated but not necessarily won by the same party. Conservative MPs could, for example, sweep a province, while the Senate election could elect a Liberal. Whose claim to speak for the people of that province would be most convincing? Already frustrated by the performance of their national government, people would have additional reason to be alienated from it if intense internecine conflict engaged the House and Senate. The will of majority would be obscured and the efficient conduct of government impeded—all to little purpose. Citizens would not be empowered (more likely they would be *dis*empowered by deadlocked governments), and they would be even less supportive of government.

The election of the Senate would be undemocratic in ways other than those mentioned. First, the distribution of Senate seats between the provinces is not now, nor does it seem likely to become, proportional to their changing populations.[82] Second, an elected party senate would be an extension of the party representation that the majority of Canadians reject. Third, as they participated in Senate elections, citizens would be encouraged to identify themselves, even more strongly, as members of a provincial or regional bloc competing with others for influence on the central government. Fourth, we are now confused by the buck-passing that goes on between federal and provincial governments; that would be added to with two empowered legislative chambers in Ottawa. Fifth, it is more common to find modern democracies abolishing second chambers than enhancing their powers. There are good reasons for this. In the 21st century, we need government that is responsive to us and can provide good government. An elected senate would be a barrier to both.

Current proposals to elect and, in so doing, empower the Senate, are characterized as democratic, when in fact they are *undemocratic*. Influential citizens are already overly represented in our political life through both the interest-group and party systems. They do not need an elected senate, too. It is the general citizenry—the kept-silent majority and specific parts of it: the economically marginalized, the aboriginal population, women, the young and old, some ethnic minorities, and others—who are not adequately represented. Policies that would improve the quality of their lives are hard to get and keep in partyocracy. The policy democracy model would increase their representation and that of all other Canadians.

Abolition of the Senate and the redirection of the resources used to support it to a network of 308 elected constituency parliaments across the country would be a real step toward transferring the control of government from party elites to citizens.

Parliamentary reform: summing up. The acid test of the talk, and some action, related to reform in the Commons and proposals for change in the structure of the Senate is whether these proposals would strengthen the

---

82   The troubled American political system is the (poor) example that inspires most of the ideas of Alberta reformers, including those in that province who have advocated a Senate with equal representation from each province.

performance of government and reduce political alienation. A report of the Library of Parliament is telling on the latter issue: "Public opinion polls suggest that upwards of twenty years of reform directed to "restoring the role of the private member, and thus the role of Parliament" have had little positive impact on public perceptions. Indeed, public perceptions of the effectiveness of members of Parliament in their fundamental task of representation appear to have continued to grow more negative, even as the successive cycles of parliamentary reform since the late 1960s have taken effect."[83]

A new element—citizens organized in constituency parliaments—must enter our political life and change the balance of political power in the country before parliamentarians can become true "tribunes" of the people and the House of Commons a respected forum of the nation.

Conclusion

Our comparison of the benefits (?) of current reform proposals to those we could expect from adoption of the policy democracy/constituency parliament model is not yet complete. Examination of the attempt to strengthen the political system through reform of party and party finances remain. However, before turning to those in the next two chapters, we can reach some general conclusions based on what has been discussed thus far.

Long gone are the days when John Diefenbaker could bring a crowd to its feet with a rousing endorsement of traditional parliamentary government. Now audiences hear critiques of parliament and other aspects of politics, often delivered by politicians themselves. Their interest in change is not just rhetorical. Some tidying up of objectionable features of party-parliamentary government has actually occurred, and other reform proposals are being pursued.

There is a consensus on the need for change, change that satisfies the desire of citizens for more self-government. Reform proposals considered in

---

83   Jack Stilborn (prepared by), "The Roles of the Member of Parliament in Canada: Are They Changing?" (Ottawa: The Library of Parliament, 2002), 13. www.parl.gc/ca/information/library/PRBpubs/prb0204-e.htm

this chapter reflect this preoccupation, but the extent to which each aims to empower citizens is strikingly different. At one extreme, we have increases in tell-and-sell consultation and, at the other, measures of direct democracy. However, there is no clearly defined, overarching, truly democratic objective against which current reforms can be assessed—and discarded, if they fail to move the polity toward it. There should be. Forces supporting the status quo are well entrenched, and Canadians cannot afford to dissipate their energies on adjustments in the system that do not significantly strengthen our role in it.

An enormous amount of energy has to be expended now to get even trivial reforms adopted, and the exaggerated expectations associated with them generally lead to disappointment. They are swallowed by a system that quickly adjusts back to its unsatisfactory equilibrium point, or one that is even more undemocratic, i.e., based more than ever on the manipulation of citizens rather than on their representation.

The interests of elites, more than citizens, are reflected in all the current proposals for reform and, markedly, in the way those already adopted are functioning. Political leaders are engaged in an ongoing personal struggle to reconcile their commitment to democratic values with their stake in partyocracy. The commitment calls for them to support the democratic aspirations they share with their fellow citizens. Their vested interest demands that they hang onto as much of the existing system, their security blanket and source of status, as they can. They are in a strong position to do so.

Leaders ask us to devote some of the limited time and energy we have for politics to bolstering the legitimacy of an obsolete system. We are urged to vote in larger numbers; join parties; attend town-hall sessions; fill out insulting, loaded, party questionnaires; applaud parliamentary reforms (a century overdue) that do little to enrich citizenship; and so on. There is, however, real danger in prolonging the life of a fundamentally obsolete political system with "reforms" that do not go to the heart of its undemocratic features.

Party leaders are trapped in a system that, in a host of ways, makes it impossible for them to support truly representative government and survive in their current roles. That leaves it to us to reject the political palliatives the leaders offer and insist on having the mode of democratic representation we, and many parliamentarians, believe is appropriate to our time and needs.

The adoption of the policy democracy/constituency parliament model would represent a significant step forward in encouraging, over time, the evolution of an engaged citizenship willing to give *our* government the support it requires to meet its challenges. It would bypass a long, confused struggle to implement a variety of reforms that, at best, would help to keep a dysfunctional system in place.

Parties on the Public Payroll: Democratic Reform?

Parties that develop public funding sources in order to insulate themselves from the ebbs and flows of public support will inevitably distance themselves from those they represent. Running elections and governing by marketing principles may be successful in the short term for parties, but this strategy may well undermine the democratic process in the long term.

Russell J. Dalton and Martin P. Wattenberg

... There are grounds for wondering whether their [the parties'] continuing survival is more of a worry than their supposed decline. Is it so very comforting that parties can lose members, worry less about ideas, become detached from broader social movements, attract ever fewer voters, and still retain an iron grip on politics? If they are so unanchored, will they not fall prey to special-interest groups? If they rely on state funding instead of member contributions, will they not turn into creatures of the state?

The Economist

Introduction

Elections are the only formal link between us and the governing party. As long as this remains the case, the legitimacy of government will depend heavily on how elections are organized and, in particular, on how the party competitors are financed. This chapter will consider the most significant of the changes in regulations governing party/election finance introduced in the 1974 to 2010 period. My intent is to consider whether changing party/electoral finance is a promising approach to strengthening the limited democracy and the government we presently "enjoy." If it is, the case for more fundamental political change is weakened. If it is not, we should put aside the hope that changes of this kind will significantly vitalize our current political system.

This brief review of the regulation of party/election finance also provides an excellent example of how reforms are manipulated to benefit the party initiating them. If reforms are to primarily benefit us, we will have to take charge of the reform process.

Overview

The regulation of party/election finance is one of the many problematic areas in our political system that has been recognized, addressed ineffectually, and allowed to fester for years. Our forebears, sensitive to the threat to honest government posed by certain financial contributions to the parties, started regulating campaign funding as early as 1874. At that time, candidates were required to report their campaign expenses following the vote.[84] Other regulations followed. In 1908, for example, corporations were barred from making campaign contributions.[85] The same prohibition was proposed again in 2003 by Prime Minister Chrétien.

The regulations adopted early on had little effect, because they were not enforced effectively, i.e., the party government adopting the regulations and its successors chose to evade them. From the 1920s to the politically tumultuous 1960s, the issue of party/election finance was set aside. Then, two government committees, and later a royal commission, examined the issues involved and recommended changes, some of which were adopted.[86]

---

84 Jean-Pierre Kingsley, Chief Electoral Officer, "Money and Elections," (Paper presented at the XVIII World Congress of the International Political Science Association, Quebec City, August 4, 2000, 4. www.electionscanada.ca
85 Jay Makarenko, "Federal Campaign Laws in Canada," Maple Leaf Web, 2. www.mapleleafweb.com
86 Canada. Committee on Election Expenses. (Barbeau Committee) 1966a. (Ot-

The cycle of changes following the studies was initiated by Prime Minister Trudeau in 1974. The prime minister headed a minority government and needed to refurbish his early image as a reformer.[87] He might not have done so had his government not been pressured by the NDP, the principal beneficiary of the changes being considered, on whose votes his government depended for support. Additionally, with the advent of television advertising as a major campaign expense, all the parties were interested in new ways of raising funds. The act adopted in 1974 has seen significant amendments up to the present.[88] The changes made were radical but not without precedent. Some Canadian provinces and many other countries had already adopted regulations similar to those initially proposed by Trudeau and to others adopted later.

The governing party of the moment (Liberal, Progressive Conservative, or Conservative) has always chosen to draft the changes in electoral law itself, rather than delegating the task to a more impartial agency. As a result, the interests of the party authors were, naturally, reflected in the adoption or rejection of the recommendations of the commissions that had studied the issue. Many expected that the changes would quite dramatically improve the quality of Canadian politics. Readers may ask themselves whether they have noticed a qualitative change in our politics since 1974.

Public Financing/Restricting Competition

In rough order of their appearance, the focus of the major changes proposed and adopted in the period from 1974 to the present was on: stimulation of individual contributions to parties with tax write-offs; state contributions

---

tawa: Queen's Printer); Special House of Commons Committee on Election Expenses (Chappell Committee) 1971, 13:19; Canada, Royal Commission on Electoral Expenses and Party Financing, (the Lortie Commission), (Ottawa: Minister of Supply and Services, 1991).

87   Support existed for the reform. A survey sponsored by Elections Canada revealed

that (93.8 percent) of Canadians supported limits on party and candidate spending, i.e., the actions the government took. Data extracted from a letter sent by the chief electoral officer to Mr. Peter Adams, Chair, Standing Committee on Procedure and House Affairs, on February 5, 1998. www.elections.ca.

88   Canada Act. 1974 [R.S., c.14 (1st Supp.), s.1.] 7–55.

to "approved" election expenses of parties and candidates; requirements for party registration and for registered party and candidate expenditures established; a new level of transparency about party/election finance; limitations on, and then complete prohibition of, corporate, union, and association contributions to parties; an annual subsidy to registered parties; expansion of the right to party registration and its benefits; and, finally, a proposal to eliminate the recently adopted subsidy to registered parties. Changes galore—but progress toward a more citizen-responsive political order based on parties?

The most significant feature of the changes was the introduction of public/taxpayer direct and indirect funding of some of the party candidates' election expenses and of those of the central party.[89] The new statute stimulated individual contributions by allowing donors to deduct a percentage of their contribution to a registered party, up to a maximum of $500 from their taxes. A donation of $100 would allow the donor to deduct $75. Since all citizens would have to make up the resulting loss of $75 in tax revenue, this can be seen as a combined form of public and individual financing of parties. This tax write-off remained stable for a number of years, but in 2003, it was increased to provide a maximum benefit of $650 for a donation of $1,275. Corporate contributions to parties had always been treated as a business expense, so allowing citizens a tax credit could be seen as, belatedly, extending to individuals a similar inducement to contribute.

It is consistent with the negative feelings we have for parties that, despite the financial encouragement, it was found that "only a tiny percentage of Canadians contributed to a party and/or candidate, even with the tax inducement. The percentage of electors contributing to any federal party was 1.26 percent in 1984 and 1.18 percent in 1988. If we add the number of contributions by individuals to candidates, the percentages rise to 1.78 percent in 1984 and 1.77 in 1988."[90] The tax write-off did help the parties

---

89   The changes are set out in the Election Expenses Act, 1974, C51.

90   W. T. Stanbury "Regulating the Financing of Federal Parties and Candidates," in *Canadian Parties in Transition,* 2nd ed., eds. A. Brian Tanguay and Alain-G. Gagnon (Toronto: Nelson, 1996), 382.

raise larger amounts from individuals, however, reducing their dependence on contributions from organizations: corporations, unions, etc.[91]

The largely ignored inducement to individuals to contribute was accompanied by spending limits on the parties and their candidates. Candidates were reimbursed for some of their election expenses but only conditionally. If they received at least 15 percent of the vote, they were reimbursed for a portion of their approved expenses up to a maximum allowable amount set by Elections Canada.[92] By 2004, the 15 percent had been lowered to 10 and the reimbursement raised from 50 to 60 percent of approved expenses.[93]

The 15 and then 10 percent thresholds were high enough to prevent candidates of small parties from benefiting from the reimbursement. Discrimination against them was a characteristic of all the changes made in the 1974–2007 period. This was the case despite the recommendations of the committees and royal commission that "fairness" and "levelling the playing field" should be emphasized in any changes made in party/election finance.

The limits on spending established in 1974 were presented to the public as a major reform. But, like much political terminology, the use of the term *limits* was misleading. Referring to them, political scientist Ronald Landes wrote, "Limits that are set so high that no party approximates them in no way curtail party spending in campaigns. In fact, since the public now subsidizes these expenses, the costs of the campaigns have soared to unprecedented levels."[94] All through the multiple changes in election regulations from 1974 to the present, the major parties have made sure that their financial resources were enhanced.

A decade after the 1974 changes, the system of public finance was expanded dramatically in a way that continued the discrimination against the candidates of small parties and initiated reimbursements of election

---

91   Kingsley, "Money and Elections," 6. The nominal value of tax credits increased from $3 million a year in 1977 to $17.5 million in 1988.
92   Election Expenses Act, 1974, C51, S 63.1 (1).
93   Andrew Heard, "Canadian Election Laws and Policies," 4. www.sfu.ca/~aheard/elections/laws.html
94   Ronald G. Landes, *The Canadian Polity,* 2nd ed. (Scarborough, Ont.: Prentice-Hall Canada Inc., 1987), 266.

expenses to their national organizations on a similarly discriminatory basis.[95] Registered parties—those contesting 50 seats and meeting other requirements—were entitled to a reimbursement of a percentage of their allowable expenses. Initially, the percentage was 22.5. It increased to 60 percent for the 2004 election and then reverted to 50. The reimbursement was conditional on the party receiving 2 percent of the national vote or 5 percent of the vote in the constituencies which they contested and spending at least 10 percent of their allowable expenditure.

Of the minor parties, only the Greens, running a full slate of 308 candidates and receiving 4.3 percent of the national vote in 2004, have so far qualified for these reimbursements and the annual allowance to parties (see below). After a considerable campaign, the Greens were allowed to participate in the 2008 leaders' debate and won 6.8 percent of the vote in the ensuing election.

Next to the Greens, the major beneficiary of the system of reimbursements to candidates and parties has been the Bloc Québécois, with its campaign to dismember Canada. In 2007, 86 percent of the Bloc's revenues came from the federal treasury, compared to 37 percent for the Conservatives.[96]

When the policy of public funding of parties was initiated in 1983, the Bloc, organized in 1991, was not on the scene. Had it been, the policy might not have been adopted in its existing form. Indeed, Lucian Bouchard, who led the breakaway group of Conservatives and Liberals to form the Bloc, might not have done so without the assurance of federal financing. As we are often reminded, change may have unexpected consequences.

In 1983, parliament also adopted rules governing the distribution of free and purchased broadcast time for the parties during election campaigns. The chief electoral officer described this distribution as "equitable" but, as usual, it was based on a sliding scale that gave the largest amount of air time to the major parties.[97] Members of the public have many opportunities to hear from the dominant parties between elections. Our interest in hearing more from less-familiar voices was set aside by those drafting the rules.[98]

---

95   Kingsley, "Money and Elections," 4..
96   Makarenko, "Federal Campaign Laws in Canada," 25..
97   Kingsley, "Money and Elections," 3.
98   Perhaps, for example, a louder Green voice would have alerted more of us earlier to

It should be noted in passing that the discrimination against small parties extended into the House of Commons. There, a party had to have won 12 seats to qualify for recognition as a party and to be entitled to the various benefits attached to it.

The Royal Commission on Electoral Reform and Party Financing (the Lortie Commission), appointed by the Mulroney government, reported in 1992. (Astonishingly, this commission on electoral reform was precluded by its terms of reference from considering a new electoral system, i.e., proportional representation, a matter of particular interest to reform-minded members of the public.) As usual, the government acted on only those recommendations of the Commission that favoured its interests.[1]

The following year, immediately prior to the 1993 election, the governing party adopted further protection for itself and its colleagues in the House—as if the rule that to register and be eligible for public funds a party had to run 50 candidates were not enough.[2] An amendment to the Canada Elections Act increased the deposit for candidates from $200 to $1,000. A candidate receiving less than 10 percent of the vote—reduced from the initial 15— would forfeit half that, and be refunded the rest only after filing the financial statements required by Elections Canada.

As political scientist Heather MacIvor commented, this additional imposition was devastating for small parties. To stay registered, they were already required to field 50 candidates. Now they also had to raise $50,000, payable to the government, to field those candidates and could expect to recover only half that amount after the election.[3] In effect, a $500 penalty for running for public office was established. No amount of protection from new competitors seemed sufficient for the dominant parties that, as MacIvor

---

the environmental problems that now beset us.

1   On this point, see Alexandra Dobrowolsky and Jane Jenson, "Reforming the Parties: Prescriptions for Democracy," in *How Ottawa Spends 1993–94: A More Democratic Canada,* ed. Susan D. Phillips (Ottawa: Carleton University Press, 1993), 44–81.

2   The few quoted words are taken from Heather MacIvor, "The Charter of Rights and Party Politics: The Impact of the Supreme Court Ruling in Figueroa v. Canada (Attorney General)," Choices 10, 4 (Montreal: IRPP, 2004), 8. www.irrp.org. I am heavily indebted to Prof. MacIvor's insightful and comprehensive study of the issues under discussion here. The interpretation of them is, of course, mine.

3   Ibid., 8.

writes, behaved like a cartel when acting on the regulation of party/election finance.[4]

Approximately a decade later, prime ministers Chrétien and Harper took the final steps in the progression to an almost-exclusively government and individual system for funding of the established parties and in restricting competition to them. Chrétien became a reformer on the point of his retirement in 2003, when his reputation was badly tarnished by scandals. Without consulting his colleagues, he proposed that corporate and union contributions to the parties be banned. This provoked outrage within his party. MPs who would be staying on to fight in the political arena after his departure objected to both the prospect of being deprived of any of their financial weapons of war and to the PM's not-unusual failure to consult before announcing his proposed changes. Again, we see the arbitrary power of a PM being exercised on a highly sensitive issue.

The revenues lost by the ban would be compensated for by an annual grant from the treasury, based on the number of votes the party received in the most recent election. This would be in addition to increases in election reimbursements and boosting of the tax rebate for individual contributions mentioned earlier. To be eligible for these grants the party had to be registered and meet either the 2 or 5 percent threshold. The first grant was $1.75 per voter; provision was made for the amount to escalate with inflation.

The formula for distributing the grant avoided giving Canadians the opportunity to complement their occasional paper vote with an annual "financial ballot." We might have been allowed to check off on our income tax forms the party—or none—that we wanted to receive "our" $1.75 (now, in 2010, $1.95). Of all the parties, only the then-out-of-office Conservatives supported that idea. Leading a minority government for five years, the party has not proposed changing the distribution formula from which they benefitted. Now (2011) with a majority it proposes to eliminate the annual grants altogether over several years. For the other parties, involved in adopting the annual grant, it seemed that having to face one popular election every four or five years was demanding enough. Adding another each year, where the "vote" was monetary, was too much.

---

4   See Heather MacIvor, "Do Canadian Political Parties Form a Cartel?" *Canadian Journal of Political Science* 29, 2 (June, 1996): 317–33.

Chrétien's proposal for a complete ban was modified by him to allow very modest corporate and union contributions to constituency organizations. However, after he came into office in 2006, Prime Minister Harper banned these altogether. The difference between a legal and an effective ban should be noted. Quebec, whose ban predated that of the national government, has found itself mired in scandals, as parties and donors evade the party finance regulations.[5] Federal politicians may well succumb to electoral pressures and find ways around their ban, as well. The Conservatives are already facing criminal charges for allegedly evading some of the new rules in what is known as the "in-and-out" scandal.[6]

Our system of financing registered parties is now (in 2010) very simple. Parties are financed entirely through grants of public monies and contributions from individuals that are limited to $1,100 in total per year to any of the political parties, riding associations, and individual candidates. A significant portion of the approved election expenses of candidates (60 percent) and parties (50 percent) are reimbursed by the state, i.e., by us.[7] There is little likelihood that the present financing arrangements will remain fixed, however. They will probably continue in play as each governing party seeks to secure a competitive advantage for itself through amendments to them. [8] [9]

Third-Party Spending

A set of supplementary regulations was required to curb possible evasion

---

5   Rhéal Séguin, "Scandal-ridden Charest welcomes recess," *Globe and Mail* (June 11, 2010), A7.

6   Campbell Clark, "Tory ad scheme in Quebec was illegal, watchdog says," *Globe and Mail* (October 23, 2008).

7   Canada, Elections Canada, "Contributions and Expenses at a Federal Election or By-Election: Candidates and Registered Parties," 3–4. http://www.elections.ca/asp?s... .

8   Mark Kennedy, "Harper vows to take taxpayer cash from political parties," *Vancouver Sun* (January 13, 2011), B3.

9   An "academic" case for eliminating the allowance to parties and offering greater inducement to individuals to contribute to the party of their choice is presented in Tom Flanagan and David Coletto, "Replacing Allowances for Canada's National Political Parties?" 3:1, SPP Briefing Papers (Calgary: University of Calgary, School of Public Policy, 2010).

of the regulations on party spending by independent-of-party organizations ("third parties") intended to influence election outcomes.[10] Those proposed initially were challenged in the courts that found they violated the freedom of speech provisions of the Charter.[11] Over a period of years and after successive court challenges, however, agreement was reached on regulations that required the registration of third parties wishing to advocate independently of the political parties and limited the amounts they spent on their advocacy.[12] Elections Canada was charged with the added responsibility of administering these regulations. One set of regulations gave rise to the need for another.

The Figueroa (Communist Party) Challenge

The series of provisions discriminating against small parties, written into the legislation on party/electoral finance, did not go completely unchallenged. Unfortunately, the majority of us, unorganized and feeling powerless in political matters, just accepted what the dominant parties were doing. Indeed, then as now, most Canadians were so divorced from the political scene that they were unaware that changes were being made.[13] However, the tiny, poorly financed, but feisty Communist party of Canada took up the cudgels on its own and, depending on one's perspective, our behalf. With the help of the Supreme Court, it dramatically altered the intentions of the governing party vis-à-vis its small competitors, actual and potential.

---

10   For the history of legislation on third-party expenditures, see Canada, Elections Canada, "Regulation of Election Activities by 'Third Parties.'" www.elections.ca

11   The campaign against the regulations was organized by the National Citizen's Coalition, a right-wing lobby group then headed by Stephen Harper, later leader of the Conservative party and prime minister. For the decision of the Supreme Court that settled the dispute, see Harper v. Canada (Attorney General) [2004] S.C.C. 33.

12   The terms: third parties, including corporations and unions, are allowed to spend up to $150,000 overall to influence voters during an election campaign, but no more than $3,000 in any one constituency. If a third party spends more than $500, it is required to register with Elections Canada and account for its expenditures to the Chief Electoral Office in much the same way as parties and candidates. Andrew Heard, "Canadian Election Law and Policies." www.sfu.ca~aheard/elections/laws.html

13   Asked, "Are you aware or unaware that each federal political party received $1.75 of taxpayer money per year for every vote they received in the most recent federal election?" 75 percent of respondents said that they were unaware. SES/Public Policy Forum Poll, September 7, 2005. www.sesresearch.com.

Here are the details: the strengthened regulations against small parties adopted in 1993 and in effect for the election of that year "caught" the Communist party. Unable to field 50 candidates, the party, along with several others, was deregistered and required to wind up its affairs. Referencing Section 3, the political freedoms section of the Charter,[14] the party challenged sections of the Elections Act and, in particular, the constitutionality of the penalty for failing to meet the 50-candidate requirement.[15] A protracted series of lower-court hearings followed, with the party winning on some points and losing on others. Finally, in 2003, the Supreme Court sided with the party's position and gave parliament a year to reconsider the offending legislation.[16]

In proceedings leading up to this decision, government lawyers used their usual rationale in defending the regulations: they were constitutional because it was in the interest of good government to discourage these small parties.[17] They split the vote, making the formation of stable one-party majority governments more difficult, as well as confusing the electoral process with a multiplicity of voices. Avoiding these difficulties was a more important public interest than allowing voters a wider range of choice of parties at the polls or the freedom to organize a new party without facing unreasonable barriers.

For the Supreme Court, Mr. Justice Iabucci ruled, "While on its face, S 3 [of the Charter] grants only a right to vote and to run for office in elections,

14   "Every citizen of Canada has the right to vote in an election of members of the House of Commons or of a legislative assembly and to be qualified for membership therein." Canadian Charter of Rights and Freedoms, Part 1, S3.
15   Miguel Figueroa v. Canada (Attorney General), S.C.C. 37, June 27, 2003. When the cycle of changes in the legislation governing party/election financed started in 1974, the Charter and its protection of individual rights against government were almost a decade away. Party government, invoking parliamentary sovereignty, could legislate its values and interests without fear of the court's intervention, but that had changed by the time the Figueroa case arrived in the courts.
16   Details of the proceedings in the courts and an analysis of the judicial rulings are set out in MacIvor, "The Charter of Rights and Party Politics" and in Megan Furi, "Legislative History of Bill C-3," Parliamentary Research Branch, revised April 6, 2004. www.parl.gc.ca/information/library/PRBpubs/.
17   The government relied on Section 1 of the Charter: The rights set out in the Canadian Charter of Rights and Freedoms are "subject only to such reasonable limits prescribed by law as can be demonstrably justified in a free and democratic society."

Charter analysis requires looking beyond words of the section and adopting a broad and purposive approach. Section 3 should be understood with reference to the right of each citizen to play a meaningful role in the electoral process, rather than the election of a particular form of government."[18]

The government responded to the judgement with a bill incorporating the views of the Court. It became law in May of 2004 and was in effect for the election that followed in that year.[19] The new statute replaced the 50-candidate requirement for registration. It stated that any party meeting the reasonable provisions in the Act and running even a single candidate in a general or by-election could be registered.[20] This meant that even a one-candidate party would be allowed to issue tax receipts for political contributions between elections and to receive unspent election funds from its candidates, and other benefits.

The barrier to new parties posed by the prohibitive deposit required from candidates had already been struck down by a lower court. It had ruled that the $1,000 deposit should be returned in full if reporting requirements set out in the act were met. The lower courts had also found unconstitutional the automatic liquidation of a party not meeting registration requirements and the limitations on putting a party's name on the ballot. The government did not appeal these lower-court decisions to the Supreme Court. However, the important requirement remained that a party must receive 2 percent of the national vote or 5 percent in the ridings it contested, and 10 percent in a constituency, to receive the reimbursement of election expenses and the annual allowance to the party. A group of six small parties challenged the constitutionality of these restrictions, but they were upheld in the lower courts, and the Supreme Court refused to hear their appeal against that decision.[21]

We cannot conclude from the outcome of the Figueroa case that, despite

---

18   Miguel Figueroa v. Canada (Attorney General) Decision, S.C.C. 37, June 27, 2003.

19   The details of Bill C-3, are set out in Furi, "Legislative history of Bill C-3," 6–13.

20   The provisions called for the signed declarations of support from 250 members, one candidate for public office, and at least four party officers. Elections Canada, "Press Release re: Bill C-51," October 8, 2003. www.elections.ca

21   For the outcome of the case, Longley v. Canada (Attorney General), see "Elections Canada, Judicial Decisions and Proceedings," 2009. http://elections.ca/content.asp?s

the apparent inability of unorganized citizens in partyocracy to protect their political rights, other safeguards for our rights exist in the system. The tiny Communist Party, however much it is reconciled to democratic values, is still a weak repository of our political interests. Yet, had it not appealed the government's legislation, there would not have been a Figueroa case, and the government's choice-limiting legislation would have stood. Further, to protect our rights, the Supreme Court had to go beyond the reach of the weak Section 3 guarantee in the Charter. It cannot be counted on to do so in less egregious cases.

Where the Supreme Court's occasional decisions on cases relating to our political system will take us is difficult to foresee. To ensure that it is where we want to go, we need an agreed-on vision of how we want our political institutions to develop in order to guide us and the Court. The unelected judges came to a conclusion on important aspects of party/election finance regulations that differed fundamentally from that adopted by our elected representatives. Did the Court or "our" elected (party) representatives actually represent our interests?

Conclusion and Analysis

The full account of party governments struggling to come to grips with the issue of party/election finance is long, tortuous, complicated, and ongoing. It is an important story, illustrating why we must empower ourselves through constituency organization as the first step in democratizing the system. If we are not in control, opening up partyocracy to changes is likely to prove counterproductive. Parties will "reform" the system to suit, and further entrench, themselves.

From the perspective of the major parties, the changes made in the regulations governing party/electoral finance have been positive. In 2010 they have a close-to-guaranteed source of income from the federal treasury along with other support, such as free broadcast time. Small parties that might challenge their dominance are almost entirely excluded from sharing taxpayer funding by the 2, 5, and 10 percent threshold of votes at the national and constituency levels they must cross to tap into taxpayer dollars.

The challenge of the Communist party in the Figueroa case did frustrate the desire of the government to force small parties unable to meet the 50-candidate rule to close their operations and go away, but that failure was scarcely a significant problem for the dominant parties. That rule was a case of overkill. Other provisions in the reform legislation are enough to maintain the cartel of the major parties.

The parties' raid of the public treasury was accomplished without a quid pro quo from them for Canadians. The parties ignored the recommendations of the committees and commission that they should do more in such areas as public education, political engagement, and policy research.[22] They were able to carry on their activities as before but with generous financial guarantees from the state.

For Canadians, the changes did bring a higher level of transparency, however. Elections Canada, charged with enforcing the new regulations, required a full accounting of party receipts and expenditures. This documentation was then made available to the media and to us. Years of suspicion and speculation about the sources of campaign funds that contributed to lowering our respect for politicians and their governments was ended.[23]

An element of fairness, of levelling the playing field, was also introduced with the changes. The prohibition of corporate, union, and association contributions to the parties meant that all parties were dependent on government and individual contributions. The formula for distributing the government assistance still favoured the party drafting them, however. Despite that, the availability of public funds meant that a party like the NDP, which was chronically disadvantaged by the electoral system and by a smaller base of financial support than the other major parties, would be rewarded

22   For suggestions of what the parties might constructively do, see Heather MacIvor, "Medicine for our democratic malaise," *Inroads* 18 (Spring/Winter 2006):109–20..

23   Parties have a habit of passing progressive legislation and then evading its provisions. Idealism is expressed, and then it is subverted as parties respond to competitive pressures. The parties were quick find a major reporting loophole in "their" 1974 Act and exploited it for 27 years. Contributions were solicited by constituency organizations between election periods and then donated in a block sum to their candidate without identifying the contributors to it. In the 2000 federal election, several ministers reported transfers of block sums from their riding associations that made up most or all of their election funding. Campbell Clark, "'Close loophole for hidden election donations,' citizen group says," *Globe and Mail* (April 23, 2001).

with federal dollars for all of its votes until the Conservatives abolish the annual allowance. Its competitive position, and that of the Greens and Bloc, was enhanced temporarily. Most Canadians, I suspect, would consider that these changes—transparency and some levelling of the playing field—qualify as *reforms*. Clearly, however, these positives have not resulted in more citizen empowerment and less political alienation.

After the changes, politics for the vast majority of citizens is little changed and might even seem to have deteriorated further. [24] The expectations that many politically engaged citizens had for changes in the regime of party/election finance were unrealistic from the outset. For example, Linda McQuaig, a critical journalist, welcomed them with the comment that "It's hard to think of anything more fundamental to what's wrong with our political system than the enormous role corporate money plays in influencing government."[25] It is *not* hard. The absence of a responsible role for citizens in determining public policy is the fundamental weakness in our system.

The exaggerated expectations were understandable. The relatively underfinanced political left had turned the affluence of the establishment parties against them with the superficially appealing argument that "he who pays the piper calls the tune." The inference was that taking away the corporate and union paymasters of the parties and substituting funding from the state and individuals would let voters do the calling. But this thinking ignored the facts that (a) voters are not organized to express an authoritative majority viewpoint clearly, and (b) far more than just campaign contributions tie the parties to corporate, union, and other powerful interests.

Each of the parties shares interests with major powers in the community and is not going to abandon those simply because it no longer receives direct financial support from them. Further, even where a community of interests and financial dependence may not exist, these powers must be respected

---

24   A study done in 2000 revealed evidence of mounting public cynicism about the role of money in politics over the preceding decade of reform. Eighty-eight percent of Canadians agreed with the statement, "People with money have a lot of influence over the government," up five percent from a decade earlier." Paul Howe and David Northrup, "The Views of Canadians," in the Strengthening Canadian Democracy series, 1.5 (Montreal: Institute for Public Policy Research, July 2000), 37.

25   Linda McQuaig, "Biting the hand that feeds parties," *Toronto Star* (January 26, 2003), A13.

because of the impact their actions can have on Canadians. The strength of these pressures continues. They have not disappeared with the prohibition of their contributions to parties. The parties will only become significantly more responsive to us and able, when desirable, to stand up to pressures from organized interests when Canadians are organized and able to offer government countervailing support.

Most academics shared the desire to curtail the influence of big money in politics but some were also concerned about the method used to do it, i.e., substituting state support. Before the public treasury became the chief source of funds for parties, there was already a very substantial gap between the priorities of MPs with their governments and those they claimed to represent. The concern is that this gap will be widened, as the parties get the bulk of their funding from the state and can worry less about the public's reaction to their policies.[26]

In a number of contexts in this book—including the consideration of Prime Minister Martin's widely applauded, but unsuccessful, proposals for attacking the democratic deficit— the need to link citizens more closely with their representatives is identified as the major democratic challenge. Public finance of parties may do just the reverse. Prof. MacIvor writes, "The annual allowances may actually weaken the links between our parties and the electorate, rather than the reverse. Some experts argue that public subsidies widen the gap between parties and civil society by relieving parties of the need to raise funds from the electorate. The possible result is a vicious circle, as parties are forced to rely on the state for funding because they are losing their capacity to attract members and donations. Beyond this, European experience suggests that subsidies erode the relationship between parties and the wider society."[27]

Norway is one of those European countries with a long experience with state-subsidized parties. Recently it conducted an extensive public study of the state of its democracy. State funding was identified as a major *cause*

---

26   "The comparison between elites and general public suggests that, as with priorities, a profound gap exists between the public and decision-makers in the area of preferred government values." Ekos Research Associates Inc., *Rethinking Government '94: An Overview and Synthesis* (Ottawa: Ekos Research Associates Inc., 1995),12.

27   Heather MacIvor, "Medicine for our democratic malaise," 112.

of their country's democratic deficit—not an answer to it! "With falling membership ranks, political parties are reinventing themselves. They are becoming professional political machines in which members matter less and have less sway. This is made possible [in Norway] by tax-funded subsidies for political parties on a grand scale. (British parties have, as is well known, become dependent on private contributions, in particular from business. Many dislike that and want public subsidies instead.) For democracy it is bad news, whichever way, and who can say which is worse?"[28]

It is also the case that the minimal expectation of changes in public finance and limitations on spending, i.e., that it would clean up politics, has been disappointed.[29] If a satisfactory way of financing party/elections cannot be found, perhaps it is because any way of integrating an undemocratic institution, i.e., a party, into an aspiring democracy is bound to prove unsatisfactory.

The time and energy spent on changing our method of regulating party/election finance has diverted attention from our central democratic challenge, i.e., involving citizens constructively in their own governance. Similar diversions will frustrate our democratic progress as long as the reform process is in the hands of party politicians who, naturally, seek only to bolster *their* system. Proposing and debating alternatives to our dysfunctional political arrangements is a task we must undertake ourselves. If an alternative democratic model is circulating in the body politic, party-inspired diversions can be tested against it to determine whether they will further democracy or will simply entrench partyocracy. Such a test might well have dissuaded us from investing in changing the way parties are

---

28   This quotation is taken from a commentary on the contents of the report cited in Stein Ringen, "Where Now, Democracy?" 2003, 4. The main report: Power and Democracy (Norwegian Official Reports, 2003:19, in Norwegian only) 2004. www.oedc.org/dataoecd/63.

29   Considering continuing scandals, Guy Peters notes, "Interestingly, many of these scandals arose in countries with public financing of parties and limitations on campaign expenditures." "Democracy and Political Power in Contemporary Western Governments: Challenges and Reforms," in *The Art of the State Governance in a World without Frontiers,* eds. Thomas J. Courchene and Donald Savoie (Montreal: The Institute for Research on Public Policy, 2003), 95.

financed. We have no interest in maintaining organizations that usurp our rights and responsibilities as citizens.

The millions of dollars of public money now spent each year in allowances to the parties, in tax write-offs for party contributors, and in administering a complex set of regulations governing party finance would be infinitely better spent on providing the means—constituency parliaments—for the public to interact constructively with their elected representatives and the governments those representatives support.[30] With either private or public funding, parties support only a rudimentary form of representation, to which an alternative needs to be offered. Replace, not refinance parties with public monies.

---

30   The complexity is now seriously interfering with the ability of candidates to recruit official agents and with Elections Canada to recruit staff. To some degree, this negates the intention of some of the reforms, i.e., to open up the electoral process. Joan Bryden, "Complex laws, onerous tasks scaring off election volunteers," *Globe and Mail* (June 30, 2009), A8.

The Great Delusion: Parties as Vehicles for Democratic Citizenship

National political parties, at least the Canadian variety, are not much more than election-day organizations, providing the fundraising and poll workers needed to fight an election campaign. They are hardly effective vehicles for generating public-policy debates, for staking out policy positions, or for ensuring their own party's competence once in office.

Donald J. Savoie

Citizenship is possibly the most important of the central institutions of the modern democratic state. It is an instrument to socialize individuals into a supportive relationship to that state. It encourages them to develop positive attitudes to membership in the political community and to view the legally constituted political authorities as legitimate, in short, to see the state as their state, in whose development they actively participate.

For the modern mobilizing democratic state, many of whose public policies cannot be successfully implemented without the support of the population, citizenship is an essential tool.

Alan Cairns

Less than 2 percent of Canadians ever have held membership in any political party. Prospects for improvement are not compelling. It is not hard to understand why.

… Membership has been devalued, their role in policy has been
diminished, and the place of parties as incubators and recruiters
of talent has been under merciless attack from various forces.
Even the most fundamental role of a political party—to choose the
platform and leaders from which voters can then choose policies,
direction, and governments—has also been diminished.

Hugh Segal

Introduction

Generations of Canadians have been born into a system labelled "democratic"
but based on competitive party elections, not citizen participation. Power
in these parties is distributed "top down," and the governments they form
are similarly organized with a party prime minister at the "apex of power."
Parties have promoted the idea that joining is an act of good citizenship and
is politically empowering. Resigned, at some level, to accepting the belief
that parties are inevitable in a democracy and that party membership is the
only way, apart from voting, to exercise their democratic citizenship, a very
few citizens do join them. Their small numbers are sufficient to maintain
these shell organizations because, at the moment, there is no democratic
alternative able to perform their functions. Maintaining at least the façade
of a popular base with their membership organizations helps the parties
legitimate their monopoly on political power. Further, strengthened with
many hired professionals and money from party headquarters, the usually
moribund party organizations are resuscitated to help party candidates
electioneer.

A critical look at the record of parties trying to accommodate the desire
of people to be democratic citizens, will, however, make it abundantly clear
that we must look beyond parties for that opportunity. Citizens wanting to
participate actively in politics should not be forced to do so through parties,
unintentionally perpetuating the existence of an outworn institution that is
blocking democratic progress.

Party Promises of Membership Control

Three parties have made noteworthy promises to "square the circle." While maintaining the fundamental basis of partyocracy— the delegation by citizens of their civic responsibilities to party leaders—they have promised to follow the policy direction of citizens as either party members or constituents. A failure to recognize the hopelessness of trying to reconcile these conflicting objectives could result in further attempts and more delays in proceeding with significant, achievable democratic reforms.

The approach of two of the three parties has been to promise its members a significant, or controlling, voice in determining party policy—government policy when their team is in office. A second and even more interesting (startling, even!) proposal of another party was to promise this, but also that its MPs would represent the policy positions of their constituents in the House of Commons, even when they differed from those of the MP or his or her party. The views of constituents would always take precedence over the views of all others—as most citizens believe they should.

The CCF, its successor the NDP, and the Trudeau Liberals promised the first approach. The Western farm parties, particularly the United Farmers of Alberta in the 1920s, and, recently, Reform/Alliance, the second. These parties recognized that it would be popular with voters if they at least promised to give citizens and/or party members a controlling voice in determining party/government policy.

The CCF/NDP and membership control. The CCF/NDP attempt to enhance the roles of its members and citizens in political life is now history, although it is formally ongoing. The examination here of the attempt focuses on the CCF experience in Saskatchewan in the years between the early 1930s, when the party was organized, and 1964 when a 20-year period of CCF government in that province came to an end.

In a study of the national political system, this now-dated excursion into provincial politics may seem out of place. The conditions in Saskatchewan were, however, unusually favourable for the successful implementation of the CCF's offer of a significantly enhanced role in political life to those who joined the party. If democratic participation through party could take place anywhere in Canada, it should have been in Saskatchewan, in that period.[31]

The CCF held its founding convention in 1933, during the Great Depression, when support was strong for radical change in many areas of life. Competing with the well-financed "free-enterprise" Liberal and Conservative parties, the CCF's leaders needed to attract a large, strongly committed membership to provide its resources. Without this, failure was inevitable. Capitalizing on the hostility in the West to the hierarchical structure of the established parties, the CCF proposed to be democratic in all its internal relationships. More generally, the party's founders emphasized the importance of political participation as an essential part of the development of the whole person.[32]

The commitment to membership control was a foundation stone on which the party was organized, and because of this, at least the rhetorical commitment to it had to be maintained through the years that saw changes in name and organization. It can no more be jettisoned without risking the party's existence than the PQ in Quebec can drop its commitment to sovereignty.

Support for internal party democracy was formally recognized in the new party's constitution. For example, it provided for the annual election of the party leader, open financial records, and consultative bodies linking legislators and the membership. At the same time as these democratic processes were adopted, however, the party also endorsed parliamentary government. Leaders of the CCF proposed to overcome the clash of values and institutions this involved by doing the impossible, i.e., integrating a fully democratic party into a parliamentary system supporting prime ministerial government.

Social conditions in Saskatchewan were initially very favourable to its

---

31   In this discussion of the CCF/NDP, I rely heavily on Seymour Lipset's classic study of Saskatchewan politics, *Agrarian Socialism: The Cooperative Commonwealth Federation in Saskatchewan* (Garden City, NY: Doubleday and Company, 1950; rpt. 1968); and Vaughan Lyon, "Democracy and the Canadian Political System" (PhD diss., the University of British Columbia, 1974), 125–215.

32   David Lewis and Frank Scott, *Make this Your Canada* (Toronto: Central Canada Publishing Company, 1943), 109–10.

attempt.[33] As Seymour Lipset noted in his study of Saskatchewan politics, the population of the province was small; its political culture was, relative to the rest of the country, "participant;" social equality was the norm; party members expected to be consulted and had experience with how democratic organizations worked; and the commitment to membership control was strongly held.[34] While party democracy was favoured by these factors, parliamentary government posed a series of barriers to it. The highest was this: if the membership was to decide on the party's policies and, in effect, direct a CCF government, then that government could not claim convincingly to be meeting its constitutional obligation to govern for all the people.

Initially, the new party's theoreticians sought to skirt this problem by arguing that the CCF would be a democratic mass movement embracing all but a handful of the very rich. They wrote, "In and through such a political movement, every Canadian can find opportunity for his initiative and enterprise."[35] Such a movement could claim to speak for virtually all the people and that would give it the authority needed to implement its program.

Theory and wishful thinking quickly met reality. Only some of the mass of citizens for whom the party/movement hoped to speak chose to break free of established party ties to join or vote for the CCF. Even after the party became well established, it could only claim that it had a larger membership than its competitors. It was impossible to suggest that the membership wing

---

33   After the Depression and the war, when the party was first in office (1944–64), postwar prosperity dampened the sense that political change was urgent.

34   Lipset wrote: "Political participation of the ordinary citizen in Saskatchewan is not restricted to the intermittently recurring election. Politics is organized to be a daily concern and responsibility of the common citizen. The relatively large number of farmers' organizations, co-operatives, and other civic-interest organizations encourages common citizens to share in the government of their communities as a normal routine of life." Lipset, *Agrarian Socialism*, 265.

35   Lewis and Scott, *Make This Your Canada,* 109–110. Elsewhere (p. 133) they state, "The CCF is a party not only for the people, but of and by the people. It is so organized constitutionally, financially, and in every other way as to be the people acting for themselves rather than an organization divorced from the people but pretending to speak for them."

of the party was an all-inclusive mass movement that could legitimately direct the government.

When the party succeeded in winning office in 1944 under the leadership of Tommy Douglas, it removed the clause in the party constitution that bound its members of the legislative assembly (MLAs) to follow the direction of the extra-parliamentary wing of the party, "On all questions of policy, tactics, and program ...."[36] Party MLAs were then able to give voters the usual promise made by politicians, i.e., that a government they formed would consider everyone's views. "We will," the new premier promised, "welcome the help of all groups in the province, irrespective of their political, religious, or occupational background."[37]

Ministers in Douglas's governments were encouraged to maintain an open-door policy and the party's MLAs were charged with holding listening-reporting sessions with constituents before and after legislative sessions. In this respect, the Saskatchewan party anticipated by decades the *non-binding* consultative approach now generally adopted, with less rigour, by most parties and by governments at all levels.

Policy democracy based on constituency parliaments would carry this approach a vitally important step further. Elected local representatives would be involved in deliberative discussions on issues on an organized basis and their views carried forward to the Commons by their MPs. Constituents would be empowered and not merely consulted on an ad hoc basis.

The CCF's leadership's offered further reassurance that the party membership was not going to dictate the policies of the government by supporting existing parliamentary institutions. It showed little interest in parliamentary reform. Tommy Douglas' governments featured an unusual amount of consultation with all those interested in the development of policy; this was feasible in that small province. At the same time, however,

---

36   Minutes of the Provincial Council, CCF (Saskatchewan Section), Saskatoon, July 14, 1942, 3, cited by F.C. Engelmann, "The Cooperative Commonwealth Federation of Canada: A Study of Membership Participation in Party Policy-Making" (PhD diss. Yale University, 1954), 215.

37   T. C. Douglas, "Report Upon Election," radio broadcast, July 1944, cited in A. W. Johnson, "Biography of a Government, Policy Formation in Saskatchewan 1944–1961" (PhD diss. Harvard University, 1963), 252.

he maintained the distribution of powers traditionally associated with prime ministerial government. He was the boss.[1]

The formal change in the constitutional status of the membership vis-à-vis its elected representatives was accepted by the rank and file. The acceptance can be attributed, first, to Douglas, a remarkably skilled leader. By dint of personality, lots of formal and informal consultation, membership-flattering rhetoric, and the persuasive powers vested in a successful leader, he finessed the conflict between party democracy and parliamentary government. The ultimate authority of the membership, he told convention delegates, rested on its ability to elect a new party leader at its annual meeting if it was dissatisfied with the performance of its government.[2] The leadership review did give members more influence than that exercised by members of the traditional parties—such reviews and accountability sessions were still unknown to them—but it was very different from members taking responsibility for determining the policies of the government.

Second, it was recognized by most in the party that to be successful in the ongoing partisan warfare, the leader must have a large measure of autonomy. He or she must be free to bob, weave, and change direction as the competitive interests of the party required. It was unrealistic to imagine that the leader could doggedly implement a "wish list," probably full of inconsistencies, drawn up at a brief party convention by uninformed political amateurs with no formal responsibility for governing. The opposition would be unmerciful in its attacks on such behaviour; the media and public outraged.

Further, members of the legislative wing of the party, their careers at stake, could not be expected to defer to the general membership of the party on matters involving the party's success at the polls. The MLA's self-interest did, however, dictate that they must defer to the leader of their party, especially if he or she were premier.

Denial and rhetoric was the third way the loss of formal control was

1   Ibid., 142. "The premier would not be told what to do by people who did not sit in the Assembly."

2   Evelyn Eager, an academic who has written extensively on party-government relations in Saskatchewan, concludes that, "Mr. Douglas reconciled opposing principles, but he did not eliminate the dilemma of conflict between party democracy and the traditions of responsible government." "The Paradox of Power," in The Political Process in Canada, ed. J. H. Aitchison (Toronto: University of Toronto Press, 1963), 134–35.

made acceptable to the CCF membership. Evelyn Eager writes: "Following the 1956 election, The Commonwealth, the organ of the party, proclaimed in a headline that 'CCF Convention will direct government policy for new term,'" and the party secretary, in making a call for members to attend the convention, stated that, "The people themselves decide the policies and programs which the government is to institute."[3]

It is common for a party to send different messages to its various audiences. When a commitment, like membership control, is a central element of a party's belief system, lip service must be paid to it, although doing so raises expectations in some members that cannot be met.

A final major barrier to membership control was the disparity of resources between the various elements of the organization. The "professionals" had information and responsibilities, and they were subject to pressures not experienced by members. Party members were busy making a living and not directly responsible to voters. They could not interact with their members of the legislature, and particularly with those in the cabinet, on the basis of anything resembling equality. Then as now, without appropriate means to deliberate on policy, thoughtful citizens will defer to others whom they consider, sometimes mistakenly, better equipped to make public policy. With the policy democracy model in place they will not be required to do so.

From a party perspective, the CCF experience in Saskatchewan was a success. The party held office for 20 years and during that time built a reputation as a progressive, people-centred, efficient administration. Its leadership devoted time and energy to encouraging "mere voters" to become "democratic citizens" to the very limited extent allowed by the party/parliamentary system. A party model was created that had some positive impact on the internal processes of other parties and on the character of Canadian politics in general.

At the end of the Douglas period in office, however, it was clear that the model was not dynamic from a democratic perspective. Indeed, observers concluded that the membership's role in the party had become progressively more formal over time, rather than the reverse.[4]

---

3   Ibid., 125.
4   See John Richards, "The Decline and Fall of Agrarian Socialism," in Lipset, Agrarian Socialism, 372–73.

Achieving power to implement its social and economic program was the overriding objective of the party, and that required embracing the existing political system.[5] Considering the failure of the left, generally, to press for more democratic politics, Professor Meyer Brownstone, a critical "friend" of the left, writes, "Their reforms have been limited to issues within the system itself, such as patronage and election funding. Indeed, social democrats are the greatest defenders of liberal parliamentary democracy and existing modes of administration."[6]

The Liberal's (Trudeau's) flirtation with participatory democracy. The 1960s were politically tumultuous times. The issues of the day activated a significant number of normally politically apathetic people and intensified the feelings and activity of those already politically engaged. People demanded to be heard, and many rejected the right of even elected officials to make policy without consulting them. It was an excellent opportunity for democratic leadership, for a politician or politicians to give creative thought to meeting the awakened participatory aspirations of many.

Pierre Trudeau—fairly recently a critical political outsider, but as of 1968 the country's Liberal prime minister—responded rhetorically. He campaigned in his first election as prime minister on the twin themes of "participatory democracy" and a "just society." Trudeau's language on the former was charged with promise of dramatic change in the system of representation and distribution of power: "The Liberal Party speaks of participation and it does so with sincerity. It knows that there is no 'middle Canada' qualified to give its mandate to a 'Liberal Establishment.' We know that if we are to retain the confidence of the people of Canada as a government,

5   As the late Prof. Walter Young wrote, "The democratic political movement which rises in opposition to the existing political and social system faces a dilemma. To achieve its ends it must have power, and it must seek that power through the existing system. It must operate within the system and engage in the very practices it came into being to oppose. Although it may work within the system purely as an expeditious approach to reform, it runs the risk of contamination." The Anatomy of a Party: The National CCF 1932–61 (Toronto: University of Toronto Press, 1971), 177.
6   Meyer Brownstone, "Moving Beyond the Limited Democracy of Social Democracy," in A Different Kind of State? Popular Power and Democratic Administration, eds. Leo Panitch, Gregory Albo, and David Langille (Toronto: Oxford University Press, 1993), 179.

we must as a party seek and find a means of offering representation and distributing the decision-making power among those voiceless thousands who have not shared in these opportunities in the past."[7]

Those looking for political change greeted Trudeau's message with excitement; expectations were raised. On a wave of public enthusiasm ("Trudeaumania"), he led the Liberals to the majority-government status that had eluded the party under his predecessor. For a brief moment, the political situation cried out for new initiatives. These could involve shoring up partyocracy or responding to the demands for more participation with a new more democratic mode of representation, i.e., constituency representation. There has always been a huge constituency for the latter, as has been noted, but it has always been unorganized and lacking a concrete proposal around which to rally. Alas, the political leadership of the country chose to see the restiveness as a threat to the system that should be met by modest reforms in it.

Trudeau and his colleagues seemed not to have thought through what institutional changes participatory democracy would require. For them, it was primarily a vote-getting slogan. Liberals, however, had to do something to respond to the expectations aroused by their leader's rhetoric. The something was similar to the approach adopted earlier by the Saskatchewan CCF. The party message was, "Join our democratic party; help determine party policy that will become government policy when the party is in office." Richard Stanbury, the party president, enthusiastically and creatively took up the challenge of opening up the party to a much higher level of membership engagement in setting party policy. Initially, Trudeau appeared to support his efforts.

Those active in national politics in the 1960s were, however, different, and more difficult to organize and satisfy, than those in the small province of Saskatchewan in the 1930s and later. The Liberal Party was old, wedded to traditional politics, and struggling to maintain its dominant position in the national party system in the face of new pressures. The politically alienated,

---

7   Liberal Party of Canada, P. E. Trudeau, "Remarks to Liberal Policy Conference," 1970, Mimeo, 18.

urban, middle-class political actives to whom it needed to appeal had to be convinced that the "natural governing party" could change its spots.[8]

Lorna Marsden, a sociology professor and key party activist during the period of Trudeau's leadership, analyzed the party's experience as a vehicle of political participation.[9] She noted that while Trudeau was preoccupied with channelling the widespread political unrest into the system through the Liberal Party he, like Douglas, was determined to preserve the cabinet's control of policy. He saw participation more as a learning experience for citizens than as a means of empowering them, although his early rhetoric, as shown above, suggested otherwise.

Richard Stanbury, on the other hand, shared much the same dream as the early CCF theoreticians of what the membership wing of the party could become. The party's challenge, as he set out in a lengthy memo, was to convince Liberal Party members and prospective members that the party had really changed. Membership opinion would be taken seriously in developing party policy.[10] With Trudeau's acquiescence, an elaborate consultative and accountability structure—somewhat less extensive than that of the Saskatchewan CCF but still impressive for a national party—was set up to show that the leadership was intent on fulfilling its commitment. However, Stanbury's vision, too, was bounded by his acceptance of the ultimate authority of the PM and his cabinet on policy questions.

The Liberal loss of majority status in the Commons in the 1972 election shocked the party and raised questions about the vote-getting appeal of the "new politics" to the broad swath of "non-political" voters. Marsden states that with the loss, the party was too preoccupied for the next two years with winning back its majority to worry about other matters. The enthusiasm for party participation in setting the course of the government was never fully recovered.[11]

---

8   The phrase was popularized by Professor Reg Whitaker.
9   Lorna Marsden, "The Party and Parliament: Participatory Democracy in the Trudeau Years," in *Towards a Just Society*, eds. Thomas S. Axworthy and Pierre Elliott Trudeau (Markham, Ont.: Viking Press, 1989), 262–81.
10   Stanbury outlined his hopes for integrating the membership wing of the party with "its" government in Richard J. Stanbury, "The Liberal Party of Canada: An Interpretation," June 15, 1969. Mimeo.
11   Marsden, "The party and parliament," 275.

Trudeau was to qualify what he meant by participatory democracy. It did not mean participating in making current policy and taking responsibility for it.[12] Rather, he urged the party to focus on the long term in its policy discussions. Party members should become "futurists!"

With that major refinement, Trudeau could reconcile his commitment to increased participation with maintaining traditional top-down government. For party members, however, it meant being shut out of participation in making the policies immediately affecting their lives.

Referring to reforms adopted prior to the 1984 convention that replaced Mr. Trudeau as party leader, Marsden concludes, "They restricted the role of the Party and marked the end of participation by Party members at least in the ways that had been dreamt of by Richard Stanbury and others in 1968."[13] The Trudeau who came into office championing participatory democracy had become noted for strengthening prime ministerial government.[14] No transfer of power and responsibility to citizens had even been considered, beyond the party-serving invitation to join the Liberal Party, engage in its difficult-to-find constituency policy discussions and, particularly, in its election-related activities.

The national Liberal Party was even less successful in becoming an instrument for democratic citizenship than the Saskatchewan CCF had been. For substantive policy advice, party leaders turned to the bureaucracy, outside experts, powerful lobbies, and polls. The "voiceless thousands" (millions?) would remain inarticulate.

---

12   "Participation doesn't mean participating in the decisions. In a society there is always some tool or instrument for somebody making a decision at some point. In our form of government it is the cabinet   what people want to know and to be assured of is that their point of view has been considered." P. E. Trudeau, *Toronto Star* (May 26, 1970), A10.

13   Marsden, "The party and parliament," 281.

14   McCall and Clarkson described the transformation: "The former apostle of participatory democracy had become frankly authoritarian: governments, he indicated, were elected to govern as rationally as possible until they presented themselves to the atomized voters to seek their support once more. Between elections, the public should mind its own business and the elected should not compromise themselves by responding to pressure. Citizen activists were dismissed as defending vested interest, which by definition could not have the common good at heart." Christina McCall and Stephen Clarkson, *Trudeau and Our Times: The Heroic Delusion*, vol. 2 (Toronto: McClelland and Stewart, 1994), 127.

The reform energies of many, mobilized by a unique set of historical circumstances in the 1960s and early '70s, were desperately needed to bring the political system into line with popular ideals and the government's need for support. Instead, they were diverted into a futile attempt to make the Liberal Party a vehicle for democratic citizenship. That was by no means the end of the story of our being diverted by party promises in our search for meaningful citizenship.

Party-Advocated Constituency Representation: Reform/Alliance

Western reformers in the 1920s. Party-advocated constituency representation is the most important illustration of the futility of attempting to reconcile party representation with significant democratic participation. Historically, certain parties have promised voters that they would act as political public-service agencies: their MPs would give priority to representing the views of their constituents in the House of Commons and/or provincial legislatures over those of their party or their own. By inference it was recognized that the mandate the party and its MPs claimed to have received in the election could be an inaccurate reflection of the views of constituents on some, perhaps many, issues. Further consultation, and a response to it, would be needed to ensure true representation.

Millions—as voters and including the few voters who were also party members—were beguiled by this attractive notion of real constituency representation within the framework of existing party institutions. A major step toward a higher level of democracy could be taken relatively effortlessly!

The history of parties attracting—and disappointing—citizens with promises of constituency representation dates back to the end of World War I. The agrarian reformers of the 1920s, particularly those in the United Farmers of Alberta (UFA), included delegate democracy/constituency representation in their program when challenging the reigning Liberals. The UFA, with an assist from organized labour, won control of the government of Alberta in its first bid for office in 1921 and remained in power until 1935. Unprepared for their victory, its elected members were under immediate pressure to fill the traditional roles found in the party parliamentary system. They did so with only a little dissent, which died over time.

It might have been otherwise if the UFA had gone into the election committed to a clear, workable model of constituency representation. Its supporters would then have had something tangible to rally around and to hold their elected representatives to establishing. Delegate democracy was, however, just one of a mélange of democratic reform ideas that UFA members found appealing. No serious thought had been given to how it could be organized. Most UFA members, basking in the satisfaction of having their team in office, and with a living to make, were content to have their members of the legislative assembly govern conventionally.

The rhetorical commitment to democratic change lived on for a few years after the UFA government took office in Alberta through the UFA component of the national Progressive Party. As members of that party, which was based on provincial farm organizations across the country, the UFA MPs rejected the discipline of their party caucus in Ottawa, arguing that they must be free to represent the views of their constituents. Their stand, militantly advocated, did much to disrupt the internal unity and effectiveness of the Progressives. The party was a short-lived force in national politics.

Those committed to advancing democratic practice might see as admirable the continued resistance of some party MPs to conforming to the norms of party government. It was, however, a pseudo form of constituency representation that the MPs actually practiced. Students of the politics of the time argue convincingly that it was the leaders of the UFA organization to whom the UFA MPs responded. There was no organization of constituents that could present MPs with informed views shared by the majority of their constituents. That essential piece of the delegate/policy democracy model was missing, and the vacuum was filled by provincial UFA leaders claiming to speak for the interests of voters.[15]

With only a few zealous reformers surviving the winding up of the Progressive Party after the 1926 election, and defections to the established parties, for a time there was no party left articulating the desire of Canadians for constituency representation, let alone considering how it might be achieved. In the Depression years of the 1930s, the new entrants to the party system from the West—the CCF and Social Credit—showed no

15   See Denis Smith, "Politics and the Party System in the Three Prairie Provinces, 1917–1958" (B. Litt. Thesis, Oxford University, 1959), 146.

interest in constituency representation. Indeed, Social Credit, despairing of partyocracy, urged a transfer of policy control to unelected experts. If the voters had been familiar with a feasible, ready-to-go alternative model of democratic representation, they would have had that to turn to when there was a loss of confidence in traditional party government.

Although the interest of the agrarians in replacing party with constituency representation did not lead to change, their critique of party politics was a valuable contribution to the democratic cause. It reverberates today, reinforced by dramatically changed circumstances that make their message even more important and feasible.

Reform/Alliance. In the 1980s, a group of Albertans, led by Preston Manning, organized a new federal party by building, in part, on the same democratic aspirations that had inspired the UFA and some Progressives. Their party, Reform, was reorganized as the Alliance in 2000 and then merged in 2003 with the Progressive Conservatives to become, simply, the Conservative Party. In the ensuing discussion, reference will be only to Reform/Alliance, since the reform views of the party changed little with the 2000 reorganization. The Conservative Party, with Stephen Harper its chief ideologue, does not, however, share the democratic values of its Reform/Alliance predecessor.

As Reform/Alliance moved rapidly to become the official opposition in Ottawa, the party muted its reform proposals and democratic rhetoric. Initially, however, Reform/Alliance prominently featured its commitment to the package of reforms familiar as "internal party democracy," "direct democracy," and "delegate democracy"—or constituency representation.[16] The promise of constituency representation is considered here. The party's leaders could no more accept membership control of party policy than the other parties espousing it, and for similar reasons.[17] The political warfare

16   The party's commitment to these is set out in various party documents, including The Reform Party of Canada, "The Blue Sheet," 1995, 8.

17   Mr. Manning was frequently accused by members of being dictatorial, with considerable justification, but can a party compete successfully without this style of leadership? See Derek Ferguson, "Reform's grass roots think Preston Manning has 'gone Ottawa,'" *Toronto Star* (September 30, 1994), A15.

that parties wage demands that they have a commanding general wielding considerable freedom to act.

Reform/Alliance might well have hesitated before promising constituency representation. The UFA, a source of its inspiration, had been in power in Alberta for 15 years without acting on its promise to implement this form of representation. To avoid the new promise being greeted with cynicism, the party might have been expected to accompany the second-time-around promise with a practical implementation plan. Partyocracy, however, does not encourage us to pay close attention to politics. Promises unfulfilled the first time they were used to attract support can be recycled successfully, in almost the same form, without serious questions being asked.

Democratic reform was, of course, only one plank in the platform of Reform/Alliance. The party also proposed a right-wing economic and social program and supported a decentralist vision of Canada.[18] These were not sufficiently attractive to launch the new national party into orbit on their own, however. For that, the party relied on democratic reform, with its wide appeal, and on the West's long-standing sense of grievance with Ottawa. In his autobiography, Preston Manning proudly cites his slogan in the 1993 election campaign: "So you don't trust politicians? Neither do we."[19] A politician leading a party, Manning appealed to voters by distancing himself from both. We don't find the leaders of other organizations denouncing them— "soiling their own nest"—to gain popularity.

The party's commitment to constituency representation was emphasized in its literature. And, in at least one important expression of it, the party also recognized its responsibility to go beyond the collection of constituency opinion and to help constituents think through their position on issues, i.e., to "deliberate": "Reformers asserted that it is the responsibility of political representatives to encourage, inform, and focus public participation in the democratic process, and then faithfully to reflect the views of the people they represented. Reform members of Parliament play a critical role in this

---

18   See the Reform party of Canada, "The Blue Sheet," 1995.
19   One piece of evidence of the success of this anti-politics approach is that the overwhelming majority of those in the country who rejected the party system voted for Reform/Alliance in 1997. See David Laycock, *The New Right and Democracy in Canada* (Don Mills, Ont.: Oxford University Press, 2002), 109.

process. They are to represent the principles and policies of the Reform Party of Canada, to put forward the views of the constituents and bring their own knowledge, judgement, and conscience to their task. Reformers see political representation as a dynamic process where these three roles constantly interact. The Reform Party's commit to broadening democracy, however, makes it clear than when one or more of these roles come into conflict, it is the will of the electors which must predominate. Without such a commitment, true democracy cannot take root and grow in the political institutions of Canada."[20]

The likelihood of conflict between functioning as a loyal party MP in the Commons and simultaneously as a constituency representative would depend first on how often, on what issues, and how constituents were consulted. Second, it would depend on how the consultation was conducted and, finally, on the opportunities for deliberation available to constituents.

How far did Reform/Alliance progress in developing constituency representation? Unlike the adoption of direct democracy, constituency representation did not need to wait for a Reform/Alliance government to win office and pass supporting legislation. The party's MPs could have sponsored the organization of constituency parliaments or some similar organization that would have gone considerably beyond occasional consultation in town-hall meetings, mailed questionnaires, etc., in organizing local opinion. Admittedly, the task would have been difficult without state financial support, but perhaps the party could have financed at least a model of constituency representation in one or more constituencies. Taking this initiative would have shown that the party was committed to constituency representation and would have been a popular move with the vast majority of Canadians who already support constituency representation. Successful,

---

20   The Reform Party of Canada, "Final Report of the Democratic Populism Task Force II," January 1996, 1. The Task Force made it clear that when Reform/Alliance referred to "free votes" it meant a vote where the "discipline" of constituents was substituted for that of party. The MP must follow the direction of one or the other. The point is important since people commonly assume that in a "free vote" the MP would not be tied.(7) If MPs were free to act on their own judgment, their constituents would still be left without representation as most understand that concept. Powerful special interests would welcome MPs loosening their ties to both party and constituents, because it would leave MPs even more vulnerable to pressure from them.

it would have forced the other parties to emulate its initiative and in doing so perhaps making parties irrelevant. If constituents were speaking with one voice through an organization like a constituency parliament, the election of an MP would be a contest to determine which candidate could most effectively represent that opinion in the Commons. The local strength of candidates would determine their success.

Reform/Alliance MPs, like reform-minded MPs of other parties, were subject to pressure to conform to the norms of party/parliamentary government as soon as they set foot in the Centre Bloc on Parliament Hill. Rather than resisting behaviour that would interfere with representing constituents, as the Alberta Progressive MPs of an earlier time had done, they went into training to learn how to behave conventionally.[21] The rapid acceptance of traditional party/parliamentary norms was illustrated by the party's almost-immediate shift away from its promise to organize its caucus in a new way.

The party's Blue Book committed it to making public the votes of its MPs in caucus, so that constituents could then monitor how they were being represented by their MP.[22] The party altered this commitment to one promising to release an annual record of votes in caucus. The explanation for this action was the reasonable fear that the other parties would seek to exploit evidence of division within the Reform caucus.[23] It meant, however, that the MPs' constituents were not able to know the current positions their representatives were taking in caucus at a time when they might influence them.

Understandably, the party experienced other problems in implementing even its limited vision of constituency representation. The party task force studying the implementation of its democratic reforms found difficulties "with the objectivity of questions asked of constituents, with the timing and

---

21   "The party has been forced to abandon plans to do politics differently. It discovered the hard way that attacks earned them headlines and nightly sound bites on the news as compared to the politeness and decorum that doomed them to obscurity." Norm Overden, "Reform faces a make-or-break year," Toronto Star (January 3, 1996), A11.

22   The Reform Party of Canada, "The Blue Book," 10.

23   Reform Party of Canada, "Final Report of the Democratic Populism II Task Force," 7.

analysis of results …." in their MPs' consultations with constituents.[24] Without restrictions, Reform/Alliance MPs could use the results of consultations as justification for breaking ranks with their caucus colleagues. Such action would reveal divisions in the party and raise questions about whether the MP or the party was following the public will.

The party decided that these problems should be dealt with by subjecting their MPs' consultations to the supervision of party and polling experts. Caucus officers and the party's "direct democracy critic" were to be involved in deciding what issues were suitable for a constituency consultation. A procedure was established whereby potential issues were identified, listed, and discussed by caucus; appropriate consultative methods were then determined. Individual MPs were left to exercise their own judgment in deciding which of the approved methods they actually used.[25]

It was only inferred in the party document that MPs should limit their consultations to the approved list of issues. If, however, that was the understanding among MPs, it represented a significant curtailment of their freedom to respond to constituents who might want to be heard on an "unapproved" issue. If a Reform/Alliance government had been elected, the cabinet could have managed the constituency consultations through a caucus bound to support it in the ongoing parliamentary battle. The government would not want its policy preferences submitted to constituents by MPs if it thought, or knew, they would be opposed.

The last line of the task force report (an afterthought?) deserves emphasis: "The Blue Book stipulates that constituents may also initiate the process [i.e., set the constituency consultative process in motion] … so the same level of flexibility will apply to a process initiated by constituents."[26] The process constituents should use to do this was not set out. This strongly suggests that only the party MP, not his or her constituents, was intended to decide what issues would be submitted to the formal party consultative process.

Competitive pressures limited Reform/Alliance's ability to act on its

---

24   Ibid., 5.
25   Ibid., 3–5.
26   Ibid., 13. Apart from affirming the right of constituents to raise issues, the Blue Book, too, says nothing more about how they are to do this. Reform Party of Canada, "The Blue Book," 1991, 10.

promise to adopt constituency representation once it approached governing power. The greater limitation was, however, the threat to the party's policy agenda that constituency representation would present. What party, having won a victory at the polls, would be willing to relinquish control over the implementation of the policies it was organized to promote? Reform/Alliance had to approach the consultative process with caution, lest it get unwelcome messages from voters on issues that were key to it, like gun control or same-sex marriage.

In short, the vote-getting promise to give citizens the right to instruct their MP on his or her policy stance in the Commons had to be finessed, but without losing a support base drawn, significantly, from citizens who rejected conventional politics. Fortunately for the party's leaders, most party members also had a stake in the success of the finesse.[27]

The most significant dimension of the finesse of Reform's constituency representation commitment has been referred to, but it deserves emphasis. There is one best way for Reform/Alliance, or any other party, to remain in firm control of the function of representing citizens while at the same time capitalizing electorally on a commitment to constituency representation. It is to do nothing to facilitate institutional development that would give citizens a substantive and authoritative voice on a continuing basis on issues of concern to them. Such a voice could not be ignored when it conflicted with the views of the party—without exposing as fraudulent the party's commitment to constituency over party representation.

The time and effort of those citizens who were attracted to membership in the UFA and Reform/Alliance in the hope of advancing the democratic cause was not completely wasted. While joining a party amounted to an endorsement of an institution that was a barrier to democracy, that damage was offset by supporting leaders who, for a time, criticized party politics and raised the profile of constituency representation. Those leaders recognized, rhetorically at least, that constituency representation is the next logical step in our democratic evolution. They were not prepared to take that step on

---

27   The UFA government in Alberta never renounced the UFA's commitments to delegate democracy and a variety of other reforms. They just ignored or, when necessary, "talked around" them.

their watch, however. An organized push from citizens was needed to insist that they act. It was absent.

Conclusion and Summary Comment on Reforms of Partyocracy

We have completed our examination of the major reforms proposed for and implemented in partyocracy. At this point, it may be helpful to summarize our final evaluation of some of these reforms starting with our just-completed survey of attempts to convert parties into effective agencies for political participation.

- **Democratic parties?** "Three strikes and you're out!" It would be helpful if a variant of that rule could be applied to attempts to reconcile party with internal party democracy and/ or constituency representation. Proposals for constituency representation or delegate democracy have been talked about several times, under different circumstances, and each time it has been shown that these different modes of representation cannot be integrated into parliamentary government when it is based on competing parties. Recycling that proposal yet again is a waste of the limited energies of reformers.

Even if the impossible were to happen and people flocked to parties as a means of expressing their democratic citizenship, those who joined the "democratic" party would be inducted into the realm of competitive party politics. Seeking fuller democratic citizenship, they would end up party warriors engaged in power struggles with neighbours enlisted in other parties. Democratic values and interest in good government would be subsumed by the appetite for power of leaders and member citizens.[28]

---

28   Party membership is likely to corrupt the very qualities needed for democratic citizenship. Prof. John Meisel writes, "Otherwise reasonable people can come close to losing their senses in the flush of extreme partisanship .... All partisanship reduces the openness of mind of the partisan, of course .... To the degree that parties contribute to this situation [extreme partisanship], they exert a negative influence on the political system and they make it harder for themselves to perform their tasks effectively." "The Dysfunctions of Canadian Parties: An Exploratory Mapping," in *Democracy with Justice,* eds. Alain-G. Gagnon and A. Brian Tanguay (Ottawa: Carleton University Press, 1992), 415–16.

Political leaders, reformers, and citizens should all think anew about how representation and government should be organized to meet the demands of the 21st century.

- **Access to information.** Access legislation was put in place years ago, yet we now have what is universally considered one of the most secretive administrations in our history. What does that tell us about the possibilities of depending on words on paper (legislation) as a means of strengthening democracy.

Competitive pressures on the governing party supporting secrecy are much stronger than the current public and media pressures demanding respect for the letter and spirit of the access legislation. Typically, even "law and order" governments will subvert reforms that they might have adopted if they feel that the reforms will weaken their competitive position.

- **Electoral reform.** Proposals for change to a system of proportional representation (PR) will, if they get past the talking stage that has extended over the last 100 years, leave citizens "mere" voters and party elites still rulers. While PR would be an improvement on the existing egregiously flawed plurality electoral system, its pursuit is a time-consuming detour from the citizen-empowering reform that is desired and needed—now.

- **Extra-parliamentary representation.** Since formal representation based on citizens choosing between competing parties is a grossly inadequate mode of citizen political expression, citizens and organized interests turn to the informal system: representation primarily based on lobbying, street demonstrations, etc. Party governments are free to accept, reject, or manage these pressures as they see fit.

Political equality is impossible to obtain in the informal representative system where unequally distributed resources play a dominant role in deciding public policy. Governments try to inject an element of equality into the competition for its support by distributing lobbying funds to resource-poor, favoured, or feared groups, so that they can be heard. But how can equality be achieved between, say, groups representing the homeless and business in giving small grants to the former? Funds granted can be withdrawn. In trying to bring at least a measure of equality to the competition of groups for government resources, the governing party is drawn into manipulating actors in civil society in a way that favours its interests.

Democratic citizenship and effective governance are held back when even more groups are encouraged to battle for benefits from government. Government should lead in encouraging citizens to recognize and pursue their common interests and should "grow" its ability to respond to them.

- **Ad hoc non-binding consultations.** Political leaders offer these consultations as a substitute for organized citizen participation in setting the government's agenda. Citizens are, however, poorly prepared by how they are socialized by the system to participate in these consultations. They tend, as a result, to become tell-and-sell and public-venting exercises that annoy citizens more than they satisfy their desire for increased control over our necessarily large, intrusive government. On the other hand, powerful interests are pleased to have yet another means of influencing the content and administration of public policy. And governments can "fob off" demands for more participation by referring to the availability of these consultations.

- **Cleaning up party finance.** The hopes of many for better politics have rested for years—more than a century—on cleaning up party finance. However, when reforms were finally adopted restricting the funding of parties to the state and individuals, the public funds were distributed in a way that discriminated in favour of the established parties and, particularly, the governing party. The cartel of the dominant parties was strengthened at the expense of new party entrants who could not easily qualify for public funds. Parties, secure in their largely state financing, are thought to be even less responsive to their members and to the people they claim to represent than they are when dependent on outside sources.

This "reform" forces citizens to contribute to the cost of supporting parties, an institution they do not respect, which stands in the way of adopting the more democratic mode of representation they desire. They are also forced to contribute to parties that, once the regulations are in place, find legal and illegal ways to subvert them.

People receive no quid pro quo for the funds they are forced to invest in parties. Parties ignore the urging of virtually all students of politics to function in a way that would increase the political participation and sophistication of the citizenry. It is not in their interest to do so. Politically savvy and engaged citizens would be even more difficult to reconcile to the archaic party system. Instead, parties continue to appeal to voters with demagoguery and personality politics, as indeed they must to attract votes from those they have dumbed down. The media caters to the same audience with "horse-race" journalism and politics as personal melodrama. Voters who could be encouraged to become democratic citizens, if funds going to parties were spent differently, are left with an ever-more-entrenched system of competitive party politics. Public funding of parties supports parties—not citizens.

The present prime minister, Stephen Harper, if he wins a majority government, is committed to eliminating the grants to parties, the "reform" achieved after over a hundred years of effort. The government subsidy to the actual election expenses of parties and candidates would be continued. This move would deprive the Bloc Québécois of the bulk of its funds and increase the financial advantage of Mr. Harper's party over the rest.

- **Measures of direct democracy.** The loss of confidence in the formal institutional arrangements for representing citizens, i.e., voting and sending party representation to the Commons, has led, or forced, elites to supplement them with measures of direct democracy. Experience has shown, however, that referenda, etc., in the hands of the governing party turn out to be a means of managing, not empowering, citizens. Resort to referenda, for example, is often a good release for some of the public's frustration with a political system that excludes its significant participation in making public policy. Sometimes it enables a party to avoid making a vote-endangering decision on an issue. Pressure for significant system reform is weakened by these occasional concessions to popular sovereignty.

When there is the occasional resort to direct democracy, the policy-making process is made even more irrational, as ill-informed citizens are called on to answer a question related to a specific issue that may have wide ramifications on others that it is difficult to factor into the decision.

- **Reform of Commons and Senate.** This need is recognized even by MPs and senators. In the case of the Commons, however, the reforms adopted, and those proposed, largely involve an exceedingly modest shifting of powers within the institution; not enough to offset the growing powers of the chief executive. They do little or nothing to enrich the political life of citizens. The one citizen-significant reform proposed, i.e., allowing MPs to vote the views of their constituents, conflicts with the system-imposed need for party discipline. It is also impossible to implement in the absence of any organized way to determine the majority view of constituents. Although promised often, it cannot be implemented without system change.

Several approaches to Senate reform are proposed. The most significant, electing the Senate, would give Canadians more of the party politics they find alienating and would cause gridlock in our national government, as can be seen in the US model.

Reflecting their interests, elites direct their and our attention to finding a purpose for an archaic institution beyond rewarding a few (usually friends of the governing party). While the search for a purpose goes on, no, or too little, thought is given to establishing a new institution that would allow citizens the form of representation they desire, an institution that would allow them to interact constructively with their MP, government, and bureaucracy. Party politicians have little or no interest in any reforms, however significant they might be, that would threaten their dominant position in the system. Our politicians, mostly committed public servants are caught up in the throes of *their* system and their political imaginations limited.

When and if they do think anew, outside the "box" of party inevitably, it seems highly probable that they would come to the policy democracy/constituency parliament model or something very similar. Many of the current proposals for reform, like those considered in this and the previous chapters, are edging toward this model. However, they stop short when the movement threatens the lock the parties have on our polity.

Parties have served well as transitional institutions, allowing us to move in a fairly orderly fashion from autocratic rule to one where we elect our leaders. They still represent progress for third-world countries in that stage of development but, for us, after more than 150 years of party rule, they represent stagnation, a block to essential democratic development. In an era when government is large, intrusive, and essential, we need, and are ready for, more control over government policies than a competitive party system can provide.

In virtually every respect, our parties are in steep decline as citizen-based organizations. Can we afford to wait until the party-based system becomes completely dysfunctional? At that point will a rational consideration and implementation of a strengthened model of democracy be possible?

On the Cusp of True Democratic Representation

The total configuration, not bits and pieces, is what should concern
Canadians as they seek to improve their system of government.

Thomas Axworthy

The quality of public services will require new and better
mechanisms for engaging citizens and civil society in governance.

A challenge of all governments is to find innovative ways to put citizens at
the centre of the governing process, to engage youth in public enterprise,
and to give voice to those who find themselves on the margins.

The Right Honourable Jean Chrétien

Power concedes nothing without a demand. It never has and it never will.

Frederick Douglass

Introduction

We stand on the cusp of an historic democratic development—the adoption
of a truly democratic mode of representation and governance. Insist on
our long-held desire for constituency representation and we will break our
dependence on seriously dysfunctional parties to represent and govern us.
We will speak for ourselves and make government ours.

With policy democracy based on constituency parliaments, we would retain the right to elect our leaders but would also have the opportunity to participate directly in determining the policies those leaders implement between elections. Our government's agenda would be set in deliberative discussions of citizens with elected members of the House of Commons and MPs with their colleagues in the Commons. Significant input into those discussions would come from the prime minister, his or her cabinet, and members of the bureaucracy. The myth that citizens issue policy mandates to governments with an "*X*" after the name of a party candidate on a ballot every few years would die with the existence of real popular mandates. For the first time ever, the government would be firmly rooted in the people it was elected to serve.

The adoption of policy democracy based on constituency parliaments would vault Canada into a leadership position among liberal democratic states. We would have added an advanced non-party model of representation and governance to the arsenal of democratic institutions.

Implementation of the collaboratively arrived-at policy agenda would be the responsibility of a team composed of citizens elected to constituency parliaments, parliamentarians, the political executive and the civil service. No longer fearful of damaging their competitive position, leaders could promptly adopt essential public policy endorsed by us and our representatives in the House of Commons – a Commons of citizen representatives that would have replaced the "House of Battling Parties," each claiming to represent our interests. The coercion and manipulation of citizens needed now to build support for party policies would be unnecessary with our collective authority behind public policy. Access to information about our public affairs would be guaranteed. Civil servants could talk freely about their work with us as members of the governing team. Respect for, and trust in government would increase as we came as close to governing ourselves as is practical today. New opportunities to put government to our service would open up.

Most of the problems we encounter with the present political system would be overcome as the mode of representation was democratized. Our children and grandchildren will be spared dealing with those problems under what will undoubtedly be less propitious circumstances. They will have their own challenges to meet—policy democracy based on constituency parliaments is not the final stage in our quest for full democracy nor will its adoption ward off the tremendous challenges for humanity on the horizon. With a unifying, inclusive political system in place, however, future generations will be better able to meet them.

The political world would be so different with policy democracy in place that it challenges the imagination to think about it. But it is achievable, now.

Incremental Change

What stands in the way of our making the change from party to citizen representation? The belief that "parties are inevitable" presents one hurdle. Firmly as that belief is currently held, however, it will gradually dissipate if we turn our attention to asking how a more vital democracy can be achieved and hope and plans for our political future replace the present despair.

A related hurdle is the belief that policy democracy can be achieved through incremental reforms in partyocracy. We have been socialized since birth to the notion that it's normal in a democracy for citizens to delegate their democratic rights and responsibilities to our (party) professional politicians and their supporters. This pattern of delegation has encouraged most people to sit back, criticize politicians acting in response to the incentives and disincentives built into the party system, and wait for them to adopt incremental reforms. We hope the politicians' incremental reforms will lead to a more responsive, citizen-inclusive system. Politicians have encouraged these unrealistic hopes by adopting and proposing a series of "reforms" that they have labelled as "democratic."

The futility of the hope that our empowerment can be achieved in this "easy" way was shown in the several chapters in which we analysed reforms such as democratizing parties, public finance of parties, access to information, and others. We found that party leaders engaged in intense adversarial competition do adopt—and then often subvert—what they label as "reforms" or even "democratic reforms." The reforms do not touch the party monopoly of our political lives. We remain as powerless as before they were adopted.

It is not the conscious intention of most of our leaders to deny citizens empowerment. But many of them have always equated partyocracy with "democracy." For them, it follows that strengthening party rule is to extend democracy. Presented with a feasible model that really does empower us, we can hope that they will see the inadequacy of the incremental adjustment approach to change that they have been following. Continuing on this familiar path would be to ignore the truth that it has not staunched the steady rise in citizen alienation and withdrawal of support from government. Instead, the reforms have strengthened the party monopoly on representation and governance—the root cause of our political alienation.

Our challenge is to persuade our leaders that constituency representation is feasible. Most of these leaders are drawn from the pool of Canadians who are already convinced that constituency representation is the appropriate mode for a democracy. A failure to act on that view after they are fully aware of the feasibility of doing so would be a betrayal of their fellow citizens.

We need a citizen-inclusive, efficient, and responsive administration, one that we can trust and support. The failure of partyocracy to meet those conditions leads most citizens to put their primary trust in an amoral market to solve social and economic problems.[29] This is ironic and compounds our difficulties because many of the problems faced by government are created by the functioning of that same market. Neo-conservative groups propose to deal with the political alienation by reducing the size and scope of the government, i.e., leaving even more power to the market, but that is unrealistic. Even under conservative administrations pledged to cut government, its growth, of necessity, continues.

The message is clear: strengthening a political system that evolved in the 19th century to meet the needs of men who fundamentally abhorred democracy is not the route to a truly representative popular democracy. It is hastening the inevitable crisis in relations between citizens and party government. An incipient crisis is already gathering momentum—declining voter turnouts and the progressive loss of confidence in our political leaders

---

29   Asked in a 1991 poll conducted by Gallup Canada, "In general, who do you be-
lieve are more honest and trustworthy, political leaders or business leaders?" 6 percent chose political leaders, 59 percent business leaders, while 35 percent had no opinion, *Toronto Star* (November14, 1991). Opinions of political leaders have not changed for the better since the poll was taken. The reverse is more likely to have taken place.

are two examples of this. The sensible time to enter into a serious discussion of a change in the mode of representation is before the existing system is overwhelmed by citizen indifference, if not revolt. (As mentioned earlier, political developments in Canada and elsewhere during the economic crisis of the 1930s were not favourable to democracy. In Canada, Quebec turned to Duplessis's brand of quasi fascism and Alberta to Social Credit. In Europe the beneficiaries of the crisis were fascism and communism.)

A secure, stable democracy demands that citizens have the opportunity to exercise their rights and responsibilities to the fullest possible extent. (Many will, of course, choose not to take advantage of the opportunity. Their children, experiencing a different kind of political socialization, are more likely to, however.) Fortunately for us, conditions are now unprecedentedly favourable to the adoption of a truly democratic reform that would move us from our present system to the mode of representation we have long desired.

Circumstances Favouring Change Now

Conditions that have led us to the cusp of change have never been as demanding or as promising. "Demanding," because party government has shown that it fails to inspire trust and confidence at a time when governments face increasingly challenging problems. "Promising," because the conditions supporting fundamental change to constituency representation are already almost as strong as those supporting the status quo. Only the necessary organized and focussed public demand for it is missing. Consider the converging circumstances that support the move to a new level of democracy:

- **Widespread support for constituency representation.** The belief that representation *should* be based on constituency rather than party is already firmly established. It has been "lying in wait" for over a century for citizens to insist on having this more democratic form of representation. Discussion of *how* constituency representation could be implemented has to this point, however, been stifled by the party leaders who dominate the public dialogue and have an interest in preserving the system that has rewarded them with power.

- **Escape from the dictatorship of no alternatives.** Over the past century, we have been frustrated in realizing our desire for constituency representation by the absence of a realistic model of it around which we could rally. While our thinking has been "boxed in" by the belief that "parties are inevitable," little thought has been given to alternative forms of representation. *That vacuum has now been filled by the policy democracy based on constituency parliaments model.* A major barrier to reform has been removed.

- **Openness to reform.** Prime ministers, leaders of opposition parties, members of parliament, political activists, students of politics, and citizens all recognize that the existing political system is functioning poorly—better than in many other countries, but far below what is needed to give us good government.

This diverse group of Canadians who are dissatisfied with the system are united in a general understanding of what change is required: the ties between citizens and government must be strengthened—dramatically. Former Prime Minister Chrétien's words bear repeating: "A challenge of all governments is to find innovative ways to put citizens at the centre of the governing process.… " Chrétien suggests that the challenge is to government, but its incremental reforms have proven to be a dead-end, a chimera. If we are to be at the centre of the governing process, party representatives must be replaced by our representatives. That point, though obvious, has been beyond the range of thinking of most political leaders deeply engaged in party politics. They have neglected the development of the citizen-government relationship for over a century, and now we must insist on bold moves to compensate.

- **Many MPs are anxious to represent their constituents.** It is particularly significant that many MPs are among those open to reform. In the present system they are required to follow the policy line laid down by their party. They would like to be able to represent the views of their constituents. The policy democracy/constituency parliament model would meet the aspirations of these MPs: they are important potential recruits to the cause of advancing Canadian democracy.

- **Responsibility-ready citizens.** Partyocracy evolved in the 19th century when most citizens were, for a host of reasons, poorly equipped to play a significant role in shaping public policy. Since that time, however, educational levels have risen rapidly, along with a parallel rise in the standard of living. To a great extent, leaders and led are now drawn from the same middle class. There is no natural governing elite any more. In every constituency there are a significant number of citizens able and anxious to contribute to shaping the policies of the country. Given time, with modern communications we can access most of the information available to our elected representatives. What progressive democracy can afford to brush aside the desire of citizens to be more engaged, *on their terms,* in the government of their country?

- **New possibilities for organizing citizen support for change.** Modern communications technology allows formerly isolated and powerless citizens to reach out to others and bypass leaders committed to maintaining the existing distribution of political power. The widespread access to and use of the social media for the exchange of political ideas and information has made the rapid organization of citizens around ideas possible, particularly those ideas they already support in the abstract. It is difficult to overstate the importance of this dynamic new factor in political life.

- **The possibility of party-supported change.** Throughout the book I emphasize the importance of *not* depending on a party to initiate fundamental reform. That position is unchanged; a powerful tide of demand for change is necessary if we are to break out of the political stalemate that exists today. We are alienated from "our" government: we are not pressing power-holders to make the feasible changes in the representative system that we want and need. That stalemate must be broken: the forces of change would be strengthened with the help of one or more parties. Party against the party system? While we should not depend on it, that development is possible.

There are circumstances in which a party or parties, with their organizational apparatus, could support a change to constituency representation. It might do this despite the fact that it would be weakening or, more likely, supplanting the 19th-century party system in which it is participating—perhaps reluctantly since it is the only avenue available.

There are realists, in minor parties particularly, who can see that their only way to contribute to government policy now is to pressure other parties, and particularly the governing party, to adopt their policies. A party in this situation, believing that its ideas are broadly in tune with those of the public, has much to gain in supporting a challenge to the party mode of representation. Working from the ground up, i.e., through constituency parliaments, the party's members, along with other citizens, would have a better chance of having their policies adopted—if they, indeed, proved to be consistent with the policy preferences of the wider community—than they would battling in the existing House of Commons. Renouncing the pursuit of power, a party could achieve its policy objectives through policy democracy.

In breaking the grip of the parties on our politics, the minor party's members would earn the respect and appreciation of now inarticulate Canadians. Once it showed that it was successfully mobilizing the now-latent public support for constituency representation, the party in office might choose to endorse it, too, rather than suffer the humiliation of going down to defeat fighting against the extension of Canadian democracy.[1]

With this set of propitious circumstances, we stand on the verge of change that goes far beyond incremental adjustment. We have been in this position before. In the 1960s, there was wide support for Trudeau's ill-defined "participatory democracy." The idea was popular, and support for change was mobilized, but the moment passed because no thought had been given by either the prime minister or citizens to how participatory democracy could be responsibly organized. The primary objective of the

---

1   It is predictable that the first concession of a major party would be to set up a system of constituency "advisory committees" to avoid an actual transfer of power to citizens. But that "temporizing" action would not satisfy the demands of citizens.

Liberal Party was to achieve power for its leader by riding on the widespread desire for change. A citizens' movement for constituency representation, with or without party backing, would have only one objective, i.e., creating the institutional framework that would would allow citizens to become a significant force in shaping public policy.

Conclusion: Our Challenge

The challenge of moving a now (barely) tolerable political system to a better place is formidable. Under normal circumstances, most people will want to devote their energies to objectives, private and public, that seem more attainable. But conditions are not normal. They are unusually favourable to change: change to the vibrant polity needed to meet the exceptionally difficult national and global challenges our country and others face. The investment in real political reform now promises huge social and economic returns for us and future generations.

Canadians did not choose to be represented and governed by parties. Rather, most were born into a country with an entrenched political system and socialized to accept it as "democratic." That 19th-century system has proven unable to meet the challenges of the very different world of the 21st century. It is past time that citizens had the opportunity to adopt their preferred form of representation, with the new powers and social responsibilities its adoption would entail for them. It is past time, too, that MPs promising and wishing to represent their constituents were given the appropriate means to do so.

Moving a well-entrenched political system to a higher, more democratic level is an enormous challenge, even when conditions demand it and circumstances are very favourable. While most Canadians endorse constituency representation at an intellectual level, for many, actually taking the plunge, i.e., becoming active supporters, will involve personal courage. Opponents of the new model will cry that if constituency representation is implemented, "the sky will fall."[2] Reviewing the rhetoric predicting disaster if working men and, later, women

---

2   Traditional rulers in the Middle East are learning the hard way that their sky will fall if they fail to modernize their political institutions in line with the political aspirations of their peoples.

were given the vote, is instructive on whether the result of further empowering citizens would be positive. Note too, that nearly all the "reforms" introduced by party elites purport to open up the system to more participation or, in the case of voting, maintain what little there is. Their proponents know what is needed but find it hard to accept it on their watch. As a result, their reforms stop short of challenging the basis of our political malaise, i.e., the delegation of our political rights and responsibilities to parties and, particularly, to party leaders.

Other opponents will feel that it is un-Canadian for us to initiate a richer form of democracy. They believe, in the best colonial tradition, that Canadians should continue to look to the United States or the United Kingdom for political models. But we need a system that meets our unique values and challenges. Further, along with anger and frustration, there is comfort for some in the familiar, albeit malfunctioning, system to which they will cling. But, surely, our concern for our children and grandchildren who will live in a more difficult world than we have experienced will not allow most of us to do that.

The effort Canadians would have to put forward to achieve policy democracy, to overcome these fears and reservations, would be infinitely worthwhile. Success would tip the balance of power from party politicians and interest groups to an organized citizenry. Resentful citizens would no longer tell pollsters that they feel "powerless." We would no longer have to wait years, or perhaps a lifetime, for good people, acting on our behalf, to pressure reluctant governments to adopt economically feasible and socially desirable measures opposed by a powerful few. Citizens, as "governors," could consider and act on social and economic projects that must remain just dreams with our present system, where citizens are set against each other and so many do not trust government.

The other "democracies" of the world, also stalled at "electoral democracy," their citizens often having to take to the streets to be heard, would benefit from an awareness that there is an alternative to 19th-century partyocracy.

A "Quiet Canadian Democratic Revolution" would be the unifying project that would reverse the ongoing political fragmentation of our country. With its success, the pettiness and sterility of the divide-and-exploit politics of the parties would be set aside. Party priorities would be replaced by those we developed in collaboration with our elected representatives and civil servants. In a very real sense, we would be sovereign: the transition from monarchs ruling by divine right to government by the people would be as close to reality as is feasible today.

Our investment in a more democratic future for Canada would be rewarded by the knowledge that we have done something truly creative, courageous, and enormously significant with a part of our lives. Most of us aspire to make a difference. We now have that opportunity.

There is no greater power on earth than an idea whose time has come.

Victor Hugo

REFERENCES

Abelson, Julia, and François-Pierre Gauvin. "Assessing the Impacts of Public Participation: Concepts, Evidence, and Policy Implications," Ottawa: Canadian Policy Research Networks, 2006.

Adams, Michael. "Canadian Attitudes Toward Legislative Institutions." In *Canadian Legislatures: The 1986 Comparative Study*, Robert J. Fleming, ed. Queen's Park, Toronto: Office of the Assembly, 1986, 25–32.

Atkinson, Michael. "What Kind of Democracy Do Canadians Want?" *Canadian Journal of Political Science* 27, 4 (December 1994): 717–45.

Aucoin, Peter. "Responsible Government and Citizen Engagement at the Millennium: Are Political Parties Irrelevant?" In *Taking Stock of 150 Years of Responsible Government in Canada*. Leslie F. Seidle and Louis Massicotte, eds. Ottawa: Canadian Study of Parliament Group, 1999, 71–101.

Axworthy, Thomas S. "Everything Old is New Again." Kingston: Queen's University, 2008. www.queensu.ca/csd

Axworthy, Lloyd. *Navigating a New World*. Toronto: Alfred A. Knopf Canada, 2003.

Axworthy, Thomas S., and P. E. Trudeau, eds. *Towards a Just Society*. Markham, Ontario: Viking Press, 1989.

Axworthy, Thomas S., and Julie Burch, "Closing the Implementation Gap," Kingston: Queen's University, 2010. www.queensu.ca/csd

Bagley, Robin F., and Samuel Wolfe. *Doctors' Strike*. Toronto: Macmillan, 1967.

Barber, Benjamin R. *A Passion for Democracy*. Princeton, NJ: Princeton University Press, 1998.

———. *Strong Democracy*. Berkeley: University of California Press, 1984.

Barnett, Anthony. "The Creation of Democracy." In *Reinventing Democracy*. Paul Hirst and Sunil Khilnani, eds. Oxford: Blackwell, 1996, 157–77.

Barney, Darin and David Laycock. "The Decline of Party: Armchair Democracy and the Reform Party of Canada." Paper presented to the British Columbia Political Studies Association Conference, Simon Fraser University, Burnaby, BC, May 5–6, 1995. Mimeo.

Bay, Christian. *The Structure of Freedom*. Stanford, CA: Stanford University Press, 1958.

303

Bennett, Carolyn, Deborah Grey, and Yves Morin. *The Parliament We Want: Parliamentarians' Views on Parliamentary Reform*. Ottawa: Library of Parliament, 2003.

Berlin, David. "A Love Affair with Secrecy." *TheWalrus*, November 2004, 34–37.

Bissoondath, Neil. *Selling Illusions: The Cult of Multiculturalism in Canada*. Toronto: Penguin Books, 1994.

Black, Jerome H., and Bruce M. Hicks. "Strengthening Canadian Democracy: The Views of Parliamentary Candidates." Institute for Research on Public Policy (IRPP) Montreal, March 2006. www.irpp.org/indexe.htm

Blakeney, Allan, and Sandford Borins. *Political Management in Canada*. Toronto: McGraw-Hill Ryerson Ltd., 1992.

Blais, André, et el. "Does the Local Candidate Matter? Effects in the Canadian Election of 2000." *Canadian Journal of Political Science* 36, 3 (July–August 2003): 657–64.

Bogdanor, Vernon. *The People and the Party System*. Cambridge: Cambridge University Press, 1981.

Bourgon, Jocelyne. "Notes for an address to the Association of Professional Executives of the Public Service of Canada Symposium." Ottawa, May 27, 1998, 3. Mimeo.

Boyer, J. Patrick. *Direct Democracy in Canada*. Toronto: Dundurn Press, 1992.

———. *The People's Mandate: Referendums and a More Democratic Canada*. Toronto: Dundurn Press, 1992.

Bridge, Richard. "The Law of Advocacy by Charitable Organizations." Vancouver: Institute for Media, Policy and Civil Society, September 2000. http://www.canadianconstitutionfoundation.ca/files/pdf.

Brooks, Neil. *Left vs. Right*. Ottawa: Canadian Centre for Policy Alternatives, 1995.

Brownstone, Meyer. "Moving Beyond the Limited Democracy of Social Democracy." In *A Different Kind of State? Popular Power and Democratic Administration*. Leo Panitch, Gregory Albo, and David Langille, eds. Toronto: Oxford University Press, 1993.

Burke, Edmund. "Speech to the Electors of Bristol." In *The Philosophy of Edmund Burke*. L. I. Bredvold and Ralph G. Ross, eds. Ann Arbor: University of Michigan Press, 1960, 147–48.

Burnheim, John. *Is Democracy Possible? The alternative to electoral politics*. Cambridge: Polity Press, in association with Oxford: Basil Blackwell, 1985.

Cairns, Alan C. "Afterword: International Dimensions of the Citizen Issue for Indigenous Peoples/Nations." Citizenship Studies, 7, 4 (2003)

———. Citizens Plus: Aboriginal Peoples and the Canadian State. Vancouver: University of British Columbia Press, 2000.

———. Disruptions: Constitutional Struggles from the Charter to Meech Lake. Toronto: McClelland and Stewart, 1991.

———. "The Electoral System and the Party System in Canadian Journal of Political Science 1, 1 (March 1968): 55–80.

Cameron David R., and Graham White. Cycling into Saigon: The Conservative Transition in Ontario. Vancouver: University of British Columbia Press, 2000.

Cameron, David R., and Richard Simeon, "Intergovernmental Relations and Democratic Citizenship." In *Governance in the Twenty-first Century: Revitalizing the Public Service.* Guy Peters and Donald J. Savoie, eds. Canadian Centre for Management Development. Montreal and Kingston: McGill-Queen's University Press, 2000.

Camp, Dalton. "The Limits of Political Parties." In *Sovereign People or Sovereign Governments,* H. V. Kroeker, ed. Montreal: Institute for Research on Public Policy, 1981.

———. *Points of Departure.* Ottawa: Deneau and Greenburg, 1979.

Campbell, Barry. "Part Three: Sanity Found," *The Walrus* 5, 4 (2008): 72–78.

Campbell Public Affairs Institute. *Constructing Civic Virtue.* A symposium on the state of American Citizenship. E-book. Syracuse, NY: The Maxwell School of Syracuse University, 2000.

Campbell, Robert. "Coping with globalization instead of just talking about it." *Policy Options* (December 1992).

Canada. Elections Canada, "Report of the Chief Electoral Officer on the 39th General Election." October 2006, 65. www.elections.ca.

———. "A Report from the National Coordinating Committee for Organ and Tissue Donation and Transplantation to the Federal/Provincial/Territorial Advisory Committee on Health Services." Ottawa: Health Canada, 24 April 2006. www. hc-sc.gc.ca/dhp-mps/pubs/biolog/summary-sommaire_e.html.

———. Public Service Integrity Officer. 2004–2005 Annual Report to Parliament. Ottawa: Public Service Integrity Office, 2005. www.psio-bifp.gc.ca/publications/ann-rpt-2004-2005.

———. Elections Canada. "Report of the Chief Electoral Officer on the 38th General Election." Ottawa: October 2004. www.electionscanada.ca

———. Law Commission of Canada. Voting Counts: Electoral Reform for Canada. Ottawa: Minister of Public Works and Government Services, 2004.

———. Privy Council Office. "Ethics, Responsibility, Accountability. An Action Plan for Democratic Reform." Ottawa: 2004. www.bcp.gc.ca/

———. Figueroa v. Canada (Attorney General), [2003] 1 S.C.R. 912.

———. Annual Reports of the Information Commissioner, 1999–2003. Ottawa: Minister of Public Works and Government Services Canada.

———. Law Reform Commission of Canada/Fair Vote Canada. (Prepared by Dennis Pilon.) Renewing Canadian Democracy: Citizen Engagement in Voting System Reform. March 2002. www.lcc.gc.ca

————. "The Social Union Framework Agreement," 1999. www.cspsrefpc.gc.ca/Research/publications/pdfs/SUFA_e.pdf

————. National Council of Welfare. Report. "Healthy Parents, Healthy Babies." Ottawa: Minster of Public Works and Government Services, 1997.

————. Citizens' Forum on Canada's Future. (The Spicer Commission) Report to the People and Government of Canada. Ottawa: Minister of Supply and Services Canada, 1991.

————. Final Report Royal Commission on Electoral Expenses and Party Financing. 4 vols. Ottawa: Minister of Supply and Services, 1991.

————. Money in Politics Financing Federal Parties and Candidates in Canada, Vol. 1 Research Studies, Royal Commission on Electoral Reform and Party Financing (Toronto: Dundurn Press, 1993), 28–53.

————. Access to Information Act, R.S. 1985, c. A-1, S. 2(1) www.scc-csc.gc.ca/information/index_e/asp

————. Task Force on Canadian Unity. A Future Together: Observations and Recommendations, Ottawa: Task Force on Canadian Unity, 1979.

————. Economic Council of Canada. Design for Decision-Making: Eighth Annual Review. Ottawa: Information Canada, 1971.

————. Report of the Royal Commission on Bilingualism and Biculturalism. Ottawa: Queen's Printer, 1967.

————. Special House of Commons Committee (Chappell Committee) on Election Expenses. House of Commons, 1971, 13:19.

————. Committee on Election Expenses (Barbeau Committee). 1966a. Ottawa: Queen's Printer.

Carty, R. Kenneth, "The Shifting Place of Political Parties in Canadian Political Life," *Choices* 12, 4 (2006). http://www.irpp.org

Carty, R. Kenneth, William Cross and Lisa Young. Rebuilding Canadian Party Politics. Vancouver: University of British Columbia Press, 2000.

Centre for Research and Information on Canada (CRIC). "The Charter: Dividing or Uniting Canadians." April 2002. www.cric.ca

Chennells, David. *The Politics of Nationalism in Canada: Cultural Conflict since 1760.* Toronto: University of Toronto Press, 2001.

Chrétien, Jean. *My Years as Prime Minister.* Toronto: Alfred A. Knopf, 2007.

Clarke, Harold D. and Allan Kornberg. "Evaluations and Evolution: Public Attitudes toward Federal Political Parties, 1965–1991." *Canadian Journal of Political Science* 26, 2 (June 1993): 287–311.

Clarke, Harold D., Jon H. Pammett, and Marianne C. Stewart. "The Forest for the Trees: Regional (Dis)Similarities in Canadian Political Culture." In *Regionalism and Party Politics in Canada.* Lisa Young and Keith Archer, eds. Don Mills, Ontario: Oxford University Press, 2002, 43–76.

Clarke, Harold D., L. LeDuc, J. Jenson, J. H. Pammett. *Political Choice in Canada.* Toronto: McGraw-Hill Ryerson, 1979.

Clark, S. D. *The Developing Canadian Community.* Toronto: University of Toronto Press, 1962.

Cleveland, Gordon, and Barry Forer; Douglas Hyatt; Christa Japel; Michael Krashinsky. "New Evidence about Child Care in Canada." *Choices* 14, 12 (October 2008). www.irpp.org/choices/archive/vol14no12.pdf

Clokie, H. McD. *Canadian Government and Politics.* Toronto: Longmans Green, 1944.

Cole, G. D. H. *Essays in Social Theory.* New York: Macmillan, 1950.

Coleman, Stephen, and Jay G. Blumler. *The Internet and Democratic Citizenship.* Cambridge: Cambridge University Press, 2009.

Colombo, J. R., ed. *Colombo's Canadian Quotations.* Edmonton: Hurtig, 1974.

Conference Board of Canada. "Performance and Potential 2003–4: The Canadian Advantage." www.ConferenceBoard2003.4.pdf

Corbett, D. C. "The Pure Group and the Public Interest." Institute of Public Administration of Canada, Proceedings of the Fifth Annual Conference, 1953. Reprinted in Canadian Public Administration. J. E. Hodgetts and D.C. Corbett, eds. Toronto: Macmillan, 1960.

Crisp, L. F. *The Parliamentary Government of the Commonwealth of Australia.* London: Longmans, 1961.

Crosbie, John C. *No Holds Barred.* Toronto: McClelland and Stewart, 1997.

Cross, William, and Lisa Young, "Are Canadian Political Parties Empty Vessels?" *Choices* 12, 4 (2006). http://irpp.com

Cross, William. "The Increasing Importance of Region to Canadian Election Campaigns." In Regionalism and Party Politics in Canada. Lisa Young, and Keith Archer, eds. Don Mills, Ontario.: Oxford University Press, 2002, 116–28.

Cross, William, "Members of Parliament, Voters, and Democracy in the Canadian House of Commons," *Parliamentary Perspectives*, 3rd paper, n.d.

Crouch, Colin, and David Marquand, eds. *Reinventing Collective Action.* Oxford: Blackwell, 1995.

Crozier, Michel J., Samuel P. Huntington, and Joji Watanuki. Crisis of Democracy: Report on the Governability of Democracies to the Trilateral Commission. New York: New York University Press, 1975.

Dalton, Russell J., and Martin P. Wattenberg, Parties without Partisans: Political Change in Advanced Industrial Democracies. Oxford: Oxford University Press, 2000.

Dahl, Robert A. "On Removing Certain Impediments to Democracy in the United States." *Political Science Quarterly* 92, 1 (Spring 1977): 1–20.

————. *A Preface to Democratic Theory*. Chicago and London: University of Toronto Press, 1956.

Dawson, R. MacGregor. *The Government of Canada*. Toronto: University of Toronto Press, 1948.

Devereaux, P. J. et al., "Payments for care at private for-profit and not-for-profit hospitals: a systematic review and meta analysis," *Canadian Medical Association Journal* 170 (June 2004): 1817–24. www.cmaj.ca/egi/reprint/17c/12/18/7.

Dewey, John. *The Public and Its Problems*. 1927. Denver: Allan Swallow, 1954.

Docherty, David C. "Citizens and Legislators: Different Views on Representation." In Neil Nevitte, ed. *Value Change and Governance in Canada*. Toronto: University of Toronto Press, 2002, 165–206.

Docherty, David. *Mr. Smith Goes to Ottawa*. Vancouver: University of British Columbia Press, 1997.

————. *Legislatures*. Vancouver: University of British Columbia Press, 2005.

Dobell, Peter and Byron Berry. "Political Discontent in Canada." In *Parliamentary Government* 39 (January 1992.)

Dobrowolsky, Alexandra and Jane Jenson. "Reforming the Parties: Prescriptions for Democracy." In *How Ottawa Spends 1993–94: A More Democratic Canada*. Susan D. Phillips, ed. Ottawa: Carleton University Press, 1993, 44–81.

Doern, G. Bruce, ed. *How Ottawa Spends 2004–2005*. Montreal and Kingston: McGill-Queen's University Press. 2004.

Doern, G. Bruce, and Brian W. Tomlin. *Faith and Fear*. Toronto: Stoddard Publishing, 1991.

Eager, Evelyn. "The Paradox of Power in the Saskatchewan CCF, 1944–1961." In *The Political Process in Canada*. J. H. Aitchison, ed. Toronto: University of Toronto Press, 1963.

Easton, David. *A Systems Analysis of Political Life*. New York: Wiley, 1965.

Economist. "Empty Vessels." July 22, 1999.

Ekos Research Associates Inc. *Rethinking Government '94: An Overview and Synthesis*. Ottawa: Ekos Research Associates Inc., 1995.

Eldersveld, Samuel J. *Political Parties: A Behavioral Analysis*. Chicago: Rand McNally and Co., 1964.

Engelmann, F. C. *The Cooperative Commonwealth Federation of Canada: A Study of Membership Participation in Party Policy-Making*. PhD diss. Yale University, 1954.

English, John. *Just Watch Me* (Toronto: Alfred A. Knopf, 2009).

Erickson, Lynda, and R. K. Carty. "Parties and Candidate Selection in the 1988 Canadian General Election." *Canadian Journal of Political Science* 32, 2 (June 1991): 331–49.

Evans, Gareth. *The Responsibility to Protect*. Washington, DC: Brookings Institution Press, 2008.

Everitt, Joanna, and Brenda O'Neill, eds. *Citizen Politics*. Don Mills, Ont.: Oxford University Press, 2002.

Fishkin, James S. *Democracy and Deliberation*. New Haven: Yale University Press, 1991.

Flanagan, Tom. *Harper's Team*. Montreal and Kingston: McGill-Queen's University Press, 2007.

Flanagan, Tom, and David Coletto. "Replacing Allowances for Canada's National Political Parties?" SPP Briefing Papers 3, 1. Calgary: University of Calgary, School of Public Policy, 2010.

———. *Waiting for the Wave*. Toronto: Stoddart Publishing Co., 1995.

Fournier, Patrick. "The Uninformed Canadian Voter." In *Citizen Politics*. Joanna Everitt, and Brenda O'Neill, eds. Don Mills, Ont.: Oxford University Press, 2002, 92–109.

Fraser, Graham. "Sending money home." *Toronto Star*. March 11, 2000.

Friedman, Jeffery. "Introduction: Public Ignorance and Democratic Theory." *Critical Review* 12, 4 (Fall 1998): 397–411.

Fromm, Erich. *Escape from Freedom*. New York: Avon Books, 1941.

Furi, Megan. "Legislative history of Bill C-3." Parliamentary Research Branch. www.dsp-psd.tpsgc.gc.ca/Collection-R/LoPBdP/mat-e.html.

Galbraith, John Kenneth. *The Affluent Society*. Boston: Houghton Mifflin Books, 1998.

Gerth, H. H., and C. W. Mills, eds. From *Max Weber: Essays in Sociology*. New York: Galaxy Paperback, 1958.

Gibbins, Roger. *Conflict and Unity*. Toronto: Methuen, 1988.

———. "Shifting Sands: Exploring the Political Foundations of SUFA." Policy Matters, Institute for Research on Public Policy, 2.3. www.irpp.org

Giles, David E. A., and Lindsay M. Tedds. "Taxes and the Canadian Underground Economy." Canadian Tax Paper, No. 106. Toronto: Canadian Tax Foundation, 2002.

Gutstein, Donald, *Not a Conspiracy Theory*. Toronto: Key Porter Books Limited, 2009.

Gould, Philip. "Power to the People." *The Spectator* (May 18, 2002): 24–25.

Greenspon, Edward, and Anthony Wilson-Smith. *Double Vision: The Inside Story of the Liberals in Power*. Toronto: Doubleday Canada, 1996.

Godfrey, John, and Rob McLean. *The Canada We Want*. Toronto: Stoddart, 1999.

Goldenberg, Eddie. *The Way It Works: Inside Ottawa*. (Toronto: McClelland and Stewart Ltd., 2006).

Gomery, Justice John. Phase 1 Report, "Who is Responsible?" Ottawa: Minister of

Public Works and Government Services, 2005. www.cbc.ca/news/background/groupaction/gomeryreport_phaseone.htm

Graves, Frank. Rethinking Government '94. Ekos Research Associates. 1995.

Gregg, Allan. "Identity Crisis." *The Walrus* 3, 2 (March 2006).

———. "How to Save Democracy." *The Walrus* (September 2004), 26–29.

Gwyn, Richard. "No Wonder Democracy is in Trouble." *Toronto Star.* May 26, 2002, A15.

———. *The Northern Magus.* Toronto: McClelland and Stewart, 1980.

Hale, Geoffrey E. "Priming the Electoral Pump: Framing Budgets for a Renewed Mandate." In *How Ottawa Spends 2001–2002.* Leslie A. Pal, ed. Don Mills, Ont.: Oxford University Press, 2001, 30–60.

Harcourt, Mike. *Mike Harcourt: A Measure of Defiance.* Vancouver: Douglas and McIntyre, 1996.

Harrington, Michael. *The Accidental Century.* Baltimore: Penguin Books, 1966.

Hatch, Christopher, and Matt Price. *Canada's Toxic Tar Sands.* Toronto: Environmental Defence, 2008. www.environmentaldefence.ca/reports/pdf/TarSands_TheReport.pdf

Hébert, Yvonne M. ed. *Citizenship in Transformation in Canada.* Toronto: University of Toronto Press, 2002.

Heilbroner, Robert L. *An Inquiry into the Human Prospect.* New York: W. W. Norton, 1975.

Hirst, Paul, and Sunil Khilnani, eds. *Reinventing Democracy.* Oxford: Blackwell Publishers, 1996.

Hockin, Thomas A. "Pierre Trudeau on the prime minister and the Participant Party." In *Apex of Power.* Thomas Hockin, ed. Scarborough: Prentice-Hall, 1971, 96–107.

Hodgetts, H. B. *What Culture? What Heritage?* Toronto: Ontario Institute for Studies in Education, 1968.

Hodgins, Bruce W. "Democracy and the Ontario Fathers of Confederation." In *Profiles of a Province.* Edith G. Firth, ed. Toronto: Ontario Historical Society, 1967, 83–91.

Hoppe, Hans-Hermann. *Democracy: The God that Failed.* New Brunswick, NJ: Transaction Publishers, 2001.

Hou, Feng, and Garnett Picot, "Visible Minority Neighbourhoods in Toronto, Montreal, and Vancouver." Ottawa: Statistics Canada, Cat. No. 11-008, 2004, 10–11. www.statcan.ca/bsolc/english/english/bsolc?catno=11-008.

Howe, Paul, Richard Johnston, and André Blais, eds. *Strengthening Canadian Democracy.* Montreal: Institute for Research on Public Policy, 2005.

Howe, Paul, and David Northrup. *The Views of Canadians.* Montreal: Institute for Research on Public Policy, *Policy Matters* 1, 5 (July 2000). www.irpp.org.

Hurl, Lorna F. "Privatized Social Service Systems: Lessons from Ontario Children's Services." *Canadian Public Policy* 10, 4 (December 1984): 395–405.

Inter-Parliamentary Union. *Electoral Systems: A Worldwide Comparative Study.* Geneva: Inter-Parliamentary Union, 1993.

Jennings, Ivor. *Party Politics: Volume 2: The Growth of Parties.* Cambridge: Cambridge University Press, 1961.

Jenson, Jane. "Beyond Brokerage Politics: Toward the Democracy Round." In *Constitutional Politics.* Duncan Cameron, and Miriam Smith, eds. Toronto: James Lorimer and Company, 1992, 204–14.

Johnson, A. W. *Biography of a Government: Policy Formation in Saskatchewan 1944–1961.* PhD diss. Harvard University, 1963.

Johnston, Donald. *Up the Hill.* Montreal and Toronto: Optimum Publishing International, 1986.

Johnson, Nevil. *"Adversary Politics and Electoral Reform: Need We Be Afraid."* In Adversary Politics and Electoral Reform. S. E. Finer, ed. London: Anthony Wigram, 1975.

Johnston, Richard, André Blais, Henry E. Brady, and Jean Crêt. *Letting the People Decide.* Montreal and Kingston: McGill-Queen's University Press, 1992.

Kingsley, Jean-Pierre. "Money and Elections: The Canadian Experience." Paper presented at the XVIII World Congress of the International Political Science Association, Quebec City, August 4, 2000. www.electionscanada.ca

Kingwell, Mark. *The World We Want.* Toronto: Penguin Group, 2000.

Kernerman, Gerald. *Multicultural Nationalism.* Vancouver: University of British Columbia Press, 2005.

Kroeker, H. V., ed. *Sovereign People or Sovereign Governments.* Montreal: Institute for Research on Public Policy, 1981.

Ladner, Kiera L. "The Alienation of Nation: Understanding Aboriginal Electoral Participation." *Electoral Insight* 5, 3 (November 2003): 21–26.

Landes, Ronald G. *The Canadian Polity*, 3rd ed. Scarborough, Ont.: Prentice-Hall Canada, 1991.

———. *The Canadian Polity*, 2nd ed. Scarborough, Ont.: Prentice-Hall Canada, 1987.

Lawson, Kay, ed. *Political Parties and Linkage.* New Haven: Yale University Press, 1980.

Laycock, David. *The New Right and Democracy in Canada.* Don Mills, Ont.: Oxford University Press, 2002.

———. *Populism and Democratic Thought in the Canadian Prairies, 1910 to 1945.* Toronto: University of Toronto Press, 1990.

Lazar, Fred. *How Ottawa Rewards Mediocrity.* Toronto: University of Toronto Press, 1996.

311

LeDuc, Lawrence. *The Politics of Direct Democracy: referendums in global perspective.* Peterborough, Ont.: Broadview Press, 2003.

———. "Consulting the People: The Canadian Experience with Referendums." In *Citizen Politics.* Joanna Everitt and Brenda O'Neill, eds. Don Mills, Ont.: Oxford University Press, 2002, 247-267.

Leib, Ethan. *Deliberative Democracy in America.* University Park, PA.: Pennsylvania State University Press, 2004.

Lewis, David, and Frank Scott. *Make this Your Canada.* Toronto: Central Canada Publishing Company, 1943.

Lijphart, Arend. *Patterns of Democracy: Government Forms and Performance in Thirty-Six Countries.* New Haven and London: Yale University Press, 1999.

———. *Democracies: Patterns of Majoritarian and Consensus Government in Twenty-One Countries.* New Haven: Yale University Press, 1984.

Lindblom, Charles. *Politics and Markets.* New York: Basic Books, 1977.

Lindquist, Evert A. "How Ottawa Plans: The Evolution of Strategic Planning." In *How Ottawa Spends 2001-2002.* Leslie A. Pal, ed. Don Mills, Ont.: Oxford University Press, 2001.

Lipset, S. M. *Agrarian Socialism.* 1950. New York: Doubleday, 1968.

Little, Bruce. "Canada's latest report card has disappointing marks." *Globe and Mail,* October 4, 2003, B3-B4.

Lowi, T. J. *The End of Liberalism.* New York: W. W. Norton, 1969.

Lyon, Peyton V. *Canada in World Affairs 1961-1963.* Toronto: Oxford University Press, 1968.

Lyon, Vaughan. "The future of parties: inevitable ... obsolete?" *Journal of Canadian Studies,* 18, 4 (Winter 1983-84): 108-31.

———. *Democracy and the Canadian Political System.* PhD diss. University of British Columbia, 1974.

Macdonald, Donald C. "Modernizing the Legislature." In *Government and Politics of Ontario.* Donald C. Macdonald, ed. Toronto: Macmillan, 1975, 93-113.

MacIvor, Heather "The Charter of Rights and Party Politics: The Impact of the Supreme Court Ruling in Figueroa v. Canada (Attorney General)." *Choices* 10, 4 (2004). Montreal: IRPP. www.irpp.org

———. "Do Canadian Political Parties Form a Cartel?" *Canadian Journal of Political Science* 29 (June 2, 1996), 317-33.

———. "Medicine for our democratic malaise." *Inroads* 18 (Spring/Winter 2006), 317-33

Macpherson, C. B. *The Rise and Fall of Economic Justice.* Oxford: Oxford University Press, 1985.

———. *Democracy in Alberta*, 2nd ed. Toronto: University of Toronto Press, 1962.

Makarenko, Jay, "Federal Campaign Laws in Canada," Maple Leaf Web, 2. www. mapleleafweb.com

Mancuso, Maureen, Richard G. Price, and Ronald Wagenberg, eds. *Leaders and Leadership in Canada*. Toronto: Oxford University Press, 1994.

Manning, Preston. *Think Big*. Toronto: McClelland and Stewart, 2002.

Mansbridge, Jane J. *Beyond Adversary Democracy*. New York: Basic Books, 1980.

Marsden, Lorna. "The Party and Parliament: Participatory Democracy in the Trudeau Years." In *Towards a Just Society*. Thomas S. Axworthy and Pierre Elliott Trudeau, eds. Markham, Ont.: Viking Press, 1989, 262–81.

Marsden, William. *Stupid to the Last Drop: How Alberta is Bringing Environmental Armageddon to Canada (and Doesn't Seem to Care)*. Toronto: Alfred A. Knopf, 2007.

Martin, Pierre, and Richard Nadeau. "Understanding Opinion Formation on Quebec Sovereignty." In *Citizen Politics*. Joanna Everitt, and Brenda O'Neill, eds. Toronto: Oxford University Press, 2002, 142–60.

Mathews, David. *Politics for People*. Urbana and Chicago: University of Illinois Press, 1994.

May, Elizabeth. "Clearing the Air on Climate Change." Address to Manitoba Wildlands Organization, Winnipeg, Manitoba. 20 June 2006. www.elizabethmay.ca/ speeches/Clearing-the-air-on-climate-change.php

McCall, Christina, and Stephen Clarkson. *Trudeau and Our Times. Volume 2: The Heroic Delusion*. Toronto: McClelland and Stewart, 1994.

Meekison, J. Peter, ed. *Canadian Federalism: Myth or Reality?* 2nd ed. Toronto: Methuen, 1971.

Meisel, John. "The Dysfunctions of Canadian Parties: An Exploratory Mapping." In *Democracy with Justice*. Alain-G. Gagnon, and A. Brian Tanguay, eds. Ottawa: Carleton University Press, 1992, 407–31.

———. "The Decline of Party in Canada." In *Party Politics in Canada*, 4th ed. Hugh G. Thorburn, ed. Scarborough: Prentice-Hall, 1979, 119–35.

———. "Recent Changes in Canadian Parties." In *Party Politics in Canada*, 2nd ed. Hugh G. Thorburn, ed. Scarborough: Prentice-Hall, 1967.

Mendelsohn, Matthew. "Healing Social, Political and Regional Divisions." In *Memos to the Prime Minister*. Harvey Schachter, ed. Toronto: John Wiley and Sons, 2001, 10–20.

———. "Public Brokerage: Constitutional Reform and the Accommodation of Mass Publics." *Canadian Journal of Political Science* 33, 2 (June 2000): 245–72.

———. "Introducing Deliberative Direct Democracy in Canada: Learning from the American Experience." *American Review of Canadian Studies* 26, 3 (1997): 449–68.

Mendelsohn, Matthew and Andrew Parkin. "Introducing Direct Democracy in Canada." *Choices* 7, 5 (June 2001)

Michels, Robert. *Political Parties*. Glencoe: Free Press, 1915.

Milne, David. *The Canadian Constitution*. Toronto: James Lorimer and Company, 1991.

Milner, Henry. "Fixing Canada's Unfixed Election Dates." IRPP *Policy Matters* 6, 6 (December 2005). www.irpp.org/indexe.html.

———. *Civic Literacy: How Informed Citizens Make Democracy Work*. Hanover: University Press of New England, 2000.

Mishler, William. *Political Participation in Canada*. Toronto: Macmillan, 1979.

Morton, W. L. *The Progressive Party in Canada*. Toronto: University of Toronto Press, 1950.

———. "The Social Philosophy of Henry Wise Wood." *Agricultural History* 22, 2 (1948).

Naylor, James. *The New Democracy*. Toronto: University of Toronto Press, 1991.

Nevitte, Neil. *The Decline of Deference: Canadian Value Change in Cross-National Perspective*. Peterborough, Ont.: Broadview Press, 1996.

Nevitte, Neil, Andre Blais, Elisabeth Gidengil, and Richard Nadeau. *Unsteady State: The 1977 Canadian Federal Election*. Don Mills, Ont.: Oxford University Press, 1999.

Noel, S. J. R. "Political Parties and Elite Accommodation: Interpretations of Canadian Federalism." In *Canadian Federalism: Myth or Reality?* 2nd ed. J. Peter Meekison, ed. Toronto: Methuen, 1971, 121–42.

Norris, Pippa, ed. *Critical Citizens: Global Support for Democratic Government*. Oxford: Oxford University Press, 1999.

O'Malley, Eoin. "The Power of Prime Minsters: Results of an Expert Survey," *International Political Science Review* 28, 1 (2007), 7–27.

Osbaldeston, Gordon F. *Keeping Deputy Ministers Accountable*. Toronto: McGraw-Hill Ryerson, 1989.

Ostrogorski, M. *Democracy and the Organization of Political Parties II (1902)*. Chicago: Quadrangle Books, 1964.

Page, Benjamin I., and Marshall M. Bouton. *The Foreign Policy Disconnect*. Chicago and London: University of Chicago Press, 2006.

Pal, Leslie A., ed. *How Ottawa Spends 2001-2002*. Don Mills, Ont.: Oxford University Press, 2001.

———. "How Ottawa Spends 2001-2002: Power in Transition." In *How Ottawa Spends 2001-2002*. Leslie A. Pal, ed. Don Mills, Ont.: Oxford University Press, 2001, 1–27.

Paltiel, Khayyam Zev. "Political Marketing, Party Finance, and Decline of Canadian

Parties." In *Canadian Parties in Transition*, 2nd ed. A. Brian Tanguay and Alain-G. Gagnon, eds. Toronto: Nelson, 1995, 403–22.

Pammett Jon H., and Lawrence LeDuc. "Explaining the Turnout Decline in Canadian Federal Elections: A New Survey of Non-Voters." Executive Summary Elections Canada 2003. http://www.elections.ca/content.asp?section=loi&dir=tur/tud& document=index&textonly=false

Pateman, Carole. *Participation and Democratic Theory*. Cambridge: Cambridge University Press, 1970.

Peat Marwick Associates. *Economic Impact of the Tobacco Industry in Canada*. Montreal: Canadian Tobacco Manufacturers' Council, 1979.

Perkins, Anne, and Robert P. Shepherd. "Managing in the New Public Service: Some Implications for How We Are Governed." In *How Ottawa Spends 2001-2002*. Leslie A. Pal, ed. Don Mills, Ont.: Oxford University Press, 2001, 95–121.

Perlin, George C. "The Progressive Conservative Party." In *Party Politics in Canada*, 4th ed. Hugh G. Thorburn, ed. Scarborough, Ont.: Prentice-Hall, 1979, 161–8.

Peters, B. Guy. "Democracy and Political Power in Contemporary Western Governments: Challenges and Reforms," in *The Art of the State Governance in a World without Frontiers*. Courchene, Thomas J., and Donald Savoie, eds. Montreal: The Institute for Research on Public Policy, 2003, 81–108.

Peters, B. Guy, and Donald J. Savoie, eds. *Governance in the Twenty-first Century: Revitalizing the Public Service*. Montreal and Kingston: McGill-Queen's University Press, 2000.

Peters, Joseph. "E-Consultation: Enabling Democracy between Elections." IRPP *Choices* 15, 1 (January 2009). http://www.irpp.org

Petry, Francois, and Matthew Mendelsohn. "Public Opinion and Policy Making in Canada 1944–2001." *Canadian Journal of Political Science* 37, 3 (September 2004): 505–29.

Phillips, Susan D. "SUFA and Citizen Engagement: Fake or Genuine Masterpiece?" IRPP Policy Matters 2, 7 (December 2001). http://www.irpp.org

Phillips, Susan D., and Michael Orsini. "Mapping the Links: Citizen Involvement in Policy Processes." CPRN Discussion Paper No. F.21. Ottawa: Canadian Policy Research Networks, April 2002. www.cprn.com

Pitkin, Hanna F. *The Concept of Representation*. Berkeley: University of California Press, 1972.

Plattner, Marc F. "From Liberalism to Liberal Democracy." *Journal of Democracy* 10, 3 (July 1999): 121–34.

Pross, A. Paul, and Iain S. Stewart. "Breaking the Habit: Attentive Publics and Tobacco Regulation." In *How Ottawa Spends 1994-95: Making Change*. Susan D. Phillips, ed. Ottawa: Carleton University Press, 1994, 129–64.

Qualter, T. H. *The Election Process in Canada*. Toronto: McGraw-Hill, 1970.

Rae, Bob. *From Protest to Power*. Toronto: Penguin Books Canada, 1996.

Reed, Paul B., and L. Kevin Selbee. "Patterns of Citizen Participation and the Civic Core in Canada." Paper presented at the 29th ARNOVA annual conference, New Orleans, Louisiana, November 16–18, 2000. Mimeo.

Reform Party of Canada. *Principles and Policies* (The Blue Book). Calgary: Reform Fund Canada, 1991.

Resnick, Philip. *The Politics of Resentment: British Columbia Regionalism and Canadian Unity*. Vancouver: University of British Columbia Press, 2000.

———. *Twenty-First Century Democracy*. Montreal and Kingston: McGill-Queen's University Press, 1997.

———. *Parliament Vs. People*. Vancouver: New Star Books, 1984.

Revel, Jean-Francois. *Without Marx or Jesus*. New York: Doubleday, 1971.

Richardson, N. H. "Insubstantial pageant: the rise and fall of provincial planning in Ontario." *Canadian Public Administration* 24, 4 (Winter 1981): 563–85.

Ringen, Stein. "Where Now, Democracy?" Commentary re Power and Democracy. Norwegian Official Reports. 2003.19 (in Norwegian only) 2004. www.oedc.org/dataoecd/63.

———. "Wealth and decay: Norway funds a massive political self-examination and finds trouble for all." *Times Literary Supplement,* 13 February 2004.

Robertson, Gordon. *Memoirs of a Very Civil Servant*. Toronto: University of Toronto Press, 2000.

Robinson, Donald L. *Government for the Third American Century.* Boulder, Colorado: Westview Press, 1989.

Rokkan, Stein. "Norway: Numerical Democracy and Corporate Pluralism." In *Political Oppositions in Western Democracies*. Robert A Dahl, ed. New Haven: Yale University Press, 1966, 70–115.

Rolph, W. K. *Henry Wise Wood of Alberta*. Toronto: University of Toronto Press, 1950.

Rose, Richard, and Guy Peters. *Can Government Go Bankrupt?* New York: Basic Books, 1978.

Rowat, Donald C., ed. The right to know: Essays on government publicity and public access to information. Ottawa: Department of Political Science, Carleton University, 1980.

Russell, Peter H. *Constitutional Odyssey: Can Canadians Become a Sovereign People?* Toronto: University of Toronto Press, 1992.

Sagoff, Mark. *The Economy of the Earth: Philosophy, Law, and the Environment*. Cambridge: Cambridge University Press, 1988.

Sartori, Giovanni. *Democratic Theory*. New York: Frederick A. Praeger, 1965.

Saul, John Ralston. "How we will make Canada ours again." The LaFontaine-Baldwin Lecture. *Globe and Mail* (March 24, 2000): A16.

Savoie, Donald J. "The broken chain of answerability." *Globe and Mail* (May 17, 2008): A19.

———. *Breaking the Bargain*. Toronto: University of Toronto Press, 2003.

———. "Reshaping National Political Institutions." In *Memos to the Prime Minister*. Harvey Schachter, ed. Toronto: John Wiley and Sons, 2001.

———. *Governing from the Centre*. Toronto: University of Toronto Press, 1999.

———. "The Rise of Court Government in Canada." *Canadian Journal of Political Science*. 32.4 (December 1999): 635–64.

———. "Reforming Civil Service Reforms." *Policy Options*, April 1994.

Schachter, Harvey, ed. *Memos to the Prime Minister*. Toronto: John Wiley and Sons, 2001.

Schattschneider, E. E. *Party Government*. 1942. New York: Holt, Rinehart and Winston, Inc., 1967.

———. *The Semisovereign People*. New York: Holt, Rinehart and Winston, 1960.

Schlozman, Kay Lehman, and John Tierney. *Organized Interests and American Democracy*. New York: Harper and Row, 1986.

———. "More of the Same: Washington Pressure Group Activity in a Decade of Change." *Journal of Politics* 45, 2 (1983): 351–77.

Schumpeter, Joseph A. *Capitalism, Socialism and Democracy*, 3rd ed. New York: Harper and Row, 1950.

Schwartz, Mildred A. *Politics and Territory*. Montreal and London: McGill-Queen's University Press, 1974.

Simpson, Jeffrey. "Big Lloyd will not soon be forgotten." *Globe and Mail* (September 22, 2000).

———. *Spoils of Power*. Don Mills, Ont.: Collins Publishers, 1988.

Segal, Hugh. "The costs of partisan disengagement: the mounting democratic deficit." *Opinion Canada* 6, 27 (September 9, 2004). www.cric.ca and www. canadiandemocraticmovement.ca/Article443.html

Seidle, F. Leslie, and Louis Massicotte, eds. *Taking Stock of 150 Years of Responsible Government in Canada*. Ottawa: Canadian Study of Parliament Group, 1999.

Smiley, Donald. "Local Autonomy and Central Administrative Control in Saskatchewan." *Canadian Journal of Economics and Political Science* 26, 2 (1960): 299–313.

Smith, David E., *The People's House of Commons*. Toronto: University of Toronto Press, 2007.

Smith, S. G. D. *Politics and the Party System in the Three Prairie Provinces, 1917–1958*. Master's thesis. Oxford University, 1959

Somin, Ilya. "Voter Ignorance and the Democratic Ideal." *Critical Review*. 12, 4 (Fall 1998): 413–558.

Soroka, Stuart N. *Canadian Perceptions of the Health Care System*. A report to the Health Council of Canada. Toronto: Health Council of Canada, 2007.

Soroka, Stuart N., and Christopher Wleszien. "Opinion Representation and Policy Feedback: Canada in Comparative Perspective." *Canadian Journal of Political Science* 37, 3 (September 2004): 531–59.

Stanbury, Richard J. "The Liberal Party of Canada—An Interpretation." June 15, 1969. Mimeo.

Stanbury, W. T. "Regulating the Financing of Federal Parties and Candidates." In *Canadian Parties in Transition*, 2nd ed. A. Brian Tanguay and Alain-G. Gagnon, eds. Toronto: Nelson, 1995, 372–402.

Stanners, Michèle, and Roger Gibbins. "The Continuing Canadian Drama." *Opinion Canada* 5, 21 (June 5, 2003). www.cric.ca

Stewart, Gordon T. *The Origins of Canadian Politics*. Vancouver: University of British Columbia Press, 1986.

Stilborn, Jack, prepared by. "The Roles of the Member of Parliament in Canada: Are They Changing?" Ottawa: The Library of Parliament, 2002. www.parl.gc/ca/information/library/PRBpubs/prb0204-e.htm

Sutherland, Keith. *The Party's Over*. Exeter, UK: Imprint Academic, 2004.

Tanguay, A. Brian, and Alain-G. Gagnon, eds. *Canadian Parties in Transition*, 2nd ed. Toronto: Nelson, 1995.

Tussman, Joseph. *Obligation and the Body Politic*. New York: Oxford University Press, 1960.

UNICEF. "Child Poverty and Changes in Child Poverty in Rich Countries Since 1990." Innocenti Working Paper 2005-02. Florence, Italy: Innocenti Research Centre, 2005. www.unicef-irc.org/publications/pdf/iwp_2005_02_final.pdf

Uzelman, Scott, and Donald Gutstein. "Editorial writers don't share same concerns as general public." *Newswatch Monitor* 3, 2 (Spring 2001).

Verba, Sidney, et al. *Elites and the Idea of Equality*. Cambridge: Harvard University Press, 1987.

Watkins Mel. "Why foreign ownership still matters in 2008." Submission to the Competition Review Panel, Briefing Paper. Ottawa: Canadian Centre for Policy Alternatives, 9. www.policyalternatives.ca/documents/National_Office_Pubs/2008

Warren, Mark E., and Hilary Pearse. *Designing Deliberative Democracy*. New York: Cambridge University Press, 2008.

Westell, Anthony. *Paradox: Trudeau as Prime Minister*. Scarborough, Ont.: Prentice-Hall, 1972.

White, Ted, MP. "Freedom of the MP within a Party Structure." Presentation to Fraser

Institute Conference, November 22, 2001. Vancouver, B.C. www.fraserinstitute. org

Wilson-Smith, Anthony. "What Liberals Won't Admit." *Maclean's* (January 29, 2001): 14.

Wiseman, Nelson. Review: *Representation and Electoral Democracy in Canada*. ed. William Cross. Don Mills: Oxford University Press, 2002. In *Canadian Journal of Political Science*, 35, 4 (December 2002): 901-3.

Wood, Louis Aubrey. *A History of Farmers' Movements in Canada*. Toronto: Ryerson Press, 1924.

Young, Lisa, and Keith Archer, eds. *Regionalism and Party Politics in Canada*. Don Mills, Ont.: Oxford University Press, 2002.

Young, Lisa. "Value Clash: Parliament and Citizens after 150 Years of Responsible Government." In *Taking Stock of 150 Years of Responsible Government in Canada*. F. Leslie Seidle, and Louis Massicotte, eds. Ottawa: Canadian Study of Parliament Group, 1999, 105-36.

Young, Walter D. *The Anatomy of a party: the national CCF, 1932-61*. Toronto: University of Toronto Press, 1971.

ACKNOWLEDGMENTS

I owe an enormous debt to my partner and my family for their love and support as I brought this project to completion. With some help from the medical profession, Nonie ensured completion of the book by nursing me back to good health through several challenging episodes. My son Geoffrey helped me to "say" what I meant to on numerous occasions and suggested the title of the book. From Milan, another son, Scott, helped me expand my computer literacy and, when that failed, repaired my manuscript promptly for me. My other adult children, Doug, Karen, Mary Lou and Jack, were also an unstinting source of support.

I want to mention, too, my late brother, Peyton, in this recognition of the base of support from which I worked. He encouraged me to follow him into the academic world of political science and was a constant source of inspiration. Late in life, he still pursued the important causes to which he was committed with intelligence and courage.

My doctoral committee at UBC took a chance that a near-middle-age student with substantial family responsibilities could make a contribution to the academic world. Trent University then provided me with the opportunity to teach, write, and research in a stimulating and supportive environment. For that interesting life, I thank both. I want to continue paying back to my ultimate employer—my fellow citizens, whose political aspirations have been too long neglected.

Professor Heather MacIvor and Ross Johnson, colleagues in the discipline, each read a chapter in the book and offered important suggestions. My thanks to them. Alan Cairns, with whom I have been privileged to have a long association, has a special association with this book. He was my doctoral thesis supervisor and now, 40 years later, he agreed to introduce my book. Alan's impressive body of work—and, in particular, his stress in it on the need for an enriched concept of citizenship to take hold in Canada—has also been a source of inspiration.

Finally, I would like to acknowledge the support of our friends in Vancouver. Their interest in the progress of the book has sustained my work, and I appreciate it deeply.

Interested in advancing the
"Quiet Canadian Democratic Revolution?"

Contacts:
e-mail, vaughanlyon@shaw.ca
web, Democracynow.ca

CPSIA information can be obtained at www.ICGtesting.com
Printed in the USA
LVOW070400150212

268693LV00003B/9/P